My Dark Room

My Dark Room

SPACES OF THE INNER SELF IN THE
LONG EIGHTEENTH CENTURY

Julie Park

The University of Chicago Press   CHICAGO AND LONDON

The University of Chicago Press, Chicago 60637
The University of Chicago Press, Ltd., London
© 2023 by The University of Chicago
Published 2023
Printed in the United States of America

32 31 30 29 28 27 26 25 24 23   1 2 3 4 5

ISBN-13: 978-0-226-82475-8 (cloth)
ISBN-13: 978-0-226-82476-5 (paper)
ISBN-13: 978-0-226-82477-2 (e-book)
DOI: https://doi.org/10.7208/chicago/9780226824772.001.0001

This publication is made possible in part by the New York
University Center for the Humanities and the Paterno Family
Endowment of the Pennsylvania State University.

Library of Congress Cataloging-in-Publication Data

Names: Park, Julie, 1970– author.
Title: My dark room : spaces of the inner self in eighteenth-
century England / Julie Park.
Description: Chicago : The University of Chicago Press, 2023. |
Includes bibliographical references and index.
Identifiers: LCCN 2022049686 | ISBN 9780226824758 (cloth)
| ISBN 9780226824765 (paperback) | ISBN 9780226824772
(ebook)
Subjects: LCSH: Space and time in literature. | Self in literature.
| English literature—18th century—History and criticism.
Classification: LCC PR448.S69 P37 2023 | DDC 820.9/353—
dc23/eng/20221108
LC record available at https://lccn.loc.gov/2022049686

♾ This paper meets the requirements of ANSI/NISO Z39.48-1992
(Permanence of Paper).

For my father, in loving memory

Come; lead us to thy Chamber; there unfold
Thy secret Charms, delightful to behold;
How little is thy Cell? How dark the Room?

JOHN CUFF, "Verses, Occasion'd by
the Sight of a Chamera Obscura"

Contents

Introduction

For clearly we see many things emit bodies galore,
Not just from deep inside themselves, as I have said before,
But also from exteriors, for instance with their hue—
As red and gold and purple awnings regularly do,
When, stretched over a great theatre, hung on poles and beams
Above the crowd, they flap and billow, and their colour streams
Staining the faces of the audience in the stands below,
The stage and spectacle a-flicker in their fluttering glow.
The more the theatre's enclosed, shut from the glare of day,
The more the laughing show of colours puts on its display.

LUCRETIUS, *The Nature of Things*

At the center of the small dark room is a round white table. Overhead, a metal turret extends through an opening in the roof. Functioning as a periscope, it conducts light into the room.[1] Close the door to block out other sources of light, and the world streams in, covering the table's surface, not with static images but with the full flow and color of life's movements—slowed somehow, in hues more saturated, edges blurred and noises silenced. A captain's wheel, attached to a box on a short post alongside the table, is linked by a thin pole to the turret. Turning the wheel rotates the periscope, panning across the scene outside, bringing new views of street and beach onto the table. Yet even without this capacity to shift its gaze, the camera obscura functions as a pair of virtual feet, covering ground you cannot reach with your own body while standing in its dark chamber.

Within this small, elevated room, the crowds on view become characters in a silent drama. As tourists cross the street, their bare legs appear to undulate in unison, an effect unseen at street level, where the noise

FIGURE 0.1 Camera obscura projection table, aperture, and pole attached to wheel for maneuvering rooftop turret (2018). Santa Monica Art Lab. Photograph by the author.

of their voices drowns out thought. Here, silent, they are fascinating ob-jects of contemplation, moving with, not against, the formation of your thoughts. As you watch them heading toward the tour bus parked in front of the hotel, you begin to identify with them. Will they make the bus on time? Where will they go next? Then cars take over the street where the tourists just passed, gliding as if on skates. And when the turquoise bus, passengers finally on board, pulls away from the curb, you feel an inner sense of celebration at witnessing something once so still begin to move, showing one of the very signs of life. Drawing visitors into a dream state induced by way of projection, this enclosed space transforms even a prosaic tour bus into something like Sleeping Beauty waking up from a century-long slumber.

Within the dark room, the white table is only the most obvious surface displaying internal projections of the external world. The floor on which you stand becomes the road. As you watch cars drift along the wood grain, you sense a rippling motion close to the floor out of the corner of your eye and wonder whether a cat has entered the room. It is only the cars in the distance—or rather, the image of them—coming closer. You watch, not without a sense of wonder, how images of the world outside land on surfaces of the room—and not just the designated screen—and realize that the room creates an experience in which external reality is transfigured within parameters set by the particularities of a physical space and by your own imagination. Wooden floorboards and Ocean Avenue traffic interfuse to recreate the surfaces of the world, becoming your own internal space, the realm of interiority.

The room I have just described belongs to the Camera Obscura Art Lab, a community center in an oceanfront park in Santa Monica, California. The device brings the external world inside in a way that renders it indistinguishable from both the architectural and mental spaces of the interior. This replicates the experience of spaces of fascination that were prevalent throughout the seventeenth and eighteenth centuries. Take, for example, Alexander Pope's grotto at his Twickenham home. Pope encrusted the ceilings and walls of the grotto, connected to his house by an underground tunnel, with carefully selected stones and crystals from English mines, and shells "interspersed with pieces of looking-glass in angular forms." Above the entrance, an inscription by Horace, "Secretum iter, et fallentis semita vitae"—translated by an eighteenth-century visitor as "A hid Recess, where Life's revolving Day, / In sweet Delusion gently steals away"—anticipates the experience that would much later be hosted at the Santa Monica Camera Obscura.[2] At one point, the grotto by the Thames did function like the beachfront projection room. Pope described in a letter to his friend Edward Blount how, "when you shut the doors of this grotto, it becomes on the instant, from a luminous room, a camera obscura; on the walls of which all the objects of the river, hills, woods, and boats, are forming a moving picture in their visible radiations."[3] The lovingly designed grotto functioned as a space for domestic retirement and also as the setting for his imagination, where "the Muse he found."[4]

FIGURE 0.2 Camera obscura view of Ocean View Hotel façade (2018). Santa
Monica Art Lab camera obscura. Photograph by the author.

As Pope's grotto illustrates, seventeenth- and eighteenth-century subjects conveyed imaginative experiences not only through text but also
through spatial enclosures found in architecture, landscape design, and
dress. The camera obscura prompted the understanding that fiction and
the passages of the imagination it facilitates emerge in both textual and
nontextual—representational and real—spaces. Inner life in seventeenth-
and eighteenth-century England resembled the camera obscura in being
simultaneously a "dark room" (translation of the Latin *camera obscura*)
and a medium for receiving and revealing the projections of external reality within an internal space. The device was a persistent and widespread
paradigm for the mediation of feeling, perceiving, and, above all, imagining. In its simplest and earlier guise, it was—and still is—a darkened
and enclosed room to which light rays are admitted by a small aperture,
projecting images of the outside world on the opposite wall.[5] A historically pivotal structure, the optical device demonstrated that spatial environments in lived reality not only coexist with the psyche and imagina-

tion but actively deepen and expand their reaches. Imagined worlds, a writing closet, or a sheet of paper were all spaces for dwelling, building, and thinking.

In this book, the meeting points of the real and the fictional, and the material and the mental, form a conception of home. This conception is basic to the development of interiority as a property of selfhood, in both senses of the word *property*.[6] I use the term *possessive interiority* to describe the dual condition where interiority is a characteristic of selfhood as well as a means for self-possession.[7] The various spaces examined in this book, like the camera obscura, made possible the process by which individuals accessed their interiority and in doing so laid hold of the private domain of their own identities.

George Mackenzie's *Mirror* 61 (1779) presents perhaps the most extended meditation on the architectural environment of the home as a wellspring for possessive interiority and the imagination. His periodical essay addresses the way in which "a certain attachment to place and things by which the town, the house, the room in which we live, [has] a powerful influence over us." This, the author explains, is "the sentiment of *Home*."[8] As a vivid example of how the idea of home, architectural environments, the imagination, and individuation are bound together, Mackenzie intro-

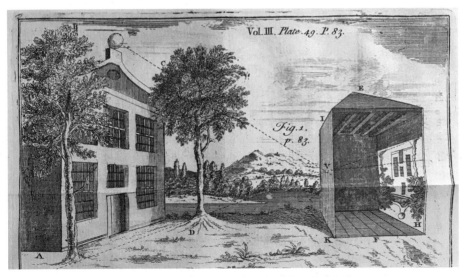

FIGURE 0.3 Eighteenth-century representation of an architectural design
for a camera obscura. Benjamin Martin, *Philosophia Britannica*, vol. 3 (1759).
Photograph: Huntington Library, San Marino, California.

duces Mr. Umphraville, an eccentric friend whose antiquated country house, with its "old yew trees" and "stiff, rectangular walks," allows the homebody "who has retired from the world" to indulge in the "pensive pleasure" of nostalgia and remembrance.[9] Just as the age of the house's furnishings and servants stimulate the "tenderness" of his recollections, so does its very architectural structure, which is described as having "large rooms, lighted by small Gothic windows, and accessible only by dark narrow stair-cases."[10]

The design and function of these rooms recalls the camera obscura. In rooms made dark by the smallness of the windows, the parade of memories inspired by the objects in the house is made lovelier by those same windows, which environmentally and visually perform the softening work of temporal distance on the mental images of memory and their projections. Temporal distance reimagines the past as it "gives us back the affections, the regrets, the sentiments, of our former days . . . their joys without tumult, their griefs without poignancy, and produces equally from both a pensive pleasure."[11] Distance, in other words, sweetens the reality of the past, and memory is but the act of the imagination. Thomas Hobbes reminds us they "are but one thing, which for divers considerations hath divers names."[12] Mr. Umphraville prefers to dwell in this setting, whose elements he refuses to update.

Much like Mr. Umphraville's dark rooms, the spaces in this book—from the private closets of seventeenth- and eighteenth-century English aristocracy and gentry to eighteenth-century women's detachable pockets, owned by servants and mistresses alike—are, in distinct ways, dark, enclosed spaces with strategically placed apertures for projecting and reframing reality. As such, their formal and conceptual coherence with the camera obscura facilitates the means by which a person could become individuated through the possession and expression of an interior life while responding to the design and features of their material surroundings.

Spatial Formalism

Under the name "spatial formalism," this book develops a critical method for revealing these vital interactions between human subjects and their physical environments, and between the spaces of textual creations and those of eighteenth-century England's material world. Not just a critical method, spatial formalism is also the term I give to the wide-ranging ways in which historical subjects, whether real or fictional, materialized inner realities through the resources of form that inhere in the spaces of the material world. In both senses, spatial formalism views architecture, landscape, and other features of the material world as kinetic, interactive sites of design and experience, not as static, fixed sites whose particularities are more or less incidental.[13]

The book emphasizes above all spatial *experience* rather than spatial *description*. The distinction is significant, not least because spatial experience indicates that the relationship between humans and spaces is interactive and mutually constitutive. Spatial formalism attends not to how Marvell describes a country house, for example, but to how the experience of the house as a material space with particularities of design makes it possible for him to envisage his own mental processing. Nun Appleton's architecture and landscape exist not as immobile objects of unilateral description and perception, but as dynamic spaces that shape the passages of the mind in a relationship of reciprocal definition. Architects like John Webb, in innovating the double pile design for houses that preceded his design for Nun Appleton, promoted and practiced spatial formalism in creating new pathways for proceeding through domestic environments that allowed inhabitants and guests greater freedom to be alone with their thoughts, as well as privacy. Yet I argue that Marvell, in a fashion, was a spatial formalist too, especially in the final portion of both the poem and his walk through the Nun Appleton estate, where he finds a woodland sanctuary during the flooding of the meadow and turns the natural environment into a dark room for lodging his innermost thoughts, thereby building a home for his possessive interiority. Subsequent subjects in the book, such as Alexander Pope, Samuel Richardson's heroine Pamela, and Margaret Cavendish, practice spatial formalism more concretely, with actual materials and spaces in the physical world that they shape, design, alter, and inhabit.

As a critical method, spatial formalism looks at these interactive relationships between people and spaces. As a historical phenomenon, spatial formalism characterizes the way people intentionally designed spaces to achieve a fluid state of unity between interiority and space. Pope, I argue, was a spatial formalist who designed his grotto as a space that extended the regions of his poetic imagination to include the arrangement of stones and shells, creating dramatic contrasts of shadow and light, and rhymes in shape and texture. The effect of such juxtapositions and pairings induced states of reverie and intense awareness of the fanciful visions in one's head. By turning his grotto into a camera obscura, he further turned his grotto into a spatial form for nourishing the life of his imagination.

Despite its emergence in other genres, such as poetry, nowhere in eighteenth-century English literature has the space for interiority been more widely recognized than in the developing genre of the novel.[14] The novel in its new eighteenth-century guise differs from romance, its predecessor in fictional prose, by the very quality of interiority, its proclivity "thoroughly to unfold the labyrinths of the human mind" and "paint the inward mind" rather than to "amuse" readers "with a number of surprising incidents and adventures."[15] The imaginative genre of the novel was formulating a fresh paradigm of literary representation by situating the unfolding of characters' inner lives in direct correspondence with physical environments made ever more visible through newly detailed descriptive language in textual representations.[16]

Importantly, however, neither this interiority nor this book is restricted to the novel, for it was not the only site, literary or otherwise, in which the physical features of the domestic interior had become more discernible. At the same time that the novel was developing its representational language for interiority, eighteenth-century subjects were cultivating creative and imaginative states of being by setting the unfolding of their own inner lives in designs for private environments that promoted interiority.[17] The interior itself became a more visible and articulated area of definition in architectural plans and treatises of the period.[18] *My Dark Room* excavates seventeenth- and eighteenth-century inner life by drawing on personal letters and diaries, poems, architectural designs and plans, and sketches, prints, and paintings for records of houses, gardens, rooms, and pockets that existed in reality and in fantasy. These are associates of spaces appearing in or evoked by literary sources as interactive sites of becoming.

My Dark Room also considers spaces inspired first by literature, not just spaces that appear to precede literary ones. For instance, Pope's grotto was created after he wrote *Eloisa to Abelard*, the long poem whose Gothic nunnery setting models the play of enclosure and of light and shadow that defined his grotto. Pope's grotto, as a veritable camera obscura, turned those effects into material reality. This book applies spatial formalism to provide close readings of spatial themes in literary works, but also to consider how the interiority expressed in eighteenth-century literature emerges across the diverse media of textual genres, architectural designs, landscape buildings, paintings, visual devices, and intimate garments. Some chapters will closely read literary texts that depict the merger between spatial settings and inner experience, such as Andrew Marvell's *Upon Appleton House* and Samuel Richardson's *Pamela*, but others are as attentive, if not more, to analyzing the formal features of visual, topographical, and architectural spaces, such as grottoes, writing closets, and garden follies.

Spatial formalism reveals that interiority, traditionally considered the abstract province of mind, is a relational condition contingent on the structures of the material world, and develops in reciprocal relationship with them. If literary texts, especially environmentally specific ones with psychological orientations, express and channel the thoughts and fantasies of human subjects, so too do the spaces of eighteenth-century material culture. When placed in dialogue with each other, texts and spaces reveal more about how English culture of the long eighteenth century viewed the interior self and its domain of interiority than either would reveal alone.[19] Ultimately, this is the abiding contention of spatial formalism in my study: when we talk about interiority, we are talking about the spaces we inhabit and interact with, not only the mind that perceives them.

Projective Spaces

Spatial formalism is modeled critically on the camera obscura. No other space in material reality epitomized the interplay between the real and the represented more richly for eighteenth-century subjects than the camera obscura, which reveals new insights about interiority and how setting operates across literary works and in daily life. This dynamic is illustrated in a much-quoted passage from John Locke: "For, methinks, the *Understanding* is not much unlike a Closet wholly shut from light, with only some little openings left, to let in external visible Resemblances, or *Ideas* of things without."[20] Much as the camera obscura processes the images of views outside of its walls inside its own architectural space, the mind is made busy processing and responding to the physical settings that are a part of day-to-day life. The camera obscura shows us that if physical environments are a feature of "external" reality, they become aspects of "internal" reality as well, if only momentarily, through the mediating transit of images resembling it.

The fact that the camera obscura appears as a figure of consciousness in the most quoted passage from Locke's *Essay* has worked only to conceal its pervasiveness as an artifactual space of seventeenth- and eighteenth-century material culture that engaged and mediated imaginative activity while supporting scientific pursuits. By showing how the affective and psychic dimensions of inner life in seventeenth- and eighteenth-century culture are embedded in the built environments of the period, my book departs from recent studies of eighteenth-century literature that reckon with interiority in terms of mind, consciousness, or cognition.[21] This book shifts interiority from the mind to space. In doing so, it situates interiority in the realm of becoming known as life and redefines the literary notion of setting as deeply and materially constitutive of it.[22] Brad

Pasanek's database and study of eighteenth-century metaphors of mind have shown that the camera obscura widely circulated as one. Sean Silver's study of material objects that model cognitive processes from the same period has shown it to be an ocular "gadget" that offers a "relatively crude production of the sovereign mind" while manifesting operative concepts of empiricist philosophy.[23] More than a metaphor or model for mind alone, and much more than a gadget, the camera obscura was—and is—a dynamic and encompassing space for embodied experiences of beauty, wonder, and the imagination.

The camera obscura has a long history in European material and visual culture that predates the Enlightenment. What is thought to be the first illustration of the camera obscura, in Reinerus Gemma-Frisius's *De Radio Astronomica et Geometrico* (1545), depicts it as a small room encased with architectural molding details.[24] Later, in 1671, an engraving in Chérubin d'Orléans's *La Dioptrique Oculaire* also illustrates an architectural camera obscura, but this time inside a room designed to be a study. Against one of the walls not being used as a screen for the projected image stands a built-in bookcase, with volumes of different sizes arranged on the bottom three shelves and, on the top shelf, an armillary flanked by two globes. Presenting the camera obscura as a place that contains all the sources of study about the world, the engraving also suggests that the space, with its key architectural components—two walls opposite each other, one with a

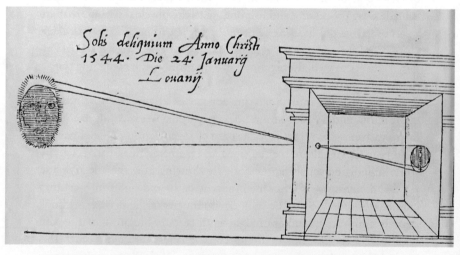

FIGURE 0.4 Earliest known illustration of a camera obscura rendered as an architectural space. Reinerus Gemma-Frisius, *De Radio Astronomica et Geometrico* (1545). Photograph courtesy of the John Carter Brown Library (CC BY 4.0).

FIGURE 0.5 Image of a camera obscura as a study. Chérubin d'Orléans's
La Dioptrique Oculaire (1671). Photograph: Huntington Library,
San Marino, California.

hole, the other intact—is its own source of study, its own world and universe. Renaissance artists used it for rendering perspectival depth and pictorial space as well as for demonstrating "natural magic." Since the Middle Ages and early modern period—and probably antiquity—it was also used for observing such celestial phenomena as solar eclipses. And throughout the seventeenth century, it was used for the study of optics.

D'Orléans's engraving indicates that camera obscuras of the period were aspects of domestic architecture. As John Hammond puts it, although the technology for camera obscuras is the same today as it was several centuries ago, the early modern camera obscura "was a room of a house made dark by closing the shutters, whereas today it is a structure designed specifically for the purpose."[25] Elizabeth Graeme Ferguson, in Milcah Martha Moore's commonplace book, describes her 1764 visit to fellow Quaker Thomas Goldney's landscape garden in Bristol. Here, in addition to its shell-encrusted grotto (discussed in chapter 3), Ferguson enjoyed a camera obscura made out of one of its follies, the Octagon (now removed), a two-story summer house on a hill. "The Windows of this Building," she wrote, "are so disposed at the outside, to see a Camera Obscura, of the whole Country & the objects around."[26]

Rooms could be made into camera obscuras with the help of specific devices, such as the scioptic ball. An inventory for Goldney Hall from 1768 reveals that Goldney also kept in his study a scioptic ball, which he described as an "Ox Eye or Camera Obscura to fix to Window Shutters for viewing objects."[27] Invented in 1636 by Daniel Schwenter, a professor of mathematics and oriental languages, the scioptic ball is a portable spherical device with a compound lens and a swivel construction that allows its user to draw panoramic views by capturing unbroken images of the view outside. Recognizing that the camera obscura was first and foremost a domestic architectural space is critical for appreciating how it functioned as a spatial medium for inhabiting and interacting with the world. Its dimensions and relationship to the body varied, as the example of the scioptic ball indicates. Not just a tool, it was also a spatial environment and created spatial environments for seventeenth- and eighteenth-century subjects.

John Harris's early eighteenth-century dictionary entry describes the camera obscura in its architectural guise as "this most Wonderful and Glorious Experiment, tho it be very common," intended to "represent all outward Objects in their proper Colours, Distances and Proportions, on a White Wall, a Frame of Paper, or Sheet hung up for that purpose in a Darkened Room."[28] Without a double convex glass or mirror placed at the aperture, the projected image appears both upside down and in lateral reversal, reminding you that it is a projection, not the "real thing." Harris's captivation is clear when he describes the projections as images that "appear" and are "expressed" on the cloth with more beauty and sense of life than one can imagine, transforming the cloth into the world itself, with its movements and colors exquisite objects of contemplation:

> Another thing in which this Representation exceeds Painting is, That here you have *Motion* expressed on your Cloth. If the Wind move the Trees, Plants or Flowers without, you have it within on your Lively Picture; and nothing can be more pleasant than to see how the Colours of the moving parts will change as they do without. . . . The Motion of any Flies or Birds, is painted also in the same Perfection: And the exact Lineaments of any Persons walking at a due Distance without the Glass, will be also expressed to the Life, and all their Motions, Postures and Gestures, will as plainly appear on the Cloth, as they do to any ones Eye without.[29]

Abraham Rees's *Cyclopædia* (1786) provides detailed instructions for the "construction of a chamber camera obscura" that bears a remarkable resemblance to the Santa Monica device, with a projecting mechanism situated in a movable domed roof and controlled from within the room by a long rod (albeit without the captain's wheel) and a white tabletop on which to view the projected images. These do-it-yourself instructions

FIGURE 0.6 Model for an eighteenth-century camera obscura similar in
construction to that at the Santa Monica Art Lab. Abraham Rees, *Cyclopædia: or,
An Universal Dictionary of Arts and Sciences* (1786). Photograph: Thomas Fisher
Rare Book Library, University of Toronto.

also inform us that temporary rooms were built specifically for making
camera obscuras, which suggests just how common a domestic architectural feature the camera obscura had become toward the end of the eighteenth century.[30] Opticians such as Messrs. Jones, of Holborn, sold camera boxes that came with the requisite glasses for proper reflection and
projection, expressly for the purpose of creating camera obscuras out of
rooms at home.[31]

The device was a source of entertainment across different classes and
age groups throughout the eighteenth century, with traveling showmen
in America and Britain paid to demonstrate its workings. Poems were
written about its wonders.[32] Contemporary descriptions placed greater
significance than does today's commentary on the camera obscura's abil-

ity to replicate the colors and movements of objects—their qualities of liveliness and lifelikeness.[33] Echoing Harris's sense of wonder about its moving, colorful projections, as well as Joseph Addison's in *Spectator* 414, Ephraim Chambers's *Cyclopædia* of 1728 describes the images it projects as "perfectly like their objects, and each clothed with their native colours, and by expressing at the same time, all their motions: which latter, no other Art can imitate."[34] From dictionary definitions and technical manuals to the beguiled descriptions in poems, Addison's essay on the pleasures of the imagination, and Pope's letter to Edward Blount, eighteenth-century sources find remarkable the camera obscura's ability to represent "the Lively Representations of External Objects, and their various Motions as well as Shapes and Colours," as Robert Boyle put it.[35] Edmund Stone saw in these projections both wonder and practical potential:

> The Representations of Objects in this Machine are wonderfully pleasant, not only because they appear in the just Proportions, and are endued with all the natural Colours of their Objects, but likewise shew their various Motions, which no Art can imitate; and a skilful Painter, by means of one of these Machines, may observe many Things from the Contemplation of the appearing of Objects therein, that will be an Help to the Perfection of the Art of Painting; and even a Bungler may accurately enough delineate Objects by Means of it.[36]

What allows the camera obscura to aid painters, and would-be painters, is its ability to make apparent "many Things" that would not otherwise be seen. Thus, even as a medium purportedly intended for the accurate delineation of a directly perceived physical reality, the device creates an occasion for wonder, discovery, and experiencing life as a dream state.

External space turns into internal space, but the device is not only a model for the mind. This book considers the camera obscura as an architectural model for the generative qualities of space as well. In other words, the camera obscura models the process whereby humans come to inhabit the world through acts not just of reflecting on but also of being *with* and of becoming *through* the spaces in which they dwell. The camera obscura's mechanism was recognized as one of *throwing* the image onto the requisite white surface—a painted wall, sheet of paper, or piece of cloth—that renders it visible while housing it temporarily.[37] James Mann, peddling a microscope camera obscura in 1760, writes, "The Image or Picture of the Object is thrown in a most exact, beautiful, and surprising Manner, upon a white Screen or linen Sheet, placed on Purpose to receive the same." Given that "throwing" is another word for "projecting," Mann's description of his device intimates the protocinematic aspects of the camera obscura's function.[38] Moving beyond the more evocative verbs that his contemporaries used to describe what light does in the camera obscura's operation ("paint" was especially popular), Mann chooses one that concurs with a term that is standard for describing the mechanism of the camera obscura, magic lantern, or movie camera in our own time. Whereas the word's sense of causing "(an image or representation of an object) to form on a surface . . . as a result of action elsewhere" was used as early as 1692 and throughout the eighteenth century in optical discourses, the receiving surface was always the retina of the eye, not a screen.[39] The usage of "project" to mean the act of causing "(a figure, image, or shadow) to appear or stand out *against* a background" would not be in place until 1832.[40] And its usage specifically in relation to a screen would not appear until 1897, and then only in regard to the media of photography, film, and slides.[41]

Yet even as eighteenth-century sources use words other than *project* to describe the camera obscura's technique—by far favoring verbs that suggest its capacity to operate as an apparent proxy for the artist, a notion Joshua Reynolds deplores—the apparitional qualities they attribute to the device indirectly suggest the meaning of the word that prevailed in the eighteenth century.[42] As Maximillian Novak explains, the term *projector* originally referred to men who set out to swindle innocent people.[43] At the end of the seventeenth century, however, Daniel Defoe, in *An Essay upon Projects* (1697), rehabilitated the term to describe those who overcome difficult circumstances by devising inventive plans for business and institutional initiatives, expressing the "mixture of hope and optimism with an expectation of failure" that characterizes the period Defoe referred to as "the Projecting Age."[44] In either sense, pejorative or sympathetic, the term *project*, as it was used in the eighteenth century, is relevant to the way the camera obscura was regarded as making possible realities visible to those who might not otherwise see them.

Poetic descriptions of the camera obscura's basic mechanism exemplify the period's prevailing attitude toward the device as a medium for apparitions. The midcentury poem "The Camera Obscura" enthuses:

> Thus have I seen Woods, Hills, and Dales appear,
> Flocks graze the Plains, Birds wing the silent Air,
> In darken'd Rooms, where Light can only pass
> Through the small Circle of a Convex Glass:
> On the white Sheet the moving Figures rise,
> The Forest waves, Clouds float along the Skies.[45]

These lines narrate the transformation of a landscape scene from an object of vision to an object of conveyance that "pass[es]" with a ray of light
through a narrow channel—"the small Circle of a Convex Glass"—and
magically resurfaces in the dark room. Moving and rising on a white sheet,
what would otherwise be an everyday scene turns into a ghost landscape,
unmoored from reality but appearing as such. The landscape is even more
animated than it was in its original form: "The Forest waves, Clouds float
along the Skies." In "throwing" the image of an existing scene so that it
appears in a different location, the camera obscura accomplishes an act
of projection that evokes the supernatural. The device's inclusion in a late
eighteenth-century book of magic tricks demonstrates that its ability to
miniaturize reality and make its images "appear painted in their natural
colours on the opposite side" of a pasteboard or wooden box rendered it
nothing short of an act of conjuring.[46]

Moreover, as the architectural theorist Robin Evans can help us see,
the notion of projection has to do not only with the mechanical proce-
dure by which the camera obscura and other visual technology media
make their images but also with the speculative, and thus inherently fictional, mode of architectural design. In more ways than one, the projective cast was an intrinsic feature in the camera obscura and spaces similar
to it, from writing closets to grottoes.

Just as the projective element of architecture lies in the way it produces "a reality" that will exist "outside the drawing" as well as prior to
it, so too does it lie in the camera obscura's productions, but in reverse.
That is, the scene on the wall of a camera obscura is one that exists after
the fact of the original, which is located outside its space. The same reversal is present in the dimensional translation of each form—whereas
architecture creates two-dimensional images that will eventually be rendered in three-dimensional constructs, the camera obscura creates two-
dimensional representations of three-dimensional entities. In both cases,
the entity created is a virtual one. On one hand, architecture produces
virtual buildings. On the other, the camera obscura produces virtual windows in addition to landscapes. The very translation between different
dimensions, and between actual and virtual constructs, whether with architecture or camera obscuras, exemplifies how projection "operates in
the interval *between* things." In this way, projection is "always transitive"
as well as mobile.[47] As Evans explains, in the practice of architectural design, vision is transitive, sustained by the interplay between the hand's
movements and the inscriptions they produce. The ideas that ensue are
produced by the transference from mind to hand and page in activity that

is both visual and based on motor skills. Thus, the projective space of architecture is "inextricably bound up with mobility and imagination."[48]

This dynamic interaction between eye, hand, and imagination also brings to mind the camera obscura's kinship with the practice of writing, as well as its protocinematic function, suggested by the repeated emphasis in eighteenth-century poems and dictionary definitions on the white wall, cloth, or sheet of paper on which the image is made to appear. This surface coincides, in its whiteness and flatness, with the other white surface privileged as a medium for the mind's processes—paper. As will be shown in chapter 2, the ground on which the thoughts of Margaret Cavendish marched out from her pen was a sheet of white paper. So too was the empty surface Locke envisioned as the space for the furniture of ideas. In both instances, the medium converges with the camera obscura. As Locke puts it, "Let us then suppose the Mind to be, as we say, white Paper, void of all Characters, without any *Ideas*; How comes it to be furnished?"[49] The camera obscura as a form of visual technology that, in Pope's case, overlaps with the space of domestic architecture, then, offers itself not only as a model for the operation of the mind but also for that of writing. Pope appears to have been aware on some level of the relation between writing and using the camera obscura; the sketches that show him writing in the grotto indicate he used the space as much for processing his thoughts on paper as for his visual perceptions on the grotto wall.

This points to a critical distinction between the photographic camera and the camera obscura: the latter is a device of ephemeral reproduction. The arresting motions and telling gestures discerned by the camera obscura never solidify into a stable and enduring image or record, as architectural drawings and writing do. In this respect the camera obscura is closer to life itself than is painting, photography, or writing, and this property is vital for understanding its function as a prototype of narrative art. Locke is attuned to this provisional aspect of the device's images in his oft-cited comparison of its workings with human cognition: "*would* the Pictures coming into such a dark Room but stay here, and lie so orderly as to be found upon occasion, it would very much resemble the Understanding of a Man."[50] Other commentators in the eighteenth century remarked wistfully on "the fleeting figures of a camera obscura."[51] Among them was the anonymous author of a poem, "On the Camera Obscura," that appeared in 1746–1747 in *The Museum*, a publication edited by Mark Akenside, who depicts the melancholy ending of a camera obscura's projected scenes as a moment in which pleasing phantoms disappear: "Pleas'd we observe— when ah! intruding Light / From the dark Chamber drives the Noon-

FIGURE 0.7 William Kent or Dorothy Boyle, Duchess of Burlington, ink drawing
of Alexander Pope writing inside his grotto (ca. 1730–1740). Photograph
© The Devonshire Collection, Chatsworth. Reproduced by permission of
Chatsworth Settlement Trustees/Bridgeman Images.

day Night; / Skies, Ocean, Mountains, vanish swift away, / And every
lovely Phantom sinks in Day."[52]

The camera obscura's act of "capturing" the otherwise invisible qualities of an object in its state of motion is one of perceiving life and its
phenomena as they happen rather than preserving them archivally for
the future. It represents life as experience and not as universal truth—we
view things not as they are but as they are perceived, from a particular point of view. The image of the world it brings to its dark room is as
mobile and mutable as the life it sees and the dream state it summons,
turning external reality into an internal world of one's own. This effect is
brought on by the features the camera obscura reveals in its objects, such
as new qualities of motion. The author of a dictionary entry on the camera obscura describes its ability to delineate "the motion of the object itself," such as a man walking, who appears to "have an undulating motion,
or to rise up and down every step he takes," though "nothing of this kind
is observed in the man himself, as viewed by the naked eye."[53]

The camera obscura is not just a space that resembles thinking. It is also a place where the particular faculty of thinking that Hobbes identifies as the fancy or the imagination becomes active, turning real life into both its experience and its object.[54] Accordingly, objects have "qualities called Sensible" that "presseth our organs diversely." Their "apparence to us is Fancy, the same waking, that dreaming." It is "in Ecchoes by reflection, wee see they are; where we know the thing we see, is in one place; the aparence, in another."[55] In his rendition of fancy as a faculty that makes equivocal the distinction between reality and fantasy, or waking and dreaming, Hobbes evokes the camera obscura and its properties.

Camera Obscuras as Book Spaces

Toward the end of the seventeenth century and throughout the eighteenth, the room-size camera obscura was rescaled as a movable object and appeared as a portable box, with Robert Boyle allegedly its inventor in the mid-seventeenth century.[56] *Oculus Artificialis Telediotricus sive Telescopium* (1685) by Johann Zahn, a German optician, inventor, mathematician, and priest, depicts in its figure XXI an array of such movable optical devices, including magic lanterns (with protruding projection or objection lenses) in the top two panels and, in the bottom panel, a camera obscura whose wheels signal its portability, with side flaps to recreate the environment of a darkened room. Zahn made a camera obscura that was twenty-three inches long, in addition to designing several portable ones.[57]

During the eighteenth century, coinciding with the cultural moment in which the value of books (novels in particular) rose as commodities, one could acquire in France and England what looked like a folio-size volume but opened to become a camera obscura. Some of these book camera obscuras—such as one attributed to the eighteenth-century instrument maker Benjamin Martin, now in the Harvard University Collection of Historical Scientific Instruments, and another belonging to Joshua Reynolds, in the Science Museum—come with a curtain to block out light when one inserts one's head into the box. This feature, like the side panels of Zahn's machine, allow the portable device to be used in external settings. That the book camera obscura attributed to Martin has "CAMERA OBSCURA" stamped in gold on its binding explicitly communicates the desire to mix the function of seeing with reading: they were mutually immersive activities that induced interiority.

The camera obscura's "title" also suggests that such activities might be more readily housed within the material spaces of books. With the eighteenth-century invention and popularity of the book camera obscura,

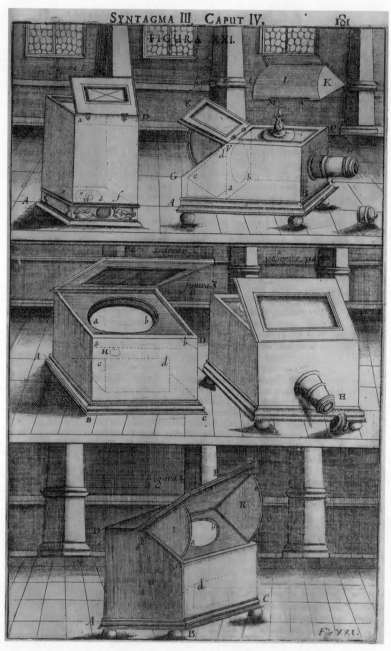

FIGURE 0.8 Early models of portable camera obscuras. Johann Zahn, *Oculus Artificialis Telediotricus sive Telescopium* (1685–1686), figure XXI. Photograph: Getty Research Institute, Los Angeles.

the shift from the camera obscura as a room to a portable object had been realized. Not only does the transformation indicate that camera obscuras were viewed and experienced as commensurate with books, but also that books were viewed and experienced as commensurate with rooms, portable or otherwise, for they shared their properties of enclosure and interiority. The novel especially was a commodified literary form whose absorbing properties derived from its ability to offer identifiable worlds to step into and inhabit while it remained a material book object held and carried in the hand. Its close identification with the bound codex format is underscored by the fact that, as Ian Watt points out, the novel was the first literary genre "essentially connected with the medium of print."[58]

By the age of romanticism, the camera obscura had become so solidified as a model for the novel's plausible projections of an interiority situated in lived reality that Samuel Taylor Coleridge, in *Biographia Literaria* (1817), complained about "devotees of the circulating libraries"—that is, readers of novels—whose reading serves as a form of "beggarly day-dreaming" by which they fill their minds with "a sort of mental *camera obscura* manufactured at the printing office, which, *pro tempore* fixes, reflects, and transmits the moving phantasms of one man's delirium, so as to people the barrenness of a hundred other brains afflicted with the same trance."[59] Here, Coleridge complains that the novel works too well as the instrument of a readymade and commodifiable interiority, and yet the fault appears to lie less with the camera obscura itself than with the printing process.[60] Coleridge's romantic period recognition of the close relationship between the novel and the camera obscura as interconnected media of both subjectivity and imagined reality—for better or worse—warrants recovery.[61]

Hester Thrale Piozzi's comparison of *Cecilia* (1782), the latest novel by her frenemy Frances Burney, with a camera obscura only confirms Coleridge's characterization of the novel genre. Deeming it "the Picture of Life such as the Author sees it," she uses the same terms as Coleridge. Burney's picture of life is one that is viewed through a camera obscura and as such, is "astonishingly perfect." She attenuates her praise, however, by comparing Burney's skill to that of Samuel Richardson, whose work will have "Principle of duration." "Burney's Cecilia is to Richardson's Clarissa," she proclaims, "what a Camera Obscura in the Window of a London parlour,—is to a view of Venice by the clear Pencil of Canaletti [*sic*]."[62] In light of the fact that Canaletto was long believed to have used a camera obscura for his perspective views of Venetian cityscapes, and that he owned a portable device (currently in the Museo Correr, Venice), the

FIGURE 0.9 Attributed to Benjamin Martin, book camera obscura (ca. 1765), shown open (*above*) and closed (*facing page*). Calf skin, felt, glass, wood; "CAMERA OBSCURA" inscribed in gold tooling on spine. 5½ × 24½ × 18 in. (14 × 62.2 × 45.7 cm). Photograph: Collection of Historical Scientific Instruments, Harvard University.

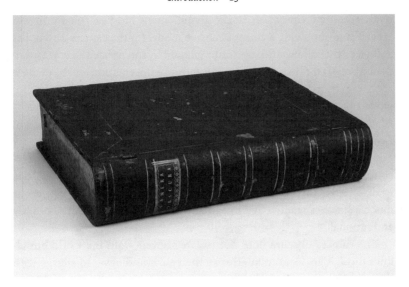

comparison seems slightly less unflattering.[63] In designating her friend's novel as a more familiar, domestic, and ephemeral view of life, mediated through a camera obscura, and Richardson's view as one that endures, having been painted by a master draughtsman who was known to have used a camera obscura, Thrale acknowledges the work of the camera obscura as a standard of artistry for novels.

In more recent times Jonathan Crary has emphasized, with great influence, a notion of the camera obscura as a "space of reason" and as such a paradigm for regulatory epistemologies of knowledge and vision that he identifies in the writings of seventeenth- and eighteenth-century philosophers such as Isaac Newton, Descartes, Locke, and Berkeley.[64] The examples he chooses from them conform with a picture of the viewing experience as an estranging and clinical one. For Crary, Newton's description in *Opticks* of using a prism inside a dark room presents the putative observer standing inside the darkened chamber as, in part, a "disembodied witness to a mechanical and transcendental re-presentation of the objectivity of the world." Ultimately the observer is "a marginal supplementary presence independent of the machinery of representation," with their body "a problem the camera could never solve except by marginalizing it into a phantom."[65] Crary sees Locke presenting the camera obscura viewer in a more dominant role. He extends to the camera obscura Locke's figure for the brain, as a "presence-room" (a chamber in a palace where a monarch receives guests) where sense impressions "from without" are selectively admitted. Crary sees Locke giving "a new juridical role to the observer" and supplying a comprehensive model for the camera obscura as a device "that allows the subject to guarantee and police the correspondence between exterior world and interior representation and to exclude anything disorderly or unruly."[66] In doing so, it "offer[s] an orderly projection of the world" and immobilizes it "for inspection by the mind."[67] *My Dark Room* presents an alternative view to Crary's understanding of Locke: the lure of the camera obscura for eighteenth-century viewers lay not so much in its immobilization and regulation of the world as in its ability to project the world in its very state of motion, whether orderly or disorderly. The camera obscura was for eighteenth-century viewers as much a space of wonder and imagination as an instrument of the orderly and rational.[68]

The camera obscura does not isolate viewers from the world but allows those it encloses to interiorize their surroundings—to engage with the world in a new way by bringing them more deeply into the self. Matter and imagination are made indistinguishable, and external reality all the more enchanting, for being inseparable from a remarkably vivid internal reality and perception.

Textual/Textural

As it turns the critical focus from objects to spaces—and considers certain objects as spaces—this book views material spaces as interactive environments for living, feeling, moving, imagining, and creating, as well as thinking.[69] By bringing examinations of spaces in material culture and their phenomenological resonances into mutual relationship with readings of literary works, I soften the boundaries between what anthropologist Tim Ingold distinguishes as the "textual" and the "textural." Material designs and qualities of real spaces are just as much objects of analysis as passages from literary texts.

This study thus enlists the approaches and insights of several disciplines outside of literary studies that emphasize the material and visual dimensions of human experience: art history, architectural history and theory, landscape design history, anthropology, media studies, film studies, and above all material culture studies (also known simply as "material culture"). The aspect of material culture that resonates in this book is its singular regard for physical structures and objects as historical-cultural subjects in their own right, endowed with the power to express, influence, and interact with human desires and to define relationships, and just as open to close reading as texts themselves. In turn, visually and materially oriented disciplines might gain from literary studies a vocabulary for perceiving how fiction and narrative are mediated through nontextual forms, from architecture and landscape design to optical devices.

In regarding space as a vital agent for shaping mental life and private experience, spatial formalism corresponds with conceptual formulations about the generative potential of enclosed situations or environments in disciplines within and outside of literary studies, from sociology to architectural theory and anthropology. Sociologist Erving Goffman, for example, offers a corresponding term for spatial formalism's notion of space as an activator of internal behavior with his frame theory, which sees social situations as theatrical. Subjects behave as actors within the *frames* that shape "the organization of experience."[70] Particularly significant to spatial formalism is the work of architectural theorist Robin Evans, already mentioned, for whom a corollary term for "setting" in the agentive sense I am pursuing it here is architecture itself, which provides "a format for social life" and "the preconditions for the way people occupy space," while playing an "instrumental role in the formation of everyday events."[71]

Offering a yet further-reaching conception of the interactive relations between organisms and environments (including spatial ones), and having even more relevance to this book's argument, is the work of Ingold. For him, organism and environmental relations form a "totality," within which they develop reciprocally, through the mutual action of their movements on each other, not just the action of the organism on the environment: "In dwelling in the world, we do not act *upon* it, or do things *to* it; rather we move along *with* it. Our actions do not transform the world, they are part and parcel of the world's transforming itself."[72] In calling for an approach to anthropology that takes into account "the agent-in-an-environment," as opposed to an "isolated, self-contained individual," Ingold insists on a reformation of anthropology that perceives no division between anthropology and psychology. The new discipline that will thus be "called into being . . . whatever we choose to call it" is one that studies "how people perceive, act, think, know, learn and remember within the settings of their mutual, practical involvement in the lived-in world."[73]

This study of how people behave in mutual and practical relation to the spaces of the world in which they live also characterizes spatial formalism and its examination of how the inner experiences of people in the long eighteenth century were shaped by the places in which they dwelled. Spatial formalism examines, for instance, how Margaret Cavendish occupied her writing closet as a space that allowed the places of her mind to expand while giving her greater intimacy with them. It also studies extant writing closets of the period, from their furnishings to their layouts, to understand the vital roles their material features played in creating such experiences.

Ingold writes that the relation between text and spatial experience is apparent only if we think of writing not as a verbal composition but as a tissue of lines—"not as text but as texture." Both words derive from the Latin verb *texĕre*, "to weave," and a rare usage for "text" is in fact "texture" itself. However, text, in predominant usage, refers specifically to the organization and arrangement of words in particular, whereas texture denotes tactility and the more general structured arrangement of contrasting elements.[74] Thus Ingold characterizes the relationship between text and texture as one "between the way in which words are inscribed upon a page of writing, and the way in which the movements and rhythms of human and non-human activity are registered in lived space."[75]

In the same way one might move into and out of a piece of writing, one moves into and out of buildings and other built environments throughout daily life, producing "entanglements" between built structures and the subjects who move through them and leave behind their traces. That one of the definitions for "space" is an inscriptional one—"a portion of a page, form, etc., available for or occupied by written or printed matter"— affirms the notion of the *architextural* as a concept that implicitly refuses a separation between lived, textual, and textural spaces; between rooms, paper sheets, and cloth.[76] Likewise, the scalar dynamics of the relationships between books and buildings, and objects and spaces, that this book reveals, beginning with the development of the camera obscura itself from a room to a handheld book, reinforces the understanding of the architextural as the crossing of texts with architectural environments. One need only to be reminded that "setting" is a term used in printing as well, with "set" the operative maneuver used for arranging type on a page and "setting" the result, to grasp the inherent connection between text and space.

In this book, the development of interiority in literature is inseparable from the historical acts of creating and inhabiting the interior designs of lived experience.[77] Insofar as literary criticism claims that "the privileged subject of modern literature is the psychic interior," this book examines how it began to emerge as such in concert with the rise of domestic spaces designed precisely to cultivate that interior.[78] Taking into mutual consideration the two realms—textual and architectural—in which interiority comes to the fore at the same historical moment, the eighteenth century, is made especially possible by an intermediary structure, the camera obscura.

Dynamic Settings

In rooms, landscape designs, buildings, and artifacts of seventeenth- and eighteenth-century England, impressions of the outside world were brought in, reconfiguring the world according to their own internal design and making it difficult to distinguish between what was real and imagined, outside and inside. In these spaces, the world that seventeenth- and eighteenth-century subjects lived in was becoming more vividly present than before through *projection*, whether via the imagination or an optical mechanism. These diverse and novel forms of enclosure contained and shaped subjects' innermost feelings, channeled their most creative visions and ideas, and transformed their conceptions of reality. Such spaces, like the camera obscura (as a device as well as a space), served not just as the locations but as the very mediums for inner experiences. They exemplified the dual meaning of the word *medium* as a "channel of communication or expression" and "the substance in which an organism lives."[79]

Throughout much of this period, the term *interiority*, "the quality or state of being interior or inward" or the "inner character or nature" of something, had been associated most closely with spiritual life in religious contexts, consistent with earlier attitudes.[80] In the Middle Ages, the human body was primarily an architectural edifice that sheltered or confined the interior entity of the soul. For Gregory the Great, "the flesh is the visible house (*domus carnis*), the soul the invisible indweller (*habitator*) looking out the windows or doors of the house, which are the senses."[81] In the Renaissance, as Katharine Eisaman Maus has shown, the conceptual division between inner and outer realms of being registered as an epistemological issue, with the inner distinguished as the site of personal, invisible "truth" and the outer as the site of what is socially apparent.[82] This separation between inwardness and outwardness emerged in religious culture as the grounds for God's divine power of omniscience; only God sees and knows the secret interior of human beings. In this regard, the interior was rendered by Renaissance humoral psychology as its own physical domain.[83] This domain was the human body itself, and, in contrast with the medieval attitude conveyed by Gregory the Great, the body with its organs, including the heart, comprises a material edifice that exists not in tension with the inner self but as its very site.[84] For Robert Burton in *The Anatomy of Melancholy*, the brain is "the dwelling house and seat of the Soule," and for Francis Bacon in *Historia Vitae et Mortis*, the stomach is "the master of the house . . . upon whose strength all the other digestions depend."[85]

In the latter part of the seventeenth century, the material space of interiority was recognized as an actual structure in the spatial environment and not just a figure for the corporeal one. As such, it was viewed as a space to be actively modified and arranged for an intensified spiritual experience. The guidebook *Enter into Thy Closet* (1663) by the Anglican bishop Edward Wettenhall designates the domestic space of a closet (at the time, the term for a small room) as the environment for cultivating a rich interior life through daily devotion within it.[86] By properly "fitting" the prayer closet with such furniture as "a Table, a Stool, and a Candlestick," as well as a "praying Desk," and opening the window to face the "visible heavens" while praying, Wettenhall proclaims, he has "designed" not just a "place for my devoute retirement" but also "a certain secret Chappel for my self."[87] Religious guidebooks such as Wettenhall's described how to turn preexisting domestic spaces into sites where one might "be alone" to nourish the "inward disposition of [the] soul" and above all, as Richard Rambuss puts it, "engage the self."[88] Affirming the architectural novelty of designing closets to be designated spaces of solitude in the seventeenth century, Lena Cowen Orlin argues that the Tudor closet, contrary to our modern assumptions, was more a rhetorical site of privacy and individual control than an actual one. Added on rather than built in, closets of the sixteenth century were commonly used as spaces for storing a household's growing stock of valuables rather than for privacy.[89]

Architectural writings instructed readers in how to build these spaces into one's house design, a novel practice at the time. Roger North, Wettenhall's seventeenth-century contemporary and an architect, recognized the creation of closets where one might retire as a feature of living without intrusion from others, including one's servants:

> But now ease and convenience is made the rule: wee demand these accommodations: first a passage to a back stair, for the servants in their common offices to pass by; next, a room for a servant to be within call, and lastly for a closet, where the person, who is supposed of quality, to retire for devotion, or study, whilst the chamber is cleaned, or company present.
> These are necessary, and indispensable.[90]

Whether a grotto or a closet for prayer or retirement, these ever more "necessary, and indispensable" architectural spaces of the early eighteenth or late seventeenth centuries were used for being alone with one's feelings and thoughts. In this role they redefined interiority in a recognizably more modern direction. Interiority came to encompass modes of inwardness—not only religious but now also secular—that were contingent on a world

ENTER INTO THY
CLOSET.

Sold by Io: Martyn at ỹᵉ Bell in Sᵗ Pauls C. Yard.

FIGURE 0.10 Edward Wettenhall, frontispiece for *Enter into Thy Closet* (1684).
Photograph: Huntington Library, San Marino, California.

whose material spaces were designed to fulfill individual needs and standards for solitude and privacy.

In the first half of the eighteenth century, owing to increased activity in the furniture trade, architects became much more attuned to the arrangement and décor of interior rooms as integral elements of their designs.[91] Architects had already begun considering the interior details of buildings in the seventeenth century, as indicated by chimney pieces drawn by Inigo Jones and a bedchamber design (including a frieze detail) by his student John Webb for their respective projects at Greenwich.[92] Yet by 1757, an even more developed sense of how wall coverings, paintings, furniture, and colors might appear in relation to each other became evident in such examples as James Stuart's drawing for the design of a state room at Kedleston Hall.

The growing awareness of interior spaces within homes as having increasingly specialized functions while offering a rich medium for design and individualization was registered in the fact that interiors were represented at all in architectural drawings. Charles Saumarez Smith explains that 1720 saw the establishment of a new convention for illustrating houses: the cutaway section. Previously, houses had been rendered in bird's-eye perspective, which allowed a house to be viewed externally, in relationship to its surrounding environment.[93] With a cutaway section, a vertical view of a building's interior is exposed, as if the façade had been sliced off.

Intensifying the new representational form's effect of revealing a building's inner contents, renowned architect William Chambers drew in 1759 the interior of the projected York House in Pall Mall. Allegedly the first of its kind, it shows the full design scheme for each room inside the house, including not just the different wall coverings and furniture for each room but also their *colors*. Admiring its "new level of realism," Saumarez Smith describes how the drawing illustrates "the afternoon sun making shadows on the walls of the central staircase." As a type of orthographic projection, the cutaway section uses perspective to show in two dimensions a structure of three dimensions. In its status as a perspectival projection that, furthermore, captures the colors of three-dimensional interior space, Chambers's drawing shares critical features of the camera obscura's imaging qualities. Not least are its function since the Renaissance as a painting device for creating perfect perspective, and its ability to produce images of the external world in color. The shadows, colors, and impression of depth were as much techniques for producing reality effects as for creating a sense of interiority. Meredith Martin observes that techniques like adding shadows and incorporating perspective into architectural interior drawings "were used with greater frequency and interest in the eighteenth century partly out of a desire to add psychological depth to the depiction of interiors."[94]

Another architectural method for imaging interior space that became prevalent in the second half of the eighteenth century was the "developed surface interior," as Evans calls it, which laid out all four walls of a room as panels on the same page. This type of architectural drawing required the viewer to envision the panels in an upright position to "see" the room as a three-dimensional space. Thomas Lightoler's drawings of staircases and a hall in William Halfpenny's *The Modern Builder's Assistant* (1757) are among the earliest examples. The technique not only allowed all decorative elements of a room to be viewed at once but also conveyed the importance of considering the room as one might experience it in lived reality. The drawing itself "dwell[s] lovingly on the inside faces" of the room, depicted as a three-dimensional space of *enclosure*, which one could imagine oneself occupying as a fully embodied being.[95] Furthermore, as Evans points out, by eliminating other rooms and elements, including the "thickness of the walls" themselves, the developed surface interior makes "the actual individual rooms the subject of architectural drawing."[96] In externalizing the interior rooms of a building as well as capturing their function as three-dimensional enclosures, the developed surface interior drawing supports the camera obscura's function of producing projected illusions of rooms by creating lasting records of such projections. The examples of the cutaway section and developed surface interior drawings demonstrate that the innovative imagining of rooms and their interiority during this period needs to be considered as intermedial and not solely textual developments.

Spatial formalism considers textual and material, and literary and landscape, environments as mutually implicated projects of design. Not just painted backdrops against which scenes can unfold, interior settings in literature, as in life, function as agents of subjective experience and narratives of internal drama and practical movement.[97] Resonating emotionally and bearing mutable qualities, settings in lived reality and literary texts acquire, as Jayne Lewis reminds us, the evocative and intangible character of atmosphere *through* rather than despite their material particularities.[98] As Maurice Merleau-Ponty observes, "Space is not the setting (real or logical) in which things are arranged, but the means whereby the position of things becomes possible."[99]

The material qualities and conditions of spaces themselves define and redefine inner realities and forms: for the landed gentry, a country house floor plan with a corridor affords greater choices and privacy in moving

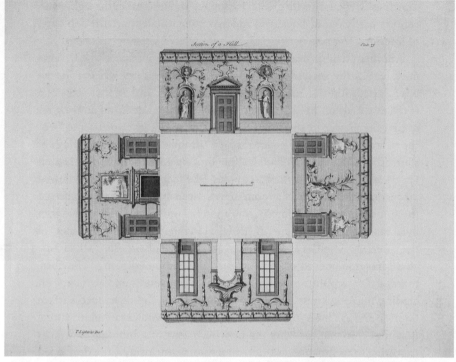

FIGURE 0.11 Example of a "developed surface interior" drawing. Thomas Lightoler, Section of a Hall. From William Halfpenny, *The Modern Builder's Assistant* (1757). Photograph: Getty Research Institute, Los Angeles.

between parts of the house. A floor plan without this neutral zone of passage forces inhabitants to walk through individual private rooms to reach their desired destination, which entails the relinquishment of solitude and the imaginative states of mind it fosters. Or, for female servants like the eponymous heroine of Richardson's *Pamela*, the woman's detachable pocket is a domestic space of privacy, intimacy, and movement. In this capacity it can function like a portable writing closet. Spatial formalism, then, reveals how material and generic forms are related—including forms of architecture, texts, and textiles—because they are co-identified and experienced primarily as space.[100]

This consideration of space can be usefully compared to literary theorist Mieke Bal's idea of space in narrative as a "frame" in which events can occur.[101] The world of narrative, in fact, is essentially spatial, for it "gives space to events, so that events can, as the phrase goes, *take place*."[102] Bal's observation also concurs to a certain extent with D. S. Bland, who views narrative space as a place in which "characters can act out their stories," with the "precision" of its rendition critical to a sense of realism. For Bland, narrative spatial environments function in this way much like "the dramatically presented description and the stage scenery of drama."[103] Moreover, narrative setting needs to be as realistic as possible to overcome the fact that it, unlike drama, cannot offer directly embodied forms of representation. Yet for Bal, the realistic nature of narrative needs to be apparent for a more direct reason than this: "The space must resemble the actual world, so that the events situated within it also become plausible." With this, Bal suggests for us how narrative spaces in particular may operate like the projective space of the camera obscura. Narrative spaces, like the camera obscura's projected images, do not so much refer to or describe the concrete world as serve as illusory projections of it. Just as the characters of a literary work might behave in a particular way given the type of space they are operating within, so too might occupants of the same spaces in lived reality.[104] For this reason, space as setting in literature must be viewed not just as a stable descriptive referent but, like its model in reality, as a site of interactivity.

The "real" in spatial formalism is this interface of literary technique and the material dimensions of lived spaces. At this point of connection, the interiority of a more broadly conceived fiction that emerges in different media and literary genres, including poetry, achieves its form and definition. An example of this broadened, intermedial notion of fiction arises in the landscape follies of chapter 5; here, newly built castles appearing to be old ruins generate an air of mystery for visitors and make them feel haunted by a far more distant past. Projections of everyday life, whether in camera obscuras, domestic interiors, or books, furnished novel spaces and experiences of interiority for eighteenth-century subjects while giving them a sense of home in unexpected places.

Interiority in this study stakes out a terrain distinct from philosophical debates (empiricism versus idealism) and their newer, related concepts (distributed cognition or extended mind). Locating the realm of interiority in camera obscuras, writing closets, the artificially abraded rocks of picturesque follies, and the plotted embroidery patterns of women's detachable pockets as well as in long poems, novels, letters, and aesthetic treatises, this book reveals what it means to have an inner life in a modern world where space is a vital medium of individuation, imagination, and fiction. Interiority, in other words, is rooted in daily life contexts—it is as much an architectural space to occupy (a writing closet or a grotto) as the inner region of mental experiences, conveyed outward through pen and paper. In these material details, stories about inner life and its adventures can be traced, discovered, and created. A country house estate, for example, does not so much reflect the owner's strength and valor as become a reflection of all who look into it. One sees oneself in its landscape as it becomes a medium for self-reflection. In turn, the poem depicting this, Andrew Marvell's *Upon Appleton House*, prompts the reader to wonder if she has been, within the space of the poem, inside a mental space or a physical one. The focus of my book is this spatial interface of imagination and material reality, the domain of inner life.

In locating the "real" in the interface of literary technique and the material dimensions of lived space, spatial formalism builds on and moves beyond Ian Watt's still influential elaboration on the novel's technical features not just as a literary genre but as a genre of the everyday, in which he identifies interiority as a function of the novel's "formal realism."[105] For Watt, formal realism is designated by, in addition to a minutely delineated time frame, the sense that a narrative is unfolding "in an actual physical environment."[106] Within these novel yet familiar narrative environments, characters in turn appear more real as individuals and, as such, more capable of undertaking the "adventures of interiority" that Georg Lukács claims the novel genre "tells."[107] Such "solidity of setting" and place might emerge through descriptions of material objects, interior spaces, or topography, as in the work of Daniel Defoe, Samuel Richardson, and Henry Fielding respectively. Despite its conceptual power, formal realism tends to treat the spatial environments it mentions as givens of daily life that are described as self-evident objects of realist description. Spatial formalism, on the other hand, asks how a more developed historical account of the houses themselves, and the ways in which their structural qualities as inhabited spaces affect passages of mind, might shed new light on Watt's proclamation "we go inside their minds as well as inside their houses."[108] As material constructs that were designed, created, and experienced during a specific time, what made these houses more conducive to going into the minds of the people who inhabited them?

As Cynthia Wall has argued, narrative space in eighteenth-century fiction cannot be seen merely as ready-made backdrops. Spatial settings in eighteenth-century fiction are instead disarticulated constructs that emerge through the flow of narrative and thus arise organically, "opening" up through detail and the movement of events in a story.[109] In a later elaboration of this argument, Wall observes that spaces in early eighteenth-century fiction, from balconies and bedchambers to windows and doorways, "arise strictly when called on by the plot" or "emerge when a character needs to encounter them."[110] For Wall, space acquires presence primarily through the vivifying powers of description, especially descriptive details: "Detail opened narrative spaces, transforming static setting into moving surface, into possibilities for action, into fluid worlds."[111] Attributing dynamic qualities to description, thereby challenging prevailing assumptions about its "static" nature, Wall's supple argument subordinates space to description as its main protagonist, with the exigencies of plot serving as the engine for its manifestation.[112]

Whereas the core subject for Wall is language itself and its power, through description, of bodying forth spaces conceived in the imagination, in *My Dark Room*, spaces and the humans who occupy, design, and create them are central, rather than language. Humans and spaces, mutually influencing each other, are formed, change, and come into being in their interactions. It is in this way that spaces are settings, or locations where things or persons are placed, not so much like a jewel as like a living organism in an environment with which it interacts. Throughout, my book redefines the literary notion of setting by first underscoring one of its definitions: as the organization and disposition of space and "the particular physical location" in which episodes or scenes take place.[113] In a more general sense, settings in literary works, particularly narrative, are the designated environments that serve as the frameworks in which the fabricated lives of fictional persons are set and the stories of their lives unfold.

Along these lines, literary setting has also been understood as general historical, social, or cultural context, within both the work itself and the circumstances in which it was created. Some of the most influential studies in eighteenth-century literature in the past thirty years have focused on tracing this context in various cultural-historical areas, from prison reform and domestic ideology to popular literary traditions and print culture. Certainly, this book is indebted to the general approach taken in such works of bringing to the foreground contextual matters that might otherwise be considered "background." Yet for this book, *setting* is not general social or cultural context but specific forms of embodied space arising in domestic built environments as they interact with the self and the imagination and mediate them.[114]

Spatial formalism shows that literary texts incorporate private spaces far more deeply and intricately into their own logic and design, and into their shaping of personhood, than has been recognized. They do not represent sites of domestic life only as manifestations of ideological developments and pressures, as literary critics such as Nancy Armstrong and Michael McKeon have demonstrated.[115] Nor do they describe only the interiors, landscapes, and physical environments in which narratives unfold. Point of view and perspective, voice, epistolary writing, and free indirect discourse have been well established as features of literary form and technique, especially for realist narrative. The very textual transmission and structuring of psychic experience in space and time are enabled by them. However, the story of their development in close and reciprocal relationship to the material designs and settings of home, dwelling, and daily life in seventeenth- and eighteenth-century England has further to be told.

My Dark Room

Focusing on a different space in each chapter, the book is organized chronologically, moving from the middle of Britain's seventeenth century to the last quarter of the eighteenth. It reveals a chronological progression of moments when increasingly pervasive spatial forms specific to each period and corresponding texts yielded interactive experiences of interiority. One spatial form prevalent throughout most of the book, in addition to the camera obscura, is the country house. A complex space of cultural interpretation, the early modern country house inevitably engenders the architectural codes of privacy, domesticity, and social distinction central to the development of literature's language of interiority, especially in the novel. I trace this architectural development from the country house poetry of the seventeenth century—and Marvell's decisive turn away from it for a more inward and directly embodied form of poetic meditation on an estate in *Upon Appleton House*—to Richardson's psychologically oriented narrative of country house realism in *Pamela,* and to the landscape follies of stately homes that give architectural shape to fantasies of the past.

In *Upon Appleton House* (written in 1651, published posthumously in 1681), Andrew Marvell (1621–1678) depicts the landscape and garden design of his patron's country house estate according to its features in real time and space. The act typifies as much conventions of the seventeenth-century country house poem as it does the "localization" that Ian Watt claims would be a defining trait of the novel genre and its innovative realist technique. D. S. Bland, expanding on Watt, uses a "rough test" for identifying localization in a novel: can one "draw a map or make a picture from the data" provided by narrative description?[116] One can certainly create such plans and pictures with the details of spatial design provided in *Upon Appleton House,* but those details also serve as the medium through which the poet's interiority expands, deepens, and becomes more real in the course of the poem by organizing the choices he makes about how to proceed during his tour of the estate.

Registering in multiple ways the effects created by a pivotal change in the architecture of domestic space, which especially gave house dwellers the space and range of motion to have a private self, *Upon Appleton House* marks a departure from traditional country house poetry. It regards the country house not as a fixed symbol of social order and tradition but as a metamorphic structure for the embodied experience of private perception. As it does so, it serves as the starting point for an interiority situated in the region where material and mental life overlap and interact. It also signals the onset of a way of living inside the interior spaces of one's mind and one's physical environment simultaneously.

Marvell's contemporary Margaret Cavendish (1623–1673) made a career out of her profoundly interiorized approach to living, and asserted her need and determination to do so. A vital setting that allowed this chosen way of life was her writing closet. Chapter 2's examination of the role Cavendish's writing closet played in her creative and intellectual processes reveals how, for historical figures, interior settings were dwellings that constituted the domain of life. The writing closet was a place where Cavendish's mental life merged with its location in architectural space, serving as an environmental medium for making real the inner processes of an exceptionally creative and philosophical mind. The cherished space let Cavendish dwell as much as possible in her mental world while maintaining a connection with the physical elements of her domestic environment. In so doing, she produced multigeneric works that are textual as well as textural experiments in giving form and expression to an interior life that is domestically bound and that are rendered through their publication as mobile surrogates of both her brain and her house.

Cavendish found through her closet that the conjoined spaces of mind and home made possible the opportunity to imagine and live inside invented worlds. Alexander Pope, also a socially marginalized subject, discovered in the early eighteenth century a similar function with the grotto at his villa home. Yet unlike Cavendish, Pope was actively if not passionately involved with designing his enclosed space to serve that role in aesthetically calculated ways. The extent of his dedication to its design is evident in the fact that Pope was almost as famous for his grotto as he was for his poetry. A visitor in 1748 described how, inside the grotto, one encounters "an undistinguishable mixture of realities and imagery." This remark captures the impression created by *Eloisa to Abelard* (1717), a poem that manipulates language to create the credible experience of another's interior life. Pope's grotto recreated the poem's manipulation of darkness to illuminate the passage of feelings and thoughts as they move through the mind of an imagined being. In effect, the physical space of the grotto transformed the poem's textual effects into a textural, material reality.

Chapter 3 argues that it was predominantly in Pope's life as a grotto de-signer and dweller, that is, as a spatial formalist, that the projections of psychological interiority in illusory spaces were most extensively per-formed and experienced.

The grotto's function as a camera obscura demonstrates how in Pope's experience of interior life—the life he carefully designed when seeking the retirement and solitude required for artistic creation—he was able to make scenes of the outside world emerge inside. He did so as much on the walls of the grotto as in the space of his mind. With matter and imag-ination rendered indistinguishable, external reality becomes ever more enchanting for its inseparability from a stunningly vivid internal reality.

Spaces of interiority need to be understood not just as architectural interiors but also as sartorial ones, such as detachable pockets, which women of the eighteenth century wore close to the body. Contemporary usage of the word *fabric* illustrates the connection between architecture and dress: originally meaning "building" or "contrivance," it was not un-til the second half of the eighteenth century that the word came to mean "textile." The woman's detachable pocket was a site where internal projec-tions of experiences in lived reality accumulated and were stored in the form of letters. As such, they functioned like the pocket-size camera ob-scuras appearing on the market around the same time, but with streaming epistolary projections that were artifactual and enduring.

Critics have long noted how Pamela's writing closets function as spaces of interiority and self-possession in the novel. Frequently overlooked is the fact that such architecturally defined interior spaces do not give her full protection from her master; he owns the houses in which the closets are built and attempts to hide in them as if they were camera obscuras affording views into her mind. The enclosed spaces of Pamela's pockets function as a portable space for hiding the letters that Mr. B attempts to steal from her closet. What appears to be an inconsequential material ob-ject in fact functions as a mobile form of possessive interiority, as well as a medium of spatial formalism for a subject born without access to landed property.

Pockets offer Pamela a setting for her most private belongings, her let-ters, but private rooms offer settings for narrative action and the acquisi-tion of spoken information that might not be available otherwise. Rooms in this way play significant roles in the novel as camera obscuras of sorts, in which characters such as Mr. B and Pamela sit in hiding and hear and see things normally hidden from them. They model in this way camera obscuras used for observing eclipses throughout the early modern period.

Letters, and in turn the pockets that carry them, turn the rooms of private households into movable spaces as they relay information about the interior worlds housed within them.

Whereas detachable pockets ensured a concealed and mobile form of possessive interiority on the body of an individual, architectural fictions of historical pasts that never happened were being incorporated into fashionable landscape gardens of country house estates to be regarded out in the open. This shift further demonstrates the movability of interior spaces, not just in relation to the body, but also to purported divisions between "outside" and "inside," and "past" and "present." These architectural fictions, made out of stone abraded to look ancient and known as "follies," were viewed through camera obscuras and black mirrors, thereby turning exterior communal space into a zone of internal reverie and fantasy. Those who visited or regarded them experienced transformations in their own interior states as they, prompted by the mysterious appearance of seeming ruins, pondered historical events that might have taken place. Follies shed light on how fiction not only creates environments for interior lives but is created by built environments.

Horace Walpole is known for using Strawberry Hill, the modest and nondescript estate he transformed into "a little Gothic fiction," as the inspiration for inaugurating the Gothic genre of fiction with his *Castle of Otranto* (1764). Yet Walpole was not the first to use a building to mediate a Gothic fiction. Chapter 5 argues that much earlier in the century, the landscape follies standing on such country house estates as Hagley, the Leasowes, and Wimpole Hall performed Gothic fictions in their own right, catching the eye and psyche in doing so. By making manifest in everyday spaces the internal visions of a projected past, eighteenth-century landscape follies exemplify how fiction can go beyond text and paper to emerge as an intermedial and transhistorical space of the psyche. The folly demonstrates that Gothic fictions were created with architectural and landscape media as well as text. The folly also functioned as a medium in itself by conducting fantasies about the past through its spatial arrangements and the embodied experience of them. The development of the Gothic novel was dependent on the prior existence and experience of Gothic form as an architectural fiction in the daily built environments of eighteenth-century Britain. In this way, the Gothic as an architectural construct demands that we reevaluate Gothic fiction as central, not alternative, to the development of "domestic realism" as a narrative category.

The folly also demonstrates that fiction-making was equally an aspect of eighteenth-century literary worlds and of material environments in everyday life, especially when viewed through a camera obscura or black mirror. By this point in time, the camera obscura was not just a model for the imagination but the imagination itself, according to William Gilpin, theorist of the picturesque. Rearranging, rescaling, and recreating the features of one's everyday environment so they appeared spectral, the camera obscura performed optically what Gothic fiction did textually through bound print objects. The portability of the camera obscura by this point allowed for spectral transpositions as well as household items to be carried in one's pocket. It also reflected a point in time when the carriage of interior spaces became a standard feature of day-to-day life. The domain of inner life, once predominantly found within an encompassing and fixed structure, was ready at hand.

My own experience with portable eighteenth- and nineteenth-century camera obscuras has shown that the accuracy of their depiction is susceptible to subjective interpretation, as well as the romantic alterations of mediated viewing. Using camera obscuras from media archaeologist Erkki Huhtamo's collection, I saw many effects that historical documents and critical writing about them do not seem to describe or capture. I was struck, for one thing, not so much by how well the device reproduces reality but, rather, by how much it captures reality as a dream experience.

If, to seventeenth- and eighteenth-century eyes, the view of the camera obscura appeared to "delineate accurately" the objects and spaces of one's immediate reality, it seems to have done so as a dreamscape, fit for the meditative act of "contemplation," not just as visual reproduction. At the same time, the reproduction in itself proves to be highly subjective and interpretive, as the disparity between tracings of the camera obscura–mediated scene created by two different viewers makes clear. So individualized are the lines of each tracing that one can hardly tell they were made using the same machine. Each is a picture of one person's inner sense of the world.

Spatial formalism and the interdisciplinary investigation of interiority in these chapters illuminate the complexities of today's spaces and our experiences of interiority. Today we are in the predicament of continually retreating to interior worlds through our electronic devices while revealing our private lives to an invisible public, as image-making technologies enlarge and disseminate projected slivers of everyday life through social media. Portable interior spaces accompany us, as people stare at laptop screens in cafés or at their smart phones as they walk down the street, oblivious to the environment around them. In these ways our lives parade in front of us on the screen, and we have become more comfortable with being immersed in virtual worlds mediated by external devices than in real spaces.

In contrast, the images of everyday life projected by the camera obscura are flowing and fleeting at once, never stable, lasting, or disseminatable, unless recorded by tracing, filming, or photographing them. Paradoxically, they anchor one in the material dimensions of one's environment by exquisitely intensifying the visual qualities of entities captured by the device's gaze, both in color and in movement. Furthermore, the moment of projection coincides with the direct moment, turning any immediate happening into a mirage or dream. One's sense of time becomes transformed, seemingly elongated, as movements becomes isolated and one's perception of them becomes far more acute. The response of tree branches to a slight breeze turns into a series of mesmerizing micromotions, and the view of the Santa Monica Mountains is more evocative of a distant memory than a direct impression of them. As the image moves inside the box, held in one's hands at chest height, one has the sense of holding a world while looking down at it, as one would with a smartphone, or an open book. Yet, what others around you might not know is that the image on the screen is of the world directly in front of you, which has turned into both your own inner reality and a dream world, an elsewhere that is actually quite close. Such were the impressions produced by my experience of looking through a portable nineteenth-century camera obscura that uses the same mechanism as an eighteenth-century design from the rooftop of UCLA's Broad Art Center on a summer day.[117]

The simultaneity is spatial as well; one is either surrounded by the space or holding it in one's hands while the reality being projected in the camera obscura's stream of images is happening. The effect is one of co-presence and intimacy with a reverie.[118] That one is either surrounded by the space or holding it in one's hands deepens this sense of copresence and intimacy. Feeling haunted by a vivid dream is inescapable, for the camera obscura's imaging of reality is a reminder of something but is never actually it. Not just a mediation of reality, it is a transformation of reality, rechanneling it according to its own temporality, intensity of color, and blurriness, turning immediate experience into a continually streaming reminiscence.

In these ways, the inner drama of emotions, as well as the ephemerality and wonder of visual projection, which play a significant part in the experience of camera obscuras, simply does not feature so much in today's image-making technologies. And yet the camera obscura's deep allure in eighteenth-century England's designs and experiences of interiority allows us to see anew our own fascination with virtual realities and

FIGURE 0.12 Views of the Santa Monica Mountains using an early nineteenth-century camera obscura (*top*) and a phone camera (*bottom*) (2018). Erkki Huhtamo Collection of Optical Devices. Photographs by the author.

FIGURE 0.13 The author using a nineteenth-century camera obscura modeled on an eighteenth-century design to view the Santa Monica Mountains from the roof of the Broad Art Center, University of California, Los Angeles (2018). Erkki Huhtamo Collection of Optical Devices. Photograph by Erkki Huhtamo.

preoccupations with delimiting the borders of possessive interiority in an era of technologically generated "home pages" and "privacy settings." It is through studying the spatial forms of inner realities in eighteenth-century England, whether in dark rooms, gardens, books, or hearts and minds in motion, that we may grasp how designing and inhabiting the diverse spaces for our inner selves has become critical to the way we live and define who we are now.

Country House

MAKING STORYLINES
AT NUN APPLETON

The country manor house remains a fixture of eighteenth-century British fiction, if not fictions of British life in general. From Paradise Hall and Bramble Hall to Brideshead and Tallis, country manor houses define the works in which they appear, turning them into worlds of their own.[1] As narrative setting, the country house estate provides the framework in which plots may develop and expresses the ethos of characters and their community. In many eighteenth-century novels, it is given at the end of the story as the ultimate reward for correct moral behavior and conduct, or it works as the medium through which a character realizes her romantic error. So pervasive a feature is the country house in novels, and so polished its integration in the narrative machinery of such authors as Jane Austen, it seems innate to the novel genre and its celebrated portrayals of life within psychological and spatial interiors. Yet the seemingly native alliances between narrative, country house setting, and interiority that achieve their full development in novels of domestic realism—perhaps the most modern and English of narrative genres—derive from a historical background of generic, architectural, and social flux. Spatial formalism reveals how the interplay between physical environments and embodied encounters with them was pivotal in this background, with the camera obscura a vital paradigm for experiencing spaces of the country house estate as inner space.

Before novels, country houses and the traditional way of life they supported were represented in a tradition of politically conservative poetry written throughout the seventeenth century.[2] Named "country house poems" by G. R. Hibbard, these texts equated the estate's architecture and grounds with the owner's virtues, as well as with "a way of life" centered on supporting the economy and social life of the community.[3] Originally, in the poems privileging and apostrophizing it, the country house existed in real time and space, as an object of veneration and an architectural extension of its lord, the poet's patron, a real person. The estate in country house poetry was most significant not as an agent for plot movement, but as an agent for upholding community and an "icon for power, legitimacy, and authority."[4] The viewpoint of such poetry is a collective and idealizing one. Country house poems following Ben Jonson's paradigmatic example in "To Penshurst" (1616) vanished after 1660, for this was when the feudal way of life they reflected began to wane.[5] Changes in the social function of the great house, as well as in architectural style, contributed most to this decline.[6]

Andrew Marvell's *Upon Appleton House* marks the last stage of the traditional country house poem; it appeared at a time when poets had begun to rely less on patrons and the country house and its great hall no longer occupied a central place in the "political, social and intellectual" life of the nation.[7] Toward the second half of the seventeenth century, such life found its new center in London. Estate poems continued to be written after *Upon Appleton House*, and well into the eighteenth century, with poems such as Alexander Pope's *Epistle to Bathurst* (1733) paying homage to a long-vanished age and what Hibbard repeatedly calls its "way of life."[8] But the fact that a new narrative genre would come to import the country house as a critical element in its textual designs, for very different ends and effects, suggests a new way of building, designing and inhabiting country houses had emerged as well.[9]

Just as innovations in the architectural design of country houses made inevitable changes in the subjective experience of domestic space, and changes in the experience of subjectivity itself, so too were transformations in the writing about such experiences made inevitable.[10] This is to say that literature's textual forms cannot be fully comprehended without awareness of the material forms of lived reality that surrounded their development. While traditional country house poetry invoked the architectural characteristics of a patron's home to reflect a greater view of his role in society, the more introspective form of country house poetry modeled by Marvell's *Upon Appleton House* enacts and builds on new designs in the domestic environment that made space for the freedom of possessive interiority. These designs introduce new pathways of embodied perspective into the domestic environment. Marvell's poem, true to the experience of introspection, resists strict categories and boundaries, and wanders as it follows an unpredictable path.[11] Rather than "a way of life," which never changes, the poem represents everyday life, which defines itself as much through routine events as through contingent ones, and through the familiar spaces that channel and shape one's movements and thoughts.

In Jonson's time, country house estates like Penshurst still retained their community function from the Middle Ages, serving as the foundation for a network of relationships that formed local social and economic structures, including the interlocked relationships between lords and their servants.[12] Through acts of housekeeping, offering food and drink in the great hall to all classes, lords expanded the boundaries of their estate to include those who served them. Giving more than sustenance, landlords provided in their great halls "a common meeting ground" to all classes that allowed them to "feel members of the whole."[13] By the time Jonson wrote his poem, though, such customs of housekeeping and the use of the great hall were on the wane, supplying the source for the poem's nostalgia.

As the name would suggest, great halls of country houses were rooms of immense size. At Penshurst, which was built in the fourteenth century, the great hall measures sixty-two by thirty-nine feet, with a ceiling sixty feet high. Its twenty-foot-long trestle tables, dating to the fifteenth century, indicate that the hall served as a gathering place for a community, and its open hearth signals that comfort was experienced communally. That "the kind of society Pope approves of was already no more than a ghost" at the time he published *Epistle to Burlington* in 1731 indicates that building country houses as showpieces for individual wealth and power had become the norm, and that those who contributed to and constituted the "life of the community," as celebrated by Jonson, had disappeared.[14] The hall's loss of dominance in country house architecture was not just a function of changes in social structures and the waning of feudal orders; at the same time, families began to seek private rooms for dining and other purposes.[15] As rooms become more specialized, the prior function of the great hall as a space where food and drink were shared gave way to its new purpose as a vestibule. It became, in other words, a space for waiting and expectation, not hospitality. Such changes in the function and design of country houses corresponded not just with the decline of the country house poem but also with the occupants' growing demand for domestic privacy.[16]

As early as the late fourteenth century, families had begun to withdraw from the company of others and to dine separately, in rooms adjoining the hall known as the solar or great chamber.[17] Later, in the sixteenth century, owners of older country houses signaled the departure from the Middle Ages by further dismantling the architecture of manorial housekeeping;

this entailed subdividing great halls and creating new, smaller rooms for day-to-day functions: parlors, withdrawing rooms, closets, study chambers, bed chambers.[18] Owners added ceilings to the great halls, halving their heights to control drafts. Other structural changes included the introduction of staircases and corridors, which created passageways from communal spaces to private ones for family members.[19]

In direct correspondence with domestic architecture's unceasing movement toward promoting privacy and the ability to be apart from those not one's intimates during everyday rituals, private property emerged and developed steadily as "an economic aspect of individualism." The collapse of the medieval property systems allowed for the development of a system that treated land as a commodity and transformed its "basic unit of ownership" from the household to the individual.[20] Diplomat and writer Henry Wotton, in *The Elements of Architecture* (1624), recognized as "the first complete English treatise of classical architecture," articulates an opportunity for independence and autonomy in country house ownership.[21] The country house estate, for the man who owns it, is "a kinde of private *Princedome*":

> Every Mans proper *Mansion* house and Home, being the *Theater* of his *Hospitality*, the *Seate* of *Self-fruition*, the *Comfortablest part* of his owne *Life*, the *Noblest* of his Sonnes *Inheritance*, a kinde of private *Princedome*; Nay, to the *Possessors* thereof, an *Epitomie* of the whole *World*.[22]

So complete are its multiple functions in a man's life, defining his public identity while contributing to his private comfort and ensuring the posterity of his family line, that the country house, both as "house and Home," represents (as Utopia and all utopian communities might) "an *Epitomie* of the whole *World*." Central to this status is the fact that public and private spheres coexist even in privately owned space. Both a "*Theater* of his *Hospitality*" and "the *Comfortablest part* of his owne *Life*," the country house is the domain for a man of property's public identity as well as for his private life.

What the camera obscura offers inside its space is also aptly described as an "*Epitomie* of the whole *World*." It is no accident that Wotton, who eloquently described the boundaries of selfhood within the architectural context of a country house estate, also penned the most vivid description of encountering a portable camera obscura. In it, he addressed its application to managing one's private property by speculating about how it could be used as a tool for mapping and describing the landscape. As this chapter reveals, Marvell's poem in a similar fashion presents the possibility of experiencing the spaces and grounds of a country house estate within the space of a mobile camera obscura that continually envelops the outer world within its architecture of interiority.

In this way, the experience of the country house and its landscapes in *Upon Appleton House* resembles the model of "the built environment in motion," as architectural historian Kimberley Skelton puts it, that appears in Vincenzo Scamozzi's *L'idea della architettura universal*, a text owned and read by influential seventeenth-century architects John Webb, Inigo Jones, and Sir Roger Pratt.[23] Webb, in fact, designed Nun Appleton around the early 1650s. In Scamozzi's *L'idea*, an architectural space is illustrated in which light rays are projected through different apertures into the room, suggesting an interior space subject to the movement and modulation of light that takes place throughout the day and across the seasons (fig. 1.1).[24] This drawing illustrates that architectural space is, much like the camera obscura, a receptacle for receiving the play of light, whose shifting qualities transform the subjective experience of the space dramatically. Likewise, as spatial formalism further reveals, Marvell's country house poem is a medium for the interactive relationship between the mind, its environment, and the topographically and architecturally located transformations in perspective that ensue, and not just a static representation of a manor house and the lord who owns it. *Stanza*, after all, means "room" in Latin. And the stanza serves, throughout Marvell's poem, as a camera obscura as well as a unit of textual composition that interiorizes what it depicts, connecting architectural and landscape spaces with shifting stories of inner life. In this sense, the poem exemplifies the "crossing of texts with architectural environments" referred to earlier as the "architextural."

The Architecture of Mental Experience

The dynamic interchange between the public and the private within the country house itself was the result of a significant seventeenth-century architectural innovation: the double pile house plan. Created by placing two rows of rooms parallel to each other, with a corridor running between them, the double pile gave houses a compact and symmetrical external appearance. The key innovation was the corridor, which allowed inhabitants to walk into rooms from a common space rather than through adjoining private rooms. Though the double pile was in use as far back as the early sixteenth century, as exemplified in East Barsham (ca. 1520) and Hengrave (1525–1538), it epitomized seventeenth-century architecture, reaching a state of refinement during this period. Notable examples of the

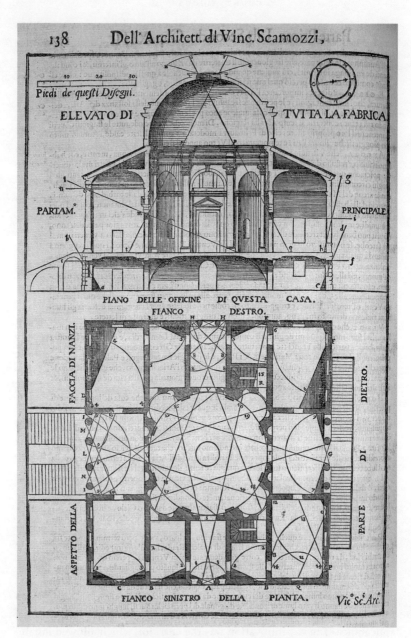

FIGURE 1.1 Vincenzo Scamozzi, "Elevato di Tvtta la Fabrica,"
in *L'idea della architettura universal* (1615).
Photograph: Getty Research Institute, Los Angeles.

double pile plan include Inigo Jones's Queen's House (1616–1636), Roger Pratt's Coleshill (ca. 1658–1662), and John Webb's Amesbury (1661).

The double pile design facilitated the "the delicate and elegant balance . . . between public and private" in seventeenth-century England.[25] Strengthening the boundaries around private spaces, marking a clearer

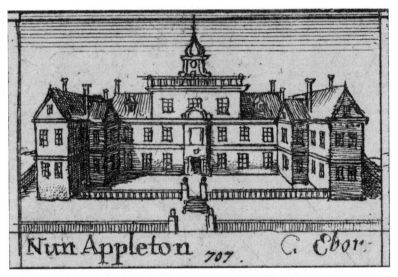

FIGURE 1.2 Daniel King, design for Nun Appleton House: front (*top*) and back (*bottom*) elevations (ca. 1655). Bodleian MS Gough 1, fol. 1. Photograph: Bodleian Libraries, University of Oxford.

distinction between private and public areas, and accelerating movement through the house were all important consequences of the corridor. Yet, more significant than its enforcement of separations and creation of unobstructed pathways were the *options* it made available, the increased nuances and possibilities it produced in the subjective perception and negotiation of the interchange between private and public space.

Addressing the social impact that the spatial innovation of the corridor brought to architectural design, Robin Evans writes, "No longer was it necessary to pass serially through the intractable occupied territory of rooms, with all the diversion, incidents and accidents that they might harbor . . . these thoroughfares were able to draw distant rooms closer, but only by disengaging those near at hand. And in this there is another glaring paradox: in facilitating communication, the corridor reduced contact."[26] By distinguishing private from communal space, the corridor simultaneously created a connection between the two domains and facilitated the fluid movement between them. To be in private and interior spaces, as modeled in the quintessentially seventeenth-century floor plan of the double pile, entailed awareness of the immediate options for crossing into public spaces even while having greater access to private ones.

Though scholars argue over which house Marvell encountered during his stay at Nun Appleton House as the family tutor (ca. late 1650–1652), it is now impossible to determine whether it was the modest old house built after the Dissolution in the middle of the sixteenth century or the grand new one designed by Webb in the 1650s and illustrated in the King engraving of ca. 1655–1660. Knowledge of Webb's role in the design of Nun Appleton is critical, for he was a seventeenth-century architect who "achieved [the] finest architectural expression" of the double pile house plan. It may have been too early for him to have perfected the plan by the time he worked on Nun Appleton House, but Webb was already designing with a view toward creating more freedom of movement and circulation, as his plan for the house he worked on just before, Maiden Bradley (1646–1640), demonstrates. If the scholars are correct who believe that Marvell lived in the new house, or at least was present when work on it began, then he would likely have encountered the double pile plan, or a plan that would lead to it later.[27]

If not the double pile itself, the affordances and consequences of the architectural form—the experience of domestic space as a state of potential crossing between public and private, or communal and solitary, states—would have been available elsewhere and difficult for Marvell to escape in his world. The *Oxford English Dictionary* lists 1620 as its earli-

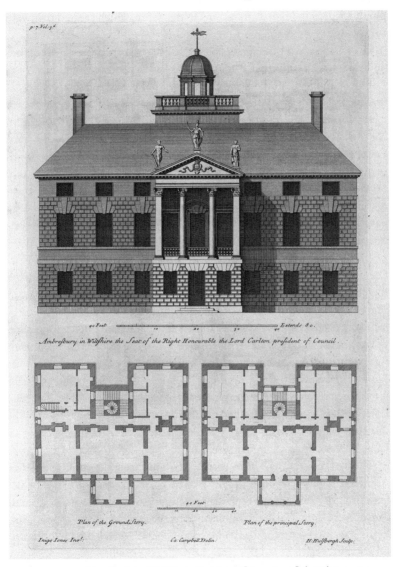

FIGURE 1.3 Plan for John Webb's Ambresbury [Amesbury] (1661), based on
designs by Inigo Jones, in Colen Campbell, *Vitruvius Britannicus*, vol. 3 (1715).
Photograph: Getty Research Institute, Los Angeles.

est usage citation for "corridor" as "a passage . . . between two places."
Certainly, Marvell evinces an awareness of the element of choice and
possibility that devices like corridors afford in passing between different modes of occupying the interior world of a country house estate.
Bringing this awareness to bear on the literary form of the country house

poem resulted in pivotal alterations to the genre, which created pathways to new ones.

If Jonson in "To Penshurst" claims that the estate's owner, Robert Sidney, distinguishes himself from owners of such prodigy house estates as Longleat and Wollato because they have "built" their edifices, whereas he "dwells" in his, then one might say that Marvell enjoyed an advantage in constructing his ambitious heap of a poem because he, unlike Jonson, had dwelled in the house he is celebrating.[28] As the hired tutor to Lord Fairfax's daughter Mary—the young heiress whose arrival on the landscape ends the poem—he had the opportunity to experience the estate on the level of a live-in employee rather than that of a guest. *Upon Appleton House*, that is, departs from country house poetry tradition in large part by basing itself on the richly subjective associations Marvell developed in his time as a dweller on Fairfax's estate.[29]

Marvell came to Nun Appleton from London to work as Mary Fairfax's tutor late in 1650, and he left in the spring or summer of 1652. Being a member of the household for nearly two years would certainly have given Marvell an opportunity to experience the estate intimately. And because intimacy produces complexity as well as the richness of inner experience, the abbreviating polarities that at once drive "To Penshurst" and keep its proportions balanced and contained would have been unsuitable for Marvell's poem.[30] In *Upon Appleton House*, the estate is as much the site for his own retreat and contemplation as it was for his employer, Thomas, Lord Fairfax, when he retired from military life as commander-in-chief of the New Model Army in 1650. Fairfax's retirement from public life is in fact the occasion for the poem.

The first ten stanzas, with their focus on the architectural character of Appleton House, establish the house not just as a symbol for Lord Fairfax's integrity but as an agent for narrative. At the outset, they imitate Jonson's rhetoric of flattery in his country house poems by equating the house's architectural modesty and elegance with its owner's excellence. Other critics have noted the conventionality of the first stanza; in using architectural details of the house as the vehicles of encomium, it and the nine stanzas following remain within the country house poem tradition. Yet the first eight lines, even in following literary tradition, stray from panegyric and begin to generate narrative flow. Not just describing the house as an extension of its lord, they create a fanciful equation between the man-made structure and man himself:

> Within this sober frame expect
> Work of no foreign architect;

That unto caves the quarries drew,
And forests did to pastures hew;
Who of his great design in pain
Did for a model vault his brain,
Whose columns should so high be raised
To arch the brows that on them gazed.[31]

House and human mirror each other in this stanza: the house resembles a human face, and the human face a house. Rising to perceive the building's columns, the brows themselves become "arches." At the same time, reflecting the Vitruvian notion that the proportions of temples must follow those of the human body, and referencing the Constantijn Huygens poem *Hofwyck* (1651), which figures the house and garden as the head and body of a human, the house resembles a human head, replete with a "brain" and columns that raise the brows.[32] While these arching brows belong to a human viewer, the subject referred to in "on them gazed" is ambiguous: the gazer could be the columns as they regard the brows, or the brows as they regard the columns. The features and identities of observing self and inanimate building become interchangeable and indistinguishable; the text registers the process by which the self and the space become mutually constitutive. Similar ontological tricks arise and are registered throughout the rest of the poem.

When invoking architectural counterexamples for the "sober frame" of Appleton House—itself a metonym for the Fairfax line—Marvell cannot help but explore rather than simply denounce them. The relation between human and building, both fanciful architectural creations, goes beyond vanity and social image. It is one in which human imagination and physical material merge. The baroque façades that display the mental exertions of their designers appear to breathe in unison with the viewer, whose own face betrays the physical exertion required to make out the extravagant architectural details. By the end of the stanza, the reader has experienced the mental torsions required to trace Marvell's play of images and words, thereby enacting between mind and words a reciprocal relationship corresponding to the one between human body and building depicted on the page.[33] In the very first stanza, then, Marvell "digresses"—to apply Anne Cotterill's analytical terminology for the poem—from the encomiastic mode of country house poetry to create a work that approaches the act of writing about a country house estate as an occasion for tracing the internal wanderings of the mind as it roams that environment.[34] Moreover, rather than embracing the permanence of meaning that buildings appear to connote—an attitude exemplified in Jonson's "To Penshurst"—

Marvell's poem reveals the mutability and instability of meaning that apparently fixed architectural structures provoke. They function as containers not just for the human body and human belongings but also for the flow and enlargement of mental activity.

The poem's tidy equilater or quadrangle stanzas of eight lines of eight syllables each, packaged to resemble the "sober frame" of the house they celebrate, continue to be undone by the heady baroque imagery and syntactical complexity they contain within their own frames. The subtle tension between explicit order and implicit disorder in Marvell's poem suggests that the mutability and pliability of creative activity ensue *because* and not in spite of the formal constraints that domestic architecture provides as a setting for subjective experience. No other lines in the poem exemplify this central notion more compellingly than those of stanza 7, which contains the fantastic image of a house that sweats, swells, and stirs when its Master enters:

> Yet thus the laden house does sweat,
> And scarce endures the Master great:
> But where he comes the swelling hall
> Stirs, and the square grows spherical;
> More by his magnitude distressed,
> Than he is by its straitness pressed
> And too officiously it slights
> That in itself which him delights. (lines 49–56)

These lines stage the drama of inert, inorganic matter becoming animate and organic, thus mirroring the first stanza's vignette of a human face turning into a reflection of an architectural façade ("Whose columns should so high be raised / To arch the brows that on them gazed"; lines 7–8). Moreover, Marvell's "short but admirable lines" invoke the ancient geometrical problem of squaring the circle—or here, circling the square.

Much like the provocative presentation of works by a foreign architect, the poem emulates architectural ambition through verse, creating perceptual effects with its own play of perspective and distortions of scale. Clearly, stanza 7, registering Fairfax's patronage of Marvell, pays respect to the employer's eminence. Its fanciful imagery suggests that the house's Master, by virtue of his greatness, forces the building into a new shape and size to accommodate his own. Also suggested is the poem's continual inability to resist exploring the way this particular place and space—Nun Appleton—goes beyond embodying its owner's power and strengths. Emulated and stimulated in verse are the movements of the individual human mind. Above all, however, the stanza demonstrates the poem's pervasive notion that material form and spaces expand to accommodate and induce changes in interior life. The interior dwelling that stirs in response to the intrusion of an external element is a striking image of the workings of interiority itself.

Despite the fixity of its square form, the stanza is an emblem of Baroque technique and style, wherein expression, irregularity, and distortion prevail over formal symmetry and "in a single word, the motions of souls, not their states of rest," prevail.[35] The visual effects of Baroque art—"some strangeness in the proportions," as well as "constant novelty and unexpectedness"—were equally prevalent in Baroque prose, with its rhetorical diction marked by signs of mental processing.[36] The purpose of "Anti-Ciceronian rhetoric," Morris Croll's alternate label for Baroque prose style, was to "portray not a thought, but a mind thinking."[37] Mobility, above all, is the characteristic of "a mind thinking," as opposed to the static unit of a thought. Employing asymmetry—or the breaking of symmetry—is one way to create such mobility. While the poem's series of ninety-seven uniform stanzas appears to contradict the strange proportions and loose form of the Baroque style, its progressions through scenes that follow "the movements of a mind discovering truth as it goes, thinking while it writes," sustain it.[38]

The poem's provisionality and tendency to divagate, and the poet's own uncertainty over "what was about to happen next" in the scenes he depicts while inhabiting them, reveal an approach to representing life as lived experience rather than as universal truth.[39] This approach reveals the method not only of inductive reasoning identified with Francis Bacon's natural philosophy and writing style but also of Baroque sentence patterns, with their "loose" periods or sentences.[40] In an architextural maneuver, Marvell displays such looseness in the continual openings he creates *between* stanzas. If Marvell appears to model the closed style of classical symmetry with his perfectly regular stanzas, the uniform little "rooms" within the vast house of his poem, he undoes the symmetry through the coordinating conjunctions that begin many of the stanzas and function much like architectural corridors, linking the disparate stanzas while allowing for movement between them. The many conjunctions—"but," "and," "yet," "so," "while," "whereas," "nor," "for," "or," "where," "when"— ensure the boundaries of each stanza remain open-ended, conducive to further movement, rather than neatly contained.

In addition to rendering permeable the boundaries of poetic stanzas to accommodate the peregrinations of "a mind thinking," Marvell further performs architexturalism by making elastic the division between humans and architectural matter. The first stanza unsettles the definition of inanimate matter by merging it with human activity, and at the same time destabilizes generic definition. It also playfully distorts the country house poem's maneuver of locating the material for encomium in the house's architectural details by creating outright equivalences between such details and humans themselves:

> A stately frontispiece of poor
> Adorns without the open door;
> Nor less the rooms within commends
> Daily new furniture of friends. (lines 65–68)

These well-known lines, the first half of stanza 9, evince a Mannerist attitude, copying in reverse Arcimboldo's paintings of human faces composed of inhuman entities such as fruits, flowers, books, fish.[41] Here, inhuman objects such as the frontispiece and furniture—presenting "the face" of the estate—are composed of humans. These lines too mock gently one of the set pieces of country house ideology. Not just presenting an eternal tableau of grateful tenants, friends, and supplicants, Marvell casts them as literal architectural and decorative fixtures. In the context of a poem written on the occasion of a great man's retirement from public life, it appears fitting that the house's real purpose exceeds its immediate function of hosting guests, and that the house allows its own form to become supplanted by mendicants, flatterers, and acquaintances:

> The house was built upon the place
> Only as for a mark of grace;
> And for an inn to entertain
> Its Lord a while, but not remain. (lines 69–72)

Whereas other country house poems make much of the manor house's function as "an inn to entertain" guests, *Upon Appleton House* inverts that notion by presenting the house as "an inn," not for guests, but for the lord himself.

Just as the Nun Appleton house serves only as a temporary lodging for its Master on his way to heaven, so too is it a momentary stopping point for the poet in his divagations on the estate. Indeed, the poem's section on the house of Nun Appleton serves as a frontispiece in itself, an entryway into the architecture not only of the manor house but also of the poem as a built structure that encloses an interior space. Accordingly, there is a pun in "frontispiece of poor," which ties Fairfax's architectural property to Marvell's textual one.[42] "Frontispiece" can refer both to a building's ornamented entryway and to the title page of a book. That *Upon Appleton House* existed only in manuscript during Marvell's lifetime makes the evocation of the frontispiece in his poem all the more ironic, and underscores the coextensive relationship between material forms and mental conceptions. Marvell's frontispiece is a threshold for the poem itself as a dark room, or series of dark rooms, whereby its narrative appears to be set in external settings but, like the camera obscura, in fact goes further inside the estate and its interlinked interior worlds.

The Nunnery

It is into narrative itself that the "frontispiece," the poem's architectural section, leads, but only after summarizing the spaces it intends to plot: "fragrant gardens, shady woods, / Deep meadows, and transparent floods" (stanza 10, lines 79–80). Stanza 11, in appropriately Baroque fashion, undoes this plan by proposing to revisit, instead, the story of the house's past incarnation as a Gothic nunnery, which now exists as surrounding ruins:

> While with slow eyes we these survey;
> And on each pleasant footstep stay,
> We opportunely may relate
> That progress of this house's fate.
> A nunnery first gave it birth
> (For virgin buildings oft brought forth),
> And all that neighbour-ruin shows
> The quarries whence this dwelling rose. (lines 81–88)

The earlier image of the house that expands to register the new happening within it—the entrance of the lord—recalls pregnancy, Rosalie Colie has observed. Stanza 81 repeats this image of a life-bearing house, and it is an equally outlandish one, for the body is allegedly a "virgin" one, and its household a nunnery. What it might spawn is not a domestic household but a religious one abounding with female creativity and sexuality, where nuns pray and embroider, make balms, sugar pastes, perfumes, and candied fruits, and delight in each other's bodies at night.

This section, stanzas 11 through 35, provides not just the history of the estate and the Fairfax line, but a glimpse of England's heritage as a Catholic nation. Stepping outside the house after exploring its architectural properties, the poet faces a choice for his next source of creative inspiration and admiration of Fairfax. His opting to address next the ruins neighboring the house demonstrates a continued fascination with the life of architectural matter—evinced in the earlier image of a sweating house—as well as an ability to see and hear life in a discarded dwelling in ruins. Ironically, when he continues to explore the life-generating qualities of matter, it is to decry Catholicism, a religion that enacts them in its own ceremonies and rituals.

The section offers "a small gothic fiction," according to Nigel Smith.[43] Indeed, its story of Fairfax's great-grandparents Isabel Thwaites and William Fairfax, and of the Cistercian priory that spawned the family's estate, provides the most coherent narrative in the poem. Predating Sophia Lee's or Ann Radcliffe's novels of the last quarter of the following century, Marvell's gothic narrative also concerns an imprisoned maiden, the threat of sexual and social deviance, crooked authority figures, and the fate of a powerful dynasty.[44] It is also set in the historical past, but with ruins that are real. Such correspondences not only anticipate later developments in narrative patterns but also reveal Marvell's robust instincts for narrative. Providing the history for the ruins that adjoin the house he had finished describing appears a fitting opportunity—"We opportunely may relate / That progress of this house's fate"—to continue the panegyric vein that motivates the poem.

Yet the lure of transport inspires this history, prompted by the mystery of ruins. (This scenario anticipates the effect of follies, the fake ruins of eighteenth-century British landscape garden design examined in chapter 5.) As an element of the "spatial design" of Nun Appleton, the nunnery ruins evoke the "magical power" generated "when the experience of moving through the material world of the garden in present time transports visitors into the different world and temporality of a narrative."[45] For Marvell, such power arises in the opportunity to invent a narrative of how the ruins came to be.

Accordingly, he creates a romantic fiction in which William Fairfax not only rescues his betrothed from nuns who have refused to relinquish her, thereby obstructing the heterosexual, procreative union required to continue the Fairfax line ("Yet, against fate, his spouse they kept; / And the great race would intercept"; lines 47–48), but also takes possession of their land and demolishes their cloister:

> But the glad youth away her bears,
> And to the nuns bequeaths her tears:
> Who guiltily their prize bemoan,

Like gypsies that a child had stol'n.
Thenceforth (as when th'enchantment ends,
The castle vanishes or rends)
The wasting cloister with the rest
Was in one instant dispossessed. (stanza 34, lines 265–72)

In this stanza, the story of a Protestant, heterosexual, procreative union prevailing over Catholic, female-female, nonprocreative couplings is cast as a magical quest romance and yoked to a heroic conquest of property. Two pieces of property are seized—Isabel Thwaites, the virginal bride and future Fairfax matriarch, and the land that will become the Fairfax seat. Marvell's version of the story rewrites both family and national history. William Fairfax did not himself dispossess the nuns of the priory and claim the land for his family. It was nearly twenty years later, in 1539, during Henry VIII's second dissolution of the monasteries, that William's two sons with Isabel, Thomas and Gabriel, took possession of the estate.[46]

Thus, Marvell accomplishes an act of mystification that contributes to the obscured features in England's "secret history of domesticity."[47] The widespread dissolution of monasteries during the sixteenth century resulted in "a huge re-shaping of the built environment of early modern England."[48] Two Acts of Parliament, in 1536 and 1589, enforced the closure of approximately eight hundred monastic houses throughout England.[49] In short order, government powers turned sites of religious institutions into secular, domestic spaces. Nun Appleton was one of those sites. The interiority of spiritual life—an interiority Marvell imagines as voluptuous and carnal—is replaced by a secular interiority that locates itself not so much in the individual members of the Fairfax family as in the poet who surveys their estate and experiences shifts of consciousness within his own interior chamber of imagination.

Most interiorized and obscured in the nunnery section of the poem are the desires and voice of Isabel Thwaites, the human medium through which the house of Fairfax is able to generate and extend itself. She is both a susceptible auditor for the words of a persuasive prioress—"the nun's smooth tongue has sucked her in" (line 200)—and the subject of a smooth-tongued male poet whose own voice is omitted from the scenes he observes and depicts. The only indication of her viewpoint is ambiguous: "But truly bright and holy Thwaites / That weeping at the altar waits" (263–64). We have no way of knowing whether she is weeping for joy or for grief before "the glad youth away her bears, / And to the nuns bequeaths her tears" (265–66).[50] With her body carried away by her fiancé and her tears left for the nuns, Isabel's own perspective remains unrevealed, as will Maria Fairfax's later in the poem. The poet's perspective will prevail, and it expresses kinship with these silent women whose bodies serve as vessels for the continued growth of a family line. The body of Marvell's poem shares that purpose too. His own digression from that role, in using the poem's body so much to mediate his own perspective, suggests the potential for women's voices and perspectives to achieve greater expansion and depth in narratives of precarious inheritance, property, and enclosure in the following century.

Through the medium of words, the poem constitutes the plot of the land itself and even "mimes the estate," as T. Katharine Sheldahl Thomason puts it.[51] Of course, in doing so, it represents the estate as an embodiment of "the self-control of its wise creator," the honorable Lord Fairfax. The estate's remaining topography suggests that just as the next section of the poem, beginning with stanza 36, is the general's garden, so too was it the next area of the estate after the nunnery ruins.[52] A recently unearthed map of the estate, from close to Marvell's time, confirms both this notion and the fidelity of his poem as a whole to the estate.[53] Through the positioning of his stanzas, the poet produces an estate map of his own. The blank space between the two stanzas serves as the pathway between two areas of the estate. From a site that recalls female enclosure, Marvell moves to a site that simulates a male enclosure—the military fort.

Lord Fairfax's Military Garden: Internal Landscape Made External

Where the nunnery section represented a space devoted to the estate's past and Lord Fairfax's ancestors, the garden section represents the house's present and Lord Fairfax himself:

> Who, when retired here to peace,
> His warlike studies could not cease;
> But laid these gardens out in sport
> In the just figure of a fort;
> And with five bastions it did fence,
> As aiming one for ev'ry sense. (stanza 36, lines 283–88)

Unlike the nunnery, which could only be imagined on the basis of viewing its ruins, and the house, whose own features become obscured by the estate of the poet's imagination, the garden appears to be depicted as it stood.[54] Built to continue the retired general's "warlike studies [that] could not cease," the garden gives shape with earth and plantings to the militaristic thoughts that persist in his mind. According to a twentieth-century visitor of the estate, Marvell's description of Fairfax's garden was accurate: the extant landscape design, as described in the poem, lays out "ten gardens . . . in two rows, with a 'bastion' of sorts placed at the head of each of the five columns."[55]

Fairfax's garden, designed to appear in "the just figure of a fort," not only recreates the military environment the general could not forget but functions as a theater for reenacting his life in that environment. As such, it shares the purpose of other built landscape environments in this book, such as grottoes and follies that were designed, created, and occupied to engender specific frames of mind in states of solitude. In drawing attention to the retired patron's garden design, this section also presents a detailed picture of Fairfax's mental life in retirement. The poet here functions like a narrator who describes features of the garden from his patron's imagined perspective. Accordingly, the flowers are anthropomorphized as obedient soldiers. Beginning a typical day at Nun Appleton, the bee beats a drum for reveille, and

> Then flowers their drowsy eyelids raise,
> Their silken ensigns each displays,
> And dries its pan yet dank with dew,
> And fills its flask with odours new. (stanza 37, lines 292–96)

The next stanzas continue the martial play of bees and flowers. The flowers, discharging "odours new" in "fragrant volleys" (298), salute "their Governor" and "their Governess" during their morning walk. They hold fire, however, when Maria passes, as she "seems with the flowers a flower to be" (302). The shots, not primed with gunpowder, are silent; their "shrill report no ear can tell, / But echoes to the eye and smell" (307–8). That perceiving the salute of flower soldiers engages different senses than does the salute of human soldiers reinforces the understanding that, for the Lord General, military life has gone inward. It is an inwardness defined as much by its domestic setting as by its mental one, and as such prefigures the other interiorities examined in this book that are generated by reciprocally defining relationships between self and space. Marvell, in his position as an onlooker privy to the spaces and routines of Fairfax's domestic life, functions as the mediator for his perspective, and the poem as its medium. The poet in effect works as a narrator. In the garden stanzas, so thoroughly does he fulfill this role that the perspective encompasses aural and olfactory perceptions as well as visual ones.

He also shifts from a familiar and fanciful perspective to a distanced and grave one by likening the garden to England and to Paradise itself:

Oh thou, that dear and happy isle
The garden of the world ere while,
Thou Paradise of four seas,
Which heaven planted us to please, (stanza 41, lines 321–24)

And by likening gardeners to soldiers:

The gard'ner had the soldier's place,
And his more gentle forts did trace.
The nursery of all things green
Was then the only magazine. (stanza 43, lines 337–40)

The poet brings the two metaphors—garden as England and gardener as soldier—together in stanza 44 by identifying Fairfax as one who had the power to cultivate the garden of England to "spring / Fresh as his own and flourishing" but withdrew from doing so:

And yet there walks one on the sod
Who, had it pleased him and God,
Might once have made our gardens spring
Fresh as his own and flourishing.
But he preferred to the Cinque Ports
These five imaginary forts:
And, in those half-dry trenches, spanned
Power which the ocean might command. (stanza 44, lines 345–52)

Thus, while Marvell delineates the political and national resonances of Fairfax's retirement and turn to inwardness, he does so by presenting it as a psychological condition, and he occupies that position himself by perceiving the garden as Fairfax might—as "five imaginary forts" and the magazine for imaginary artillery. What appears to be a laudatory description of a garden is in fact another example of the properties of matter—and property itself—becoming absorbed by properties of mind, taking the space of external reality into a dark chamber (a camera obscura, that is) of introspection. Ineluctably, the poet's tour of Appleton House continues as a mentally oriented journey. At the end of the garden section, he shifts his gaze to the next area of the landscape—"But o'er the meads below it plays, / Or innocently seems to graze" (stanza 46, lines 367–68)—and takes us there.

As he does so, he carries with him the violent images of military battle held in abeyance in the orderly garden, and perhaps in the Lord General's conscious memory. Thomas Keymer reminds us that it is in the "pastoral margins" of the estate, the meadows, that we see

> A campe of battle newly fought:
> Where, as the meads with hay, the plain
> Lies quilted o'er with bodies slain:
> The women that with forks it fling
> Do represent the pillaging. (stanza 53, lines 420–24)

Not merely describing Fairfax's garden as a fond image of a war hero in retirement, the poet processes the image.[56] Any association with war, no matter how buoyantly represented, suggests damage. Keymer claims the poem realizes this notion: "As the poem goes on, the whole landscape, traditionally an expression of its proprietor's self, becomes ineradicably coloured by visions of slaughter." The poem's distinction, he claims, lies here, in its departure from presenting the landscape as wholly "an expression of its proprietor's self." *Upon Appleton House* departs from country house poem ideology to become something else. While the question of to whom the "visions of slaughter" belong is unanswered, I suggest they belong to the poet, for whom the landscape represents as much an expression of Fairfax's inner self as it does an expression of his own experience of the landscape as an expression of that self.

The poet leaves the garden weary of the vigilance its world requires, "the vigilant patrol / Of Stars [that] walks around about the Pole" while the tulips sleep with "Their leaves, that to their stalks are curled" (lines 313–15) and the bastions fencing the fort-shaped garden beds "point the batt'ry of its beams" at Nun Appleton's neighbor, "proud Cawood Castle" (361–62). Vigilant, too, must the poet himself be, when entering a space frequented by his patron and his family, and when describing a garden he knows the patron, or the patron's family, was responsible for designing. He exits the garden in stanza 46 in the middle of a landscape "quarrel" imagined between the bastions of Nun Appleton and the distant view of Cawood Castle, which Fairfax had in fact captured during the war and turned into a camp for prisoners of war.[57] The poet begins his exit by shifting the view to the space beyond: "But o'er the meads below it plays, / Or innocently seems to gaze" (l. 367–68). The word *but* acts as the device for this shift, as it does in many other stanzas. Beyond the military world of the garden, the suggested space promises to be playful as well as innocent—an ideal setting for a hired tutor to escape his employer's notice, and the formalities of interacting with and serving him, formalities Marvell depicts the flowers and bees as observing.

Theater of Metamorphosis: Meadow and Mind

Beginning the meadow section (stanzas 47–59) with the conjunction *and*—a word that operates as the feet to follow the gaze that first turned with the word *but* two lines earlier—the poet immediately registers a sense of relief when describing the depth of the grass. Such depth may offer a space for hiding and relaxation after the garden's rigorous environment. At the same time, in moving to another area of Fairfax's landscape, he finds a space to relocate the "visions of slaughter" that would mar the garden's image of orderliness, created as much by its daily formal rituals as by its symmetrical design. The poet's "reading" of the meadow—a reading accomplished through the activity of walking that coincides with seeing—is connected to, and transformed by, his experience of the garden.

That Marvell spends so much time in, and devotes so much space in his poem—with its emphasis on transformation through perceptual shifts—to the landscape surrounding Nun Appleton, rather than remaining within the architectural edifice, suggests the estate house itself is less a site for introspection and variable perspectives than are its grounds. In this, it corresponds with Wotton's treatise on the making of a "seate":

First, I must note a certaine contrarietie betweene *building* and *gardening*: For as Fabriques [buildings] should bee *regular*, so Gardens should bee *irregular*, or at least cast into a very wilde *Regularitie*. To exemplifie my conceit; I have seene a *Garden* (for the maner perchance incomparable) into which the first Accesse was a high walke like a *Tarrace*, from whence might bee taken a generall view of the whole *Plote* below; but rather in a delightful confusion, then with any plaine distinction of the pieces. From this the *Beholder* descending many steps, was afterwards conveyed againe, by severall *mountings* and *valings*, to various entertainments of his *sent* and *sight*; which I shall not neede to describe (for that were poeticall) let me onely note this, that every one of these diversities, was as if hee had beene *Magically* transported into a new Garden.[58]

Whereas Fairfax's garden appears at first glance to contravene Wotton's recommendation for an irregular design, one might say its symmetrical design, made visible by its occupying a lower plain and experienced in direct contrast with the "unfathomable grass" of the meadows, yields the sense of "a very wilde *Regularitie*." The experiences of "transport" and "diversity" that Wotton encourages register in the circuitous and digressive—yet strangely deliberate—movement from house, ruins, and garden to meadow, and later to wood and wharf. The account of Marvell's perceptual transformations in response to walking around Fairfax's estate, in its expanded scope, conveys the diversity of the different areas in relation to one another. Internal dramas attend these experiences of diversity. They are elicited by the "severall *mountings* and *valings*" and the "various entertainements" of "*sent* and *sight*" on Fairfax's estate. Wotton recommends cultivating diversities in garden experience above all because they give the impression of being, while within one estate, "*Magically* transported into a new garden." Fairfax's garden design—as encountered by Marvell in the space of the poem—does not induce such an experience, yet the design of his estate as a whole does. It creates the effect of being transported into a new world, from one area of the estate to another. Taken as a whole, the poet's reactions to the estate design comprise a plot of inner experience that corresponds with the contingencies of external circumstances.

Nowhere else on Fairfax's estate does the poet experience more of the "delightful confusion" that Wotton advocates than in Nun Appleton's meadow. The section has been noted for its "scalar shifts" and optical trickery, but the move from the decorous yet vigilant environment of the garden to the "unfathomable" green abyss of the meadow creates perceptual incongruity.[59] The first stanza of the section plunges us into this confusion:

> And now to the abyss I pass
> Of that unfathomable grass,
> Where men like grasshoppers appear,
> But grasshoppers are giants there:
> They, in their squeaking laugh, contemn
> Us as we walk more low than them:
> And, from the precipices tall
> Of the green spires, to us do call. (stanza 47, lines 369–76)

Stating that "I pass" to the meadow—for the first time introducing himself in the first person, as an embodied presence—the poet suggests that he enters the space as if in a dream. The stanza presents one of the poem's most celebrated absurdities: grasshoppers, atop "unfathomable grass," are perched higher than men, and thus resemble giants, even as their voices remain "squeaking" and small. They lord over an estate of grass, luring the poet to pass through a frontispiece that is at once architectural and vegetative. With this stanza, the poet reframes, in camera obscura fashion, another section of Nun Appleton's topography as an enclosed interior space that reveals and alters reality.

Much like the space of the camera obscura or Scamozzi's light-ray-penetrated room, the meadow is a theater of metamorphosis. The meadow section, with its imperceptible transitions of perspective and size, concentrates the overall movement of the poem, of passing from one space to another, and of passing from one state to another. The earlier sections also depict metamorphoses—the house turns spherical when its master enters, a nunnery vanishes and becomes a country estate, and bees and flowers turn into a garden militia. The metamorphoses in the meadow section, however, are more explicitly rendered as "actual" occurrences, tracing the way in which a localized mind—the "I" that passes "to the abyss"—sees and reads those occurrences. The first stanza reinforces the impression that we are viewing things not as they are but as they are seen from an alternate point of view. The poet presents the meadow not in direct terms but as it appears to him—not merely a field but an abyss of "unfathomable grass"—thereby announcing his point of view. Insofar as the meadow section is a theater of metamorphoses, it is also a theater of internal perspective.

Such suggestions of the theater in a nondramatic context that persistently emphasizes visual events are fitting when considering, as Alastair Fowler reminds us, that the word *theatre* derives from the Greek for "a place for viewing."[60] *Upon Appleton House* registers this meaning by consistently calling attention to acts of seeing and looking as spectacles and dramas in themselves. The Renaissance art of memory, realized in Giulio Camillo's fabled theater of memory, exemplifies an early understanding of memory as an interior space within which a material repository of aids might be arranged to structure universal knowledge. Because the wooden space Camillo built—a "constructed mind and soul" as well as "a windowed one"—also draws on the act of "corporeal looking," he decided to call it a "theatre."[61] Given this background of an internally oriented notion of theater, which emerged in seventeenth-century England through Hermetic philosopher Robert Fludd, it is unsurprising that nondramatic theatrical environments pervade Marvell's reimagining of Nun Appleton's domestic setting. Wotton, too, indicates this propensity when referring to "Every Mans proper *Mansion* house and Home" as being, among other things, "the *Theater* of his *Hospitality*." Fairfax's garden shows not just how war and military life have entered domestic gardens, but also how the concept of theater allowed him to realize his garden as a private space for reenacting his enduring preoccupation with war and military life.[62]

The design and experience of landscape as a form of domestic theater converges with a more explicit form of theatrical production that took place in private homes: the masque. It is in terms of the meadow's masquelike scenes that critics have commonly interpreted the theatrical elements of the poem.[63] The meadow section explicitly uses images and conventions from masque production, its "changing scenes" in particular:

> No Scene that turns with Engines strange
> Does oftner than these Meadows change.
> For when the sun the grass hath vexed,
> The tawny mowers enter next (stanza 49, lines 385–88)

The lines portray nature functioning as both stage and stage director; it determines when the scenes change, and the players—"the tawny mowers"—enter after "the sun the grass hath vexed." Throughout, the stanzas in the meadow section, while making biblical, classical, and military allusions, and encoding references to the Civil War, depict the activities of daily life on a country house estate.[64]

In his recourse to "solitary meditation" for creative energy, Marvell uses elements of the masque (its metamorphic nature and conception of stories through settings and scenes) as an instrument of self-revelation, as opposed to political "self-delusion."[65] When the next announced "scene change" begins, in stanza 56, the laborers are done with their work and, having finished mowing the meadow—with one slicing a low-flying bird, a rail, by accident—pile the "new-made hay" into cocks and celebrate their "triumphs" with a dance. In the course of these activities, they have recreated the landscape, turning the grassy "abyss" into a "calm sea" from which emerge haycocks resembling "rocks." It is at this point that the poet announces—and effects—the transition to the next scene:

> This scene again withdrawing brings
> A new and empty face of things;
> A leveled space, as smooth and plain,
> As cloths for Lely stretched to stain.
> The world when first created sure
> Was such a table rase and pure. (stanza 56, lines 441–46)

The laborer's efforts have created, not just a landscape, but a whole new world—a "table rase and pure." The reference to the tabula rasa—a metaphor for the mind articulated before John Locke's celebrated evocation of it in *Essay Concerning Human Understanding*—affirms that such a world exists as much in the mental realm as in the concrete.[66] If entering Nun Appleton's fortified garden becomes an occasion to access Fairfax's mental world, a stage for displaying and enacting his habits of mind, passing into the meadow offers an opportunity to witness the theater of the poet's mind.

An aspect of interiority is inherent to experiencing masques, insofar as their continual changing of scenes resembles the metamorphoses of dreams, as A. W. Johnson reminds us: "In dreams, as in the masque, abrupt transformations of settings and cast replace the sinuous causative links which bind together dramatic plot or the illusion of mundane reality."[67] Hobbes, however, might point out that if masques are like dreams, they are also like thinking itself, for it is "impossible to distinguish exactly between Sense and Dreaming." Such a notion obtains plausibility when one considers "that being awake, I know I dreame not; though when I dreame, I think my selfe awake."[68] The nature of thinking, too, or at least one "sort" of "Trayne of Thoughts," which is "Unguided, Without Designee, and inconstant," resembles dreaming as well,

> Wherein there is no Passionate Thought, to govern and direct those that follow, to it self, as the end and scope of some desire, or other passion: In which case the thoughts are said to wander, and seem impertinent one to another, as in a Dream.[69]

The meadow, which takes the poet away from his patron though he remains on Fairfax's property, creates physical distance from one who might govern him both physically and mentally, and allows his thoughts to wander, "as in a dream." The poem's peripatetic and locodescriptive nature—the poet's footsteps in the environment of the estate determine the structure and content—also coincides with Hobbes's philosophy of the imagination.[70] Underscoring the notion that "all Fancies are Motions within us," Hobbes identifies a "Mentall Discourse" or "Trayne of Thoughts" as a "succession of one Thought to another." The principle of succession is key: "It comes to passe in time, that in the Imagining of any thing, there is no certainty what we shall Imagine next; Onely this is certain, it shall be something that succeeded the same before, at one time or another."[71]

The poet's experience of nature as an interiorized masque anticipates an eighteenth-century trope of the mind that, like Locke's, evokes the camera obscura, namely, David Hume's depiction of the human mind as a "kind of theatre," presented almost one hundred years later in *A Treatise of Human Nature* (1739–1740). In this theater, "several perceptions successively make their appearance; pass, re-pass, glide away, and mingle in an infinite variety of postures and situations."[72] In its emphasis on entities whose movements "pass, re-pass, glide away" and on the variety of their positions and "situations," Hume's theatrical figure reflects the dramatic style of masques rather than traditional theatrical production. At the same time, these movements, like Hobbes's imagination, describe the movements of the camera obscura's projections of everyday life as dreamlike events that move, undulate, and vanish.

Camera Obscura

Earlier in the century, in a letter to Francis Bacon about "the commerce of philosophical experiments," Henry Wotton described his first encounter with the camera obscura. "Let me tell your Lordship a pretty thing which I saw coming down the Danuby," he wrote from Vienna in December 1620. While visiting the study of Johannes Kepler in Lintz, Austria, he spied a landscape drawing, "masterly done," and asked who its "author" was. Kepler answered "with a smile it was himself; adding, he had done it *non tanguam pictor, sed tanguam mathematicus* (not as a painter, but as a mathematician)."[73] This, Wotton reports, "set [him] on fire." Responding to his enthusiasm, Kepler explained how the feat was performed:

He hath a little black tent (of what stuff is not much importing) which he can suddenly set up where he will in a field, and it is convertible (like a windmill) to all quarters at pleasure, capable of not much more than one man, as I conceive, and perhaps at no great ease; exactly close and dark, save at one hole, about an inch and a half in the diameter, to which he applies a long perspective trunk, with a convex glass fitted to the said hole, and the concave taken out at the other end, which extendeth to about the middle of this erected tent, through which the visible radiations of all the objects without are intromitted, falling upon a paper, which is accommodated to receive them; and so he traceth them with his pen in their natural appearance, turning his little tent round by degrees, till he hath designed the whole aspect of the field.[74]

Wotton finishes the account of his introduction to the camera obscura with a suggestion that "there might be good use made of it for chorography," for although "to make landscapes by it were illiberal," nevertheless "surely no painter can do them so precisely."[75] As suggested earlier, that Wotton encountered the camera obscura and thought of its usefulness for mapping a geographical region four years before the publication of *Elements of Architecture* (1624) suggests the device's influence on his conception of the experience and ownership of a country house estate.

The object that drew Wotton's admiration was a landscape picture, a static entity. The camera obscura, for Kepler, served as a tool for drawing spatial relationships that replaced the other resources an artist might use, including perspective through geometrical means, a technique that Italian artists systematized in the quattrocento.[76] With the mathematical arrangement of lines to create "vanishing points" at the level of viewers' eyes, it became possible for artists to create the illusion of three-dimensional space on a two-dimensional plane. The means for creating the illusion of depth and volume, in other words, had been invented. The camera obscura obviated the need to recur to mathematic calculation, in that it automatically translates the spatial relationships of three-dimensional objects onto a flat surface—the wall onto which the light carrying the image is projected. Simply by tracing the projected image, one could create a drawing true to life. Kepler was not completely correct, then, in saying that he had executed his drawing not as a painter but as a mathematician. He had achieved such perspectival exactitude, rather, as a machine that automatically performed the work a mathematician might.

That the image needs to be traced indicates the technical nature of the camera obscura as a device of ephemeral reproduction. The image it projects is impermanent, as it lacks a mechanism to preserve the momentary record. And yet, this aspect of the device also indicates its faculties. Such faculties are frequently elided in art historical accounts of the camera obscura's use in creating seventeenth-century Dutch paintings of domestic interiors.[77] They are missing in Wotton's account too. Not only a tool for drawing—a resolutely static medium—the camera obscura was also valued for representing, as mentioned in the introduction, "the colors and movements of objects better than any other sort of representation is able to do."[78] Not long after Wotton's letter, in 1622, Constantijn Huygens wrote about his experience encountering Cornelius Drebbel's camera obscura: "It is impossible to express its beauty in words. The art of painting is dead, for this is life itself, or something higher, if we could find a word for it."[79] Implicit in Huygens's remark is a dual notion of painting's "death"—painting can be regarded as dead because it could be supplanted by the camera obscura, and it can be regarded as dead because it is a medium that lacks movement. In its faculty of representing the movements of life, the camera obscura is closer to life than either painting or its own later descendant, the photographic camera. These aspects of the device are crucial to its role as a prototype for literary projections of interiority.

Whereas Rosalie Colie claims that the magic lantern is the proper analogue for understanding the scenic metamorphoses in the poem, the camera obscura, with its mechanism of interiorizing the objects and movements of external reality, seems a more apt model, both conceptually and chronologically.[80] Christiaan Huygens (son of Constantijn), considered the magic lantern's inventor, did not conceive of the device until 1659; animation was not yet a regular feature of presentations using it in the seventeenth century; and, most important, it is rarely a room, but more commonly a handheld apparatus. The mechanism of the magic lantern involves a built-in light that serves as its projector and a concave mirror that channels the light through a glass slide inserted into the device. Vignettes and images that have been painted onto the slides are thus projected on a screen. Magic lantern scenes, in other words, are entirely manufactured and independent of the spatial context in which they are viewed. The camera obscura, by contrast, receives and processes the projections of an external environment that is real and immediate, and for this reason it has been an apt model for the mind.

Just as Wotton recommends using the camera obscura for mapping and creating landscapes by walking across land with the portable device, Marvell figuratively does so in his plotting of the estate, demonstrating the mechanism's potential for inducing reflection. This potential especially pervades the sections of the poem that focus on his subjective impressions of a particular area, from the meadow to the wood, to the river, and back toward the house. In the meadows, the notion that his viewpoint is mediated initially emerges in the perception of an "abyss . . . of unfathomable grass." The need to register "depth" here recalls the artistic use of perspective, and the use of the camera obscura to automate its work of creating impressions of depth. The next stanza refines the impression of depth by presenting another scene:

> To see men through this meadow dive,
> We wonder how they rise alive.
> As, under water, none does know
> Whether he fall through it or go.
> But, as the mariners that sound,
> And show upon their lead the ground,
> They bring up flowers so to be seen,
> And prove they've at the bottom been. (stanza 48, lines 377–84)

Mixing elements in this passage—water for earth—and motions—rising and falling—the stanza presents images of depth perception as a physical activity. Moreover, the figuration of mowers who "dive" into "unfathomable grass" as mariners who "sound" the depth of a body of water trades agricultural labor for epistemology, and human bodies and flowers for measuring tools such as sounding leads. Embedded in this elaborate imagery is the ultimate fathomer of inner depths, the poet himself, whose written lines drop leads to indicate the presence of unknown interiors, in the meadow scenes of country house estates and elsewhere. By using poetic figures, Marvell conveys to us both the physical depths of the meadow and its metaphysical ones. In addition, by creating views of scenes not just as they are but as how he perceives them in a given moment, he enacts the empirical premise of the individual mind as a camera obscura. The stanzas of his poem function as dark rooms of subjective consciousness through which we see the world of Nun Appleton.

Glasses of Perspective

The poet ends the meadow section by viewing it *in* and then *through* a glass, transforming it from the "painted world" of William Davenant, referred to satirically in stanza 57 and populated with cattle, to a glass one in which

> They seem within the polished grass
> A landskip drawn in looking glass.
> And shrunk in the huge pasture show
> As spots, so shaped, on faces do.
> Such fleas, ere they approach the eye,
> In multiplying glasses lie.
> They feed so wide, so slowly move,
> As constellations do above. (stanza 58, lines 457–64)

The glass devices invoked in this stanza underscore how specific and individualized the poet's point of view is. The mowed meadow now appears "A landskip drawn in looking glass," the cows transformed in scale, as the grasshoppers were at the beginning of the meadow section. But where the grasshoppers were made very large, the distancing perspective here makes the cattle as small as insects, and in doing so, recalls the magnifying power of the microscope. The landscape too becomes very small, and offers itself as a reflection of the sky; the cows "feed so wide, so slowly move, / As constellations do above." With the cows, now rendered as fleas, reflecting "constellations . . . above," the microscope turns into a telescope.[81] By moving images of the landscape from the screen of the camera obscura—or the painted stage backdrop of the masque—to a pane of glass, the stanza makes it available for reflection. That the medium changes yet again, from one in which the view is presented as a reflection to one in which it is seen through a device, suggests the primacy of perspective. The word *perspective* itself is derived from the Latin *per-spicere*, meaning "to see through" as well as "to regard mentally."[82] As explained earlier, perspective was an integral feature of the camera obscura, for perspective is what the device produces when converting a three-dimensional space to a two-dimension plane that is "virtual," a term film theorist Anne Friedberg has underscored.[83]

As the poet's mind fluctuates, so too does the point of view from which he surveys his patron and employer's estate. Such a notion of the variability of "reality" as rendered by perspective contradicts Joseph Moxon's claim in *Practical Perspective; or, Perspective Made Easie* (1670) that the rules of perspective allow "all painters, engravers, architects and others" to "give every figure its true place and size" and "so shadow his work that shall seem more like the thing it represents than a representation of the thing."[84] Moxon maintains, in fact, that perspective depicts the appearance of a house on a "ground plot," a notion that would allow Marvell to accomplish what he has attempted to do: "And the architect may draw on his ground plot the appearance of several sides of his building, and place on them either doors, windows, balconies, &c. each in its proper shape and scituation."[85] Rather than subscribing to the notion that perspective enables the rendition of one "proper" view, Marvell throughout the poem expresses the notion that perspective reveals the variability of "proper" views. These views in turn are determined by the multiplicity of perspectives. While Marvell's poem contradicts the belief that perspective reveals an unvarying reality, it registers Moxon's claim that perspective entails representing "the appearance" of things in terms of their context, scale, and situation. Certainly, the poem's length derives in great part from its continual efforts to depict these qualities in nearly every aspect of the estate and the poet's subjective experience of it.

Marvell's deployment of perspective as the product of mediation coheres more with Jean Dubreuil's definition. *La perspective pratique*, Dubreuil's manual on perspective, appeared in French in 1642 and in English, as *Perspective Practical*, in 1672, and then in different editions throughout the eighteenth century. Dubreuil writes:

Perspective is the art which representeth every object, seen by some diaphane or transparent medium, through which the visual rayes penetrating, are terminated or bounded at the object: and generally all that is seen through something, as through the air, through the water, through the clouds, through glass, and the like, may be said to be seen in perspective. And because we can see nothing, but through these things, we must say, that all that we see is seen in perspective. [86]

Repeated throughout Dubreuil's definition is the word *through*, which is attached to each medium that causes an object to be seen in a certain way: air, water, clouds, glass. Marvell's poem, with its rendering of views through multiple perspectives, registers not only Dubreuil's emphasis on the array of perspectival media in nature, but also his belief that no act of seeing is free of perspective. The poem's sheer range of perspectives demonstrates this: the visitor's perspective when looking at the house for the first time, Sir William Fairfax's when rescuing Isabel Thwaites and Nun Appleton, the Lord General's when regarding his garden, and all the poet's own fantastic ones when regarding the estate from different points of an increasingly remote natural landscape.

At the end of the meadow section, the composure of a landscape recreated by glass surfaces and optical devices is undone by the natural function of flooding, a regular occurrence in the low meadows of Nun Appleton. Yet even the flood is rendered as an optical act, and linked with visual illusion. Answering stanza 58's last two lines, which depict cattle as slowly moving constellations—"They feed so wide, so slowly move, / As constellations do above"—stanza 59 begins, "Then, to conclude these pleasant acts, / Denton sets ope its cataracts; / And makes the meadow truly be / (What it but seemed before) a sea" (lines 465–68). Both a flood and a condition of the eye by which its lens is clouded—and vision blurred—the cataract absorbs the meadow, much as Marvell's eye (with a lens he perhaps considers just as clouded) absorbed it earlier, making it, too, "a sea." With this pun, Marvell produces the understanding that while humans may subject nature to the reshaping function of perspective as effected by artificial devices, nature itself functions as the ultimate perspectival medium, reshaping landscapes with its own natural rhythms and processes.

The Wood: In the Poet's House

Having moved through frontispieces, conceptual corridors, landscape scenes, and stanzas, bringing each encountered space into the dark room interiority of the poem's architecture and the different perspectives it mediates, the poet retreats to the wood, moving more deeply into nature. Such deepening inwardness is announced with his second reference to himself in the first person when he enters the wood: "But I, retiring from the flood, / Take sanctuary in the wood" (stanza 61, lines 481–82). Though the wood is the part of the estate most removed from the house, it is rendered as, for the poet, the most homelike location on the estate. Like the woodpeckers he describes in stanza 69, who find trees in which to create dwellings, he makes a home for himself in the wood. Figuring the space of the wood as an ark in the next lines of stanza 61—"And, while it lasts, myself embark / In this yet green, yet growing ark;"—he makes his first reference to the wood as a shelter. Even in this secluded space, he remains mindful that the wood belongs to Fairfax as his family seat, so he likens in stanza 62 the "double wood of ancient stocks" (line 489) to "two pedigrees" that are "On one hand Fairfax, / th'other Vere" (491–92). In doing so, he adapts dutifully the perspective of a poet remembering the patronage relationship that allows him to enter the wood at all.

Yet with a reference to "the eye" and how it "this forest sees," the poet shifts the perspective back to a point of view that perceives the woods not as a symbol for his patron's lineage, but as a space of individual experience:

> When first the eye this forest sees
> It seems indeed as wood not trees.
> As if their neighbourhood so old
> To one great trunk them all did mould.
> There the huge bulk takes place, as meant
> To thrust up a fifth element;
> And stretches still so closely wedged
> As if the night within were hedged. (stanza 63, lines 497–504)

The stanza mediates the same eye that perceived the mowers as mariners diving into a sea of grass, or as grasshoppers in an unfathomable abyss. This is to say, it is an eye enchanted by the tricks perspective plays on it, fully conscious that even as it registers the material specificities of the objects, figures, and landscapes before it, his point of view may not be allowing the poet to see things as they "really" are. Instead, perspective allows him to create an alternate reality, interior to himself, that unfolds in a flowing manner, like a story that carries him to places different from those he might experience otherwise. Instead of trees, the wood appears as "one great trunk." The poet indicates its otherworldly nature by associating it with the "fifth element," or quintessence—the ancient medium of heavenly bodies that the gods lived in and breathed. Such a tree constitutes a vast yet tight enclosure that "stretches still so closely wedged / As if the night within were hedged." The wood is nothing short of a shelter, a house. With its dark interior, the wood-as-house functions as the dark room of a camera obscura.[87] Therein, internal movements and transformations stretch on without limit, even as the physical space remains enclosed. It is here, in the area of the country house estate where the poet has found the most privacy, that the clearest evocation of the camera obscura is found.

Stanza 64 reinforces the notion of the wood as a camera obscura by recreating its effects of light filtering into a predominantly dark space: "Dark all without it knits; within / It opens passable and thin" (lines 505–6). Typographically, the semicolon that breaks but connects the spaces "without" and "within" in line 505 conveys the possibility of the inside coexisting with the outside, and of light coexisting with darkness, thus embodying what the camera obscura thematizes. The poet views this house—his house, as James Turner puts it—as just as grand as one created by a human architect. Perceiving in it "Corinthean porticoes," arches, columns, and "winged choirs," he transposes the naturalistic elements of architectural details back to nature. This house grows too, as Nun Appleton, the architecturally designed country manor house, did in the poem's introduction, but its growth proceeds from natural process, not human intrusion or intervention. Human beings such as the poet accommodate themselves to the shapes and movements of nature, not the other way around.

In such a setting, the poet finds his first-person voice: "Thus I, easy philosopher, / Among the birds and trees confer" (stanza 71, lines 561–62). He is complete here, as the plants are in themselves: "And little now to make me, wants / Or of the fowls, or of the plants" (563–64). He also longs to be one of the natural beings: "Give me but wings as they, and I / Straight floating on the air shall fly" (565–66). Unlike his meandering, earthbound path, his path through the air promises to be straight and direct.[88] Yet he need not fly; he can also stay rooted on the ground, for as a man—harking back to Platonic and Aristotelian anthropomorphizing figurations of trees—he is but an "inverted tree" (568). Showing his willingness to accommodate himself to nature's rule, he describes how "The oak leaves me embroider all, / Between which caterpillars crawl: / And ivy, with familiar trails, / Me licks, and clasps, and curls, and hales" (stanza 74, lines 587–90). Rather than use vegetal forms to decorate human design— a visual motif common in baroque design—he allows vegetal form to use human form for its own design.[89]

Fully connected with his body, he has the freedom to move further inward, into his own thoughts. The wood gives license to his imagination to flow, and to create new fabrics and patterns as it does so: "Out of these scattered sibyl's leaves / Strange prophecies my fancy weaves:" (stanza 73, lines 577–78). In a space empty of other humans, he has, moreover, space to find a home for those thoughts, like the designing hewel (woodpecker) who finds a home within a tree by gauging from the outside its affordances of depth and hollowness: "But where he, tinkling with his beak, / Does find the hollow oak to speak, / That for his building he designs, / And through the tainted side he mines" (stanza 69, lines 547–50).[90]

By giving full embodiment to his experiences, the wood gives him an opportunity to experience the setting with his body and all his senses. That the sensations are his alone is conveyed by the first-person pronoun that accompanies them. Such sensations occur in connection with the activity of the creatures that share the world of the wood with him. He freely shares the sensual pleasures of that world with his reader, as a lord might the bounty of his estate: we feel the cold strawberries under his feet, see the leaf tremble in the wind, and hear the songs of a nightingale and stock-doves as he does.[91] This is his realm of possessive interiority.

In the wood, he is no longer a mere spectator, or an imaginer of others' genealogical or interior dramas, but an actor in his own private theater. His voluntary servitude to oak leaves that embroider on him, and caterpillars that crawl on him, make him the very medium of nature and its designs. With this shift, he reverses the structure in "To Penshurst," where natural creatures on the estate submit to human designs and desires. Turning into the object of ivy's intimately creeping lines, his "I" becomes a "me": "And ivy, with familiar trails, / Me licks, and clasps, and curls, and hales" (stanza 74, lines 589–90). Yet through this inversion of the relationship between human and nature, he paradoxically finds in the next lines much greater agency and range of motion, turning back to an "I": "Under this antic cope I move / Like some great prelate of the grove" (591–92). Punning on "cope" as both a garment for religious ceremony and an architectural covering, he figures the insects and plants not so much as his captors, but as the creators of a beautiful robe for him to wear. Thus, unlike his role as flatterer of a social superior's taste in domestic design and architecture or spectator of his laborers' activities, he is promoted in this setting to a position of high rank: "great prelate of the grove." The wood becomes a true home for him insofar as it brings awareness of his body, and in turn makes it a pleasurable site to occupy. Because this is so, the space of his mind is more pleasurable to inhabit as well. Here, he is "safe" as well as "strong," and has found a place to "encamp" his mind: "How safe, methinks, and strong, behind / These trees have I encamped my mind" (stanza 76, lines 601–2).[92]

So intense are his pleasures in the wood that he imagines sadistic-seeming captivity as a delicious state of passivity. Imprisoned by the natural beings that live in the wood, he has an excuse to dwell forever with them:

Bind me ye woodbines in your twines,
Curl me about ye gadding vines,
And oh so close your circles lace,
That I may never leave this place:
But, lest your fetters prove too weak,
Ere I your silken bondage break,
Do you, O brambles, chain me too,
And courteous briars nail me through. (stanza 77, lines 609–16)

He submits, thus, to the architecture of vegetal life and natural growth, contributing to a design far lovelier, more intricate, and more vivid, than any he has observed elsewhere on the Nun Appleton estate. Vines create lace, their bondage silken, and briars are courteous for nailing him "through," securing his domestic architecture. Thus beautifully decorated, the poet's house allows him to have dominion over his thoughts. Here, in the wood, he discovers and creates an estate of the mind that exists apart from the rest of Fairfax's estate. Here, in a figurative way, he practices the spatial formalism that the subjects in subsequent chapters of this book pursue at even greater length, with actual materials, and with more concentration.

John Locke, soon after, in 1689, articulated this estate of the mind as a feature of human understanding: "the Dominion of Man, in this little World of his own Understanding, being much what the same, as it is in the great World of visible things."[93] As a sanctuary for body as well as mind, the wood intensifies the awareness of mental activity directly related to sense impressions. In this way especially, it functions as the camera obscura. In addition, it anticipates the sovereign personhood that Locke would present at around the same time, in *Two Treatises of Government*, as a natural condition: "every man has a property in his own person."[94]

The poet's sovereignty in the camera obscura space of the woods is only temporary. To remain in the setting that endows him with first-person pronoun status, largely absent elsewhere on the estate, requires his being enchained, nailed through, and staked down. The last stanza of the wood section presents an image of how he might become a permanent part of the estate topography through bondage to the land:

Here in the morning tie my chain
Where the two woods have made a lane,
While, like a guard on either side,
The trees before their Lord divide;
This, like a long and equal thread,

Betwixt two labyrinths does lead.
But, where the floods did lately drown,
There at the evening stake me down. (stanza 78, lines 617–24)

With his chain of brambles extending beyond him to the pathway
between the two woods, he offers a thread, like Ariadne's, to guide visitors through the depths of the estate's wilderness land. He volunteers
not only to become a permanent part of the estate property by being
in its possession but also, with the reach of his chain, to be a guide to it
and, in turn, to possess the land. He is throwing out a line this time—the
chain of brambles—not to measure the estate land's depths, but to provide a means to navigate them, a service that the lines of his poem have
all throughout provided. Yet, he asks "At the evening"—the present time
in the poem—to be "stake[d] down" at the meadow, "where the floods
did lately drown." In asking to be tethered outside the wood, he provides
the transition to bring himself back to the place from which he had fled,
thereby completing the circumscription of the exterior within the stanzas he has built.

Storyline: Walking, or Perspective in Motion

To be a true guide requires that he move continually across the estate,
much as the forces of nature continue to move and change, a fact revealed
by the meadow's lush appearance after the flood:

But now the waves are fall'n and dried,
And now the meadow's fresher dyed;
Whose grass, with moister colour dashed,
Seems as green silks but newly washed. (stanza 79, lines 625–28)

Nature again works as a medium in itself, offering a new perspective of the
field and creating a new textile of the grass—"fresher dyed," "moister colour dashed," "seems as green silks," and "newly washed." While the poet
experienced the transformations the interior space of the wood enabled
for him, nature has undergone its own transformation.

The similitude between walking and reading and, by extension, Marvell as a walker and his non-Fairfacian reader, is reinforced by Michel
de Certeau: "Readers are travellers; they move across lands belonging
to someone else."[95] It is reinforced, too, in the notion of the reader as a
"poacher," whose "different world . . . slips into the author's place." Much
as Marvell's embodied and ambulatory reading of the estate's landscape

makes it his own, so too reading "transforms another person's property into a space borrowed for a moment by a transient." Reading "makes the text habitable," and reading texts and reading landscapes are commensurate acts.[96] The conditions of renting, poaching, and being transient suggest movement; Marvell's own stay at Nun Appleton lasted for only a year and a half. If in reading one covers texts with one's moving eyes to piece together a story, then stories themselves "traverse and organize places; they select and link them together." Stories are in this way "spatial trajectories," and "every story is a spatial practice."[97] By putting different parts of Lord Fairfax's estate in relation to each other, making sense of those parts through his wandering perspective and the imagined perspectives of others, Marvell creates stories.

If walking is a form of reading, it is a form of writing too. For Ingold, the walker creates lines on the ground with her footsteps the way "a draughtsman traces a line with his pencil." Walking is "an act of inscription, of writing in the original sense of drawing a sharp point over a surface, of furrowing a track." Walking, however, in leaving "the traces of a moving body as it goes along," can only leave impressions. Rather than "stamps" made on "the solid earth"—inscriptions that suggest not only "intentions already engraven in the mind" but also "immobility and omnipresence"—the footprints left by a wanderer register the "interface between the mental and the material" that emerges from unpremeditated motions.[98]

Ingold recognizes the possibilities for fiction-making in the activity of walking or, as he prefers to call it, "wayfaring," the "open-ended" form of "going along" in "improvisatory movement" on the ground, through the medium of air.[99] The wayfarer, unlike a surveyor who might work to classify and arrange, "draws a tale from impressions in the ground" and in doing so situates "each impression in relation to the occurrences that paved the way for it, presently concur with it, and follow along after." The wayfarer's knowledge, then, is "not classificatory but storied, not totalizing and synoptic but open-ended and exploratory."[100] The simple fact that Marvell's poem is several times longer than most country house poems indicates that he chooses an "open-ended and exploratory" approach to the genre rather than a "totalizing and synoptic" one. Consequently he opens up further possibilities for creating storylines in his country house poem.

He also creates the space for making the estate his own, making sense of it through his point of view, his faculty of vision, deployed as much by the eyes as by the movement of his feet *through* the estate. As Marvell increasingly owns the vision of Nun Appleton as a product of his own perspective, the estate becomes a medium of self-reflection that momentarily displaces awareness of its proper lord as owner and controller of its image.

When Wotton claims that the movements of "the feete" and "the eye" on a country house estate in themselves enact "a Lordship," he suggests how such authorial slippage can take place:

> Some [architectural precepts] againe may bee said to bee *Optical*? Such I meane as concerne the *Properties* of a well chosen *Prospect*: which I will call the *Royaltie* of *Sight*. Fore as there is a *Lordship* (as it were) of the *Feete*, wherein the Master doth much joy when he walketh about the *Line* of his owne *Possessions*: So there is a *Lordship* likewise of the *Eye* which being a raunging, and Imperious, and (I might say) an *usurping Sence*, can indure no narrow *circumscription*; but must be fedde, both with extent and varietie.[101]

While Wotton's intent in the passage is to offer advice on how the owner of an estate might choose the best location for building his house, he introduces the arresting concept that the eye, in gazing on an estate, as much as the feet, in walking "about the *Line* of [one's] owne *Possessions*," creates "Lordship." Just as the viewer's position in the camera obscura—and, for that matter, Marvell's in the enclosed wood—endows him with the sovereign status of subjectivity, walking, which is determined by the volition and choices of the walker, does so too. Wotton, by virtue of terming eyesight, in general, "an *usurping Sence*," grants the privilege of lordship to anyone walking "about the *Line*" of an estate.

Walking is instrumental in generating the lines of plot and story, as well as the mobility of point of view. It is also conducive to novelistic perspective, which hinges on "a constant manifestation and testing of a developing point of view," not on "the fixed character or status of the hero."[102] Without the poet's actions—self-consciously walking the expanse of Nun Appleton, with his own feet touching its ground, and moving through its air, guided by the incalculable directions of his mind—there would be no perspective through which the reader can perceive Fairfax's estate. There would be no interiority, either, in the experience of the estate, for perspective is in itself a private world.[103]

Regarding the changed landscape of the meadow after the flood gives the poet another opportunity to recall the variability and relativity of perspective:

> See in what wanton harmless folds
> It ev'rywhere the meadow holds;
> And its yet muddy back doth lick,
> Till as a crystal mirror slick;

> Where all things gaze themselves, and doubt
> If they be in it or without. (stanza 80, lines 633–38)

No longer a "sea" or an opening "cataract," the meadow "holds" the mystery of "folds," and of the depths and contractions they create. It is still a visual device, however, as it resembles, after its mud has been "licked" away, a "crystal mirror slick." Here is the poem's most significant image of visual illusion, one that announces a decidedly modern notion of subjectivity.[104] The refreshed river, in being likened to "crystal" as opposed to the steel of older mirrors, is presented as much as an object of modern luxury as it is as an evocation of an episode in the book of Revelation. Moreover, offering a reflection of the beings looking into it, rather than pointing them to a "moral or spiritual lesson" or an "ontology of similitude," bespeaks the modern notion of the mirror as "a metaphor for human consciousness and originality."[105]

Above all, the "crystal mirror" announces a more modern view of the country house estate in that it views one of its locations not as a reflection of its owner's strengths and valor, but as a reflection of "all things" that look into it. One sees oneself, in other words, when visiting Nun Appleton. The place functions as a medium for self-reflection. In turn, the poem itself—taking up a traditional metaphor for poetry—functions as the device for showing how the place of Nun Appleton mediates self-reflection. The puzzle it presents, of making its gazers "doubt / If they be in it or without," stands for one of the poem's richest conceits and camera obscura maneuvers: turning external space into internal space. That maneuver makes the reader as a viewer wonder if she has been, during the space of the poem, inside a physical space or a mental one.

Once his charge Maria, heir of Nun Appleton, arrives, nature self-consciously adjusts, but the outside becomes inside again when nature, with its shadows, performs the architectural function of a house that closes its shutters to allow its inhabitants to settle in for the evening, turning the whole world into a dark room:

> So when the shadows laid asleep
> From underneath these banks do creep,
> And on the river as it flows
> With ebon shuts begin to close (stanza 84, lines 665–68)

The most telling sign that the world of Nun Appleton is preparing to end its day is the appearance of the halcyon, whose appearance makes the air "viscous" and solidifies the "stream" that had flowed in the previous stanza, under the shadows of the setting sun. The halcyon's "jellying" and "fixing" influence turns nature from a moving inner theater into a static picture, a tableau of brilliant hues of blue—"azure" and "sapphire" from the bird's plumage and the air in which she flies, the air that "sucks" her "dye"—and of the fishes she has caught, still, "stupid," and "hang[ing]" like crystallized flies. If occupying natural space has, for the poet, resembled the experience of the camera obscura, where projections of the outside world shift and change while the colors become more intense, the halcyon's solidification of such projections suggests the picture-making process is complete. Maria's arrival enforces this completion: "See how loose Nature, in respect / To her, it self doth recollect" (stanza 83, lines 657–58).

Because of her, the heiress, "nature is wholly vitrified" (stanza 86, line 688). Again, nature is rendered as an expanse of glass—like the meadow earlier, after the flood—and here the connection is as much to the Bible as it is to the poem's other forms of crystallization and vitrification and to the new perspectives they bring. This final act of glassmaking signals that the plotting of the poem has reached its ultimate destination, the arrival of Maria Fairfax. She is not only the embodiment of virtue and author of the future Fairfax line, but also author of the spaces of natural beauty the poem has plotted with its own lines. All natural spaces and resources on the estate in fact derive from Maria Fairfax:

> 'Tis she that to these gardens gave
> That wonderous beauty which they have;
> She straightness on the woods bestows;
> To her the meadow sweetness owes;
> Nothing could make the river be
> So crystal-pure but only she;
> She yet more pure, sweet, straight, and fair,
> Than gardens, woods, meads, rivers are. (stanza 87, lines 689–96)

This stanza brings us back to the landscape locations—garden, wood, meadow, and river—that structure the poem, and that were listed earlier, in stanza 10, as a preview of attractions to come in the poem, or a table of its contents. With Maria's authorship of these spaces solidified, all of Nun Appleton's natural spaces repay her by turning into her "house," much as the woods did earlier for the poet:

> Therefore what first she on them spent,
> They gratefully again present:
> The meadow carpets where to tread;

The garden flowers to crown her head;
And for a glass the limpid brook,
Where she may all her beauties look;
But, since she would not have them seen,
The wood about her draws a screen. (stanza 88, lines 697–704)

Turner reads the poem's "outdoor scenes" as being "presented more and more as domestic interiors"—indeed, here, "the entire estate offers itself to Maria as an interior."[106] It offers itself, with its comfortable carpeting, looking glass, and screen, as her dressing room, that most private and inward space built expressly for women in domestic architecture since the seventeenth century, and a close relative of the writing closet, the subject of chapter 2.[107]

At this point in the poem, the poet largely "draws a screen" around "the beauties" of his own mind, drawing instead the digressive lines of entailment ("And goodness doth itself entail / On females, if there want a male") that allow Maria to factor as heir of Nun Appleton (stanza 91, lines 727–28). Such a "translation" of female offspring into male roles—Maria "supplies beyond her sex the line"—accords with the malleable nature of women in the poem. They, like the poet himself, are susceptible to transformation, turning into something other—especially nature and natural elements—than what they are initially.[108] Just as the poet merges with and metamorphoses into the estate's landscape, so too does Maria; when she walks through the garden, she "seems with the flowers a flower to be" (line 296).

Conclusion: The Poem's Heiresses

Insofar as the view of the poet's mental structure is distinguishable at all, *Upon Appleton House* departs from other country house poems. Furthermore, because the view of the poet's mental structure remains inseparable from the material structures and natural formations surrounding it, and vice versa, the poem anticipates and shares kinship with narratives in which physical setting and interior experience interact. One of the most elaborated examples of such narratives emerges when, in Jane Austen's *Pride and Prejudice*, Elizabeth Bennet first sees Pemberley, and only through viewing it fully understands the value of its owner:

Elizabeth, as they drove along, watched for the first appearance of Pemberley Woods with some perturbation; and when at length they turned in at the lodge, her spirits were in a high flutter.

The park was very large, and contained great variety of ground. They entered it in one of its lowest points, and drove for some time, through a beautiful wood, stretching over a wide extent.

Elizabeth's mind was too full for conversation, but she saw and admired every remarkable spot and point of view. They gradually ascended for half a mile, and then found themselves at the top of a considerable eminence, where the wood ceased, and the eye was instantly caught by Pemberley House, situated on the opposite side of a valley, into which the road with some abruptness wound. It was a large, handsome, stone building, standing well on rising ground, and backed by a ridge of high woody hills;— and in front, a stream of some natural importance was swelled into greater, but without any artificial appearance. Its banks were neither formal, nor falsely adorned. Elizabeth was delighted. She had never seen a place for which nature had done more, or where natural beauty had been so little counteracted by an awkward taste. They were all of them warm in their admiration; and at that moment she felt, that to be mistress of Pemberley might be something![109]

Not much in the passage appears to depart from the viewpoint of traditional country house poetry. That the culminating line of the passage begins with the observation "they were all of them warm in their admiration" reinforces the prevailing collectiveness of viewpoint. Yet the semicolon that immediately follows intercepts the collective reception of the estate to introduce one particular subject's point of view: "and at that moment she felt, that to be mistress of Pemberley might be something!"

The emphatic inner statement—exemplifying the "represented speech and thought" of free indirect discourse—is the climax to an encounter between "the mental and the material."[110] Individual subjectivity bursts through the impersonal viewpoint that otherwise prevails in the passage. Elizabeth's subjectivity becomes most salient in the moment of projecting ownership over everything she and the others have seen and admired. Similar to the path of country house poetry itself, and to pathways in country house architecture that move from private to communal spaces, the passage in Austen's novel moves from touristic appreciation to an altogether more emotional and individual response. The passage also represents the phenomenon of poaching that takes place when "the traveling eye" moves "across lands belonging to someone else," whether textually or geographically realized, and "transforms another person's property into a space borrowed for a moment."[111] Such is the condition of readers, too, "poaching their way across fields they did not write." In the moment when Elizabeth sees herself in the estate of Pemberley, she has "transported" herself, slipping her world "into the author's place," and creates the space of interiority for herself that the narrative point of view reveals through free indirect discourse, even as she remains in the company of others.

Elizabeth's encounter with Pemberley distills the main dynamic I set out to explore in this chapter through Marvell's *Upon Appleton House*: inner psychology comes alive as it not so much responds to but interacts with the landscape environment of a country house estate. The concrete realm of physical setting and the abstract one of psychological event conjoin to form the third realm of interiority. That the process is an interactive one is conveyed when the landscape—the "disposition of the ground"—is described in terms of objects that move in relation to Elizabeth's point of view, which in turn moves through the windows of different rooms in the house:

> Elizabeth, after slightly surveying [the room], went to a window to enjoy its prospect. The hill, crowned with wood, from which they had descended, receiving increased abruptness from the distance, was a beautiful object. Every disposition of the ground was good; and she looked on the whole scene, the river, the trees scattered on its banks, and the winding of the valley, as far as she could trace it, with delight. As they passed into other rooms, these objects were taking different positions; but from every window there were beauties to be seen.[112]

As fantasies of what might have been intersect with the present reality, the place of Pemberley moves in another fashion: it becomes as enmeshed with the narrative that first brought it into being as with the psyche of the heroine. Responsible for rousing her feelings for a man, and thus inextricable from those feelings—as well as from the man's identity as its owner—the country house estate transforms Elizabeth's inner life by engaging her perceptions. The transformation leads to a change in the direction of the novel's storylines and results in Elizabeth's eventual occupation of Pemberley as its mistress.

This chapter has attempted to trace the background for the textual world *Pride and Prejudice* epitomizes, wherein a country house estate plays such a profound role in the narrative that it is both its destination and an environment for rousing the inner awareness that is required to reach it. Andrew Marvell's country house poem *Upon Appleton House* is foundational in literature's turn toward a practice that has heretofore been attributed to novels: using domestic architectural settings to develop narratives of inner awareness.

It is often understood that only free indirect discourse could linguistically maneuver the perpetual motion between the mental interior of a character and her highly articulated material exterior. Yet it is a maneuver that assumes the function of the camera obscura in its endless streaming of the exterior world into a spatial interior that may be either stationary or mobile. Marvell's poem creates that motion in its translations of perspective into verbal images and its progression through the spaces of Nun Appleton. The image of the river that licks its own "muddy back," "till as a crystal mirror slick," and creates a scenario in which "all things gaze themselves, and doubt / If they be in it or without," is thus all the more significant. It not only makes concrete the spatial irony that Marvell depicts as integral to interior experience but exemplifies the possibilities making renditions of interiority possible through literary technique. This is to say that literature's technology of shifting imperceptibly from general viewpoints to those of individual psychologies was introduced well before Austen appeared to perfect it through free indirect discourse.

Rosalie Colie hints at this narrative role without explicitly identifying it when she remarks on Marvell's "personality with no fixed boundaries" that "glides through a series of experiences rendered . . . in very different contexts, literary languages, and literary moralities." Presenting himself as a character, she observes, "the poet moves through his landscape and through his poem, writing as if he were actually living the scenes and experiences that are his subject, as if he were himself uncertain of what was about to happen next."[113] Here, Colie describes the poem from the perspective of Renaissance literature. Yet in doing so, she unwittingly describes how Marvell accomplishes in poetry a maneuever frequently attributed to literature of later periods: the act of perpetually oscillating between the roles of omniscient narrator and self-enclosed protagonist.

By the end of the poem, with the plotting complete, Marvell's identification with Maria Fairfax becomes fully apparent. Just as she continues a dynastic line through a feat of digressive entailment, so does he as a poet through digressive lines of poetry. Much as Maria will enjoy the estate as a transitional owner, so too does Marvell in his experience of it as a transient servant, not least in his writing about it. The poem will eventually be given over to the estate's true owner, his patron, Lord Fairfax. Its full title makes official the poet's awareness of his creation's ultimate destination: *Upon Appleton House, To My Lord Fairfax*. Whereas Maria's perspective—like that of her ancestress Isabel Thwaites in the poem—remains unknown, the poet turns the task of celebrating a lord and his estate, making political commentary, and mapping the lines of his property into an experiment in presenting and exploring his perspective and the interiority it brings. The poem's final stanza allows the poet to give one last glimpse of the estate and its world through his perspective:

> But now the salmon-fishers moist
> Their leathern boats begin to hoist;
> And, like Antipodes in shoes,
> Have shod their heads in their canoes.
> How tortoise-like, but not so slow,
> These rational amphibii go!
> Let's in: for the dark hemisphere
> Does now like one of them appear. (stanza 97, lines 769–76)

The poem ends at a point when the world itself appears like fishermen going home for the day, seemingly upside down—"like Antipodes"—wearing what should be at their feet on the tops of their heads. The stanza shows the fishermen moving—breaking the fixed frame of the emblem to which the image alludes—and thereby also shows the poet's mind moving as it makes a connection between what he sees from his perspective and what is really in front of his eyes.[114] "Appear" is the very last word of the poem, yoked with "hemisphere" as its rhyming word in the previous line of the final couplet. These two words, "appear" and "hemisphere," emblematize the entire poem's exercise of showing the distinction between the world as it is and the world as it appears. The spaces for subjectivity in and around the country house, like the poem's narration, are shaped through this distinction. And the crisis and drama of realizing such a distinction will be one of the defining features of both spatial and literary settings for interiority in the next century.

With the fishermen appearing inverted, "like Antipodes in shoes," the final, epitomizing view of the world belongs equally to the camera obscura and to the country house. By now "the dark hemisphere" is shown to be whole and complete; the projection of the fishermen going home, apparently upside down, is but a scene of the whole world miniaturized, the camera obscura's consummate trick. The poem's final command—"Let's in"—so often a pleasing point of conclusion for scholars performing the exhausting feat of writing on this long and difficult poem about a country house and its world, is hardly a point of closure. Instead, it is an opening for further points of examination as it breaks ground and makes way for literature that is ever more digressive, resolutely moving inward even while it turns outward to look at the world around it.

Closet

MARGARET CAVENDISH'S
WRITING WORLDS

Wherefore, for my Pleasure and Delight, my Ease and Peace, I live a Retired Life, a Home Life, free from the Intanglements, confused Clamours, and rumbling Noise of the World, for I by this Retirement live in a calm Silence, wherein I have my contemplations free from Disturbance, and my Mind lives in Peace, and my Thoughts in Pleasure.

But this Retired Life is so Pleasing to me, as I would not change it for all the Pleasures of the Publick World, nay, not to be Mistress of the World.

MARGARET CAVENDISH, *Sociable Letters*

Margaret Cavendish's writing closet was her favorite place to be. Publicly, too, she was identified with her closet and the mental activity it housed; a much-reproduced engraving depicts her inside the closet, at her desk, not writing in the instant, but either pausing or about to begin. There is no other visible function for the closet but to serve as a space for writing. A balustrade—similar to ones used to allocate the bed area of an early modern state bedchamber—bears an inscription that explains the room's spareness:

> Studious She is all Alone
> Most visitants when She has none
> Her Library on which She looks
> It is her Head her Thoughts her Books
> Scorninge dead Ashes without fire
> For her owne Flames do her Inspire[1]

The space, lacking even the practical comfort of a fireplace, is without furniture but for the luxurious cloth of estate, or baldachin (a fabric canopy for exalted subjects), that encloses her and the desk at which she sits. On her desk, a cloth-covered table, her writing tools are ready: a standish carrying her pen in its holder and inkwell, a pounce pot, a sheet of paper, a bell for summoning her servants, and a clock. A pair of cherubs carry the canopy drapes around her, and another pair holds a crown of laurels above her head. If she has paused from her writing, it appears she has done so to receive the crown.

As the main contents of the closet include the essential tools for Cavendish's writing, the putti hovering around her head represent the figments of thought that issue from writing. Though in a different visual style, the engraving evokes the striking interiority—of space, activity, and occupation—seen in Dutch paintings of the same period by such artists as Gabriel Metsu, Gerhard Ter Borch, and Jan Vermeer, in which women write, read, and engage in contemplative activity in the privacy of their homes.[2] Created by artist Abraham van Diepenbeeck, the image was invariably used as a frontispiece for Cavendish's books.[3] Margaret sought out his service to capture her performing her own cherished domestic skill and daily activity, just as her husband William had hired Diepenbeeck to illustrate his feats of horsemanship for his dressage manual *La Méthode et invention nouvelle de dresser les cheveaux* (1657–1658). The image, as the consistent bibliographic "frontispiece" to the house of her writing, suggests that to read Cavendish's books is to enter the innermost aspect of her residence, the writing closet of her mind. According to the image, Cavendish's mental life takes place in a concretely spatial setting, with contemporary material features.

Here, as in her writing, we might view Cavendish's thoughts as embodied rather than evoked. On one hand, they are embodied by the putti, which also enact her wish to receive fame and recognition for her writing and ideas.[4] On the other hand, according to the inscription, her thoughts are embodied as the library subsumed by her head. If the frontispiece represented Cavendish's thoughts according to her own authorial visions, they would appear not in the conventional idiom of flying baby boys, but in one of the many unique forms she gives to them in her writing: ice skaters sliding on a frozen river, struggling to stay upright; actors on the stage of her brain, who play the fool, dance, and make her laugh; or a visiting consort of learned and witty men, including natural philosophers, theologians, and poets.[5] Having entered the chamber of her mind through the frontispiece of her book, one might encounter such strikingly physical enactments of what her mind is *doing*. Indeed, the very pairing of the "philosophical" with the "physical" in the title of one of the books in which the frontispiece appears, *Philosophical and Physical Opinions*, alerts us to

Studious She is and all Alone,
Most visitants, when She has none,
Her Library on which She looks
It is her Head her Thoughts her Books.
Scorninge dead Ashes without fire
For her owne Flames doe her Inspire.

FIGURE 2.1 Margaret Cavendish in her writing closet. Frontispiece for the Huntington Library's copy (HEH RB 120148) of Cavendish, *Philosophical and Physical Opinions* (1655). After Abraham van Diepenbeeck, engraved by Pierre Louis van Schuppen. Photograph: Huntington Library, San Marino, California.

the continuity of the immaterial with the material in Cavendish's mental world.

By fusing mental life with its locations in architectural space, giving physical form and shelter to the contents of that life, and occupying a liminal status of fantasy and naturalism, the frontispiece presents the central terms of an interiority realized through architectural space that this chapter will explore in Cavendish's life and work. An author of works in many genres, natural philosopher, and reclusive noblewoman given to flamboyant dress that sometimes involved cross-dressing, Cavendish famously evinced a love for retirement from social life that matched her concerns as a writer. According to Anna Battigelli, Cavendish "explored interiority more openly and more publicly than any other writer of her time."[6] Such explorations of interiority emerged as a polemic in a scientific treatise, *Observations upon Experimental Philosophy*, which appeared in 1666 with the fantasy narrative *The Description of a New World Called the Blazing World* attached to it.[7] Cavendish's use of writing to create the spaces—as much real as imagined—that made visible and material the "creatures" and contents of her mind, an endeavor the frontispiece thematizes in both its illustration and inscription, is a consistent act of spatial formalism. Her ideas about the writing process and the work of the imagination are directly tied to her views on the spaces of the mind as well as spaces *for* the mind. Both types of spaces are, for her, ineluctably material and mobile, and at the same time indistinguishable from each other.

Yet most critics have placed greater emphasis on the particularities in Cavendish's philosophies of mental life, ignoring the fact that they were developed not just in social-intellectual settings but in spatial ones as well, whose distinct material features and cultural-historical functions played shaping roles.[8] Simultaneously, she practiced spatial formalism in exerting the creative control on her surroundings that would turn one space in particular, her writing closet, into a generative environment for her mental life. Like the country house's double pile plan, discussed in chapter 1, the writing closet promoted possessive interiority and an everyday experience of space that prompted private awareness of her inner processes and sense of individual identity. Whereas the double pile floor plan and its attendant corridor were paradigmatic for experiences of interiority as a state of mobility, a notion that Kepler's portable camera obscura with its little black tent reinforced, the writing closet was a space where one might stay in the same place to enter states of interiority. One might pace within its perimeter, as Cavendish did, but the writing closet's stationary situation facilitated mental activity that far exceeded such circumscribed movement, allowing her to create imagined spaces and worlds and bring them to others through print.

At the time the frontispiece was made, Cavendish was living in exile in Antwerp, a haven for displaced Royalists, renting a house that formerly belonged to the Flemish artist and diplomat Peter Paul Rubens, who himself had been the teacher of Diepenbeeck. According to Cavendish, Antwerp was "a place of great resort for Strangers and Travellers."[9] Before settling in Antwerp, she and William lived in Paris and Rotterdam during his banishment for being a "traitor and enemy" to the English government. Her position inside the writing closet seems stable and enclosed, but the outer conditions of her life at the time the frontispiece was made resembled more the rootlessness and mobility of the floating putti that frame her in the image.

With its floating cherubs, the Diepenbeeck illustration appears at first too stylized to indicate what Cavendish's writing space in Antwerp might have looked like. Rather than depicting an actual room, it shows her at a desk set inside a canopy of state, a distinctly ceremonial rather than homey setting. Just as the balustrade marks the boundary between the writer and others, the putti lowering a laurel wreath on her head emphasize her distinguished status.[10] Yet, the tabletop and writing accessories are true enough to life, consistent with images of other writing desks of the time, as is the damask pattern of the canopy's wall hanging, which resembles a wall-hanging pattern now found in the Duke of Lauderdale's closet at Ham House. Furthermore, in contrast with another portrait frontispiece she commissioned Diepenbeeck to create, in which she fashions herself as a classical deity by wearing a robe and standing contrapposto inside an architectural niche, the image of her sitting at her writing desk in informal contemporary dress promotes a far greater sense of her everyday life.[11] Ultimately, placing her daily activity of writing in the setting of a canopied dais and using the image as a frontispiece for her books indicates her desire to be known publicly for an activity she conducted in the privacy of her dwelling.[12]

Mary Baine Campbell has argued that Cavendish is "truly a forerunner of the modern novelist," as much for her world-making enterprise in *The Blazing World* as for her "mobile and marginal" status, which in turn brings her closer in identity to the protagonists of eighteenth-century novels.[13] Yet there is more to Cavendish's role in the history of the novel; whereas Campbell emphasizes the alterity and, by extension, antimimeticism of Cavendish's world-making (she is allegedly "more alter than idem"), I maintain instead that, for Cavendish, textual world-making relied on incorporating and transposing rather than rejecting the familiar dimensions of real-life spaces. These spaces, which include the ruins of her husband's impounded estates as well as her writing closet, factor significantly in her prevailing use of space as the environmental medium for making interior processes of the mind real. In this sense, the approach to interiority exemplified here distinguishes itself from the previous chapter's. In Marvell's case, the exterior world is internalized and, through the medium of space, constituted and made known as an internal perception.

For Cavendish, the process of dwelling was repeatedly enacted in her imaginative use of physical spaces to create mental ones, as well as in her circumstance as a Royalist refugee who moved several times during the fifteen years she lived in exile on the continent with her husband. In these ways, her approach to inhabiting space evinces "the dwelling perspective" Ingold defines as "the premise that the forms humans build, whether in the imagination or on the ground, arise within the currents of their involved activity, in the specific relational contexts of their practical engagement with their surroundings."[14]

Insofar as she finds in specific spaces of her life the locations (her writing closet) for the inner experience of thinking, and creates newly imagined spaces (her "Minds Architecture" and "Airy Castles") through that experience, she establishes a relationship to space that realizes that the act of existing is one of "dwelling," to use the term Ingold appropriates from Martin Heidegger. This dwelling is inextricable from building, or "constructing locations," which creates and enables spaces and leads to "presencing."[15] Thus, "the nature of building is letting dwell"—as well as *thinking*: "building and thinking are, each in its own way, inescapable for dwelling."[16] Such heady formulations about the relationship between humans and the physical structures that shelter them, organize their activities, and allow them to engage with their thoughts pertain to Cavendish's seventeenth-century life. The architectural sites that served as her "dwelling places"—materialized in thoughts, buildings, and words—allowed her to dwell as deeply as possible in the space of her mind while remaining engaged with the physical features of her environment, whether perceived directly or indirectly. Spatial formalism allows us to discern how, as objects of direct or indirect perception, these sites permitted her to create worlds that were realized as much in her domestic environments as in the imagined spaces of her writing. The possessive interiority presented in Cavendish, with the writing closet her medium for it, sets itself apart from Marvell by the way it derives from a practical experience of daily life that takes place on an intentional and sustained basis rather than an incidental one that emerges through an act of wandering.

World in a Closet

In *Sociable Letters*, Cavendish describes her "retired Country life" at Welbeck Abbey, begun when she and her husband returned from exile to England after the war. There, she "set down" her "Thoughts, Fancies, and Speculations" in her "Closet," with only her "Waiting-maids" as witnesses to her activity. Cavendish recounts to her imaginary friend a remark her housekeeper made to her: "you are Naturally Addicted to Busie your time with Pen, Ink, and Paper" (Letter #150, 212). As a consequence, her neighbors say, her "Waiting-Maids were Spoil'd with Idleness, having nothing to do, but to Dress, Curl, and Adorn themselves." She affirms the neglect: "I seldom took any Notice of them, or Spoke to them . . . I living so Studious a Life" (Letter #150, 211). Against assumptions that Cavendish's retreat to her writing closet in the country might bespeak the life of "obscure and sluggish security . . . buried in oblivion" that her character the Duchess deplores in *The Blazing World*, she indicates that she equated her chosen way of life with pursuing "the adventure of noble achievements" and the "glorious fame" it brings.[17] Addressing her eminent husband in the biography she wrote of him, she points out:

> It is better to be Envied, then Pitied . . . *they'l make no doubt to stain even Your Lordships Loyal, Noble and Heroick Actions, as well as they do mine, though yours have been of War and Fighting, mine of Contemplating and Writing: Yours were performed publickly in the Field, mine privately in my Closet. Yours had many thousand Eye-witnesses, mine none but my Waiting-maids. But the Great God that hath hitherto bless'd both Your Grace and me, will, I question not, preserve both our Fames to after Ages.*[18]

With her description of being observed only by her household staff as she immerses herself in writing, she creates the scene depicted in many Dutch paintings produced around the time she began her writing career: that of a woman in a domestic environment, writing or reading, usually alone, but sometimes with a servant standing next to her.[19] If the format of the letter allows Cavendish to write her "mind and thoughts" virtually in "the Company" of her absent friend, the architectural format of the place from where she wrote, her writing closet, allowed her to use the sheet of paper as a dwelling for her mind and its thoughts.

We have no definitive information about the physical elements of

Cavendish's own writing spaces, aside from what can be gleaned from the frontispiece image and inscription, Richard Flecknoe's poem "On the Duchess of Newcastle's Closet," and her comments in *Sociable Letters* and her autobiography, *A True Relation of My Birth, Breeding, and Life* (1656). Flecknoe's poem (1655–1670) registers Cavendish's closet as a small room: "What place is this? Looks like some sacred cell / Where holy hermits anciently did dwell."[20] Although the location of the closet is unspecified, the fact that the poem appears next to "On Welbeck" in Flecknoe's *A Farrago of Several Pieces* suggests it refers to her closet at Welbeck Abbey—where Flecknoe was a guest of William, his patron—as opposed to Antwerp.[21] Describing the closet in terms of how it does not resemble conventional lady's closets, Flecknoe indicates, as does the frontispiece inscription, the absence of furnishings, including mirrors or any other indicators of vanity, or even of books:

> Is this a lady-closet? 'T cannot be,
> For nothing here of vanity we see,
> Nothing of curiosity, nor pride,
> As all your ladies' closets have beside.
> Scarcely a glass, or mirror in't you find,
> Excepting books, the mirrors of the mind.
> Nor is't a library, but only as she
> Makes each place where she comes a library,
> Carrying a living library in her brain
> More worth than Bodley's or the Vatican.

Its bareness gives the impression of an eremite's abode while indicating that the main occupant of the room is the Duchess's brain. As in a dimly lit Golden Age painting, the main source of light in Cavendish's closet comes from the subject herself:

> Here she's in rapture, here in ecstasy,
> With studying high and deep philosophy:
> Here those clear lights descend into her mind,
> Which by reflection in her books you find.[22]

The room's light source and library are situated in Cavendish's mind, and in turn are reflected and processed in the books she produces from within the space of the closet. The books themselves are permutations as much of her brain—to be discussed later in this chapter—as they are of her writing closet.

That thinking was simultaneous with the physical act of writing is indicated in her remark, "I, in my Conversation, Speak, as I may say, without Thinking . . . but when I Write, I think without Speaking."[23] Indeed, just as a pen writes on paper, "*Thoughts* as a Pen do write upon the *Braine*."[24] If she is to write, she needs the space that allows her to manipulate and move her pen across the page and generate her thoughts. While the pen is the tool that allows her to create and move through a world of her own invention, the writing closet is the *environment* that allows her to use the pen at all to access the connection between her hand and brain. It is also the environment through which she moves her body to exercise it minimally, as she indicates in her memoir: "I . . . exercise little . . . only walking a slow pace in my chamber." This form of exercise gives precedence to her thoughts, which in turn influence her body: "my thoughts run apace in my brain, so that the motions of my minde hinders the active exercises of my body." More vigorous forms of exercise than this would cause her to lose her thoughts: "for should I Dance or Run, or Walk apace, I should Dance my Thoughts out of Measure, Run my Fancies out of Breath, and Tread out the Feet of my Numbers."[25]

This detail indicates the extent to which Cavendish controlled her physical activity and environment to support her mental processes—a faculty largely diminished in Marvell's own position as a hired tutor rather than lord or lady of the manor at Nun Appleton—and it provides a clue to the dimensions of her writing closet in Antwerp, the city in which she was living at the time she wrote her memoir. Large enough for her to exercise in by walking its perimeter, Cavendish's closet contradicts assumptions that all writing closets were necessarily small and intimate rooms. The frontispiece engraving presents either an isolated section of her closet or a setting entirely invented for the image. By presenting Cavendish's writing space inside a covered dais where a dignitary might sit, that image both presents Cavendish as an exalted subject and reduces the dimensions of her writing space. This spatial reduction, in decreasing the range for her external movements, suggests the expansion and intensification of the internal ones taking place when she writes. In such a space, she could never move vigorously enough to "dance" any "thoughts out of measure," or "run . . . fancies out of breath."[26] Even in its fictitious construction or selective representation of her writing space, the frontispiece communicates a critical aspect of the writing process and its effect of expanding and filling the spaces of the mind while seeming to make the surrounding world smaller.

Certainly, Cavendish's attitude toward this space was one that privileged it over the social world. Reluctant to leave the closet and exercise more vigorously or travel in her "Coach about the Town" of Antwerp, which would cause grief by requiring she leave the company of her own "harmless fancies," she spends an inordinate amount of time in the closet, situating the bulk of her daily life within its space.[27] She states as much: "for my part I had rather sit at home and write, or walk, as I said, in my chamber and contemplate."[28] She stayed so immersed in her writing that William's brother Charles likened her thoughts to imaginary fairies and teased Cavendish for spending so much time with them:

> Sir *Charles* into my chamber coming in,
> When I was writing of my *Fairy Queen*;
> 'I pray,' said he, 'when *Queen Mab* you doe see,
> Present my service to her Majesty:'[29]

Despite her apparent dialogue with fairies, her materialism arises in her devotion to writing and her rootedness in the very space of her writing, the writing closet.

The interiors of Welbeck, where the Cavendishes lived upon their return from exile, have been altered by subsequent generations so completely that only one room, the so-called Horsemanship Dressing Room, remains from the seventeenth-century ownership of William Cavendish.[30] There are no floor plans for the seventeenth-century incarnation of the house. Yet the traces of these spaces in their specific material dimensions are discernible in the literature that refers to and thereby memorializes them, literature that issued from within their walls.

Closets in early modern and eighteenth-century aristocratic homes were small rooms, ranging from seven by nine feet to twenty-four feet square, where their inhabitants were able to enjoy the informality and freedom that true privacy allows. In the homes of nonaristocratic families, or those that could do without the luxury of having rooms for different specialized purposes, the names and functions of the closet vary, sliding from "closet" and "cabinet" to dressing room, prayer closet, or study. Whatever the space was used for or called, it was the most private room in the house and reserved for its occupant's retirement. In contrast to bedrooms, where one could still receive social visits from larger groups of people, closets were spaces where one wrote letters, read, studied, prayed, rested, daydreamed, and enjoyed the company of only a few close family members or friends. As its alternate name, "cabinet," suggests, the closet might be used for display, as with the curiosity cabinet Celia Fiennes caught sight of during her visit to Burghley House, or the collection of miniature paintings in the Green Closet at Ham House.[31]

According to Peter Thornton, historian of furniture and domestic interiors, whatever their special function, "Ease, comfort and relaxation were sought in closets."[32]

Although closets for reading appeared in the sixteenth century, the seventeenth century marks a distinct period when closets began to be incorporated deliberately into the designs of domestic architecture as a form of "convenience" that sustained the development of selfhood through the provision of increasingly desired space for solitude. In the 1690s, architect Roger North (1653–1733/34) signaled that closets had become a necessity in the floor plans of domestic buildings belonging to private gentlemen, and not only princes and noblemen, by criticizing homes whose designs did not allow for them. Of Sir Henry Parker's house in Honiton, Warwick, he noted "the fault of the mode itself, which is not capable of inner rooms and closets, without prodigious waste of the best room and lights."[33] However, the "square pyle" style, or "model of 4 rooms," exemplified at "the house of my lady Rachel Haskard, at Stoke neer Windsor," met his approval for the way it allowed closets to be "pincht out of the 2 rooms on each end."[34]

In his designs for his own house, Rougham, North was obsessed with closets, making them out of available spaces whenever and wherever he could. The matter is one of "cast[ing] how the distribution would fall." Referring to the closet as "a piece of a chamber," he indicated its dimensions ("24 foot wide") as needing to be in fact larger than the room "for lodging." Throughout his descriptions of designing Rougham, he repeatedly expresses the need for privacy and solitude answered by closets. In his model for the house's pavilions, he found the west, next to the garden, proper "for retired uses" and the east, "neer the houthousing," proper "for the family." Allowing for "one chamber, and some closet, or inner room," he gave the closet in the west pavilion, next to an "inner room for a servant," a window view to the west. On the floor below, he took the same care to create spaces for privacy, including an "eating retired parlor" next to the stairs and beneath the library, which "in truth" was "a superfluous room . . . intended for my owne absolute retirement." Not stopping with this, he continued within the room to create "a room under the servant's room," which he "made into a closet."[35] Above the closets for himself and his bailiff, he built one for his wife, demonstrating his love for her by finishing it with Norwegian oak and "an angle chimney in the best manner." The corner of the east pavilion side was "dedicated to closets" entirely; one was for his household business papers, with one door opening into "the square room" and another into the parlor. Most intriguing is the additional closet he "carved out" next to the back door for his bailiff, which was connected to his room by a "passage" that allowed him to "have re-course at all times to his books and papers, etc."[36]

Accounting for his fixation on building closets into his home, North declared, "These conveniences are such ease and delight in the practice of human life and buisness [sic], that it compensates the charge of building, without which it is seldome to be had."[37] Indeed, they are "necessary and indispensable," and in the homes of less exalted inhabitants, "the placing an easement is at liberty to be done anywhere, as the places shall happen to invite, with least annoyance to the best room." In more formal homes, the proper structure, much like the design of Ham House, entailed adding to the closet a dressing room for a man and a woman each, with individual chambers for their servants close by. This allows the couple to "retire apart" once "rising" and have "severall accommodations compleat." For North, such an arrangement was "the perfection that one would expect in the seat of a prince or nobleman," but "too much for a private gentleman," whose guests are rarely as fine.[38]

Among the best known and still intact seventeenth-century closets belonging to nobility are the Duke and Duchess of Lauderdale's Private Closets at Ham House, the Fettiplace Closet at Chastleton House, and, of course, the Marble Closet and Heaven and Elysium Closets at William Cavendish's Bolsover. The spatial setting of the closet in the greater structure of the seventeenth-century country house heightened the solitude and relaxation meant to be experienced there. From within his suite of rooms, including the bedchamber (which his wife would later take over) and dressing room, the Duke of Lauderdale's closet at Ham House in Richmond upon Thames was, like most closets, sited as far as possible from a point of public entry. Located in a corner of the east wing of the house, it can be reached only by entering other rooms first, such as the north side of the bedchamber, directly off the West Passage. It can also be reached through the enfilade running from the centrally located Marble Dining Room to the Duke's dressing room and then to the west side of the bedchamber. Even though his wife took over the bedchamber through which he needed to pass to enter the closet, a set of double doors, covered by a portière made of the same material as the wall hangings, "black and olive colloured Damask hanging wt a scarlet fringe wt silver & black edging," according to a 1677 inventory, covered them and insured his privacy.[39] Another set of curtains, hanging from a canopy over the cane-bottomed couch, suggests that the Duke enjoyed lying on the couch, his relaxation enhanced by turning the space immediately around it into the soothing and contemplative atmosphere of a dark room, a veritable camera obscura.[40]

In 1679 the cane-bottomed couch was replaced by a highly fashionable "sleeping chair." With an adjustable back and footrest, it accommodated both sleep and daydreaming; one can imagine the Duke sitting in the chair with the curtains drawn around him, watching his own thoughts enter and move through his mind in the room made dark and silent. Drawing the curtains around the chair made a space free from the view of absolutely everyone, including servants in the surrounding room. Not just rooms, but furniture and textile furnishings were registering the increased desire to be alone in one's own space, in a "room" impenetrable to anyone else. The name given the room in 1677, the Closet of Repose, confirms its purpose as a space where one could feel relaxed and entertain meditative states of mind, if one so desired.

A scriptor, or Anglo-Dutch–style writing desk that began appearing in the 1660s and that closes like a cabinet, belonged to the room—and was later replaced by a larger one—further suggesting the introspective activity that took place inside it. Writing is an activity that requires solitude and the absence of interaction with others. Writing brings you more deeply into your thoughts, much as Marvell's act of wandering through a landscape brings him more deeply into his thoughts. Writing is, as Cavendish, Pope, and Richardson's heroine Pamela demonstrate, an activity par excellence of individualism and solitude. Above all, as the example of Cavendish demonstrates, it is an act as demanding of separateness and seclusion as prayer. In her seventeenth-century context, the everyday need for a special room where writing could be performed was recognized. Cavendish found in her writing closet a critical setting for the very functioning and output of her imagination. For Cavendish, unlike Pope, the spaces the closet allowed her to envision in her mind were the main objects of design, rather than the space itself in which she imagined them. In *Natures Pictures* she describes a full estate that exists in inner life: "in the Architecture of the Minde there are wide Rooms of Conception, furnish'd richly with Invention; and long Galleries, which are carved and wrought with Imaginations, and hung with the Picture of Phancy."[41] Yet contemporary examples of writing closets such as the Duke and Duchess of Lauderdales' suggest how their very design in the material plane might have functioned as channels for the play of imagination and fantasy in everyday life.

The Duchess of Lauderdale's private closet, designed in the 1670s, was used for the private activities of reading and writing that Cavendish also conducted in her closet. The furniture, reflecting this, included a scriptor, mentioned in the 1677 inventory. Described as being made of walnut, or perhaps replaced by a walnut scriptor in 1679, the desk was complemented by the arrival that year of two japanned bookcases. Showing that the closet was used for contemplative but also intimate social pursuits, the bookcases were affiliated with furniture meant for entertaining; they matched a black and gold (most likely japanned) table "en suite" with six chairs. A "carv'd and gilt" lacquered tea table, added in 1683, with "one Japan box for sweetmeats, & tea," completed the room's role as a space for cozy socializing. Filled as it was with exquisite and stylish furniture, the room did not have the space for walking and exercise that Cavendish's sparsely furnished closet did. Nor was it as dedicated to sustaining the progress of the mind through solitary experience.

But like Cavendish's closet and that of her husband, it was devoted to creating the sense that its inhabitant was dwelling in another world. The japanned and Javanese furniture, along with a little Indian box, that occupied the small room created an exotic atmosphere that was both modish and fanciful. The six chairs make manifest the room's greater effort to create a virtual Orient. Not from Japan, but intended to appear as if they were, the chairs were designed as an imagined simulation of japanned technique and style.[42] These and other items of Orientalist furnishing worked to create a virtual space that replicated the features of a different place—as one imagined it—inside the space of a room. Whereas the Duchess of Lauderdale's closet produced the impression of inhabiting another world by imitating the features of that world, the Duke of Lauderdale's closet, with its canopied couch and, later, sleeping chair, did so by inducing the cognitive perception of immersion in a place different from one's greater surroundings. Conceptually, it was a camera obscura furnished out of furniture itself.

The Duchess of Newcastle's Camera Obscura

Cavendish would have enjoyed occupying a camera obscura. Its darkened state would have allowed the diamonds and stars for which she evinced such love in *The Blazing World* to shine all the more brightly in her mind. Cavendish's friendship with Constantijn Huygens in Antwerp, who bought his in London in 1662 and showed it to the enchanted Henry Wotton (as mentioned in chapter 1), most likely brought her into direct contact with a portable model.[43] Certainly, when she describes shadows in chapter 118 of *Philosophical and Physical Opinions* (1655), she demonstrates full knowledge of what a camera obscura is and how it works. The entire entry is a description of the camera obscura, beginning with the claim that "shadows are copies, and pictures, drawn, or printed, or ingraven

FIGURE 2.2 The Duchess's Private Closet, with writing cabinet, tea table, and japanned chairs (ca. 1670–1680). Ham House, Richmond upon Thames. Photograph © National Trust Images/John Hammond.

by dark motions." Accordingly, light "is the paint, [and] the solid body on which shadows are cast, is the ground or substance to work on." The amount of darkness and light needs to be exact, for "there would be no such representments, if darkness were not; and too much light drowns the figure, or is as it were plash'd, or dabbed out, or if so much paint were spilt, or cast on the ground without order." She points out the operative distinction between shadows that fall on their own and those that are viewed within the camera obscura:

> Yet all shadows are not as if they were painted, but printed in black and white, as against a wall, or on water, or the like, but on a looking-glasse, or on a piece of paper through a little hole, in a dark room, it is as painted, the colours being represented as well as the figures.[44]

Shadows that, without the mediation of the camera obscura, render projections of reality as "images in the air"—to use Renaissance terminology—have no color.[45] When sixteenth-century natural philosopher Giambattista Della Porta describes the camera obscura as a process of "see[ing] all things in the dark, that are outwardly done in the Sun, with the colours of them," he suggests the "natural magic" of a place like Cavendish's Blazing World, which appears to have been imagined under the influence of the camera obscura.[46] That the camera obscura's projected images were portrayed not only in color, but in highly saturated color, was, as mentioned in the introduction, a quality that captivated those who experienced it, which eighteenth-century commentators especially make clear. In 1764 Venetian philosopher Francesco Algarotti praised the colors of the images projected by the camera obscura for their "vivacity and richness that nothing can excell."[47] Cavendish's Blazing World is characterized as much by its glittering light effects as by its bright and varied colors, apparent in its rainbow-hued, jewel-encrusted architecture and its people of "several complexions," from "deep purple" to "grass-green," "scarlet," and "orange-colour," not the standard "white, black, tawny, olive or ash-colored."[48]

In the Blazing World, all the elements of the real world are present, but they are made up of materials and colors that can exist only in fantasy, such as chariots drawn by unicorns and seas made of gold cloth.[49] Moreover, the domains of fact and fiction, conjoined throughout the narrative, not only experiment with the fictionality that Catherine Gallagher claims originates in the middle of the eighteenth century, but also carry out the inversion and reversal of the camera obscura's projected image.[50] Della Porta makes an observation that anticipates Marvell's envisioning of the world of Appleton House as the inside of a camera with fishermen at the end of the poem going home apparently upside down, "like Antipodes in shoes" (stanza 97, line 769). Focusing on its lateral rather than its vertical reversal, Della Porta observes that the camera obscura's projected images show figures that appear to "walk in the streets, like to Antipodes, and what is right will be the left, and all things changed."[51]

The boundary between fact and fiction is the hinge on which reversals and inversions of fictionality turn in the Blazing World. The Duchess and Duke of Newcastle, living personages, are presented as if they could be figures of fancy by being shown in interaction with their fictional counterparts, the Emperor and Empress of the Blazing World. Places such as Welbeck and Bolsover, actual Cavendish homes, are represented alongside the Emperor's gemstone and gold castle and stables and the Empress's diamond-lined chapel. New perspectives of daily life ensue, much like those yielded by the camera obscura, such as the view of Cavendish's homes in Nottinghamshire and Sherwood Forest from the vantage point of souls traveling in an "aerial vehicle," or the view of a world where nighttime is brighter than day for "reason of the blazing-stars" that twinkle there.[52] Quite possibly, the design of Bolsover itself served as the inspiration for Cavendish's imaginings of the Blazing World's architectural spaces. A description of the Emperor's bedchamber, with its jet walls, black marble floor, mother-of-pearl roof, and moon and blazing stars composed of white diamonds, seems a composite of two notable rooms at Bolsover: the Marble Closet (described below) and the Star Chamber, a large banqueting room with two hundred fifty-four gold stars covering its sky blue ceiling.[53]

William's design of Bolsover warrants its own discussion for the way it staged fiction as an architectural construct and experience. While his father Charles first worked on the country house estate with the architect Robert Smythson, William was responsible for its interior and garden designs, as well as the creation of a terrace range. He continued his father's efforts by working with the architect John Smythson, the son of Robert. From the beginning, with Charles's remodeling of the eleventh-century structure into a castle built to evoke the romances of Tasso and Spencer, Bolsover served as a fantasy world evoking a different period, to which its owners could retreat when in need of pleasure and recreation. It seems fitting, then, that a drawing by John Smythson for Bolsover's Little Castle, showing a marble-vaulted small room with a balcony and apparently used as a model for the Marble Closet, has been identified by Charles Saumarez Smith as the earliest surviving drawing of an English architectural interior.[54] Whether or not other drawings of architectural interiors

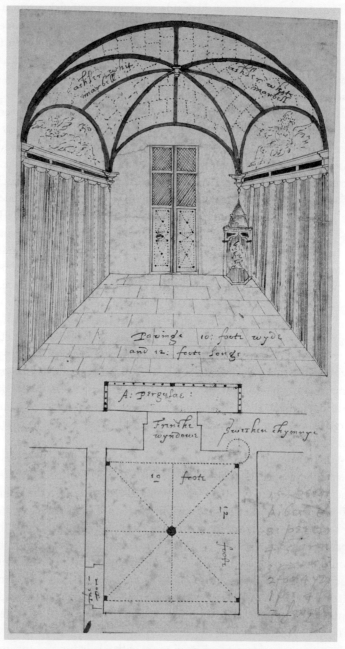

FIGURE 2.3 The earliest surviving drawing of an English architectural interior.
John Smythson, design for William Cavendish's Bolsover Castle, Derbyshire:
plan and central perspective of room vaulted with marble in
the Little Castle (1610). Photograph: RIBA Collections.

preceded Smythson's, it is clear that Bolsover was on the vanguard in imagining interior spaces as a new area of architectural emphasis. The example of Bolsover demonstrates above all that Margaret Cavendish, in her marriage to the lord of this castle, was familiar with architectural attitudes of her time that prioritized the cultivation, creation, and design of interior space as a realm for the imagination.

William Cavendish poured much energy and considerable finances into designing and decorating the interior rooms to create specific moods for those who entered the walls of Bolsover. Allegedly, he designed and built the Little Castle as much for his own pleasure as for an anticipated visit from the king and queen, who might grant him the favor of advancement. Perhaps most remarked upon by architectural historians is the series of closets, or small rooms, with evocative wall paintings, accessed through different exits and doors off the Great Chamber. William remodeled the Marble Closet in around 1619, according to a John Smythson design. The room's name refers to its being made up almost entirely—including the chimneypiece, vaulted ceiling, and floor—of Italian black and white marble. Red silk hangs against the walls, which are painted green panels. Complementing the geometrical stylishness of the room's building materials and the striking simplicity of its color scheme is a series of lunette-shaped pictures depicting the Virtues in erotic postures. Based on engravings by Hendrik Goltzius (1558–1617), the lush paintings show naked women against pastoral backdrops embracing or kissing each other. Not all the virtues depicted in Goltzius's series are present, however. The missing virtues, Timothy Raylor has argued, were said to have been supplied by the king and queen themselves: during their visit, they would be ushered into the Marble Closet, where the window would frame them as embodiments of the virtues Peace and Concord.[55]

In contrast to her husband's vision—and realization—of an architectural structure that might allow royalty to step into closets and so into preformulated roles, like actors in a play, Margaret Cavendish, within the enclosure of her own closet, created a form of literature that allowed non-monarchical subjects to step into roles of the highest nobility. Reflecting the growing tendency of great houses toward privacy, which we have already encountered in Marvell's world, closets for Cavendish were for a far more personal form of play, one that took after the play of the camera obscura rather than that of theater.

Cavendish's creation of different worlds in books from *Sociable Letters* to *The Blazing World*—as well as the lyrical vignettes in *Poems, and Fancies* that muse on the semblances between topography and human brains

FIGURE 2.4 Fireplace, vaulted ceiling, and lunette painting detail
in the Marble Closet, Bolsover Castle, Derbyshire (ca. 1629).
Photograph by the author.

("Similizing the Head of Man to the World," "Similizing the Braine to
a Garden") and the endless possibilities of "worlds in this world"—set
their own standard for a textual and textural formulation of interiority.
The fact that, for Cavendish, the camera obscura's space is merged with
that of the mind is suggested when she claims in *The Worlds Olio* that
"writing is the picture of thoughts." This very idea supplies a reason for

"Why men write Books."[56] The fullest elaboration on this conception, in the poem "Thought Similized," presents the mind as not so much a space of writing as a surface for it—on which thoughts are as much inscribed as projected—as well as a medium for camera obscura–like effects. If the pencil writes thoughts, "fancies mixt as colours, give delight."[57] Yet in order to access the "picture of thoughts" at all, a writing closet is required.

Similar to Marvell's refuge in the wood of Nun Appleton, where in its trees he "encamped" his mind, the conception of Cavendish's writing closet in Antwerp apprehends the camera obscura in its architectural guise as well as its role in demarcating the limits of solitude and sociability.[58] Unlike Marvell's accidental sanctuary, though, Cavendish's place of retreat, her writing closet, is one where she may find habitual refuge for herself and her thoughts, and design her life around being inside it. When Cavendish declares, "I had rather sit at home and write, or walk, as I said, in my chamber and contemplate," she indicates a need to be alone with her thoughts, which the enclosed space of her writing closet allows. Even so, occasional outings may be minimally necessary:

> but I hold necessary sometimes to appear abroad, besides I do find, that severall objects do bring new materialls for my thoughts and fancies to build upon, yet I must say this in the behalf of my thoughts, that I never found them idle: for if the senses brings no work in, they will work of themselves, like silk-wormes that spins out of their own bowels.[59]

Throughout her work, Cavendish weighs similar arguments for a life of sociability, and through it, "new materialls for my thoughts and fancies," against her choice to live in solitude. In the "Several Feigned Stories in Prose" section of Natures Pictures, a debate titled "The Body, Time, and Mind, disputed for Preheminency" is staged. Offered some thirty-three years before Locke's presentation of a closely similar idea in his Essay, Cavendish's argument for the primacy of the body hinges on a conception of the mind as a domicile and camera obscura to which the senses bring knowledge and understanding:

> Neither doth Time give the Minde Knowledge and Understanding, but the Senses, which are the Porters that carry them in, and furnish the Minde therewith; for the Eyes bring in several Lights, Colours, Figures, and Forms; and the Ear several Sounds, both Verbal and Vocal; the Nose several Scents; the Tongue several Tasts, and the Body several Touches; without which, the mind would be as an empty, poor, thatch'd House with bare Walls, did not the Senses furnish it.[60]

The Duchess of Newcastle's closet is free of luxurious furnishings, like an "empty, poor, thatch'd House with bare Walls," but her mind, self-consciously conceived as a camera obscura, is filled with the furnishings of sense impressions that make it as opulent as the Duchess of Lauderdale's closet. The space surrounding her needs to remain bare so she can expand the world in her head. Environmental simplicity and bareness are what allow her to come up with fanciful notions in the first place, such as the poem "A World in an Eare-Ring," in which a "vast" world is "held" by an earring. In this world "Cityes bee, and stately Houses built" while "Islands be, where Spices grow therein" and other forms of geographical plenitude thrive, including "fresh, and greene" meadows and "gardens fresh" with "Birds which sweetly sing."[61] The poem richly embodies the camera obscura's paradigm of carrying "as in a nutshell," as John Cuff put it in his 1747 poem "Verses, Occasion'd by the Sight of a Chamera Obscura," the "new creation" produced by its own projections.[62]

Della Porta, too, using a locution that Henry Wotton would later draw on to describe a man's country house estate, describes how "the beholder" shall see in a "small circle of paper (that is put over the hole)" of a camera obscura "as it were an Epitomy of the whole world" the external scene of "Birds flying, the cloudy skies, or clear and blew, Mountains that are afar off."[63] Cavendish, like Marvell, brings together the figures of camera obscura and country house as epitomes of the world, but she does so by arguing that one can in fact exist in solitude because the mind constitutes a country house estate in itself:

> the Minde is so well attended, so richly furnished, such witty Companions, such wise Acquaintance, such numbers of Strangers, such Faithfull Friends, such industrious Servants, such various Pleasures, such sweet Delights, such spatious Walks, such safe Habitations, and such a peacable Life, that it neither needs to converse or commerce either with the Senses, Mankinde, or the World, for it is a World within it self.[64]

This country house estate of the mind is the domain of the imagination, a realm where Cavendish is free to formulate and examine "the interior parts" of things that feature in her natural philosophy's complex theory of matter.[65] Therein, nature is the organizing principle of matter, which itself is self-moving, self-conscious, and possessed of reason. As such, its interiority is not a static entity but a mobile one that continually determines its "interior figure" and thereby eludes the attempts of such devices as the microscope to discover its presence and qualities.[66] The terms of the debate emerge most vividly in the following passage from *Observa-*

tions upon Experimental Philosophy, the work to which *The Blazing World* was attached:

> But as for the interior form and motions of a creature, as I said before, they can no more represent them, than telescopes can the interior essence and nature of the sun, and what matter it consists of. For if one that never had seen milk before should look upon it through a microscope, he would never be able to discover the interior parts of milk by that instrument, were it best that it is in the world—neither the whey, nor the butter, nor the curds.[67]

By referring to whey, butter, and curds as "interior parts of milk," Cavendish is making integral to milk the products that emerge from it as it undergoes processes of transformation. In this light, interiority is not an immobilized object that lies behind the mask of an exterior surface—as microscope-wielding experimental scientists belonging to the Royal Society would have it—but an object of potential becoming that is mutable and mobile. Such a notion of interiority translates to the many moments throughout her writing where mental activity is described in exquisitely concrete and embodied terms.[68]

While *The Blazing World*, which has routinely been described as the first science fiction narrative, has certainly received its due lately, less attention has been paid to the critical contexts and spaces of everyday life from which the worlds it creates and reflects on were made, including Bolsover's interior designs and Cavendish's writing closet. To examine those spaces is not only to apply spatial formalism and reveal the interactivity of Cavendish's relationship with her physical surroundings, but to underscore the intimacy between place and her own processes of thinking and creating that spaces such as her writing closet brought her. In this way, the interiority that Cavendish depicts in such concrete terms in *The Blazing World* and *Sociable Letters* intersects with the inwardness powerfully evoked in contemporary Dutch paintings of women like her, enclosed by the interior worlds that mental acts of reading and writing inside writing closets create.

Domestic Realism: Looking, Reading, Being

Recent and not so recent critical works have made us aware of the resonances between seventeenth-century Dutch paintings of domestic interiors and the novelistic genre of domestic realism.[69] The genre was putatively inaugurated by Samuel Richardson and developed further by nineteenth-century novelists such as the Brontës, George Eliot, and Honoré de Balzac. One of the first to make this connection was Romantic-era writer Anna Laetitia Barbauld, who wrote, "The style of Richardson . . . has the property of setting before the reader, in the most lively manner, every circumstance of what he means to describe. He has the accuracy and finish of a Dutch painter, with the fine ideas of an Italian one. He is content to produce effects by the patient labour of minuteness."[70] Cavendish's hybrid, multigeneric writings are just as much related to Dutch painting as are Richardson's narratives: *Sociable Letters* in particular shares a concern with expressing in prose the experience of psychological interiority within domestic spaces, and in turn forms a critical precedent for Richardson's fiction.

Dutch painting and Richardson have been looked upon as being mimetically faithful to what exists as everyday spaces of external life, from kitchens to designated rooms where letters are written or read and music played and listened to. Cavendish, for the most part, appears to transform the features of quotidian spaces according to her internal visions of them. As her writings similarly give expression to the inner processes of the mind in domestic contexts, she furnishes environments and worlds for them that boldly experiment with the status of the real at a time when lines of fiction and reality had yet to be established.[71]

The fictional missives of *Sociable Letters* imagine a correspondence between "two ladies, living at some short distance from each other" as a way "to express the humours of mankind, and the actions of man's life."[72] Though never directly named or identified, the letters' author is largely taken to be Cavendish herself. Therein she presents herself as an ordinary woman one might encounter in real life—albeit a titled and fiercely ambitious one—reflecting on the stream of events and activities in her day-to-day existence.

The letters in the formally innovative volume are "an imitation of a personal visitation and conversation." Their author, as she declares in the preface, thinks them "better" than letters written in the model of "romancical letters, which are but empty words, and vain complements" (42). This naturalistic epistolary style serves, as in Cavendish's earlier collection, *Worlds Olio*, as a vehicle for expressing views on diverse topics—from female gossip, the fashions of both sexes, feasts, pastimes, and country versus city life, to Shakespeare, government, natural philosophy, marital infidelity, and free will. Many of the letters concern domestic subjects that might be featured in genre and still-life paintings, especially those that depict food and feasts, applying a level of close attention to the details of daily life that was at the time rare in imaginative prose writing.

Such a focus on prosaic reality was intentional, as the writer of the first letter indicates when she urges her imaginary correspondent to

> converse by letters, as if we were speaking to each other, discoursing our Opinions, discovering our Designs, asking and giving each other Advice, also telling the several Accidents, and several Imployments of our home-affairs, and what visits we receive, or entertainments we make, and whom we visit, and how we are entertained, what discourses we have in our gossiping-meetings, and what reports we hear of publick affairs, and of particular Persons, and the like. (Letter #1, 47)

The accounts of prosaic matters and stories provide circumstantial details of the sort of interpersonal episodes and domestic affairs that readers have come to expect in eighteenth- and nineteenth-century domestic fiction as well as in household manuals: why cream and butter make cake and piecrust heavy; the effectiveness of taking cooling juleps and cordials for illness; the dinner table arrival of a chine of beef that provoked a married couple to fight and throw food at each other in front of their guests; a neighboring husband's attempt to woo the letter writer's servant girls by throwing into their chamber window a package of sweetmeats wrapped in a linen handkerchief (#160, 223; #140, 200; #32, 82; #124, 180). Heightening the reality effects, the influence of material factors on the correspondents' subjective, embodied experiences in day-to-day life are described as well; in a letter expanding on the use of feathers in fashion, the writer describes buying a cap with "many Feathers," explaining that "falling Feathers shadow my Face from the Burning Sun, and Fan a Gentle Air on my Face, that Cools the Sultry Heat" (#178, 244). Restating the intention to provide internal views of quotidian reality through the medium of letter writing, the writer of Letter #103 writes to her imaginary friend, "It is your Pleasure we should Write to each other, as if we were Personally Conversing, as Discoursing of what we Think, Say, or Act, of the several Imployments of our Time" (157). Here, emphasis is placed on the way time is spent and on the different subjective events that take place in it on the levels of thinking, speaking, and behaving.

   With its hybrid qualities, as a work of both fiction and autobiography, and a series of letters that for the most part went nowhere because the recipients did not exist, *Sociable Letters* uses epistolary form to render mental experience and activity within the time and space of daily life. As the letters of a "semifictional, semiautobiographical gentlewoman," as Lara Dodds puts it, the book is "primarily an exercise in genre."[73] In it, "epistolary form becomes a flexible medium for literary invention" and allows Cavendish to merge several genres, including "autobiography, satire and social commentary, and essayistic inventions"—to use the letters, at once, to record personal experiences and to "experiment with a variety of fictional personae."[74] By finding in the epistolary form a capacious medium for literary experimentation, especially with a form of literature that frames fictional episodes as well as autobiographical ones within the context of domestic dailiness, she models in part a narrative strategy that Richardson would become famous for advancing, a point first put forth by B. G. MacCarthy.[75]

As will be explored further in chapter 4, the device for creating the portrayals of "inner life" in daily contexts that Richardson's readers found so compelling was precisely its epistolary format, a medium eminently capable of capturing the inner play of consciousness and its "ceaseless flow of thought, feeling and sensation." Cavendish's writings prefigure Richardson's technical accomplishment in *Pamela* as they demonstrate how writing operates as the mobile and material medium of interiority that Richardson more decisively situates in the furnished spaces of private homes owned by everyday people. J. J. Jusserand, who pointed this out earlier in the late nineteenth century, claims that in writing *Sociable Letters*, Cavendish "may be credited with having anticipated Richardson," for in it "she tries to imitate real life, to describe scenes, very nearly to write an actual novel."[76]

For Dutch Golden Age painters, as well as Richardson and Cavendish, the letter has a special status in the intermedial depiction of domestic life and its interiority. The epistolary medium that Richardson and Cavendish both use in their representations of domestic interiority, as well as the temporality of the *textual* medium, gives a different experience from what is offered in *visual* representations of domestic interiors that feature letters purely as visual objects. Svetlana Alpers emphasizes this notion when claiming that in seventeenth-century Dutch paintings that depict women holding and reading letters, or writing letters while seated at a carpet-covered table, interiority is amply shown but not *unfolded*, that is, narrated. Accordingly, "there is also something fugitive about considering letter paintings as the representation of texts, since the viewer of the painting is not permitted to read any of the words. But it is just this fugitive quality that makes them of interest. . . . The letters are commonly the object of attention within the painting, but we do not see the contents."[77]

In contrast, when epistolary narratives or *Sociable Letters* use letters as their medium, the "minute-by-minute" descriptions and transcriptions of the writer's consciousness, fictional or real but in either case veiled, are made fully available to readers through the medium of words.[78] This access is possible because the work that incorporates the letters uses the same medium: text. Although letters are *seen* in Dutch painting, they cannot be *read*; these letters are drawn and painted, rather than written. The written contents of letters in Dutch painting remain inaccessible, which contributes to their "fugitive quality," to use Alpers's words, whereas the novel and Cavendish's *Sociable Letters* preserve and open those contents to the reader.[79]

In Vermeer's *A Lady Writing*, the well-dressed young woman in a yellow jacket with ermine trim bent over her writing at a desk looks up sideways to meet the viewer's gaze, much like Cavendish in her frontispiece portrait engraving. Her expression is gentle and friendly, yet pensive, as if she has been interrupted in the middle of a thought but is not irritated by the intrusion. Her sidelong gaze suggests to the viewer that the written contents of her letter and her mind are not available in the painting itself but must be found elsewhere, beyond the picture frame—perhaps in a different medium entirely: the text inside a book.

As Alpers would have it, Dutch paintings of domestic interiors seem to generate an intense interiority by showing solitary acts of writing even as what is written is occluded by the medium. Painting, in other words, is a medium distinct from writing. It can depict the activity of writing, focus "visual attention" on the written artifact, and convey the state of being absorbed by it, as if being held by the pocket that carries the letter itself (the subject of chapter 4), but it cannot enact or produce writing, and the underlying narratives of the mental worlds that painting so strikingly illustrates remain unknowable to us.[80] The discordance between personal letters depicted as visual image and personal letters presented for reading is paradoxical when one considers that, in the seventeenth century, the letter was regarded as "a prime object of vision." With letters, "what was communicated was intended for the eyes alone."[81] In the lengthy passage Alpers quotes from Comenius, he asks a pivotal question: "'for if it be not seen, how can it be read?'"[82] And yet, even though seeing provides access to the surfaces of interior worlds, such as the worlds depicted in paintings by Vermeer, it does not make the cognitive experience of those worlds legible on a moment-by-moment basis.

The textual medium, in contrast, can do so with its ability to reveal and proceed through time, the very medium for experience, and its use of language, a symbolic system more conducive to capturing the speed and fluidity with which thinking takes place. The inaccessibility of the written contents of a letter presented as a visual document is a figure for the inaccessibility of the female subject's actual thoughts in the many Dutch paintings that depict women reading or writing letters, as Alpers has ar-

FIGURE 2.5 Johannes Vermeer, *A Lady Writing* (ca. 1665). Gift of
Harry Waldron Havemeyer and Horace Havemeyer Jr., in memory of their
father, Horace Havemeyer. Photograph courtesy National Gallery of Art,
Washington, DC (CC0).

gued. However, the paintings themselves are not the mere counterpoint
to literary representations of letters. They show the setting in which letter writing takes place, an interior that is just as important to represent as
the interior contents of the letters that cannot be represented directly on
the canvas.

What Alpers and others who have commented on the interrelatedness of Dutch painting and domestic narrative have overlooked is the way that the physical features of the spaces where writing takes place are more readily captured by the visual medium. These features are just as important as indicators of internal experience as the textual medium's representations of the thoughts themselves. In other words, rather than seeing the paintings as generating "surface presence and inner inaccessibility," as Alpers does—echoing the terms of Cavendish's views on the inefficacy of the microscope—one might view the "surface presence" of the spaces depicted in the paintings as the very means by which inner experience can be accessed. The features of space, represented with such detail and precision in Dutch painting, indicate ways in which the material dimensions of private domestic spaces influence the experience of introspection, reflection, and thinking as much as the letters themselves do. Just as the attention of the letter reader or letter writer is held by the contents of the letter, so too is her body surrounded by a space that allows her to lose herself mentally.

In the case of Vermeer's *A Lady Writing*, the painting hanging above the woman's head, the brass-tacked chair with lion's head ornaments, the writing table covered with a blue cloth, and accoutrements of interiority such as a closed coffer, rosary beads with a yellow ribbon that matches her jacket, and, in the background, a standish, work together to articulate the woman's room as a space for thinking as well as for writing. The darkness of the room makes the woman's yellow robe glow, suggesting the growing interior brightness of her thoughts as she writes and becomes more aware of them. It is a picture of dwelling, and of thinking in action. The room itself and the woman immersed in activity inside the room respond to and generate each other's vivacity, and they define each other.

The woman's act of writing integrates and roots her in her surrounding environment while generating the rhythm of her daily life. As such, her writing is what Ingold would call a "task," or "any operation, carried out by a skilled agent in an environment, as part of his or her normal business of life." Tasks are "the constitutive acts of dwelling."[83] As a "practical operation" undertaken "in an environment" *during the course of dwelling*, the woman's act of writing is, then, an Ingoldian task.[84] As a representation of a space, the painting becomes an environment that absorbs us in ours in the same way the woman is absorbed by the internal world generated by her solitary task of writing. On the other hand, the open-endedness of what she is writing, that it indeed could be about anything, might be viewed as promoting rather than inhibiting a sense of the painting's access to the woman's interiority, in that thinking itself is a continual and fluid process. We are invited into that process as we think along with her to come up with what is being written. The impression of her interiority is as much a function of her facial expression and physical gestures as it is of the space in which her mutual activities of writing and thinking are set.

If virtual space defines the product of all artistic enterprise, from painting and sculpture to architecture, it is also the product of inner experience. The painting demonstrates that the space of interiority is as much a virtual space created by the artist as it is one created by the woman depicted in her act of writing and thinking. For Susanne Langer, space is the fundamental unit of creation and representation in "plastic art." As space that "exists for vision alone" and is created out of material that makes it uninhabitable as "practical space," it is "virtual," and creating it is as much a process of animation as it is of illusion: "What is it, then, this process of 'animating' a surface that in actuality is 'inert'? It is the process of transforming the actual spatial datum, the canvas or paper surface, into a virtual space of creating the primary illusion of artistic vision."[85] This transformation of space into a virtual realm is one performed not just by the woman in the painting, but also by Cavendish in her writing closet, and certainly by the camera obscura as well.

Mariët Westermann has observed the distinct impression of moral and intellectual independence with which Vermeer endows his female subjects immersed in solitary tasks at home.[86] Rembrandt had been distinctive in his representations of women in states of introspection and contemplation in interior settings. According to Westermann, "It is Vermeer's transfer of the possibility of independent thought from [Rembrandt's] epic heroines to seventeenth-century women that makes his paintings of them protomodern."[87] Such paintings as *A Lady Writing* demonstrate that the woman's physical act of writing is simultaneous with her mental act of thinking, which is the very premise of Cavendish's own fascination with writing. Vermeer's painting of a woman's mental world also coheres with her view that another frontispiece, specifically drawn for *Natures Pictures*, represents an image of her very brain. Not just a picture of a metaphor for her brain, it is described as a picture of it. The tension implicit in her choosing to situate herself in a private setting in the image while inviting the public to engage with her work is heightened by the very elements of the image that endow it with quotidian realism: her writing tools. In *Sociable Letters*, Cavendish notes the current social practice of leaving "Pen, Ink, and Paper lying upon the Table" in one's "Chamber," so one can use the "Excuse" that one is "writing Letters" to keep visitors from staying too long (Letter #44, 95)." If, for social visitors, displayed writing tools are meant to signal that they should leave the premises, for readers, they suggest an invitation to dwell in the most private and intimate preserve of the writer's mental life. In either case, the writing tools and the chamber reserved for their use support what Ingold calls a "taskscape"—the array of activities an organism undertakes "as part of his or her normal business of life"—a concept interlocked mutually with the landscape, "an array of related features."[88]

Cavendish's counterpart in visual images of subjects depicted in the "landscape" of their writing "taskscape" is another scholar and philosopher, René Descartes. In an anonymous print engraving, he sits facing the right side of the image, the same direction Cavendish faces. On the wall behind him a bookshelf hangs low to his left, and a linenfold panel or screen appears to his right. Whereas Descartes is known for denying sense perceptions as suppliers of knowledge, his evocations of the "stove-heated room" where he conceived his ideas and the scene of his writing depicted in this engraving suggest something quite different. Sensual comfort and conditions influenced the production of his philosophical views far more than the philosophy itself might encourage us to believe.[89] In *Discourse on Method*, he writes of the setting in which he conceived the work:

> While I was returning to the army from the coronation of the Emperor, the onset of winter detained me in quarters where, finding no conversation to divert me and fortunately having no cares or passions to trouble me, I stayed all day shut up alone in a stove-heated room, where I was completely free to converse with myself about my own thoughts.[90]

Elsewhere, he invokes the time and space of his intellectual work—placing it within the context of daily life—in the same meditation where he "demolishes" the notion that the senses are reliable sources of information: "So today I have expressly rid my mind of all worries and arranged for myself a clear stretch of free time. I am here quite alone, and at last I will devote myself sincerely and without reservation to the general demolition of my opinions."[91] Here, even as he formulates the notion "I think therefore I am," he is demonstrating what Vermeer's painting depicts visually: mental work and setting are inextricably linked.

Yet, in order to write at all, one needs the space and material tools with which to do so. The image of Descartes in his study affirms the role his material surroundings play in his ability to formulate his radical and influential thought experiments. A patterned carpet covers his desk, as is the case with many tables in Dutch paintings, and he carries his quill in his hand, caught in midsentence and midthought, like the woman in

RENATUS DESCARTES, NOBIL. GALL. PERRONI DOM. SUMMUS MATHEM. ET PHILOS.
Talis erat vultu NATURÆ FILIUS: unus Assignansq; suis quavis miracula caussis,
Qui Menti in Matris viscera pandit iter. Miraclum reliquum solus in orbe fuit.

FIGURE 2.6 René Descartes at his desk (ca. 1640–1700).
Engraving. 11⅜ × 8⅛ in. (28.8 × 20.6 cm). Photograph
© Portrait Gallery, London (Creative Commons).

Vermeer's *A Lady Writing*. His eyebrows are slightly raised, as if he has been startled out of a state of absorption, as he meets the gaze of the viewer. The room is specific to him and his moment of embodied intellection, demonstrating the affordances that allow him to think and pursue ideas in his mind: the shelf to his left is low enough for him to reach his books without the disruption of standing up or walking to them; his right foot rests on a book of Aristotle, as much to aid his writing posture as to show his disposition toward his predecessor; his inkpot is left open for ready access as he writes, and an extra quill lies next to it. The fact that the books' bindings are facing the wall to protect them from sunlight, a common practice of the time, amplifies the sense of domestic realism in the engraving. Unlike Cavendish or Vermeer's introspective women, he demonstrates his established position in public life by leaving his cloak on while he writes and keeping his hat on the table to his left. He, a male subject, is just as ready to be in the world as he is to build, through writing, the ideas of his interior world, while tearing down what he and others believed before.

Cavendish had ties with Descartes through her years in exile in Paris; he was a frequent guest at the dinner parties for French intellectuals and fellow Royalists that she and William hosted. She had a more painful connection with Descartes too, through the rumors that circulated after the publication of *Worlds Olio* claiming that her ideas were in fact copies of his and Hobbes's. So damaging were such perceptions to her sense of self that she felt the need to assert in the prefatory section of *Philosophical and Physical Opinions*, "Epiloge to my Philosophical Opinions," "I never spake to monsieur De Cartes in my life, nor ever understood what he said, for he spake no English, and I understood no other language, and those times I saw him, which was twice at dinner with my Lord at Paris, he did appear to me a man of the fewest words I ever heard."[92] Yet her own image of herself alone at her desk demonstrates their kinship as independent writers and intellectuals; both require the physical and conceptual medium of a space for developing their ideas and executing their writing "taskscapes." For each, the space of the room for writing is as necessary as the body that carries the brain and that, in one case, responds to the encouraging warmth that comes from the stove inside the room.

Vermeer's *A Lady Writing* provides a model for understanding how the Diepenbeeck frontispiece showing Cavendish in her writing closet with her writing tools and putti companions might be viewed not just as a portrait but as a virtual space of interiority, produced as much by the artist as by Cavendish in her occupation of that space. The frontispiece—made in Antwerp, a Dutch-speaking city, by an artist who was himself Dutch—

presents interiority partly in Cavendish's own idiom of fantasy, departing from the highly articulated naturalism of domestic interiors depicted by such Dutch Golden Age artists as Jan Vermeer, Gabriël Metsu, and Gerard Ter Borch, who depicted women absorbed in writing or reading letters. In turn, Cavendish's writings and her own descriptions of her writing process offer a means for understanding how the space of writing yields another channel to interiority, not just by showing what is written but also by indicating what it might mean to be the woman writing in the room and inhabiting its space.

The Movable Interior: Books and Minds

Driving the related addictions of contemplation and writing was an ambition that conceived writing as an opportunity to "Live, as Nature doth, in all Ages, and in every Brain." Cavendish elaborates: "I am industrious to Gain so much of Nature's Favour, as to enable me to do some Work, wherein I may leave my *Idea*, or Live in an *Idea*, or my *Idea* may Live in Many Brains, for then I shall Live as Nature Lives amongst her Creatures, which onely Lives in her Works" (Letter #90, 142). The childless Cavendish figured the work that lived on in others' brains as "a child" in *Grounds of Natural Philosophy*—"this beloved Child of my Brain"—and in *Poems, and Fancies*—"*being so* fond *of my* Book, *as to make it as if it were my* Child."[93]

While writing reifies her thoughts, print mobilizes them. When describing her writing, in various works, as an activity of sending in perpetuity the children of her brain to other brains—from the solitude of her closet—Cavendish lays hold not only of the generative capacities of contemplation and social isolation but also of a crucial feature in the culture of print.[94] This is its ability to make available to a public audience what her servants cannot see as they watch her voluntary burial by her writing, and what we cannot see, either, in contemporary Dutch paintings of women reading or writing letters: the thoughts and ideas that issue from acts of writing, and that become lodged in individual minds through acts of reading. The image Cavendish creates also registers a feature of print technology to which readers of her time were especially attuned: its ability to transport different worlds, cultures, and beings to the space of one's own home, merely by gaining entrance to a reader's mind. A dedicatory poem for *Sociable Letters* renders Cavendish's writing a mobile expression of the relationship between herself and the "creatures" and "commonwealths" that exist within it:

This Lady only to her self she Writes,
And all her Letters to her self Indites;
For in her self so many Creatures be,
Like many Commonwealths . . . (47)

Ultimately, the "thoughts," "creatures of her mind," and "common-wealths"—the names she gives her interiority—are detachable and transportable, insofar as they "Do travel through the World amongst Mankind" (48).

In other works, Cavendish evinces an awareness that print makes her brain and its contents available to a wider audience. Her address to the "Noble Readers or Spectators" of *Natures Pictures Drawn by Fancies Pencil to the Life* (1656) refers to the book as a representation of its writer's "brain or mind." Accordingly, such a representation is much closer to the original than the picture of her "person" is. In fact, in the case of her book as a "figure of [her] brain," the resemblance to the original is perfect:

> But howsoever, being customary for most Writers to set their Figures of their Persons before the Figure of their Brain or Mind, I thought fit to do the like. But I must tell my Readers, that though the Figure of my Person is not so exactly like the Original, as it might have been; yet the Figure of my Brain had a perfect draught from the Original of my Mind.[95]

As a "perfect draught" of her mind, it is vulnerable not to "false lines" by a painter or engraver, as "the Figure of my Person" might be, but to "false letters" by a printer, "illiterate fault[s]" that are "wound[s] to my work" and "may destroy the life of my fame."[96]

If her brain is a "commonwealth," it is also a dining room built for intimate family gatherings. In another paratext of *Natures Pictures*, a poem that precedes the frontispiece, she likens her brain to a "large room" built by her, "fill'd" with her husband, his children, and other friends:

> The compass of this fruitless Piece so strait,
> I could not place those Friends I did conceit
> Were gathered in a Company together,
> All sitting by a Fire in cold weather;
> Though in my Brain a large Room I had built,
> Most curious furnish, and as richly gilt,
> Fill'd with my Lord, his Children, and the rest
> Of my near Friends, and Banquets for to feast[97]

Because time itself presents constraints, she "thought to joyn all [her friends] in a papersheet."[98] However, the book, even if it serves as a "perfect draught" from "the Original of my Mind," is "so strait" it is unable to contain the "flow" of her "love," "phancy," and "such company." But while her "wit is scanty" and her "book / Hath narrow limits," her "love is infinite, eternal, kinde."[99] The book, as if attempting to overcome its own constrictions, illustrates the room she built in her brain (figure 2.7), replete with domestic interior detail and the family members and friends she wishes to have with her at her banquet, "with Imaginations Phancy's spread." A description accompanies the frontispiece:

> My Lord, and I, here in two Chairs are set,
> And all his Children, wives and husbands, met,
> To hear me tell them Tales, as I think fit,
> And hope they're full of Phancy, and of Wit.[100]

Thus, the fancifully conceived dining room of Cavendish's brain, an image that makes domestic interiority commensurate with psychological, is also brought into the interiors of other brains through the mechanism of print. Elsewhere, the writer conceives the book, in its function as a structure for her brain, as a "house" or an architectural structure. Whereas in her work of poetry and imaginative writing, such as *Natures Pictures* and *Worlds Olio*, she presents the book/brain as a building for domestic residency ("my Book, which is my House"), in her more serious work of natural philosophy she presents it as a building for an institution of learning. She explains in the second edition that when writing *Philosophical and Physical Opinions*, "I was very studious in my own thoughts and contemplations . . . for all that time my brain was like an university, senate, or council-chamber, wherein all my conceptions, imaginations, observations, wit, and judgement did meet, to dispute, argue, contrive, and judge."[101]

The seriousness and ambition with which she conceived her work of natural philosophy—a work in which, in its second edition, she revises and "enlarges" her "Former Philosophical Opinions," but also "Treats of the most Subtil and Obscure Interior Motions, Degrees, and Temperaments of Matter"—is reflected in the scale of the book as a building and the exactness with which its constituent spaces are designed: "I have endeavoured here to Build upon that Ground, not only a Larger, but a more Exact and Perfect Fabrick, wherein every several Chapter, like Several Rooms, have as Much and as Clear Lights as I can give them."[102] As

Thus in this Semy-Circle, wher they Sitt,
Telling of Tales of pleasure & of witt,
Heer you may read without a Sinn or Crime,
And how more innocently pass your tyme.

FIGURE 2.7 Frontispiece for the Folger Shakespeare Library's copy
(FSL 131-519f) of Margaret Cavendish, *Natures Pictures Drawn by
Fancies Pencil* (1656). Engraved by Peeter Clouwet. Photograph used
by permission of the Folger Shakespeare Library.

portable architectural structures, her books emerged from a context of instability that necessitated a mobile and portable interiority. In Cavendish's textual experiments, interiority is as much an architectural space to inhabit—a cozy dining room, a stately palace, a well-lit place of official learning—as a brain on the move, conveyed by the pen or printing press while "set down" in paper sheets and books.

For Cavendish, the conflict she faces with the male academy is based not just on gender but on how academicians' indecorous writing style evokes memories of homes seized and demolished by parliamentarians during the war. When reworking the works of the ancients in their writings, male natural philosophers "are like those unconscionable men in Civil Wars, which endeavour to pull down the hereditary Mansions of Noble-men and Gentlemen, to build a Cottage of their own."[103] With this remark, her equation of writing books and building architectural structures achieves new meaning. To practice and write about natural philosophy is a way for her to restore and reclaim those lost homes. Moreover, unlike "Castles of Stone, which are subject to Time, Accidents, and the Rages of War, by which they are Destroyed, or Moulder to Dust, and are Buried in Oblivion," the "Poetical Castles" she builds "are set in Fames Palace" (Letter #113, 167).

Her first book, *Poems, and Phancies* (1654), was conceived and written while she was traveling to England—staying there for nine months—from her residence of exile in Rotterdam. The purpose of her trip was to petition for the income Parliament had generated from selling her husband's confiscated estates, Welbeck and Bolsover, to procure funds to pay for tradesmen's services in Holland. Her brother-in-law Charles, to whom she dedicated the book, accompanied her on the trip. Although her efforts failed—the parliamentary committee refused her petition, calling her husband "the greatest Traitor to the State" as she stood mute in front of them at Goldsmith Hall—she found during her trip the incentive to begin writing.[104] Asking her readers to "*be not too severe in your* Censures" when reading *Poems, and Fancies*, she explains the circumstances of its inception: "*For first, I have no* Children *to imploy my* Care, *and* Attendance *on; And my* Lords Estate *being taken away, had nothing for* Huswifery, *or thrifty* Industry *to imp'oy my selfe in; having no* Stock *to work on.*"[105]

Utterly self-conscious of societal expectations that she, as a woman, will make domestic duties her main activity and the source of her identity, she acknowledges that by writing, and by publishing her writing, she has deviated from them. On one hand, she identifies her status as a political exile, dispossessed with her husband of his estates, as her reason for writing. On the other hand, she reinforces this status by writing and pub-

lishing as a woman to overcome the difficulties of being an exile. Anna
Battigelli claims that Cavendish found opportunity in her exile status
throughout her writing by "transforming her comparative social isolation
into a rhetorical stance, a position of advantage from which to address
her world."[106] By creating this position for herself in a world that had witnessed regicide, a civil war, and the violent plundering and confiscation of
family homes, including her own, she gave herself the freedom to explore
and investigate what fascinated her the most: her own interiority and its
worlds.[107] Certainly, her interest was timely; Hobbes and Descartes, after
all, were at about this time formulating and disseminating their philosophies of mind and their attendant views on inner psychology and individual selfhood. And certainly, the status of exile not only allowed Cavendish to create an identity independent of preconceived cultural models
but allowed her, also, to create an ultimately portable domestic interior.
A dwelling for her brain into which she invited others through her writing, this interior environment gave her a place on the print market, if not
in society.

Whereas external reality had wrested from her and her husband their
private property, writing and publishing gave Cavendish access to a form
of property that was inviolable, even when others accused her of plagia-
rism. In her biography of her husband, *The Life of the Thrice Noble, High
and Puissant Prince William Cavendishe*, she describes how her "Readers did wonder, and thought it impossible that a Woman could have so
much Learning and Understanding in Terms of Art, and Scholastical Expressions." The repeated phrase "my own," used in her defense—"those
Conceptions and Fancies which I writ, were *my own*," and "what was
written and printed in my name, was *my own*"—indicates how, for Cavendish, writing and publishing were forms as much of ownership as of
self-individuation.[108] Her books—variously figured as children, houses,
institutions of learning, garments, her own brain, a family dining room—
comprised an estate of which her possession was inviolable, even when
they were disseminated through and held by hands other than her own.
Although her books were much larger (a folio size of 12 by 7.5 inches) than
standard eighteenth-century novels (octavo, 5 by 8 inches, and duodecimo, 3 by 6 inches), like novels, they were among the first books that operated as movable goods circulating personal thoughts and feelings through
remote control and contact. They served as sites and media of possessive
interiority for her.

Cavendish was especially conscious of this possibility when she wrote
Sociable Letters. Acknowledging that she could have presented the wom-
en's "conversations" in the form of a play, she explains that she did not

because, in addition to their lengthiness and formality, plays incorporate "parts and plots that cannot be understood till the whole play be read over," whereas "a short letter will give a full satisfaction of what they read."[109] Further emphasizing the need for a more digestible format for literary genres, she registers the portability of interiority afforded by the form when her letter writer avows in the first letter, "wherefore I am never better pleased, than when I am reading your Letters, and when I am writing Letters to you; for my mind and thoughts are all that while in your Company: the truth is, my mind and thoughts live alwayes with you, although my person is at distance from you" (Letter #1, 47). Thus exemplifying her view toward writing and authorship as an act of making transportable the inner and private aspects of personhood—even their material representatives, such as a domestic environment or a handspun garment, as she puts it elsewhere—she also gives expression to the mobility that characterized possessive interiority in the eighteenth century, which will be explored further in chapters 4 and 5. Cavendish is invested in the propensity for textual narratives to create worlds and edifices of their own, diversely realized and derived as much from reality as from the imagination. Herein the camera obscura and its equivocation between real and virtual space encodes the critical features of Cavendish's approach to interiority, especially as a condition that is architecturally circumscribed, much like Pope's grotto, the subject of the next chapter.

For Cavendish, there was no distinction between her imagined worlds, her writing closet, and the sheets of paper on which she wrote. All were spaces for dwelling, building, and thinking, the functions that Heidegger memorably concatenates in his philosophy. Recognizable throughout Cavendish's life and writing is the notion that space is "neither an external object nor an inner experience."[110] Her example of dwelling illuminates not just how the interiority that literature innovated derived from spatial designs and experiences but how its spatial dimensions are founded on energies of instability, mobility, flux, and exile even when it locates its settings in the allegedly fixed environments of domestic life. Three-quarters of a century later, literary history will depict a different landscape of writing and dwelling in domestic interiors with Samuel Richardsons's *Pamela*, a book in which the servant girl and not the lady is bent over and absorbed by her letter writing. As we shall see in chapter 4, it will be her interiority—in all its material and mobile dimensions—that will absorb and move readers of her letters in turn, carrying them with her within the spaces of her own portable interiors.

The Last Room

If no other evidence exists for the physical conditions of Cavendish's writing closet, we know how she might have wanted her writing space to appear—and how she wished to appear within it—from the commissioned engraving used as the frontispiece for her books. In the image, she is situated to conduct the taskscape of her writing life: dipping the quill into the inkpot, moving it across the sheet of paper to convey her thoughts, sprinkling sand on her writing to dry the ink, ringing the bell to summon servants to perform tasks of their own for her.

Experiencing domestic instability and the loss of her husband's estates as an exile during the Interregnum, as well as ridicule when returning to England and seeking validation as a natural philosopher, Cavendish always identified interiority with a self-made form of homemaking and sovereignty. By conjoining socially removed mental spaces with architectural ones, both in her writing and in her daily life, she found a means for facilitating the making of worlds and spaces that were her own, independent of external precedents and circumstantial limitations. This is not to say that she disavowed materiality. Her natural philosophy viewed matter as "sentient, self-conscious, and self-moving" and was so thoroughgoing that, as Lisa Sarasohn puts it, "she saw and imagined matter in everything, and in her thought, even the imaginary became concrete."[111] The concept of interiority developed in her work, an introspective state of being that merges transient thoughts with concrete substance, is founded as much on her theory of matter as on her self-proclaimed "addiction to contemplation," matched only by her addiction to writing.[112]

Materiality was also a creative medium for the spatial dimensions of her interior world, which were themselves instrumental to the development of her materialist philosophy. Interconnected to each other, the spaces of writing closets, imagined and real homes, and, ultimately, printed books served as vehicles for her ability to lay claim not only to a "commonwealth" of her inner life but also to the habitation of that commonwealth. Her attitudes toward what writing does, where one writes, and what happens in such spaces are directly tied up with her belief in what interiority is and, accordingly, in which spaces allow and promote access to it. Similar to Marvell's interiority, which deepens as it moves outward and into the woods on Lord Fairfax's estate, Cavendish's writings and the interior worlds they create expand as they move beyond the boundaries of social life and its norms.

Let us take a last look at Cavendish inside a space of writing. After she becomes, in real life, an immaterial soul, by dying in 1673, Margaret Cav-

FIGURE 2.8 Grinling Gibbons, tombstone effigy of Margaret Cavendish holding
a book and inkhorn, North Transept, Westminster Abbey (ca. 1673–1676).
Photograph © The Dean and Chapter of Westminster.

endish occupies her last writing closet, her tomb at Westminster Abbey.
Against a black and white marble architectural backdrop with elaborate
moldings and a sculpted canopy, her marble effigy lies next to her husband's, both created by the prodigiously talented Dutch-born sculptor
Grinling Gibbons. As an effigy, she is ready to continue writing, equipped
with the accessories of a writing closet, including a small collection of
books carved into the side of the tomb, spines facing inward as in an actual library at the time.[113] She holds an open book, an inkhorn, and a pen-
case. This emphasis on her writing tools not only demonstrates that she
was a "wittie and learned Lady"—as the inscription on the monument
declares—but suggests that they take her to the next space of her existence, a writing closet of the mind that goes with her everywhere, even
inside the dark, interior chamber of death, an ultimate state of the "calm
Silence" she loved so dearly and found in her home life, inside her writing closet (Letter #29, 77).

Grotto

DESIGN AND PROJECTION IN
ALEXANDER POPE'S GARDEN

What would I do if I hadn't this little room, this
room that is as deep and secret as a shell?

GASTON BACHELARD, *The Poetics of Space*

During and shortly after his lifetime, Alexander Pope was almost as celebrated for the grotto he lovingly designed for the garden of his Twickenham villa as he was for his poetry. Well into the century after his death in
1744, the grotto was so famous as a space where Pope "caught inspiration,"
visiting it was viewed as akin to "kneeling in devotion before the tomb of
Shakespeare" and was believed to promise the ability to generate ideas of
one's own.[1] Toward the end of his life, Pope regarded the work of completing the grotto with such seriousness that he proclaimed, "I should be
more sorry to leave it unfinished than any other work."

The grotto was originally conceived as a solution to the structural problem posed by having the town high road run between his Palladian home
on the Thames and the five acres of unenclosed land he had leased to create his garden. In 1720 he began the work of building a tunnel twenty-two
feet long to connect the basement of the house with the garden across
the road. The tunnel, which opened to the wilderness area of the garden,
also led to the grotto. Thus the grotto served as an underground passage-
way between distinct worlds—the everyday domestic space of the home,
where one might expect to experience "true" interiority, and the garden,
a world unto itself. A major undertaking, creating the grotto according
to Pope's vision entailed regular hauls of valuable stones, crystals, and
minerals from English mines. With these he ornamented the interior surfaces: stalactites and lustrous stones "stellif[ied]" the roof, marbles were
embedded in the pavement, and Cornish diamonds lined the edges of a
little well. A letter to a friend and supplier, the Reverend Doctor William

Borlase, whose quarry in Cornwall transformed Pope's conception of his grotto's design, reveals what he hoped to achieve with the "bounty" Borlase had just sent him: "I would be glad to make the place resemble nature in all her workings, and entertain a sensible, as well as dazzling a gazing, spectator."[2]

A biographer, Owen Ruffhead, wrote in 1769 that the grotto "was one of the favorite amusements of his declining years; so that, not long before his death, by enlarging and increasing it with a vast number of ores and minerals of the richest and rarest kinds, he made it one of the most elegant and romantic retirements; and the disposition of these materials, the beauty of his poetic genius appears to as much advantage, as in any of his best contrived poems."[3] So widely celebrated were the contrivances of Pope's garden work that in 1809 Baroness Sophia Charlotte Howe, then owner of the property, had the house torn down to stem the flow of visitors who continued to come see the poet's garden and its grotto. Fortunately, many prints had been made of his villa, recording its appearance. Before the demolition, visitors to the grotto had stolen rocks and minerals as souvenirs, gradually removing with them the grotto's beauty and eroding the design, or "disposition," of its materials.[4]

Whereas Pope's poetry was intended for dissemination through the public-oriented medium of print, and had turned him into a public figure equally lauded and derided by others, his grotto was created solely for his own enjoyment, its pleasures meant to be shared only with his chosen intimates. His reputation as a poet is that of an abstracting moralizer and observer of human foibles whose every line submitted to the metrical format of the heroic couplet, but he was also a fantasist who, using his garden as a vehicle for shaping his inner visions and dreams to an intensely detailed degree, made an equally significant cultural contribution to the history of built environments.

Situated in a confined, subterranean space and entered through a tunnel, the grotto functioned as a "source" (it had a spring) for artistic inspiration as well as a theater for projecting internalized reality and creating brilliant light effects. Grottoes in themselves richly exemplify the intensifying effect enclosures have on sense perception: "dark, dank, and enveloping, they heighten our perception by the very fact of blunting our vision," writes Stephanie Ross.[5] Such a description suggests that what Pope appreciated about his grotto is the way enclosed spaces stimulate the imagination, triggering the experience of absorption and promoting heightened states of interior awareness. Thus, much like the ha-ha, the sunk fence that created an impression of boundless property in eighteenth-century landscape design, the grotto entailed "a manipu-

lation of space for the delight of the human mind."[6] For Pope, the space
was, in his own words, his "Plaything, the grotto." It seems fitting it should
have been an object of obsession, for it was an environmental counterpart
to the textual enclosures of couplets that he created habitually as a poet. It
was also where, as Robert Dodsley's poem on the grotto put it, he "slept
inspir'd, or sate and writ, and found his Muse." A drawing, allegedly by
William Kent or Dorothy Boyle, Duchess of Burlington, of Pope writing inside the grotto externalizes his source of creative inspiration, with
sylphlike creatures flying above the entrance. Such imagery suggests that
the grotto itself forms the poet's mind, his very mental space, much like
Cavendish's figuration, in the frontispiece for *Natures Pictures*, of the dining room as her brain or, in the frontispiece that depicts her at work in her
writing closet, of the putti floating above her head.

The grotto functioned as more than the late-career hobby of the century's most celebrated poet and a curiosity for sightseeing strangers after his death. As a private place, it was a space and object of creativity
whose impact equaled that of his most accomplished poems and gener-

FIGURE 3.2 William Kent or Dorothy Boyle, Duchess of Burlington,
ink drawing of Alexander Pope writing inside his grotto (ca. 1730–1740).
Photograph © The Devonshire Collection, Chatsworth. Reproduced by
permission of Chatsworth Settlement Trustees/Bridgeman Images.

ated divergent interpretations. For Maynard Mack, Pope's relocation to
the semirural locale of Twickenham, Richmond, at the end of 1719 and
the subsequent creation of his garden were primarily significant in allowing him to develop his later work as an author of moral epistles and satires
in the 1730s.[7] The relocation also allowed him to act out the classical idea
of retirement. For John Dixon Hunt, the move was a decisive retreat into
the private world of the imagination, away from the disappointing world
he had left behind. According to this view, the garden functioned as a medium for interiority that allowed Pope "to consult the oracles of his own

heart and reason."[8] Such interiority, in turn, was constituted as much by the experiences of contemplation that led to the "internal view" of human nature for which he was famous, as by his subjective experiences of dreams and visions. In contrast with these interpretations, which view Pope's garden primarily as a setting that influenced his vision as a poet, more recent scholarship has focused on his grotto as a vehicle for allowing diverse activities to take place: the creation and mediation of visual images, the deployment of attitudes toward nature and human control over it, and the intricate fashioning of a masculine character.[9]

Neither older nor more recent interpretations allow for the extent to which the grotto functioned as a virtual space, an alternate reality, where the boundary between exterior reality and interior fantasy was blurred, with space itself mediating the equivocation. Pope located and created the realm of escape in his landscape garden, continuing a project he had begun in one of his poems. Not just a sanctuary for developing his inner life or a spatial expression of the classically derived "retirement idiom," the grotto realized through concrete forms and materials the interiority that had first emerged in the textual space of *Eloisa to Abelard*.[10] It offered, in short, an opportunity for Pope to practice spatial formalism as well as create architextural connections between his craft as a poet and as a landscape garden designer. *Eloisa to Abelard*, published in 1717, two years before his move to Twickenham, first develops the virtuality of presence, space, and voice that characterizes one of the writer's most famous creations on and of earth.

Of all his poems, *Eloisa to Abelard* offers the most sustained experience of an imagined subject's consciousness in relation to her physical surroundings. In doing so, it builds a scene of interiority within a time and place specific to a greater narrative. It conveys an imagined subject's "voice," presenting a technical construct of textual art, as well as revealing its relationship with the physical environment. Conjuring a dark and contained space as the precondition for the expansion of the interior self, the poem demonstrates that Pope's views on space and interiority were intermedial; it both encompasses and transcends textually represented space by foreshadowing the rich interiority he experienced and designed for himself in such everyday domestic environments as the landscape garden.

Pope's literary and landscape outputs were mutually corresponding projects of design that entangled literature with the everyday as a lived experience and thereby effected the merging of the fictive with the real.[11] They exemplified the architecture of the camera obscura and generated its vivid yet evanescent scenes of fantasy. Not just a "perfected version of the rational intellect and disembodied mind" or a "gadget," as Sean Silver has argued, the camera obscura as a model for Pope's scenes of interior life was a powerful *space* of intentional design for making things happen externally and internally with incalculable effect.[12] Unlike Cavendish, Pope contributed actively to the appearance and décor of his interior space while reflecting self-consciously on its dual function as a camera obscura. His grotto was energetically made to serve as an agent for releasing the rational mind and activating the imagination, relying on the body's location and the mind it carries within it—or a space resembling it—to do so.[13]

That Pope was connected throughout his life to a world of internal dreams, including during illness, is conveyed in a letter he wrote to his close friend John Caryll on December 5, 1712, while at Binfield, his family home:

> I am . . . confind to a narrow Closet, lolling on an Arm Chair. . . . I believe no mortal ever lived in such Indolence and Inactivity of Body, tho my Mind be perpetually rambling. . . . Like a witch, whose Carcase lies motionless on the floor, while she keeps her airy Sabbaths, & enjoys a thousand Imaginary Entertainments abroad, in this world, & in others, I seem to sleep in the midst of the Hurry, even as you would swear a Top stands still, when tis in the Whirl of its giddy motion. 'Tis no figure, but a serious truth I tell you when I say that my Days & Nights are so much alike, so equally insensible of any Moving Power but Fancy, that I have sometimes spoke of things in our family as Truths & real accidents, which I only Dreamt of; & again when some things that actually happen'd came into my head, have thought (till I enquired) that I had only dream'd of them. This will shew you how little I feel in this State either of Pleasure or Pain: I am fixt in a Stupid settled Medium between both.[14]

With this imagery Pope reveals an interior life so vivid that he has difficulty separating it from the world of reality, or "truths and real accidents." Moreover, the image of a body immobilized in a small room (albeit lolling on an armchair) while the mind "perpetually" rambles with thoughts and visions that seem real evokes the experience of being inside a camera obscura. Intending to underscore the contrast between his state of idleness, born out of being ill, and his friend's vigor and health, Pope reveals nevertheless a fascination with the altered sense of reality, and of identity, that dwelling inside a closet can bring. Such a notion is suggested in the fanciful description of his infirm condition and his stating that the witch with whom he shares kinship "enjoys" her thousand imaginary excursions. In the confined space of his narrow closet, despite or even because of his infirmity, he can practice magic.

As a gardenist and designer of landscapes, Pope had an urge to shape natural environments to reflect a vision of how he wanted himself and others to be made to feel and think while in those environments. This is to say, as much as he was a poet, he was also a designer. Cavendish used her closet for creating and inhabiting worlds of her making, turning physical space into a taskscape of imagination and creativity, but the act of doing so worked ultimately in the service of conveying her ideas to other people's brains through the transmutation of her interior worlds into books. Pope, though, as his letters reveal, viewed the material creation of the grotto as a world-making enterprise of its own. To experience its world, one had to enter it with one's body and be immersed in it. Just as with a work of literary creation, such a world issues from a process of planning, thinking, and imagining that precedes its manifestation in concrete reality. Pope himself recognized that textual products of creativity were very much products of design in the way that landscape layouts are more readily recognized as being.

In *Essay on Man*, he provides what he identifies as a "Design"—a statement of intention that elaborates on his main purpose (to consider "*Man* in the abstract, his *Nature* and his *State*")—as well as the rationale for the form he chooses for delivering it.[15] Recognizing that he could have used prose, he defends his choice of verse as allowing him to express "principles, maxims, or precepts" more memorably and concisely.[16] Above all, verse allows him to make his points "without wandring from the precision, or breaking the chain of reasoning."[17] With this phrasing, he evokes a notion of textual production that resonates with the making of a landscape garden, with ideas serving as the environment through which the mind travels and its manner of doing so carefully managed by his judgment, not so much as an author, but as a designer, a role he suggests by calling his preamble a design.

Intentional Designs of Inner Life

Design, as the "the process, practice, or art of devising, planning, or constructing something . . . according to aesthetic or functional criteria," became linked with the production of commercial goods only from the late 1720s onward, with a swelling of interest taking place between 1740 and 1760.[18] It is in this branch of design that discourse on the creation of material structures to support both beauty and function can most readily be found.[19] Modernist Italian designer Bruno Munari's self-conscious notion of design applies especially well to Pope's garden spaces. For Munari, design is an element of daily life that determines how the form of a material entity relates to its function and satisfies human needs.[20] Design registers most on the level of the everyday, wherein interaction with the material world makes its qualities recognizable in terms of the actions its objects make possible for humans in their day-to-day activities. The designer is one who knows how to imagine ideas for pursuing particular objectives while anticipating the consumer's psychological experience in choosing whether to purchase a product. One can discern the stirrings of modern design even earlier than Munari's modernist context or William Morris's Victorian one, in the eighteenth-century efflorescence of tradesmen cards, furniture and architectural pattern books, and landscape design books that bespeak a culture keen on incorporating beauty and comfort—as well as luxury—into everyday life.[21] This was Pope's culture too, as *The Rape of the Lock*, with its phantasmagoric parade of luxury goods throughout the world of aristocrats, reminds us.

Whereas "form" might appear at first to be a relative cognate for "design," its multiple meanings in modern usage show it to be a more particularized framework than assumed, specifically in its role as a subset of design, and as a fixed companion to function. In addition, whether the usage is eighteenth- or twenty-first-century, "design" carries with it an indissoluble element of intention. For the early modern period and the eighteenth century, *design* was "an intention, a purpose," as Johnson's *Dictionary* puts it. As a verb, it meant also "to plan; *to project*; to form."[22] This concept of design as a function that entails planning as well as forming prevailed in 1966 as Munari's answer to the question of what a designer is: "He is a planner with an aesthetic sense."[23] Planning, in Munari's view, is definitional to design:

> What then is this thing called Design if it's neither style nor applied art? It is planning: the planning as objectively as possible of everything that goes to make up the surroundings and atmosphere in which men live today. This atmosphere is created by all the objects produced by industry, from glasses to houses and even cities. It is planning done without preconceived notions of style, attempting only to give each thing its logical structure and proper material, and its consequence its logical form.[24]

The very motivation for creating the grotto—to solve a spatial problem posed by the road dividing house from garden—was a functional one that turned into an aesthetic pursuit. Samuel Johnson's well-known observa-

tion about Pope's grotto identifies how its making fulfills the modern notion of design as a marriage between form and function: "A grotto is not
often the wish or pleasure of an Englishman, who has more frequent need
to solicit rather than exclude the sun, but Pope's excavation was requisite
as an entrance to his garden, and, as some men try to be proud of their
defects, he extracted an ornament from an inconvenience, and vanity produced a grotto where necessity enforced a passage."[25]

The planning of eighteenth-century gardens, and landscapes in general, demonstrated modern design principles that would be taken in a
more commercial and functional direction in the twentieth century. Literature anticipated this aspect of planning and design insofar as literary
works began with a stated design or a plan of their own organization and
intention, whether in the "Advertisement to the Reader" in Robert Boyle's
Tracts (1671), Pope's own *Essay on Man* (1733), or Johnson's preface to *A
Dictionary of the English Language* (1755).[26] An essentially projective quality inheres in design: similar to an argument in one of its earlier senses, a
design introduces what it sets out to present or establish. The confluence
of the conventional nomenclature used for the making of literature and of
landscape gardens was certainly one that had special resonance for Pope,
as someone who created both literary works and landscape gardens. What
might it mean to posit a physical space and a written one as correlates in
the intentional design of inner life? What are the implications of making
a poem and a physical space mutually relevant?

Whereas John Dixon Hunt has declared, "The literary history of the
eighteenth century could partly be written in terms of the development
of . . . the landscape garden," it was Horace Walpole who first posited an
equivalence between Pope's poetry writing and garden designing, declaring that in transforming his five acres of ground, Pope had "twisted and
twirled and rhymed and harmonized [it], till it appeared two or three
sweet little lawns opening and opening beyond one another."[27] Walpole appears to render the garden an elaborately designed poem through
which one progresses in the stateliest and most controlled manner:

> It was a singular effort of art and taste . . . to impress so much variety and
> scenery on a spot of five acres. The passing through the gloom from the
> grotto to the opening day, the retiring and again assembling shades, the
> dusky groves, the larger lawn, and the solemnity of the termination at the
> cypresses that lead up to his mother's tomb are managed with excellent
> judgment.[28]

Mack spells out the connection:

We have only to retain Walpole's principal value-terms ("effort," "art," "taste," "variety," "exquisite judgement"), and substitute literary equivalents for the operations of gardening, to arrive at a statement that could be applied to the effects Pope achieves in his best poetry: packed couplets, graceful transitions, effective contrasts, and easy but diversified crescendoes leading to climaxes either small or large.[29]

While acknowledging the poetic aspects of Pope's garden design named by Mack—its "turns," couplings, antitheses, and repetitions—I might add that there are proselike qualities too, most apparent in its elements of continuity and succession, its main motion of "passing through." Prose, after all, is marked by "continuity," in contrast to poetry's rhythm of "recurrence."[30] At the same time, continuity or "succession" is the trademark of thinking itself, an observation Locke makes: "humane Minds are confined to here, of having great variety of Ideas only by succession, not all at once."[31] In requiring the body to move through a space in order to view it, undergoing internal dramas in response to its physical design—with "passing through the gloom of the grotto to the opening day" as one of its most distinct episodes—gardens set in motion a distinctly narrative experience.[32]

That his description of Pope's garden might as easily be read in terms of poetic design as narrative befits Walpole's own status as the author of a work of fiction that also "passes through the gloom," his Gothic novel *The Castle of Otranto* (discussed in chapter 5). Yet, the intergeneric resonances of Pope's garden design are most pertinent to *Eloisa to Abelard*, a poem that is closer to modern narrative than any of his other poems. Among its most strikingly narrative qualities are its construction of a historical figure's voice and imagined state of mental awareness within an environment whose features self-consciously intensify her psychological state. On one hand, Pope's garden design allowed him to emulate the classical model of the villa, as scholars such as Mack have argued. But its provocative designs and features leading to discoveries of natural delights also invited self-awareness and reflectiveness. The space for interiority and wonder that the grotto opened up, coupled with Pope's posthumous celebrity, helps explain why the grotto remained a site of cultural fascination. Even if a marketplace was not a factor in Pope's private practice of design—a concern that, Munari points out, defines the modern designer's work—his grotto nevertheless appealed to a public whose reasons for seeking its delights had nothing to do with either its classical allusions or its natural history displays. The formal features of the grotto reconfigure the visitor's internal state of being, similar to the way reading or occupying a camera obscura does. The grotto appealed to a culture that was hungry for novelty and novels, appearing in such works of fiction as Thomas Amory's *The Life of John Buncle* (1756) and Sarah Scott's *Millennium Hall* (1762). Grottoes provided in narrative the experiences of revelation that landscape gardens promoted. The deepest connection that stories and garden share is their ability to provide "distance from reality" while at the same time "testifying to the transfiguring power of form." Herein lies their "magic": they "transfigure the real even as they leave it apparently untouched."[33]

Certainly, Pope's move to live in Twickenham and create a landscape garden indicates a desire to retreat from reality. The mentally transfiguring space of the grotto was a vehicle for this retreat. In 1748, just three years after Pope's death, an anonymous author wrote for the *General Magazine* of Newcastle an "Epistolary Description" of a visit to Pope's house and garden.[34] His detailed, first-person account indicates why the garden had become a tourist attraction. The visitor describes growing "agitated, with a kind of glowing ardour, flutt'ring at [his] heart" when approaching Pope's home, and reports being most impressed by the visual illusions created by strategically placed mirrors. After commenting on the waterworks and their "soothing Murmur of aquatick sounds," he registers his delight that "Mr. Pope's poetic genius . . . introduced a kind of machinery, which performs the same part in the grotto that supernal powers and incorporeal beings act in the heroic species of poetry."[35] This machinery involved

disposing Plates of Looking glass in the obscure Parts of the Roof and Sides of the Cave, where a sufficient Force of Light is wanting to discover the Deception, while the other Parts, the Rills, Fountains, Flints, Pebbles, &c. being dully illuminated, are so reflected by the various profited Mirrors, as, without exposing the Cause, every Object is multiplied, and its position represented in a surprising diversity.[36]

He goes on, describing the grotto's water effects in equally fine detail:

Cast your eyes upward, and you shudder to see Cataracts of water precipitating over your head, from impending Stones and rocks, while salient spouts rise in rapid streams at your feet: around, you are equally surprised with flowing rivulets and rolling waters, that rush over airy precipices, and break amongst heaps of ideal flints and spar.[37]

Describing the overall effect of Pope's manipulations of vision and presence, and water and movement, the visitor concludes, "Thus, by a fine

FIGURE 3.3 Unattributed drawing of grotto waterworks extra-illustrating
the Huntington Library's copy (HEH RB 106623) of John Serle,
Plan of Mr. Pope's Garden (London, 1745).
Photograph: Huntington Library, San Marino, California.

taste and happy management of nature, you are presented with an undistinguishable mixture of realities and imagery."[38] The presentation of this
mixture is also a central characteristic of the camera obscura.

The visitor's account demonstrates, above all, the narrative pull of the
grotto. On a journey of discovery, his emotions undergo transmutations
as he experiences the grotto's physical features. The grotto offers an escape from reality, creating visual illusions that are intensified by the waterworks with their sounds and movement, which in turn transform the
appearance of the rocks as well as the visitor's sense of what is real and
what is imagined. Apart from the drawings that depict Pope in his grotto,
only a few known illustrations of the grotto's interior survive. One drawing in particular, in a set of drawings extra-illustrating the Huntington
Library's copy of *Plan of Mr. Pope's Garden* (1745) by John Serle, Pope's
gardener, promises to provide a more detailed view of what might have
been the waterworks. If the drawing does not depict the actual waterworks, it at least suggests how they might have been envisioned as a central feature of the grotto in its use as a theatrical space with special visual
and aural effects.[39]

"You may make secret rooms and passages within it": The Grotto in England

The 1748 visitor, in praising Pope's grotto for its "happy management of nature" and "undistinguishable mixture of realities and imagery," recognized the features that define all grottoes in European cultural history. Pope's was not the only grotto in England in the eighteenth century, nor was it the first. Originating from classical antiquity, grottoes were established elements in the gardens of sixteenth-century France and Italy that began appearing in seventeenth- and eighteenth-century English landscape gardens in response to increased contact between England and Italy, manifested in such rituals for young elite men as the Grand Tour. The usage and design of grottoes through time suggests the cultural values of each age. By the eighteenth century, when their popularity peaked, grottoes were rich with the accumulated associations of their prior forms and meanings. In all periods, water, and its mediation, display, and incorporation in the spatial and aural experience of the grotto, was a consistent element. The development of hydraulic engineering thus plays an important role in the history of grottoes.

In antiquity, grottoes with fountains and springs were sacred spaces that were consecrated to gods and other divinities. One prominent variant was the nymphaeum, which originated in Greece and was developed in the Roman period as a temple dedicated to nymphs. Featuring fountains run by complicated hydraulic systems, the nymphaeum came to stand for architectural sites other than grottoes, including museums devoted to sculpture, theaters, hydraulic edifices, fountain displays, and ornamental waterworks.[40] Existing not only as architectural structures in daily life—forming, rather, "part of the mysterious, numinous, and erotic settings of antiquity"—grottoes also appeared in classical literary texts, including those of Homer, Ovid, and Virgil, serving diverse modes of "the pastoral, the sacred, the idyllic, the dramatic."[41]

Grottoes in the Renaissance evinced a fascination with the grotesque (a term, indeed, derived from *grotto*, or "of a cave") and its fanciful mergers between human, animal, and vegetal forms. While the intermingling of disparate species of living beings disrupts order, order is regained through the linear formatting that organizes the hybrid and monstrous creatures of grotesque ornament. That such a decorative style would derive from and appear in grottoes is unsurprising when one considers that the physical space was designed to stimulate the imagination by mediating the exchange between artifice and nature. A Renaissance paradigm for the grotto was a building, like the Grotta Grande (completed in 1593)

in the Boboli Gardens, with an architectural façade and an interior replete with stalagmites and stalactites, made out of materials extracted
from nature. Embedded in the calcareous rock formations are various figures; one might see flocks of sheep and their shepherds on one wall, river
nymphs and gods on another.[42] The effect of recognizing the natural-
seeming forms as representations of human and animal figures is one of
delight and surprise, but it also conveys the experience of Ovidian metamorphoses, wherein humans turn into forms from nature, such as trees
and animals. In contrast with the play of nature and artifice that such reversal mobilizes, alongside the fantastic metamorphoses of grotesque ornament, the widespread installation of automata propelled by hydraulic
force in Renaissance grottoes gestured to a more forcible control, management, and even usurpation of nature by artifice.

The Baroque grotto carried the fascination with automata and mastery of nature yet further through the showcasing of waterworks made
ever more spectacular by ingenious hydraulic engineering. The leading
engineers of waterworks in the period were the De Caus brothers, Salomon, author of the influential *Les raisons des forces mouvantes* (1615), and
Isaac, who wrote his own work on hydraulic creations, *Nouvelle invention de lever l'eau* (1644).[43] Highly derivative of Salomon's work, Isaac's
was translated into English by John Leak in 1659 as *New and Rare Inventions of Waterworks*. The brothers De Caus were responsible for the most
elaborate and prominent Italianate grottoes in England, including Som-
erset House, Richmond House, Queen Anne's house at Greenwich, and
Hatfield (Salomon) and Wilton, Whitehall, and perhaps Moor Park and
Woburn (Isaac). It was the grotto Isaac de Caus created for King James
in 1622–1623 underneath his Whitehall Banqueting House that is said
to have spurred the popularity of grottoes in English gardens.[44] Celia
Fiennes's late seventeenth-century response to the grotto Isaac designed
at Wilson House suggests the mixture of fancy and ingenuity in de Caus
grotto designs and the wonder they elicited:

There are figures at each corner of the room that can weep water on the
beholders, and by a straight pipe on the table they force up the water into
the hollow carving of the roof like a crown or coronet to appearance, but
is hollow within to retaine the water forced into it in great quantetyes, that
disperses in the hollow caviety over the roome and descends in a shower
of raine all about the roome; on each side is two little rooms which by the
turning their wires the water runnes in the rockes you see and hear it, and
also it is so contrived in one room that it makes the melody of Nightin-
gerlls and all sorts of birds which engaged the curiosity of the Strangers to

go in to see but at the entrance off each room, is a line of pipes that appear not till by a sluce moved it washes the spectators, designed for diversion.[45]

The account emphasizes the immersive quality of the grotto experience. Simulated rain and the tears of weeping statues strike the visitors, and the sound of mechanical nightingales and other birds entices "Strangers" to seek the singing's source, luring them past a set of pipes that appears unexpectedly and adds a further soaking. The grotto is designed in such a way that its space does more than just playfully surprise visitors; it controls their bodily experiences with simulated atmospheric conditions—an early modern HVAC system, if you will—providing rain rather than heat, ventilation, or cold air, as well as an occasion for wonder.

Whereas the Renaissance grotto trafficked in the grotesque, the Baroque grotto conveyed wonder, the close companion of science in the period. One of the most fantastic and elaborate grottoes, demonstrating their potential to serve as laboratories for scientific knowledge, was created around 1629 at Thomas Bushell's Enstone estate in Oxfordshire.[46] As a gentleman in waiting for Francis Bacon who retired to Enstone upon Bacon's death, Bushell shared his former employer's interest in scientific curiosities and wonders. This affinity was apparent in the grotto, a "desolate Cell of Natures rarities at the head of a Spring," that he created.[47] The

FIGURE 3.4 Example of elaborate grotto waterworks. Salamon de Caus, *Les raisons des forces mouuantes* (1624), plate 25, book 2. Photograph used by permission of the Folger Shakespeare Library.

marvelous effects created by its hydraulic engineering, coupled with optical effects produced by mirrors, further confirmed his "fascination with
experimentation."[48] John Aubrey, commenting on his visit to the grotto at
Enstone, provides a glimpse of this staging of wonder when he describes
its artificial rain, which, "upon the turning of a cock," is followed by "a
rainbow," and its display of automata: a duck circling around a wooden
Neptune and a spaniel swimming after the duck.[49] The grotto was so famous for its wonders that Charles I paid a surprise visit to Enstone to see
it. Bushell, a mining engineer and former seal-bearer for Bacon, obliged
the king, entertaining him with a show of "artificial thunders and light-
nings, rain, hail-showers, drums beating, organs playing, birds singing,
waters murmuring all sorts of tunes."[50]

It was in the Baroque era that the analogy between the stage and the
grotto was made most explicit, especially through the incorporation of
grottoes into theatrical designs. Sitting in a darkened theater might be likened to occupying a camera obscura, or a grotto. Mediating illusions and
enacting scenes through automata and their movements, ornamental imagery of grotesque hybrid creations or pastoral figures, and paintings depicting scenes from Ovid's *Metamorphoses* (like those at Villa d'Este and
the Boboli Gardens), grottoes were capable of staging moving dramas
that were akin to theatrical experiences. The equivalence was made even
more direct in the seventeenth century, wherein stage settings, such as
those designed by Giacomo Torelli, featured grottoes. Landscape views
functioned, however, not just as immovable backdrops but, presented sequentially (as in Inigo Jones's design for the masque *Oberon*), as a means
of simulating the experience of transformation that a grotto effects.[51]

In contrast with the rarefied context of masques and noble and royal
estates that characterized the grotto of the early seventeenth century, by
the end of the century the grotto had become a standard feature of private
landscape gardens in England. John Worlidge in 1677 recommends building a grotto in one's landscape as a practical means for keeping cool. The
inhabitants of "more southerly" countries, he writes, feeling "the acute
heat of that bright Orb about the middle of the day . . . usually sequester
themselves from their ordinary occupations, and betake themselves to
their shades and cool places of Recess for some few hours." Although the
summer heat is less "acute" or "constant" in England, "Grotts" are just "as
necessary" for the English, "to repose our selves in the time of our Summer faint heats," for a grotto is "cool and fresh in the greatest heats."[52]

Worlidge's design suggestions register how adaptable the grotto was
to individual tastes and needs, and how common a landscape feature it
had become: "It may be Arched over with stone or brick, and you may

give it what light or entrance you please. You may make secret rooms and passages within it, and in your outer Room may you have all these before mentioned water-works, for your own or your friends divertissements."[53] The grotto, much like the great innovation of domestic architecture during the same period, the corridor, made possible the *choice* of privacy and apartness from others. Whereas the corridor expanded the options for practical movement through domestic environments, and the writing closet offered reliable seclusion, the grotto provided opportunities for the aesthetic as well as the creative imagination to elect the ways in which one's company might be enjoyed.

With its initial display of waterworks for the enjoyment of self and others, followed by private and secluded rooms and passages chosen at will, the grotto had become a microcosm of the modern house, replicating its organizational principle of placing more public areas near the entrance and spaces intended for privacy in less accessible areas. These were the properties of the grotto by the time Pope began conceiving and designing his own in the following century.

Pope's Design Thinking

The widespread fame of Pope's grotto, which he began building in 1720, seems to have influenced the spread of grottoes in eighteenth-century gardens. Several notable ones were created in the 1730s, including those at Goodwood and Goldney Hall, and they continued to emerge on the grounds of different estates until the end of the century, by which time nearly half the country house estates in England had a grotto.[54] So common a feature was the grotto in the gardens of private homes throughout the Georgian era that it is regarded as definitional to eighteenth-century style.[55] Historian of landscape architecture Barbara Jones evocatively describes the great optical beauty of grottoes' features, which came at the cost of physical comfort:

> The grottoes were cold, damp, hard, spiky and utterly impractical, and they cost a tremendous amount of time and money, but nothing in all architecture can have been more beautiful than one of the great grottoes in its hey-day, pink and white with shells, glittering with spar and heightened with quartz and corals.[56]

The grotto's promotion of an enjoyment that focused on intense sensory experiences pointed to a new direction in landscape design. During the first decades of the eighteenth century, landscape gardens began moving away from requiring visitors to have classical backgrounds in order to understand the allusions made by busts, statues, and Latin inscriptions planted throughout the garden—as exemplified by Stowe's Elysian Fields, for instance—and toward creating meaning determined by private experience, both the designer's and the visitor's. Hunt, calling this a turn from "emblematic" garden design to "expressionism," declares Pope's garden a prime and "early exemplum . . . of the expressive garden."[57] Though the garden was indeed rich with inscribed urns, busts, and allusions to classical literary sources from Horace to Homer, as Mack has explicated, it had a decidedly individualistic design that drew on personal fancy and subjective experiences. It invited visitors to make sense of the garden on their own terms—the winding nature of the walks along the margins of the gardens indicate this—and promoted the awareness of their own mental activity as it encountered and engaged with the garden's sights and sounds.

What Hunt calls "expressionism" is in fact a form of garden design that allowed for interiority. Landscape designer Stephen Switzer's phrase "private or natural turn," which appears in *Ichnographia Rustica* (1718) as a descriptor for an emerging standard of garden design, forms the background for Hunt's notion of expressionistic landscape gardens.[58] The phrase arises in a sentence that declares, "It is an unpardonable Fault, as we see it almost everywhere . . . to have scarce any Thing in a whole Design, but carries open Walks." Even if the garden is "40, 50, or 60 acres, one shall scarce find any private or natural turn in the whole." Evident in this statement is Switzer's intolerance of gardens lacking enclosed spaces. Also clear are his expectations that a garden design stimulate a visitor's experience of interiority. Thus, implied in Switzer's phrase is the notion that fidelity to the nature of the mind as well as to nature itself is what makes a garden space natural.

The "private or natural turn" allowed visitors to proceed through a garden in a fashion that prompted the turnings of their minds. At the same time, it allowed garden designers to express personal fancies and tastes. This emphasis on individual desire emerged from a new conception of design that Pope himself helped to conceive. William Cavendish's design of the Little Castle of Bolsover is an earlier expression of this whimsical approach, an idea underscored by his reference to the castle as his "little romance." However, its seventeenth-century emphasis on accommodating expensive entertainment, especially of a high-stakes political nature, and its organization around a classical myth—the labors of Hercules—distinguish it from eighteenth-century expressions of the individual imagination in spatial design. The classical influence in Pope's

own grotto can certainly be discerned not just in the Horatian line inscribed on the marble plaque at its entrance, or in Pope's stated desire to
furnish it with a "beautiful antique" statue "with an inscription," but also
in its very purpose as a source for creativity.[59] As such, the grotto evoked
the nymphaeum of antiquity. Yet, the approach Pope took to building the
grotto was decidedly modern. The mind's interactions with the space and
its place in it was a primary consideration, alongside the practical purpose of creating a structural link between the house and the garden. In
exemplifying the redeployment of design as a function of individual intention rather than a collectively understood divine or allegorical one, the
grotto was the product of a new form of "intelligent design": its structure
was oriented in large part around the dweller's mind. Thus it contributed
greatly to the development of the picturesque and its upholding of darkness, shadows, and ruin as triggers for the imagination.[60]

Switzer demonstrates the secular notion of intelligent design by quot-
ing from a poem by "Mr. Gardiner" that characterizes the landscape designer's plan:

> Villa's and Gardens you will best command
> If timely you engage a Master's Hand,
> Whose artful Pencil shall on Paper trace
> The whole Design, and figure out the Place.
> Review the Plan yourself, you may descry
> Errors escaping the Designer's Eye.
> With Ease reliev'd, while yet to each new Thought
> The slightest Touch reforms th'obedient Draught.[61]

The last two lines show a notion of design as highly responsive to thought,
much as gardens themselves are designed to create desired experiences
in human visitors. The "Master's Hand" here presumably belongs not to
God but to a professional designer, whose materials for making the plan
are quotidian ones: pencil and paper. The hand is hired to "trace / The
whole Design, and figure out the Place," using the pencil to draft a plan.
Attesting to the plan's receptiveness as a modern document, changes can
then be made according to the impulses of human thinking and touch,
rather than divine action.

The critical difference between eighteenth-century grottoes and earlier ones issues from changing conceptions of the universe.[62] Rather than
staging a view from a single perspective, eighteenth-century gardens and
their grottoes allowed for successive openings and turnings. The key elements of "change," "process," "constantly shifting mood," and "reflec-

tiveness" that characterize eighteenth-century gardens indicate a mode of spatial experience that promotes self-consciousness and accords with the movement of mental activities.[63] Spaces in gardens were being consciously designed to accommodate those internal activities, allowing space for the movement, not just of bodies, but of thoughts, as Switzer reveals: "In the mean time I preserve some private Walks and Cabinets of Retirement, some select Places of Recess for Reading and Contemplation, where the mind may privately exult and breathe out those Seraphick Thoughts and Strains, by which Man is known and distinguish'd as an Intelligent Being, and elevated above the common Level of Irrational Creatures."[64] Above all, in garden design of the eighteenth century, "the idea of process replaced the idea of the completed perfected artifice."[65]

The changing meaning of the term *design* itself demonstrates a tendency toward individualistic form that began to emerge in Pope's century. While the term "argument from design" was coined by William Paley in 1802, its principles were very much a part of Augustan attitudes toward nature, as realized in theology and aesthetics. Argument from design found in God the epitome of a great designer; his products, the intricate systems of nature, reveal and confirm not just his greatness but, more fundamentally, his existence. Frances Hutcheson, writing in 1726, presents the pattern of reasoning that supported argument from design: "When we see then such a multitude of Individuals of a Species, similar to each other in a vast number of Parts; and when we see in each Individual, the corresponding Members so exactly like each other, what possible room is there left for questioning Design in the Universe?"[66] Furthermore, Hutcheson articulates his notion of design when he declares that "Regularity never arises from any undesign'd Force of ours; and from this we conclude, that wherever there is any Regularity in the disposition of a System capable of many other Dispositions, there must have been Design in the Cause."[67]

Pope's poems *An Essay on Criticism* (1709) and *An Essay on Man* exemplify this attitude as well. A line from *Essay on Criticism* conveys a sense of nature's role as the very measure of design: "Nature to all things fixed the limits fit."[68] Pope's supplier of minerals and rocks, William Borlase, naturalist and antiquary of Cornwall, offered an understanding of design, like that found in natural history, as providential. This is clearest when he proclaims "the principal use therefore of Natural History is, that it leads us directly to Religion: it shews us every where the plain footsteps of design and intelligence, and points out to us all the attributes of GOD."[69] For Borlase, the pursuit of natural history was as much a way of "giving a recital and detail of the whole visible Creation" as it was a source of pleasure and satisfaction for the mind that "thirsts after variety, and a fresh succession of objects."[70] In their very ability to give sensual pleasure—displaying "tints, delicacy, and lustre"—natural history objects are but elements of the "works" that "bounteous Providence has laid . . . before us."[71] They are models, brought into manageable containment, for studying the otherwise uncontainable universe:

> NATURAL HISTORY is the handmaid to Providence, collects into a narrower space what is distributed through the Universe, arranging and disposing the several Fossils, Vegetables, and Animals, so as the mind may more readily examine and distinguish their beauties, investigate their causes, combinations, and effects, and rightly know how to apply them to the calls of private and public life.[72]

Such a description of natural history suggests Pope's grotto was partly a repository for rock and mineral specimens that attempted to include all that is "distributed through the universe" within the scale of private life. Yet, the idiosyncracy of his grotto design, emphasizing the "dazzle" and "glitter" of its specimen rather than their rarity, and based in a privately realized system, not a godly one, demonstrates a marked departure from the notion of "argument from design."

The plan Pope drew in 1740 of his grotto, included in a letter from his friend William Oliver to William Borlase, indicates the ductile properties of the plan as an instrument of design. Architectural alterations he suggests include placing a "basin" to the right of the central room "receiving the small waterfall," a bagnio below the central room to the left, and features referred to as "not Pillars but left rough to support ye arches." According to Oliver, who shared the drawing with Borlase when requesting new rocks from the geologist on Pope's behalf, Pope's aim was to showcase "the Riches of our [Britain's] native soil" and "the Several Productions of Nature, which are properly to be found under ground."[73] Insofar as Pope drew his plan in order to have changes made to it as designated by the impulses of his own mind ("he has a mind to make this Passage a beautiful Grotto," wrote Dr. Oliver), he fully occupies the role of a designer in the modern terms articulated by Munari: "a planner with an aesthetic sense."[74] In turn, the plan he draws is a document of his imagination at work, reconceiving the grotto as a "glittering" minelike space.[75]

On the top left corner of the plan, Pope poses two questions—"Quare what proper for a Natural Roof? What for a Natural Pavement?"—which point to the fiction at play in his gardening pursuits. This form of fiction, one that Robin Evans points out inheres in all architectural plans, lies in

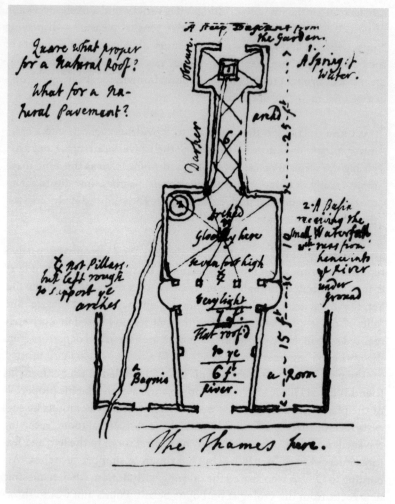

FIGURE 3.5 Alexander Pope, plan of alterations in the Twickenham grotto included in a letter from William Oliver to William Borlase (1740). Photograph by kind permission of the Morrab Library, Penzance, Cornwall.

its "projective cast."[76] Rather than showing a space that exists, the plan shows, provisionally, one that has yet to be. Accordingly, the architectural plan, as a tool, is "a form of speculation rather than a form of documentation."[77] In this regard, the plan is as much a depiction of an imagined reality as it is a concrete entity—a sheet of paper inscribed with a drawing. It serves as a device for imagining as well as for thinking, a function coextensive with the very space it imagines.[78] Pope himself recognized the role of the imagination in creating architectural plans. To his friend

Jervas he wrote while planning his move to Twickenham and designing his new house, "Much more should I describe the many Draughts, Elevations, Profiles, Perspectives, &c. of every Palace and Garden propos'd, intended, and happily raised, by the strength of that Faculty wherein all great Genius's excel, Imagination."[79] Despite mocking himself in the same letter for having "been a Poet, [who] was degraded to a Translator, and at last thro' meer dullness is turn'd into an Architect," he communicated an intermedial view that the various forms of projective drawing entailed by architecture and landscape design are as much vehicles for the imagination as poems are.[80]

Interior Surfaces: Rocks and Shells

Grottoes of the eighteenth century registered an approach to design that was responsive to states of mind. Allowing men and women to exercise their creativity, grottoes channeled their inner thoughts and feelings while at the same time altering them. This took place mainly through the acts of selecting, arranging, and displaying objects from the natural world to cover the grotto's inner surfaces. Almost every conceivable element of nature was used. Minerals, rocks, stalactites, and shells were most prevalent. Coral, bark, twigs, pine, cedar, and fir cones, mosses, ostrich eggs, and such manufactured materials as wine glass stems and bits of mirror, glass, and wool were also used at such sites as Wimborne St. Giles, Carton, and Oatlands (the last destroyed in World War II). As Barbara Jones puts it, any material could be used that "provide[d] glitter and a rich texture."[81] In compiling and organizing these materials, men and women served as "the maker" of designs, rather than an almighty deity. Grottoes performed the trick of using nature as the medium for transforming a natural space into an artificial one through alterations made to its interior surfaces.

Nowhere was this more evident than in John Serle's *A Plan of Mr. Pope's Garden, as it was left at his Death*, the account written and published by Pope's former gardener in 1745, a year after the poet's death, purportedly as a guide for visitors. In addition to plans of the grotto, the pamphlet included a catalog of its mineralogical materials. The catalog format underscores by contrast what made the grotto unique in its status as a space. It is easy to forget that the contents of the grotto, arranged on the pages of Serle's *Plan* as a directory of specimen names, like the handlist for an exhibition, appeared in the grotto in an altogether different physical manifestation—not stored inside a cabinet, case, or box, but embedded in or hanging on the very walls. When inside the grotto, the inhabitant was as much housed by the collection as the collection was housed by the grotto. The drawback with allowing visitors such direct proximity to the geological materials and shells, of course, is the items' vulnerability to being prized out of the walls and stolen, which unfortunately is precisely what happened. When Mary Delany, after her 1756 visit to the Goldney Hall grotto in Clifton, lamented that its shells were subjected to the elements, she cast light on both the excellence of Goldney's collection and the conventions for preserving and storing collectible items: "I could not but grudge at the shells sacrificed there, and exposed to the ruin of damp and time, that would have preserved their beauty for ages in a cabinet!"[82]

Clearly, Pope, too, ignored such precautions in choosing to dwell with his minerals, rocks, and shells rather than house them in a box. Addison indicates what might have been a source of delight for Pope too when reflecting on the collection of rocks and minerals that surrounded him: "those accidental Landskips of Trees, Clouds and Cities, that are sometimes found in the Veins of Marble, in the curious Fret-work of Rocks and Grottoes, and in a Word, in any thing that hath such a Variety or Regularity as may seem the Effect of Design, in what we call the works of Chance."[83] Within the materials that made up his interior landscape were further landscapes, which might appear to be products of human design but in fact are products of pure chance—of nature's own design, that is. Pope conveyed this pleasure in discovering the designs of nature to Ralph Allen, describing in a letter the appearance of Plymouth Marbles he had cut "into pieces": "I find they are very beautiful, sparry, & various color'd."[84]

The textual format of Serle's *Plan* divides the grotto into numbered sections, listing the materials in each. The rocks, crystals, and minerals were significant both for their beauty and geographical origins and for their status as gifts from friends and distinguished admirers. Specimens on the walls came from, in addition to Reverend Doctor William Borlase, the Duchess of Cleveland, who supplied "large clumps of Amethyst and several pieces of white spar," and the Earl of Orrery, who contributed "several fine Fossils from Ireland." Not just ornaments, the colorful and gleaming stones and crystals that covered the walls were artifacts of sentiment, tying Pope emotionally to each person who had marked their bond with a gift of geological materials for his beloved grotto.

One can imagine how Pope, who used the grotto as a writing space (as the two extant drawings depicting him in the act of doing so demonstrate), might have interacted with the objects: glancing up at the ceiling or looking out the window, he would catch sight of an arrangement of glass, shell, mirror, or rock, and his perception of the materials' different textures and glimmering effect would intermesh with whatever thought was passing through his mind, or would inspire a new one. The design of the grotto, with its inescapable emphasis on the textural and visual qualities of natural objects, meant to "dazzle a Gazing, spectator," was inseparable from the experience of mind.[85] Borlase suggests this correspondence when he writes, "For if the mind thirsts after variety, and a fresh succession of objects, where can she find for contemplation so numerous and various a treasure? . . . Is studious of beauty, shape, and colouring, where such gracefulness as in Man, such tints, delicacy, and lustre, as in Flowers, Birds, Fishes, and Precious-Stones?"[86] Such questions reveal the impact the sensual qualities of natural history objects were thought to have had on the human mind.

Pope's grotto was a space that functioned as an object insofar as it was approached as a product of design—and a product of mental exertion. Yet its purpose as a product of design was to create specific effects in the mental experience of the grotto *as a space*. The amount of effort and thought Pope put into the organization and display of the natural history objects he collected to display within it points to the role of these objects of fascination, not as entities separate from the space but as an integral part of it. If an architectural structure is a body, then the quartz, amethyst, fool's gold, and seashells that covered the walls and ceiling of the grotto functioned as its interior "skin."

From the middle of the seventeenth century, seashells were the primary medium for grotto design.[87] As a contemporary home economics manual for young women indicates, the pastime of making floral or geometric designs and festoons out of shells to ornament domestic surfaces belonged to women.[88] Pope's friend Mary Delany, known for her accomplished shellwork and botanically correct cut-paper flowers, joined him in the pleasures of "grottofying," as well as the solitude it brought. In a September 2, 1736, letter to Jonathan Swift, she describes "making a grotto" at her uncle's North End London house out of shells she had collected in Ireland. The process was so engrossing a summer activity that she "found living quite alone a pleasanter thing than [she had] imagined." In the letter, she also mentions an incident in which Pope attempted to assist a young lady onto a boat: "her foot missed the side of the boat, she fell into the water, and pulled Mr. Pope after her." The letter thus demonstrates the connection between Delany and Pope as well as the social channels through which the grotto rose as a popular landscape component.[89] Delany went on to make several more grottoes adorned with shellwork throughout her life, including the grotto at Bulstrode, a joint project with the shell collector and natural historian Margaret Cavendish Bentick, the Duchess of Portland (and a descendant of Margaret Cavendish).[90]

Pope appeared to place greater emphasis on geological than on conchological acquisition and display in his grotto, going so far as attempting to imitate a "quarry" or "mine," according to some scholars.[91] He valued the aesthetic qualities of brightly colored and glimmering stones, which, as mentioned earlier, were either gifts or chosen more for their beauty than for their collectability. Yet shells, too, played a significant role in his grotto design. One might say that, while decorating his grotto was an act of "stellifying," to use his term, it was also one of "shellifying." In a letter to Edward Blount dated June 2, 1725, he describes walls that are "finished with Shells interspersed with Pieces of Looking-glass in angular forms."[92] He mixed shells with mirror fragments for the grotto, but he used only shells for his Shell Temple, another prominent architectural feature in his garden. Serle's account of the grotto at the time of Pope's death in 1744 suggests that shells were used sparingly—it lists black cockle "interlaced" with white spars in only one area—in comparison with the preponderance of several types of minerals and metals that filled the rest of the cave.

Yet Pope, in a letter of August 12, 1741, asks one Judge Fortescue, "as a Devonian," to contribute to his grotto "a Hogshead of scallop shells."[93] A recent visit to the grotto reveals that even with so many of its sparkling elements pilfered by visitors, the coiled shapes of ammonites remain on the walls. And a letter of July 30, 1741, from Thomas Edwards to Richard Owen Cambridge, describes Pope's plan to "add two rooms" to his grotto, "one to be covered with shells, and the other with Minerals."[94] Presumably the hogshead of shells Pope requested from Fortescue was intended for the proposed shell room.

Just as shells were part of the 1725 design, so too were they an element of the altered grotto design. Though Serle barely mentioned them in his 1745 account, the visitor writing for the *General Magazine* in 1748 describes them as being integrated among the "Variety of Flints, Spar, Ores" stuffed "in the Fissures and angular Breaches." The visitor also describes shells hanging next to moss, both dripping with water that emerged from the spring located in the cave.[95] In using shells for at least part of his design, Pope joined others who turned to the material when adorning their grottoes. These included not only Delany and the Duchess of Richmond and her daughters at Goodwood in West Sussex, but also Goldney at Goldney Hall in Bristol and John Scott at Ware in Hertfordshire. From the outset, the idea that material belonging to an entirely different element—water—could be incorporated into a domestic space located among rocks and earth is unexpected. In their classical origins, grottoes

FIGURE 3.6 Ammonite shell decorating the wall of Pope's grotto, Twickenham, Richmond upon Thames (ca. 1741). Photograph by the author.

were naturally formed caves found close to bodies of water—along the Mediterranean coast, for instance—which may account for the common combination of shells and rocks in grotto decoration. At the same time, the primary materials of English grottoes would certainly have connoted to eighteenth-century subjects England's imperial status as a conqueror of land and sea.

Quaker merchant and grotto owner Thomas Goldney's connections in the triangular trade route between England, West Africa, and the West Indies most probably allowed him to acquire the rare and beautiful shells from those areas seen in his grotto. Overall his grotto, in excellent condition today, unlike Pope's, boasts an estimated one to two hundred thousand specimens of individual molluscans.[96] Throughout, Goldney blended his shells and corals with local minerals from Derbyshire, Cornwall, and Bristol to extremely striking effect.[97] Presumably, the walls of Pope's grotto were just as arresting in their juxtapositions and antitheses of different minerals and shells before they were looted by tourists.

Whether the materials were acquired at home or abroad, by the eighteenth century the creation of grottoes, in centering on the disposition of painstakingly acquired materials, accomplished an act of transposition, as well as one of imposition—the human imposition of form on nature.[98]

FIGURE 3.7 Exotic seashells collected by Thomas Goldney III encrusting the wall of Goldney Hall grotto, Hotwells, Bristol (ca. 1711–1752). Photograph by the author.

The shells, moved from the ocean floor to a new, subterranean context, had themselves served as movable dwellings for their original occupants. The shape of the ancient ammonite, with its spiral shell closing in around a hollow interior, evokes a notion of homey, inwardly oriented yet transportable security. Scallops, on the other hand, are known as "cosmopolitan" and "free-living" mollusks for their migratory living patterns and ability to swim rapidly. Referring to tortoises and their shells in the second stanza of *Upon Appleton House*, Andrew Marvell reminds us of the virtues of a home that, like a bird's nest, fits the occupant's body:

> Why should of all things Man unrul'd
> Such unproportion'd dwellings build?
> The Beasts are by their Denns exprest:
> And Birds contrive an equal Nest;
> The low-roof'd Tortoises do dwell
> In cases fit of Tortoise-shell:
> No Creature loves an empty space;
> Their Bodies measure out their Place. (stanza 2, lines 9–16)

In the last stanza of the poem, Marvell notes as well the appealing transportability of such compactly proportioned homes when he compares the salmon-fishers, carrying their boats on their heads at the end of their day, to tortoises.

Though the shells in Pope's grotto might not have had the exotic charms of Goldney's South Pacific and East Indies finds or the rarity of the Duchess of Portland's shells, they could not have escaped evoking the metaphysical resonances that belong to all shells. Gaston Bachelard describes the shell, originally the home of a living creature, as a model for the solitude and shelter we long for in our lives. After all, "we know perfectly well that to inhabit a shell we must be alone. By living this image, one knows that one has accepted solitude."[99] The grotto, then, might be viewed as itself a shell, offering to human bodies and souls a close-fitting shelter. Indeed, it provides rooms "as deep and secret as a shell."[100] From the country house of the first chapter and the writing closet of the second to the grotto of the present, the spaces of the inner self move toward a more deliberate sense of portability and become more amenable to modifications based on idiosyncratic fancies.

According to the 1739/40 plan of prospective improvements, Pope's grotto was at that time fifty feet long, with sections ranging from six to ten feet in height. Given the narrowness of the space, the grotto felt snugger and more intimate than other domestic environments, even for Pope's allegedly four-foot-four-inch frame, evoking the snugness of a mollusk's shell around its body. And yet the attraction of the grotto as a solitary dwelling also explains its appeal to the numerous strangers who visited it after Pope's death. Not only did they enjoy the marvelous effects of the grotto's intricate design, waterworks, and twinkling array of minerals, as well as the aura of Pope's celebrity; in experiencing an intimate space that so clearly conveyed the desire for protection and shelter, they also were made to exercise their faculty for sympathy. "Whenever life seeks to shelter, protect, cover or hide itself, the imagination sympathizes with the being that inhabits the protected space," writes Bachelard. The expansive feeling of sympathy would be heightened by contrast with the contracting emotion of fear that is felt momentarily when entering a narrow and dark tunnel to descend into an unknown secret world.

A network of surfaces decorated with shells extended from the grotto's interior to a walkway paved with cockleshells that led to the (now-destroyed) Shell Temple. The use of shells in the grotto, the Shell Temple, and the cockleshell path serving as their hyphen demonstrates that these different parts of the garden were viewed as a unit. Pope supports this notion when he declares that the "Cockle-shells" he chose for the walk "agree[d] not ill with the little dripping Murmur, and the Aquatic Idea of the Whole Place."[101] The material of the shells thus supplied a "soft transition"—to quote *The Rape of the Lock*—from the interior space to the exterior one (canto 1, line 49).[102] Pope reinforced further the idea that the grotto and Shell Temple corresponded to each other when he wrote to Edward Blount:

> From the River Thames, you see thro' my Arch up a Walk of the Wilderness to a kind of open Temple, wholly compos'd of Shells in the Rustic Manner, and from that distance under the Temple you look down thro' a sloping Arcade of Trees, and see the Sails on the River passing suddenly and vanishing, as thro' a Perspective Glass.[103]

Describing the view of the world outside the grotto, he articulates the series of frames that shape it, from the archway through the Shell Temple and on to the "sloping Arcade of Trees." The temple, with its open structure, allows the gaze to pass straight through it. Pope's mention of garden elements outside the grotto again signals its relation to the rest of the garden while showing the areas' collaboration in creating a perspective device. Here, the perspective device created by the arcade of trees appears to be a camera obscura, for the view it captures is a moving one, with its objects, the boat sails, behaving the way camera obscura images

FIGURE 3.8 William Kent, *View in Pope's Garden with his Shell Temple*
(ca. 1725–1730). Photograph © The Trustees of the British Museum.

do: "passing suddenly and vanishing." The world outside the garden is
transformed by this device as one looks through it: commercial sailboats
on the Thames appear not as the prosaic intrusions in the landscape they
otherwise would be to anyone valuing privacy in their home, but as fleeting, dreamlike visions. Under Pope's hand, form and beauty are united
as the successful product of design, and the world is made to appear as if
seen through a camera obscura.

The *General Magazine*'s 1748 account of a visit gives an outsider's impression of Pope's design. Its author adds to the dreaminess of his river-
scape description when he discerns the sightline created by the tree arcade, shell temple, and grotto passage as a "continued Tube":

> From the [Shell] Temple, this Sylvan Arcade, together with the Passage of
> the Grotto, make a sort of continued Tube, thro' which a small Expanse of
> the Thames is beheld as in a Perspective, making a beautiful remote Ap-
> pearance; where Vessels that pass up and down the River, suddenly glance
> on the Eye, and again vanish from it in a Moment.[104]

Just as he was preoccupied with sourcing, transporting, and arranging the natural materials for his grotto, Pope was attentive to the points of view it created. Ultimately, the care he put into the grotto was directed toward creating not just a "Musaeum, a Study for Virtuosi, & a Scene for contemplation," as he explained to Bolingbroke in 1740, but also a device for viewing everyday life and its scenes anew in his own domestic space, re-rendered as a domestic fiction—that is, not as reality but as visions and scenes.[105] The grotto, with its glittering bits of mirror, quartz, and spar, was as much his blazing world as it was his dark room, a transfiguring and dreamlike theater for the inner self whose movements flicker and vanish, like boats passing up and down the river.

Pope's Dark Room

If the grotto served as a viewing device for looking outward at the world, it served for looking inward too, specifically in its celebrated role as a walk-in camera obscura. The lines from Horace inscribed above the entrance to the grotto (and mentioned in the introduction) warn those who enter of this effect: "Secretum iter, et fallentis semita vitae"—"A hid Recess, where Life's revolving Day, / In sweet Delusion gently steals away."[106] Here, the inscription explains, the passage of daily life is displaced by the experiences of dreams and fancies. Similar to Cavendish's writing closet, Pope's grotto provided a space of seclusion that allowed him to perceive the activity of his thoughts and imagination more acutely. But whereas the fundamental space of Cavendish's closet was enough for her to conjure worlds in her head, Pope's grotto insisted on the space and its material features to form a fantastic world.

An underground cave may be apparently stationary, yet being inside it is a way of journeying through life in the way the inscription outside the grotto suggests. The grotto's function as a camera obscura, with the reflections of the ships on the Thames passing through it, allowed Pope to be a part of life as it was happening while remaining distant from it. Moreover, the subterranean grotto, out of sight to passersby, reconstituted the world in its transmaterial plenitude. The crystals, marbles, stalactites, and shells from different parts of England were brought to the poet through the grotto, as were the real-time views of life outside. He enjoyed the optical tricks played by two mirrors placed in a dark stone recess behind two large pillars. In reflecting the Thames, they "almost deceive[d] the Eye," appearing not as mirrors but as two arches opening to the river, with the real view placed between them.[107] In accomplishing this trick, the two mirrors, like the camera obscura, appeared to bring more of the world into the grotto than was actually the case.

In a letter of 1712/13 to John Caryll, Pope demonstrates the reclusive temperament fit for becoming a dweller of a grotto:

> I have just now stolen myself from a tumult of acquaintance at Will's, in to my chamber, to enjoy the pleasing melancholy of an hour's reflection alone. There is an agreeable gloominess which instead of troubling, does but refresh and ease the mind, and has an effect upon it not unlike the relief a sudden cloud sometimes gives the eye, when it has been aching and too much distended with the glaring of a summer's day.[108]

The letter identifies the need for shadows to relax the mind, for a dark room apart from others that one can call one's own. Rather than creating a sense of privation, the gloom and melancholy experienced in his chamber rejuvenates Pope and restores his sense of mental ease. The dark room surrounding him converges with the dark room of the mind and allows it to function as a camera obscura–like device for creating internal views— projections as well as reflections—out of those that were once external.

Writing to Lady Mary from the medieval manor house Stanton Harcourt, Oxfordshire, in 1718, the year between the publication of *Eloisa to Abelard* and his move to Twickenham, Pope expressed an even keener desire for solitude and disappearing from public view while writing his translation of Homer's *Iliad* in a tower room:

> Indeed I owe this old house the same sort of gratitude that we do to an old friend, that harbors us in his declining condition, nay even in his last extremities. I have found this an excellent place for Retirement and Study, where no one who passes by can dream there is an Inhabitant, and even any body that would visit me, dares not venture under my roof. I could not have chosen a fitter or more likely place to converse with the Dead.[109]

Here, his very existence is beyond others' dreams, which gives him the freedom to nurture his creativity and allow his own dream life to flourish and to materialize as writing.

In the same letter to Edward Blount where he proudly described his newly created grotto, Pope wrote the oft-quoted lines:

> when you shut the doors of this grotto it becomes on the instant, from a luminous room, a Camera obscura, on the walls of which all the objects

of the river, hills, woods, and boats, are forming a moving picture in their visible radiations; and when you have a mind to light it up, it affords you a very different scene.[110]

Arresting in this description is the interplay between agency and passivity, on one hand, and lightness and darkness, on the other, that the grotto animates in its function as a camera obscura. With the action of shutting the doors, the once light-filled room darkens enough for real objects to become invisible and for an unmentioned aperture to convey, through "visible radiations," images of the outside world onto the grotto's walls. The walls, also undescribed, would have had to be bare and white for the projected images to be most fully visible, suggesting that at an earlier point at least, an aspect of the grotto's design was reserved for its function as a camera obscura. In ending his description with the room again lit up—presumably by opening the doors, reversing the initial action—and "a very different scene" presented to the viewer, Pope exerted the "crucial element of personal control over his mental activity" that characterizes the eighteenth-century turn to expressionistic garden design.[111] The account also demonstrates an element of artistic creation that inheres in Pope's choice to turn the grotto into a camera obscura and his experience of it as one.

Writing his discourses on art years later, Joshua Reynolds identifies the camera obscura's limitations as a source of artistic creation, and in doing so, helps to illuminate its function as such in the case of Pope's grotto:

If we suppose a view of nature represented with all the truth of the camera obscura, and the same scene represented by a great Artist, how little and mean will the one appear in comparison of the other, where no superiority is supposed from the choice of the subject. The scene shall be the same, the difference only will be in the manner in which it is presented to the eye. With what additional superiority then will the same Artist appear when he has the power of selecting his materials, as well as elevating his style?[112]

For Reynolds, choice and agency constitute the main distinction between the artist's and the camera obscura's renderings of the same scene. Putting aside the issue of materials and style, it is fair to say that in Pope's case, choice is a factor not so much in the camera obscura's performance as in the fact that the grotto functions as a camera obscura at all. Also worthy of examination is Reynolds's view on the status of "lightness and darkness" in artistic creation:

PLATE 1 James "Athenian" Stuart, design of a wall with chimney for a
state room at Kedleston Hall (ca. 1757–1758). Pen, ink, and watercolor.
Kedleston Hall, Derbyshire. Photograph © National Trust/Andrew Patterson.

PLATE 2 The first architectural drawing showing the complete interior design scheme for each room inside a house, including their colors. William Chambers, design for York House, Pall Mall, London, for the Duke of York (1759). Photograph: RIBA Collections.

PLATE 3 Interior view of the first floor of Bolsover's Little Castle, showing the Star Chamber from the east. Bolsover Castle, Derbyshire (orig. 1618–1619). Photograph © Historic England Archive.

PLATE 4 Peter Tillemans, *The Prospect of the River Thames at Twickenham* (ca. 1724–1730). Photograph by permission of the London Borough of Richmond upon Thames Borough Art Collection, Orleans House Gallery.

PLATE 5 Robert Havell, *The Natuorama; or, Nature's Endless Transposition of Views on the Thames* (1820). Photograph: Huntington Library, San Marino, California.

PLATE 6 Unattributed sketch (ca. 1760–1810) of a view from Pope's grotto, found in the Morgan Library's extra-illustrated copy of *The Poetical Works of Alexander Pope, Esq.* (1785) (PML 4239, p. 79). Watercolor over pencil on paper. 8 × 10½ in. (20.3 × 26.7 cm). Photograph: Morgan Library and Museum.

PLATE 7 Paul Sandby, *Lady Francis Scott and Lady Elliot* (ca. 1770).
Watercolor and graphite on medium, cream, moderately textured laid paper.
5 × 5⅛ in. (12.7 × 13 cm). Photograph: Yale Center for British Art,
Paul Mellon Collection (B1977.14.4410), Yale University.

PLATE 8 Zoe Leonard, installation view of 2014 Biennial, Whitney Museum of American Art. © Zoe Leonard. Photography by Sheldan C. Collins. Photograph © Whitney Museum of American Art. Licensed by Scala/Art Resource, New York.

If we add to this the powerful materials of lightness and darkness, over which the Artist has complete dominion, to vary and dispose them as he pleases; to diminish, or increase them, as will best suit his purpose, and correspond to the general idea of his work; a landscape thus conducted, under the influence of a poetical mind, will have the same superiority over the more ordinary and common views, as Milton's Allegro and Penseroso have over a cold prosaic narration or description; and such a picture would make a more forcible impression on the mind than the real scenes, were they presented before us.[113]

By identifying lightness and darkness as "materials" and media of control belonging to artists rather than to camera obscuras, the passage inadvertently highlights a way in which Pope's transformation of the grotto into a camera obscura was very much an artistic enterprise. If his interest did not lie in "elevating his style," it certainly did in "selecting his materials." Just as an artist as defined by Reynolds's terms might do, Pope determined how much light to "dispose" in the grotto to create the condition and effect he desired. The resulting landscape, though derived entirely from "real scenes," is far from "cold" or "prosaic"—it has all the qualities of a landscape "conducted, under the influence of a poetical mind" and has the ability to "make a more forcible impression on the mind." Indeed, the scene of the "river, hills, woods, and boats," in their formation of "a moving picture in their visible radiations," makes a forcible impression on the mind precisely because it is as much a product of the mind's response of pleasure as it is of the camera obscura's carrying an image of the external world into Pope's grotto room. The numerous sources praising and describing the device show how the figure for the mind as a camera obscura—instances of which we saw in works by authors writing earlier than Locke, such as Marvell and Cavendish—had become thoroughly naturalized as part of the cultural idiom.

The camera obscura's projective space has a relationship to mobility in which the image itself is mobile while the human viewer is immobile. A transference takes place in the viewer's awareness that the image has originated in a real space "out there" and reemerged in a space that is both real and unreal. What is real is the actual space of the camera obscura—in Pope's case, a grotto that is in itself a reformulation or assemblage of elements belonging to several other places. What is not real is the moving image of an external space being projected into Pope's domestic theater of the imagination. Not only ideas are stimulated regarding what is being seen but, also, the emotions of pleasure and surprise on realizing that a spatial-visual trick has been performed. These emotions—forms of projection in themselves—fuse the virtual and real spaces that comprise the camera obscura.

For Pope, the need to reprocess views of the outside world into the reverielike projections of the camera obscura was born out of a practical need for a solution to a source of irritation in the immediate landscape of his daily life. As mentioned earlier, the activity on the Thames that was rendered so fancifully on his grotto wall was in fact a busy and noisy intrusion that was difficult to avoid. The entire garden, in fact, located next to a river filled with commercial activity, offered little privacy, as Anthony Beckles Willson explains.[114] Pope's neighbors were busy tradesmen whose businesses appeared to disrupt the tranquility normally associated with a private garden. As Bishop Warburton observed, "Close to the Grotto of the Twickenham Bard, Too close—adjoins a Tanner's Yard."[115] Thus, in addition to solving the problem of the public road's dividing the garden from the house, the grotto provided what was truly a safe space—a shell—protecting the poet from the disturbances of the river. In bringing images of the otherwise noisome river into Pope's private space, the camera obscura not only projected it but *transformed* it into a charming "moving picture," replete with boats and surrounding hills and woods. Pope's grotto, in other words, turned the world of everyday life into one of ephemeral visions.

Whether Pope corrected the camera obscura image or left it upside down and laterally reversed is unknown. Conceptually, the grotto accomplished an act of reversing and subverting an everyday inconvenience into a pleasing dreamscape, a domestic fiction. The agency entailed in using the grotto as a camera obscura led to his transforming not just the space within it but also the space outside of it; he improved it by turning it into his mental as well as spatial territory—even as a renter of the house— through the camera obscura's process of projection.

Let us return to Pope's letter to Caryll of December 5, 1712, in which he describes the experience of reposing in his closet at Binfield to recover from an illness and demonstrates that occupying a sequestered and closed space promotes an experience in which internal thoughts are made so much livelier and more perceptible that they overtake all external action. While his infirm body is in a state of "Indolence and Inactivity," his "Mind be perpetually rambling."[116] Here, the contrast between bodily stasis and mental movement that characterizes Pope's "encloseted" condition stages the workings of the camera obscura insofar as *his body* serves as the room or box in its stationary state and his thoughts the projections streaming in, creating "a thousand Imaginary Entertainments abroad, in this world, & in others."[117]

Remarkable, too, in this letter, where Pope likens himself to a witch, is the exquisite state of projection that enfolds an experience of reverie. The passage, quoted at the start of this chapter, bears repeating:

> 'Tis no figure, but a serious truth I tell you when I say that my Days & Nights are so much alike, so equally insensible of any Moving Power but Fancy, that I have sometimes spoke of things in our family as Truths & real accidents, which I only Dreamt of; & again when some things that actually happen'd came into my head, have thought (till I enquired) that I had only dream'd of them. This will shew you how little I feel in this State either of Pleasure or Pain: I am fixt in a Stupid settled Medium between both.

Pope here reveals not only the proclivities that make unsurprising his later creation of a camera obscura and grotto, but also his attraction to the intense emotional states that would lead him to imagine a character such as Eloisa, a woman whose inner life also achieves great velocity and force in the dark solitude of an enclosed space.

The Voice in the Shadows

Serle's perspective image of the entryway to the grotto demonstrates how the space contributed to the "continued Tube" mentioned by the *General Magazine* visitor, the overall perspective view through the Shell Temple, sylvan arcade, and grotto passage. It also evokes the sense of psychological depth that Pope had created in *Eloisa to Abelard*. These impressions are reinforced by the poem's spatial setting and imagery—as well as its function as another type of device, a mouthpiece for the projection of a female character's voice.

As the poem's argument explains, Eloisa began writing to Abelard and renewed their ties after their devastating separation not because he wrote to her directly but because he wrote to someone else, giving "the history of his misfortune." This history includes the story of their clandestine romance, which began when he was her tutor in her uncle's house. After discovering the affair, Eloisa's uncle, for revenge, had Abelard castrated. The lovers elected to separate and devote their lives to God; he became a monk, and she a nun. The letter that Eloisa comes across awakens "all her tenderness." In this sense, Eloisa is a projection of her readers: she reads a letter not addressed to her, just as we read a letter—hers to Abelard, re-rendered as the poem itself—not addressed to us.

A Perspective View of the Grotto.

FIGURE 3.9 John Serle, "Perspective View of the Grotto,"
Plan of Mr. Pope's Garden as it was Left at his Death (1745).
Photograph: Huntington Library, San Marino, California.

And yet, the poem's status as a multiply translated document—between languages, genres, time periods, and genders—is not its only claim to depth. Depth prevails also in the poem's contents, which comprise the plausible-seeming thoughts and feelings of Eloisa herself. The poem overflows with references to the inner scenes of her mind, which resemble the images that move on the walls of Pope's grotto when he closes the doors to shut out the light: "One thought of thee puts all the pomp to flight, / Priests, tapers, temples, swim before my sight," declares Eloisa (lines 273–74).

At the same time, the poem depicts Eloisa as highly aware of the architectural context of her material reality. The walls are close and "relentless," the "cells are awful," and the "windows are dim" (lines 17, 1, 143). The "awful arches make a noon day night" (143). With its darkness and constant sense of enclosure, Eloisa's dwelling in the poem resembles not just a grotto—indeed, she refers to grottoes in her surroundings—but a camera obscura. Though dark, the "convent's solitary gloom" allows a certain degree of "solemn light" to be "shed" through "dim windows" (38, 144). Throughout, Eloisa persists in projecting her thoughts outside the walls of the Paraclete, as her religious abode, founded by Abelard, was called. And it is the grottolike conditions of her spiritual life—which in turn model the camera obscura—that bring visions of Abelard back to her, creating the illusion of his presence. These visions penetrate her consciousness and restructure her perceptual awareness:

> Fancy restores what vengeance snatched away
> Then conscience sleeps, and leaving nature free,
> All my loose soul unbounded springs to thee.
> O cursed, dear horrors of all-conscious night!
> How glowing guilt exalts the keen delight!
> Provoking demons all restraint remove,
> And stir within me every source of love.
> I hear thee, view thee, gaze o'er all thy charms,
> And round thy phantom glue my clasping arms.
> I wake—no more I hear, no more I view,
> The phantom flies me, as unkind as you.
> I call aloud, it hears not what I say;
> I stretch my empty arms; it glides away:
> To dream once more I close my willing eyes;
> Ye soft illusions, dear deceits, arise! (lines 226–40)

Published several decades after *Eloisa to Abelard*, Soame Jenyns's "A Translation of some Latin Verses on the Camera Obscura" recasts Eloisa's frustrated attempt to hold the phantom Abelard in her arms as an implied man's attempt to embrace the "beauteous maid" projected by a camera obscura:

> Again behold what lovely prospects rise!
> Now with the loveliest feast your longing eyes.
> Nor let strict modesty be here afraid
> To view upon her head a beauteous maid:
> See in small folds her waving garments flow,
> And all her slender limbs still slend'rer grow;
> Contracted in one little orb is found
> The spacious hoop, once five vast ells around;
> But think not to embrace the flying fair,
> Soon will she quit your arms unseen as air
> In this resembling too a tender maid,
> Coy to the lover's touch, and of his hand afraid.[118]

The two passages, in relation to one another—one evoking the camera obscura, the other directly referring to it—reveal the device as one that mediates desire. At the same time, though, it frustrates desire when the desiring agent attempts to touch its image.

Outpourings of emotions similar to Eloisa's emerge in Pope's letters to Lady Mary Wortley Montagu, who shattered his heart when she traveled to Turkey with her ambassador husband. In June 1717 he wrote, "There is not a day in which your Figure does not appear before me, your Conversation return to my thought, and every Scene, place, or occasion where I have enjoyed them are as livelily painted, as an Imagination equally warm & tender can be capable to represent them."[119] It is difficult not to see how this experience of being haunted by visions of an absent loved one may have inspired Pope to write *Eloisa to Abelard*, which he wrote around the time Lady Mary left on her journey. Much like the visionary experiences that being confined and sick in a small room bring, a "sort of Dream of an agreeable thing," of seeing Lady Mary when she is not actually there, that "exceeds most of the Dull Realities of [his] Life," comes about from the pain of separation.[120]

An earlier letter to Caryll suggests that such feelings as worked out and expressed through letters—to an actual recipient, unlike Cavendish's to a fictitious being—served as preparation for lodging and transmuting them in the persona of Eloisa. When asking Caryll to return his letters so that he might use the material in them for a "design" he was "lately engaged in," he revealed his awareness that writing involved several acts of processing, with letter writing as the first stage of developing the ideas that would be part of his poetry's designs. Allowing him "the freedom of [his] soul," as he put it, Pope's letter writing to friends served as a medium for projecting and containing his thoughts as they arose. Pope recognized that these thoughts, emerging in an informal manner—"throw[n] out that way"—might "save" him "a good deal of trouble" when composing his more serious pieces of writing. In choosing the words "throw out," he identifies letter writing as involving a process of projection—the projection of his inner thoughts in their moments of passing through his mind. Such writing requires a "flux of thought and invention" that is "constant" and several stages removed from the fresh spontaneity with which the ideas first emerged on the white sheet of his consciousness.[121]

But projection is further enacted in using the format of the heroic epistle to recast feelings of romantic loss. The heroic epistle, a poetic love letter written from the perspective of an illustrious female in history to a male who has betrayed or abandoned her, was first modeled by Ovid's *Heroides*. By virtue of adapting the woman's first-person point of view, the poet is impersonating her voice by ventriloquizing his, throwing his voice so that it appears to be coming from a different source. If the poem *Eloisa to Abelard* appears to be the camera obscura–like vehicle for projecting illusions of reality, including the imagined illusions of an imagined character, it does so predominantly through the medium of voice.

Further alterations take place in Pope's trademark use of heroic couplets for forming verbal expression. This use of smooth and "polished" couplets works against Pope's subject matter, the emotional and physical immediacy of Eloisa's passion, argues Murray Krieger. For him, "Pope's perfection of the couplet is a syntactical masterpiece of studied, self-conscious artifice."[122] As such, it impedes the "unbroken sweep of emotion" for Abelard that is inscribed in Eloisa's own hand, which "obeys" her heart, and in the tears that soak the surface of her letter.[123] Contemplating Abelard's name when she ought to be contemplating God, Eloisa utters at the beginning of the poem, "O write it not, my hand—the name appears / Already written—wash it out, my tears!" (lines 13–14) While the words themselves stay within the boundaries of the heroic couplet, the gestures and thoughts they describe stay in motion, overrunning those of piety.

One might argue that here, the use of couplets supports rather than blocks this emergence of interiority and character. On the one hand, J. Paul Hunter points out that a couplet on its own "seldom or never will . . . hold the full force of a developed thought, a genuinely powerful observation, or a nuanced argument." On the other, he observes that couplets work together through "building, accumulation and interaction," forming "verse paragraphs as a collection of statements and propositions that add up slowly to a meaningful whole."[124] Pope's design and construction of his grotto, with its accumulation of stones and shells arranged to create contrasts or antitheses of light and shadow or parallels of kind, made manifest not just the imaginary spaces he had previously built in his poems, but also their formal design as *poems* written in heroic couplets. These include Eloisa's "lone walls" with "moss-grown domes" and "dim windows" (lines 141–42, 144). They also include the "grotto, sheltered close from air / And screened in shades from day's detested glare" that is the Cave of Spleen in *The Rape of the Lock* (canto 4, lines 21–22), a similar setting where female psyche and remote space become conjoined and the boundary between reality and fantasy totally subverted.

In *Eloisa to Abelard*, verse paragraphs, demarcated by indented first lines, constitute each turn of Eloisa's thoughts and feelings, including her memories of the absent lover, the addressee of the verse epistle. The vehicle of the couplet, apparently limiting and close-ended on an individual level, when presented as a series turns into an aperture for the apparently unceasing flow of interiority. Accordingly, it moves through grief and turmoil, pleasure over recollecting the past, despair over the present reality, and acceptance. As a camera obscura for the projections of Eloisa's interiority, the poem channels not only her point of view, as *Upon Appleton House* does as the poet wanders through the estate, but also her voice. Steven Connor, in his history of ventriloquism, points out the integral relationship between voice and space when he observes, "The voice always requires and requisitions space, the distance that allows my voice to go from and return to myself."[125] In the case of Eloisa, her voice projects from a space of enclosure that influences her state and passage of mind. Without this space her voice would not be heard.

What Pope recognized first in *Eloisa to Abelard* and realized later in the setting of his own life is that the virtual realities we create through our physical surroundings and built environments constitute the very grounds of that elusive entity we call interiority. This interiority is, in turn, most readily perceived in a camera obscura, or in camera obscura–like conditions. As Locke had pointed out, the camera obscura exists *as* our own minds, meaning its phantasmagoric projections define the inner experiences of our outer realities.

In 1820 a movable picture book appeared called *The Natuorama; or, Nature's Endless Transposition of Views on the Thames*, affirming both the celebrity of the grotto and its enduring influence.[126] It is a box disguised as a book, a self-proclaimed "novelty" promising, on the inside of its cover, "a moveable scene of Pope in his grotto." An outer frame depicts the grotto, with Pope seated on the right; under the frame, the reader may pass a series of eighteen boards bearing hand-colored views of the Thames, all allegedly from the perspective of Pope in his grotto (some in fact show portions of the river far from Twickenham). *The Natuorama*, in attempting to replicate the camera obscura experience of Pope's grotto, suggests the portability of that experience, as well as a capacity to manufacture his point of view. By experimenting with the book-object form as a virtual space to stand for the place of Pope's grotto—which itself functioned as a medium of virtual space—*The Natuorama* serves as a form of biography that reconstructs the grotto's vision from the poet's point of view. Here, in other words, is a material recreation of the moving external images of individualized perspective from an interior location that, by this time in literary history, had been realized in the novels of Frances Burney, Ann Radcliffe, and Jane Austen.

Before the publication of *The Natuorama*, a visitor to Pope's grotto drew their own sketch of the passing boats on the Thames from its porch. The sketch, like the interior view of a grotto and its waterworks that may be Pope's, found in the Huntington Library's copy of John Serle's *Plan of*

Mr. Pope's Garden (as mentioned earlier in this chapter), appears in an extra-illustrated copy of the Andrew Foulis 1785 edition of Pope's collected works held in the Pierpont Morgan Library.[127] Like *The Naturorama*, the sketch uses the outermost opening of Pope's grotto as not just a frame but an optical perspective for viewing the scene outside. The illustration, unskilled in its execution, captures realistic details such as the gate at the mouth of the grotto and the ancient willow tree growing directly in front of the entrance. The river appears much closer to the grotto's opening than it is in reality, and the tree appears so disproportionately large that it blocks somewhat the view of the boats directly behind it. Rather than detracting from the image, these naïve touches speak to the individual perspective that visualized the scene. It is a perspective made possible by the physical structure of the grotto, which operated as a visualizing device, much as the camera obscura does.

In creating garden spaces such as his grotto, and retreating to it, Pope made manifest spatial forms that were responsive to his inner states and impressions while simultaneously shaping them. The effects these spaces created were so powerful and inviting that they became sought after by others who wished to experience them too. As much as these forms drew on the same principles of "building, accumulation and interaction" that characterize Pope's heroic verse, they also contributed to and participated in the growing cultural energies from which the novel emerged. This is a literary genre, after all, that also offered the potential for expansive plotting, new devices for showing perspective, and new rooms for the sustained containment of internal consciousness.

Similarly, in his recreation and mediation of a historical female's subject position in a specific space and time, Pope as much takes on the classical conventions of the Ovidian heroic epistle as he contributes to a body of literature in his own period that locates in enclosed spaces projective settings intended to mediate the interiority of imagined subjects. Samuel Richardson's *Pamela*, also an epistolary text told from the perspective of a female writer of passionate letters residing in confinement and enclosures, and sometimes experiencing hallucinations, was published four years before Pope's death in 1744. Whereas Pope himself created spatial forms in both literature and landscape architecture, in the case of Richardson's novel, it is the fictional representation of a young servant girl who finds the spatial forms for possessive interiority. She does so via portable forms of containment and enclosure that overcome her lack of access to landed property. These function as her movable forms of property and her spatial forms of possessive interiority.

✳ 4 ✳

Pocket

PAMELA'S MOBILE SETTINGS
AND SPATIAL FORMS

Oh! my dear Father and Mother, my wicked Master had hid himself,
base Gentleman as he is! in her Closet, where she has a few Books, and
Chest of Drawers, and such-like.

'Shut the Door, Pamela, and come to me in my Closet.'

but he then sat down, and took me by both my Hands, and said, Well
said, my pretty *Pamela, if you can help it*: But I will not let you help it. Tell
me, Are they in your Pocket? No, Sir, said I, my Heart up at my Mouth.
Said he, I know you won't tell a downright *Fib* for the World. . . . Answer
me then, Are they in *neither* of your Pockets?

SAMUEL RICHARDSON, *Pamela*

To focus on Samuel Richardson's first novel, *Pamela* (1740), is to return attention to a work that helps make it possible to speak today of the novel as
both a genre and an artifact of the everyday.[1] As *Pamela* tracks the movements of its heroine's thoughts and feelings in response to the events and
circumstances around her, it takes pains to show that they happen within
the spaces of daily domestic life. Innovative use of such common forms
of diurnal writing as the letter and the diary, the presentation of a servant
girl as the author of the letters, and the book's setting amid household life
bolster its status as a classic narrative of the everyday. Following Nancy
Armstrong's *Desire and Domestic Fiction*, criticism has subsumed Richardson's novel under the subgenre of "domestic fiction." Indeed, that label and "domestic realism" have been used for the kind of fiction *Pamela*
represents, though not by one of its most influential critics, Ian Watt.[2]
Never employing the term himself, Watt nevertheless identifies narratives that use as a setting the domestic interior with the innovation of
representational technique in fiction, a "more elaborate representational

technique than fiction had ever seen before," which entails the "remarkable opening up of the new domain of private experience for literary exploration."[3] We encountered earlier, in the introduction, Watt's equation of mind and home as he spells out the relationship between "the delineation of the domestic life and the private experience of the characters who belong to it."[4]

Richardson's critics have almost always equated the domestic environments of his fiction with his modern realist style. In doing so, they draw attention to the way his technique enlists different permutations of the word *setting*, whether as a noun or a verb that provides the format for where and how actions take place, or as the way in which different entities are held and arranged in space. In his hands, "the moated castle is changed to a modern parlour," observed Anna Laetitia Barbauld in 1804. The figures within this new narrative setting are transferred too, from "the princess and her pages to a lady and her domestics, or even to a simple maiden, without birth or fortune."[5] Barbauld implicated the novelty of Richardson's realism with his choice of *setting* his narratives in the spaces of contemporary domestic life. She foregrounded this notion further by comparing his style with the astonishing realism of Dutch Golden Age painting: by laboring to provide minute details "in the most lively manner," Richardson allows his readers to see "every circumstance" described.[6] In making this comparison with seventeenth-century Dutch painting, Barbauld highlights the intermedial relationship between Richardson's novels and a celebrated visual tradition of domestic interiors that preceded and anticipated them.

The point of contact between the visual and textual media is not so much their shared subjects—scenes from domestic life—as the action they take in "setting" the circumstantial details that constitute those scenes. In representing a woman writing, a Dutch painter might depict the smocking on the shoulder of her robe, or the brass studs on the back of the chair she sits on. Likewise, in representing a young man spying on his pretty maid as she confides in her fellow servant, Richardson observes, through Pamela's epistolary viewpoint, the "few Books" and the "Chest of Drawers" stored inside the "wicked Closet" in which he hides, as well as the "rich silk and silver Morning Gown" he is wearing as he rushes out of it.[7] In both cases, such details create a sense of "the environment or surroundings in which a person or thing is 'set.'"[8] In the latter, two perspectival settings determine the dynamics within the scene: the predatory closet from which Mr. B spies on Pamela, and the space of the letter that is used as Pamela's device for projecting her domestic narrative of sexual intrusion.

Despite its apparent function of fixing people, objects, and stories in place, the act of setting such entities in a material environment in fact releases their potential for movement, transformation, and reflection. It does so, above all, by making more vivid the experience of a fictional character's inner life. As Watt explains, in early fiction, an unprecedented amount of "circumambient detail" fostered an unusual sense of intimacy with the private experiences of the human figures inhabiting a work's physical settings. "We have to pick significant items of character and behaviour out of a wealth of circumambient detail," he writes, "much as in real life we attempt to gather meaning from the casual flux of circumstance."[9] Without this physical detail and the vantage points it furnishes, it would be far less possible to perceive the material world and its features as they are perceived by the characters, and as they intersect with their thoughts and feelings.

"The great excellence of Richardson's novels consists in . . . the unparalleled minuteness and copiousness of his descriptions," claimed Francis Jeffrey in the *Edinburgh Review* in 1805.[10] Jeffrey builds on Barbauld's insights of the previous year by naming the effect of intimacy to which she gestures with her visual reference to Dutch painting when he invokes the social experience of visiting a home in which an "appointment" must be made, and in which we "see and hear only what we know has been prepared for our reception." No such appointment is necessary, he insists, when reading Richardson. With his fictional works, we, like Mr. B in the closet of Pamela's bedchamber, "slip invisible, into the domestic privacy of his characters, and hear and see every thing that is said and done among them, and whether it be interesting or otherwise, and whether it gratify our curiosity or disappoint it."[11]

In the imagery Barbauld and Jeffrey develop to describe Richardson's writing, not only is realism tied directly with the privacy of domestic life but, in addition, the novelist's creation, camera obscura–like, serves as an alternate space for that life. As architectural critic Aaron Betsky observes, "The space of fiction is the space where appearances and control meet to create an alternative narrative to the activities of everyday life. It is another world, but a world that one cannot inhabit, a space in which one can be only literally, not actually, at home."[12] Though Mr. B proves unable to stand inside the room of Pamela's mind, her readers have a far easier time, accessing it through the letters that give it form and that make up the very narrative they are holding in their hands and reading. Within the narrative itself, these letters, in effect, serve as portable spaces of interiority— traveling camera obscuras that enclose and screen projections of their author's internal life in an unbroken stream that emerges on the page. In contrast with the vehicles and spaces of interiority examined in previous chapters, the interiority offered by epistolary spaces that actually get delivered (unlike those in Cavendish's *Sociable Letters*) reveals a culture where interiority has been so internalized as a facet of everyday life that its spaces have become small and portable. Like Cavendish's books, letters are detachable from their original contexts in domestic architecture. But unlike Cavendish's large folio-size volumes, letters, whether sent individually or bound together as fiction in small duodecimo volumes, could be carried inside pockets.

The alternative home presented by fiction—its entrance most readily accessed when the minds of characters serve as the windows or apertures through which one views its details—is as virtual as one that might be projected by a camera obscura. As tradesman cards for optical instrument makers, accounts of grand tours, paintings, and surviving models of varying sizes and designs indicate, portable camera obscuras were a familiar commodity item throughout the eighteenth century.[13] John Cuff, optician and spectacle and microscope maker—self-identified as such on his trade card—advertised portable camera obscuras for "exhibiting prospects in their natural proportions and colours, together with the motions of living Subjects" a few years before the publication of *Pamela*.[14] In 1747 he had printed the poem "Verses, Occasion'd by the Sight of a Chamera Obscura," which describes how "instantaneous Beauties gild the Scene" when "spread[ing] the Paper Screen" toward the garden.[15]

Demonstrating how small the device could be, and how early it appeared, is an English handheld camera obscura of 7⅝ by 3 inches in the History of Science Museum, Oxford. Its dimensions, in fact, are very close to those of the standard duodecimo novel. The gold-tooled vellum and pasteboard covering its boxwood tubes is a decorative feature found on English telescopes and microscopes of 1700–1720, and recalls the gold tooling that might appear on the most elaborate book bindings of the period. With models as small as novels themselves, eighteenth-century consumers had at least the two options—novel or camera obscura—for handheld diversions from everyday life. The smaller size of such spaces ensured that those who wished to experience these items in private could do so by carrying them to places where no one would intrude upon them.

The essential movement that accompanies the experience of reading novels is one of entering interiors that move. It is as much the reader's mind as the fictive home that is "slip[ped] invisible, into," to repeat Jeffrey's words. As glimpsed earlier, in chapter 2, with Cavendish's brains and houses on the move—the vivid figures she uses for the bibliographic products of her mental labor—movement is as much a feature of the es-

FIGURE 4.1 English pocket-size camera obscura (ca. 1700–1720). Length,
7⅝ in. (19.4 cm) with lens retracted, 10⅞ in. (27.6 cm) with lens extended.
Pasteboard, vellum, wood, glass. Inv. 75945. Photograph
© History of Science Museum, University of Oxford.

sential portability of minds themselves as it is of the material form in which the novel's domestic interiors are set: the book.[16] The very definition of a book hinges on its essential characteristic as a portable container of information that can be conveyed to many recipients.[17]

But other portable interiors are entered into, sent, and carried throughout Richardson's novel, and throughout the reader's experience of reading it or another novel. What remain to be unpacked are the concrete affordances of such interiors—the detachable pockets of eighteenth-century women's dress, in particular, which carry the letters. In turn, letters emulate the function of pockets by containing and carrying items of value. Items placed in pockets might be set apart for preservation and use; so too in the case of letters, where items might likewise be set apart for preservation, and for sharing with a designated recipient. Examining the characteristics of pockets and letters in these terms allows us to understand how such objects serve as domestic spaces in themselves, housing and enclosing the owner's personal possessions along with the flow of her mind's contents, even when they are at first perceived as things.[18] Pockets, like letters, function, that is, as spatial forms of her possessive interiority.

What is said of architecture can be said of other spatial interiors, such as detachable pockets. Architectural plans and architecture certainly structure how people take up space, but they also influence how everyday events take place, observes Robin Evans. Architecture, moreover, transcends the functions of art and literature, not only because it is useful but because it is entangled with everyday life and shapes social relations.[19] Removable pockets' designs and formats afforded their users specific modes of privacy in everyday practices, much as those of rooms in domestic architecture do their occupants. Both kinds of spaces define the social relations and conditions of their users and dwellers, including the privacy they facilitate.

By examining interpenetrations between the portable spaces of interiority in material culture and a work regarded as the prototype for domestic fiction (the very fiction of dwelling), this chapter contributes to the project of incorporating mobility into the concept of dwelling that Tim Ingold formulates. His notion of dwelling, which so often "carries an aura of snug, well-wrapped localism," needs to accommodate the "primacy of movement" and the ways in which "humans and non-humans make their ways in the world." Indeed, for Ingold, "wayfaring is the fundamental mode by which living beings inhabit the earth."[20] Nancy Armstrong first made possible the understanding that the novel as a genre, and Richardson's novel in particular, rendered the interiorized female subject the paradigmatic middle-class subject of modernity. This insight has made it possible to examine more deeply the material and embodied means by which such a process took place.[21] These are the means, that is, by which homes become female domains—not so much through processes of social inscription, whether through conduct books or political theory but, rather, through the subjective process of making one's way to dwell in material surroundings by way of their affordance. Therein, diverse and movable spaces of interiority to call one's own might be found.

Property's Forms: Space, Mind, and Body in Motion

The historical backdrop for this chapter, in contrast with previous ones, sees the novel's rise as a popular literary genre coinciding with a period of transition surrounding notions of property in English political-economic history. While landed property prevailed throughout the eighteenth century as England's "dominant social, political, and ideological paradigm," the movable properties of a rapidly expanding market economy—its "commodities, stocks, credits"—created a new one.[22] Unlike its economic situation in the nineteenth century, however, during which landed property's social and political influence waned, England in the eighteenth century supported a close relationship between state and society, with landed property as its medium. Through landed property, "private rights and public legitimacy" remained integrated in eighteenth-century England. In the seventeenth century, ideas about property defining government authority and the English constitution had comprised the core of politics and its language.[23] At the same time, property in Western society has traditionally been viewed as "both an extension and prerequisite of personality" that also gives its owner the means for autonomy and independence.[24] In the seventeenth-century background is the fact that *property* and *propriety* were interchangeable; in this way, property was a "juridical term before it was an economic one" and held both meanings of "that to which one properly had a claim" and "that which was properly one's own."[25] The semantic continuity between "propriety" and "property" that J. G. A. Pocock identifies in seventeenth-century political writing pertains to Richardson's eighteenth-century narrative insofar as it presents virtue as a female subject's right to own, which in turn has economic and narrative consequences.

Throughout *Essay Concerning Human Understanding*, Locke depicts the acquisition of knowledge as a process "remarkably parallel to the acquisition of private property."[26] Such ideas ushered in the modern subject in the last quarter of the seventeenth century. When defining what it means for this subject to be modern, Armstrong and Leonard Tennenhouse use terms of everydayness that are similar to Watt's specifications of the novel's characteristics. For example, generating the novel's form are minds belonging to "uniquely individuated and yet conspicuously ordinary" characters. After Locke, this form of subjectivity would emerge in the household, wherein "power of the state ended and that of the individual began." According to Armstrong and Tennenhouse, the ordinariness of the individual subject that developed at the time registered in her gender: the mind issuing the novel is "so ordinary, in fact, it could eventually be housed within a female body."[27] Their claim coheres with the change in the meaning of "virtue" that occurred during the time in which *Pamela* was written. *Pamela* plays out the cultural development whereby virtue transforms from a civic trait upheld by men of property to a condition previously known as female chastity.[28] Virtue, in other words, mutated from a general moral quality to a sexual one that young women in particular had great incentive to uphold as a qualification for entering the marriages that would ensure economic and social survival and advantage. As such, it operated as a form of movable private property both for the families of the young women and for the young women themselves.[29]

Not merely reflecting views on the nature of property and virtue,

Richardson's novel intervenes in the wider discourse on property of his time, especially the distinction between its "movable" and "immovable" forms.[30] Whereas landed property may be viewed as representing "older conceptions of identity and wealth," and movable property the products of eighteenth-century England's new commercial economy, neither, Wolfram Schmidgen maintains, should be viewed as all that distinct from the other. At the same time, rather than a decisive shift, as some historians might suggest, with movable property dramatically supplanting immovable as the basis for social and political power, eighteenth-century England occupied a moment of economic and political transition.[31] It would not be until the Victorian period that movable property would thoroughly displace immovable property as the basis for wealth, independence, and influence.[32] Taking Schmidgen's point that the boundary between movable and immovable properties was more elastic than others have allowed—"commodities can be immovable, land can be movable"—we see that the interchange between these forms of property also accounts for the transformative energies that create narrative and social-political movement in *Pamela*. Unlike Schmidgen, who argues against making a distinction between spaces and objects and subsumes landed property under the category of "object," I insist on space as the prevailing category. For Schmidgen, Mr. B's Lincolnshire estate would function economically and politically in a manner similar to Pamela's detachable pockets: as a movable object to carry and maneuver, as a venue for action, or for reflection. Yet, Mr. B's Lincolnshire estate functions very much as a space—a venue for action and reflection—as does the pocket itself throughout the novel. The fluid relationship between movable and immovable properties and the question of what constitutes such properties, as well as who has the right to own, access, and inhabit their spaces, illuminate the political stakes of interiority in its diverse locations throughout Richardson's novel.

Servants and workers in eighteenth-century England, like Richardson's heroine, commonly used portable enclosures such as locked boxes and trunks to contain their belongings and safeguard their privacy in shared accommodations. In this scenario, which concerns working-class subjects, we see a more fully realized sense of privacy that is entirely portable, after having traveled from country house and writing closet to grotto in previous chapters. Having the ability to keep something private if one chooses is what turns an entity into property, whether movable or immovable. Privacy itself was a basic component of individual identity in the eighteenth century. As such, it comprised "the safety of one's defences, the separateness of one's concerns and the preservation of the things of one's own," as Amanda Vickery puts it.[33] The spread of such devices as keys and locks throughout the period not only registers the intricacy of legal attitudes toward what constitutes theft or burglary (only locked premises could be viewed as being "broken into") but suggests greater investment in securing one's privacy as a form of property in itself. The continuity in the relationship between privacy and property forms the material basis of individuation in *Pamela* and its key feature of portability.

"Portable" in the eighteenth century meant both movable and handheld. Whereas Ephraim Chambers's *Cyclopædia* in 1728 defined *portable* as "something easy of carriage," Samuel Johnson's *Dictionary* in 1755–1756 defined it in its first entry as "manageable by hand." Both senses of "portability," its mobility and its manual, handheld qualities, are operative in my argument. Trading on the space of interiority in a portable object such as Pamela's detachable pockets, Richardson's novel internalizes as its own narrative rhythm the unceasing movement of inanimate yet movable goods that drove eighteenth-century England's thriving consumer culture. The novel was a literary genre written for and read by those same middling classes that fueled England's increased mercantile activities and propelled the motion of movable properties. In its printed manifestation in the eighteenth century, its small duodecimo or octavo format, the novel was a handheld object that could be carried close to the body and that, when read, detached the reader from her immediate surroundings to an intimate space inside her own head.

The diminutive and portable features of the eighteenth-century novel emerged as a critical aspect of its experience and popularity: "What was rising in the early eighteenth century, in early eighteenth-century eyes, was not so much a distinctively *novelistic* fiction as a distinctively *portable* fiction," claims Deidre Lynch.[34] She also argues that literary history, especially after the Romantics, has overemphasized the eighteenth-century novel's properties as a genre devoted to the portrayal of inner life in private domestic spaces. Such overemphasis comes at the cost of recognizing another, equally pervasive movement of commercial exchange, vehicular transport, and social mobility that also attended the novel's generic development and reception.[35]

I do not disagree but would suggest that focusing on the mobility and portability inherent in the commercial practices and material features of the eighteenth-century novel need not preclude the qualities critics have noted ever since its emergence: its apparent predisposition to "domestic realism and the exploration of private spaces and psychological depths."[36] Placing novels and individual selves in commercial relationships and exchanges may seem to set them in motion, definitively taking them *out-*

side the spaces of inner life or home. Yet the evidence of material culture explored in this chapter shows that those spaces of inwardness and interiority also travel and move along with the novel and its reader in both their outward and inward trajectories, especially in the practice of novel reading.[37]

In the same work where Barbauld extols Richardson's narrative technique by comparing his skill with that of a Dutch painter, she demonstrates his popularity by recounting that "even at Ranelagh [pleasure garden], those who remember the publication say, it was usual for ladies to hold up the volumes of Pamela to one another, to shew they had got the book that everyone was talking of."[38] On one hand, such descriptions of the novel's social impact support Lynch's argument by showing that the novel functioned as a form of social currency—and one that manifested literally, not just metaphorically, in that eighteenth-century readers carried and held up physical copies of the book as a form of social exchange. On the other hand, the fact that the anecdote appears in the same work that emphasizes Richardson's intimate portrayal of domestic life reveals that the private spaces of home—its dressing rooms, libraries, and kitchens—can be brought out and carried into the public spaces of pleasure gardens.

The Interiority of Domestic Detail

Even in eighteenth-century fiction not generally recognized as domestic, the idiom of domesticity emerged as one of the standards by which commentators measured its realism, its ability to seem like life itself. For instance, Tobias Smollett, who conceived of his picaresque fiction as part satire and part romance improved, articulated the novel's destination, in moving "near" and "nearer" to its readers, as "home." He writes in his preface to *The Adventures of Roderick Random* (1748), "Of all kinds of satire, there is none so entertaining, and universally improving, as that which is introduced, as it were, occasionally, in the course of an interesting story, which brings every incident home to life."[39] Not only is the destination rendered as domestic and intimate, despite the picaresque genre of Smollett's fiction, so are scenes represented that are "familiar," yet represented "in an uncommon and amusing point of view." Publishing under the pseudonym Thomas Thoughtless, a later commentator, in 1793, writes, despite his satirical-sounding name, a sober assessment of what constitutes the novel genre. He echoes Smollett's domestic idiom when he claims that "the impressions upon the Mind, which *Truth* invariably gives to Narrative, by bringing every incident home to Life, must, out of all Reach of Comparison, be greater."[40] In his reformulation of Smollett's notion of fiction as a vehicle for "bringing every incident home to life," Thoughtless presents truth as the factor that allows narrative to make "impressions upon the Mind." He makes plain that the act of bringing incidents home, in conflating the space of the home with that of the mind, is nothing short of a definition for the workings of narrative realism.

Richardson produced verisimilitude in all three of his novels by noting the "particulars" of the domestic settings, from Mr. B's country houses in Bedfordshire and Lincolnshire, to Clarissa Harlowe's family mansion, to Grandison Hall in *Sir Charles Grandison*. In *Pamela*, Richardson is just as attentive to the "ink in a broken China Cup" hiding in Pamela's closet (112), her carefully selected and organized bundles of clothing, and Mr. B's library and elbow chair as he is to the initial impression of Mr. B's Lincolnshire home on Pamela's freshly aggrieved mind:

> About Eight at Night we enter'd the Court-yard of this handsome, large, old, and lonely Mansion, that looks made for Solitude and Mischief, as I thought, by its Appearance, with all its brown nodding Horrors of lofty Elms and Pines about it; And here, said I to myself, I fear, is to be the Scenes of my Ruin, unless God protect me, who is all-sufficient! (108–9)

Almost every aspect of this short passage, with its temporal and spatial specificities, displays the properties of Watt's formal realism. After noting the time of day, the passage reveals the appearance of the country house estate not so much as it is, but as Pamela, the fictional character, perceives it to be. Her perceptions of the "lofty" trees as "brown nodding Horrors" and the house as "made for Solitude and Mischief" can only belong to someone in her situation.

In this passage, she has recently discovered that she has been kidnapped by Mr. B instead of being transported back to her parents' home, as he had promised her would happen. The house she is encountering is indeed a prospective "scene of [her] ruin." Her interior utterances, moreover—thoughts to herself rendered as speech: "And here, said I to myself, I fear, . . ."—tell us that this perception is rooted in the context of a broader narrative. Viewing the image of Mr. B's Lincolnshire home through her eyes, we have entered the space of a different home, the dark room of Pamela's mind, and yet that mental home is in motion and stands in exterior relationship to the house that it perceives, which is not yet her physical home. Indeed, the shaping of Pamela's identity as eventual mistress of the house that she first views as a prison—the very narrative force that allows such a circumstance to happen—depends on her occupying an outsider perspective in relation to the property.

A diary written in 1762 by John Parnell, a young man visiting southern England from Dublin, similarly develops interiority by regarding the domestic setting from the outside, suggesting a general cultural predilection toward fusing interior experiences with the perception of domestic design belonging to others. The experience of domestic realism, in other words, was a feature of day-to-day life, and not only of novels. The material in the diary, Parnell explains, was copied out from notes he made in another notebook while in the moving enclosure of a coach. This original notebook functioned as a portable receptacle in which he recorded, while visiting many local country house estates, his impressions of the houses, especially their landscape design, and occasionally accompanied his detailed descriptions with sketches.[41]

Parnell's observations have a prosaic quality: "Shipton is an ugly old town, remarkable for nothing as I could find, but good Bread and Butter."[42] Most compelling is a statement he makes when visiting one of the great houses in Richmond: "Ill not pretend to go through the appartments regularly but just mention what struck *me* most as I make it a rule to set down nothing here from any other person's observation as my own." Just as he recognizes the distinctive character of each house he visits and assiduously notes the physical traits that create it, he comes into his own character by recording his subjective responses—"what struck *me* most"—in the notebook he carries with him, much as Marvell shares his own responses and perceptions in his tour of Nun Appleton. That the houses he contemplates and explores belong to others matters little when he has ownership of the thoughts that emerge out of his encounters with them. As they run through his mind in response to the encountered sights, these thoughts are internalized and captured in his portable notebook, which functions like a camera obscura that is able to preserve its impressions.

The space of private property (the house) and the space of private consciousness (the mind) similarly interpenetrate throughout Locke's *An Essay Concerning Human Understanding*. Locke uses metaphors of domestic architecture and household management to describe consciousness and its operations. Understanding, for instance, is an activity of "getting": it "get[s] all the ideas it has," even as ideas also simply "come into the mind."[43] The objective for such "getting" is to "furnish" and "stock" the understanding "with ideas" (150). Through reflecting "on its own operations," the mind deepens the "impressions" of ideas such that they turn from "floating visions" into "clear distinct lasting ideas" (107). Such deep-

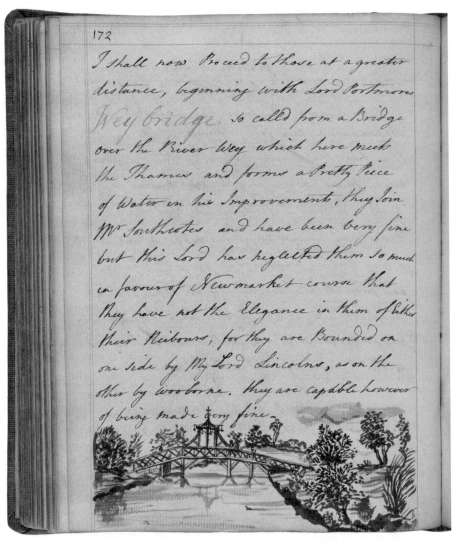

172

I shall now Proceed to those at a greater distance, beginning with Lord Portmores Wey bridge So called from a Bridge over the River Wey which here meets the Thames and forms a Pretty Peice of Water in his Improvements, they Join Mr Southcotes and have been very fine but this Lord has neglected them So much in favour of Newmarket course that they have not the Elegance in them of either their Neibours, for they are Bounded on one side by My Lord Lincolns, as on the other by Wooborne, they are capable however of being made very fine —

FIGURE 4.2 An illustrated page from John Parnell, "An account of the many
fine seats of noblemen etc. I have seen with other observations made
during my residence in [southern] England" (1763) (M.a.11).
Photograph used by permission of the Folger Shakespeare Library.

ening aids the retaining faculty that turns the mind into a "repository," the
space of memory itself, for the "laying up of our Ideas" (150). Therein
ideas may be "lodg'd," Locke writes, his most decisive representation of
the understanding and memory as domestic space (56, 153). Before such
lodgers arrive, the mind is a "yet empty Cabinet" (55).

In his signature image of the mind as a sheet of white paper, Locke presents it also as the ultimate destination for the material world's stock-taking:

Let us then suppose the Mind to be, as we say, white Paper, void of all Characters, without any *Ideas*; How comes it to be furnished? Whence comes it by that vast store, which the busy and boundless Fancy of Man has painted on it, with an almost endless variety? (104)

The mind is as much an interior space to "furnish" and "store" with ideas as it is a flat surface on which to write with "Characters" or "paint." "White paper" here connotes not only writing paper but also the camera obscura, whose screen was often white paper. Although several scholars have discerned a reference to the camera obscura in Locke's passage on the mind as a "Closet wholly shut from light," none appear to have noticed that this passage too, with its image of the mind as a blank surface, comes to have "the busy and boundless Fancy of Man" not written but *"painted* on it." Given that the camera obscura's act of projecting images onto a screen was at the time likened to an act of "painting," Locke's choice of words—painting in a dark room—is critical. In its work of mediating interiority, the camera obscura figured prominently as a correlate to writing as well as painting.

At the same time, the very equivocation between room and paper as projective as well as inscriptional space is a critical model for the work eighteenth-century novels accomplish in their designs of everyday life and its interiority. Whereas one white-paper medium may serve as a substrate for a permanent record (writing), the other offers only a fleeting one (the camera obscura projection). With *Pamela*, Richardson experimented with a textual strategy for transforming the flat substance of an inscribed sheet of paper into the empirical structure of mind as a fully dimensional room, as much like a storehouse as a camera obscura, which is to say, a camera obscura with the capacity to make lasting records. This textual strategy was epistolary narrative.

For Richardson, as for his characters Pamela and Mr. B, the seemingly flat medium of letters is an extension for the interior chambers of a female mind and body. The pen and the printing press—implements that penetrate and cover surfaces with characters—effect both the metamorphosis of white paper into the interior space of the camera obscura and the preservation of its impressions. Within this space, materials of daily experience, such as the lists of objects denoting Pamela's interior motivations and physical circumstances, are not just stockpiled but projected, as moving representations in a dark room. The store is "painted" onto, the verb favored for describing the means by which a camera obscura's images are made to appear on the projection wall or screen. Yet in this passage, Locke allows for a measure of stability, insofar as the ideas that enter the mind constitute a "store." From mind back to actual page, the act of stockpiling transforms writing itself into rooms filled with objects—arranged into sentences, shelved in rows of paragraphs, and ultimately housed inside book covers—that document experience and internalize it while making it available for public consumption.[44]

Locke's ideas are crucial for the relationship they draw not only between land and body as forms of property, but also between body and mind as interrelated domains of the individual self. As his exploration of consciousness and its relation to the body in a state of sleep reveals, the body is the permanent container for the mind, which continues in a state of movement and activity even when the body remains still (114). The connections between body, mind, room, paper, writing, and property propel the narrative movement of Richardson's *Pamela* as they do Locke's theory of mind. Countless episodes in the novel demonstrate this; perhaps the most direct and evocative are the two separate times Mr. B enters Pamela's chamber at night to spy on her. He does this once at his Bedfordshire estate when she is still employed as his servant, and once at his Lincolnshire estate when she is his prisoner. While Mr. B's intrusion in Pamela's private space is putatively undertaken to attempt to rape her, his reactions to the experience reveal that he garners more than the possibilities of sexual conquest. He as much seeks possession of her thoughts as he does possession of her body, acquiring them as if to fill the contents of his mind with hers. Whereas throughout the novel he attempts to acquire those thoughts through the movable medium of her letters, in the attempted rape scenes he does so by entering the room where she reveals her thoughts in speech and dialogue. Because such revelations take place where and when she removes her clothes in preparation for bed, the act of speaking candidly about recent past events is equated with the act of undressing, and the architectural function of the bedroom, encoded as "private," is its medium.

The "textual world" of *Pamela* enacts the tense interactions of immovable and movable property vying to be the basis of ideological control. That the novel's central tensions concern ownership and control over property—namely, over Pamela's body and letters—further makes debatable the notion that because the novel takes place within a domestic context, its female subject is removed from the "public" arena of politics to which men belong.[45] Pamela's letters and pockets, movable property that, in the absence of actual rooms that are hers, she turns into private enclosures and spaces of her own, constitute her spatial forms and basis of possessive interiority.

Certainly, the fact that movable property—Pamela's material possessions and her virtuous body—can function as a significant form of property at all challenges the basis of Mr. B's power over her and others of her class and gender. His power rests on, apart from his own class and gender, his ownership of the putatively immovable property, the landed estate, where she is employed and imprisoned. Without some type of conflict, there can be no narrative; it is the as yet unresolved tension between these forms of movable and immovable property, which are also different forms of space, that drives Richardson's narrative forward.

Pockets of Interiority

In *Pamela*, the material object that functions as a container for an interiority that crosses public and private spaces through its portability is not so much Pamela's collection of handwritten letters, which, on their own, too easily become dispersed, but her pair of detachable pockets. The transfer of Pamela's letters from her pockets to Mr. B's pocket facilitates the intersubjective exchange that causes Mr. B to begin viewing Pamela not as sexual prey for his consumption, but as an individual subject worthy of becoming his wife.[46] The whole estate of Pamela's personhood and the interiority it entails is best maintained, Richardson thus shows, when mediated by her pockets. The narrative continually tracks what things such as letters, money, and keys go into and what they come out of: pockets. They are used not just to hide things and protect them from view but also to propel the plot and carry its contents. The first pocket in the book appears in the first letter, which begins the narrative (12).[47] Pamela's sending some of the contents of her lady's pocket, the money that is distributed among the servants, serves as one of the reasons for writing this operative letter. The money itself is enclosed in "one of the little Pill-boxes" given to her by her lady, "wrap't close in Paper, that they mayn't chink" when brought to her parents by John, the household's footman (12). Later, she writes to her parents, when preparing to return to them, "I Write again, tho', may-be, I shall bring it to you in my Pocket myself," making her pocket the projected vehicle for the epistolary observations she is making at that very moment (82).

Other characters also own and use pockets, including, as just mentioned, Pamela's mistress. Taking things out of and placing things into pockets are narrative actions that might go unnoticed, but they are critical to creating the layers of interiority that make up Richardson's depiction of domestic realism and its perpetual dramas of concealment and exposure. Just as objects go into and come out of pockets throughout the novel, bodies enter and leave rooms and closets, with doors opening and shutting—all actions that control access to states of interiority.

Since at least the last quarter of the seventeenth century, women of all classes in eighteenth-century England and America had worn pockets that were not sewn into their garments, as they were for men, but instead hung from a fabric ribbon that was tied around the waist and hidden from view. In costume history these pockets are called "detachable pockets," "detached pockets," or "tie-on pockets." Their detached status meant the wearer could wear them or not as desired, and wear them with different garments. Detachable pockets were mainly worn in pairs but sometimes as a single pocket. Earlier, from the Middle Ages to the end of the sixteenth century, European men and women had worn bags visibly hanging from girdles. One costume historian claims it was the brief appearance of the bustle on women's gowns in the late seventeenth century that first afforded the space to conceal detachable pockets in a woman's dress construction.[48] Detachable pockets remained in use through most of the eighteenth century, losing ground between 1790 and 1820 to reticules, which gave way to the handbags that replaced detachable pockets entirely by 1840.

This moment in European costume history, in which detachable pockets worn concealed under skirts became more popular than the external bags, receptacles, and purses that enjoyed favor both beforehand and after, coincided with a new concept of femininity, wherein interiority and private property were interlinked. Placed between the outer and inner garments of a woman's dress, detachable pockets were worn at an intermediary position: under the outer gown and upper petticoat, and above the under petticoat and shift. The Lady Clapham doll in the Victoria and Albert Museum shows where the pocket was situated within the layers of a woman's standard dress. Imperceptible overlaid slits in the outer skirt and petticoat afforded access to the pockets and the items stored inside them. The passage for the hand to the inner regions of eighteenth-century women's attire suggests as well a channel to their selfhoods. Some of course point out that, with their slits, oval or flasklike shape, and proximity to a woman's private parts, detachable pockets also resemble a woman's internal sexual anatomy. The satirical mezzotint *Tight Lacing, or Fashion before Ease* conveys the sexual implications of such propinquity as it shows the woman's pocket in use, in a state of pear-shaped fullness, hanging against the thigh, with its long slit facing the viewer.

Costume historian Ariane Fennetaux evocatively describes the close-

TIGHT LACING, or FASHION before EASE.
From the Original Picture by John Collet, in the possession of the Proprietors.

FIGURE 4.3 *Tight Lacing, or Fashion before Ease* (ca. 1777).
Hand-colored mezzotint (777.00.00.10). Photograph: Courtesy of
the Lewis Walpole Library, Yale University.

ness of women's detachable pockets to the body: "Made in soft materials,
and worn close to the body, pockets were in direct contact with the wearer's body warmth and scent with which they would have come imbued.
Soft and warm when worn, they became almost organic extensions of the
self."[49] The stains on an English block-printed pocket of 1720–1730 from

Winterthur suggest this, while indicating the ways in which pockets—
and any historical garment—are organically extended from their environment. Although it is impossible to determine whether the brown stains
resulted from contact with the original wearer's hands or from subsequent
handling, they certainly indicate the pocket's connection to the environmental element of air, which has deepened the stain's color and sealed
it into the fabric.[50] Visually, the organic qualities of women's detachable
pockets are reinforced by the floral patterns and motifs that were often
stitched onto them, even though no one else could see them. Eighteenth-
century women frequently made and embroidered their pockets them-

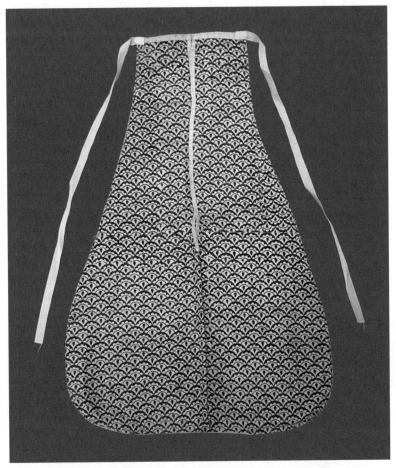

FIGURE 4.4 Pocket, unknown maker, England, United Kingdom
(1720–1730). Cotton and linen block print. 17 × 11½ in. (43.2 × 29.2 cm).
Museum purchase (1960.0248). Photograph courtesy of Winterthur Museum.

selves, and thus designed and plotted secret gardens to wear between their skirts.

The various names given to eighteenth-century women's pockets by costume historians suggests their complexity as intermediaries between interior and exterior worlds and between self and other. "Tie-on pocket" construes them as creating an attachment between the material object and the subject, while "detachable pocket" suggests a distancing. Just as pockets mediated between the outer and inner garments of a woman's attire in the eighteenth century, so too did they mediate between privacy and publicity, functioning in effect as their interface. It is this interface, as opposed to the domain of privacy and solitude—the more customary view—that characterizes the experience and location of interiority in eighteenth-century England.

Pockets, in their liminal status as private garments that could be worn in public places, and interior spaces that housed the ephemera of daily life, resemble the eighteenth-century novel, an equally liminal object, often carried close to the body, that housed interior worlds inaccessible to everyone but the reader. Considering that women's pockets were thirteen to fifteen inches long and close to eight inches wide, one can imagine novels (7 by 5¾ inches in duodecimo, or 12mo, format) fitting easily inside them. Indeed, one of the usage examples in Chambers's *Cyclopædia* (1740) for the word *portable* reads, "Books in 12mo are valued for their being *portable*, easily put in the pocket."[51] Barbauld's description of how women at Ranelagh held up "volumes of Pamela to one another" further indicates that novels accompanied readers in their pockets as they went about their daily activities. Secret worlds as well as secret gardens were carried by women's pockets.

The detachable pockets found in historical costume collections tell stories about how they mattered as objects of design, inscription, and use. We can discern, for example, the differing levels of care and intention with which they were created. A pair of pockets at the Winterthur Museum, remarkable for having both pockets intact on their original ribbon, comes from England and is dated 1735–1745, the time in which *Pamela* was written (fig. 4.5). Its block-print floral pattern, running off the edges of the pockets, indicates that the design was conceived and printed separately from the pockets themselves.

By contrast, the pattern on a pair of pockets in the Los Angeles County Museum of Art costume collection (fig. 4.6) was "embroidered to shape." This practice, plotting the embroidery to the particular shape of the pockets, suggests an approach to materiality that regarded detachable pockets as a specific medium of graphic design. The crudeness of the

FIGURE 4.5 Pair of pockets, unknown maker, England, United Kingdom (1735–1745). Cotton and linen block print. 16⅞ × 11⅜ in. (42.9 × 28.9 cm). Museum purchase (1969.3102). Photograph courtesy of Winterthur Museum.

stitching suggests the pockets were made by a young girl to demonstrate her needlework proficiency—a common practice among young girls in the eighteenth century, for whom needlework was a form of education. As such the pockets are a medium for individual talent as well as possession and authorship, which the plotting of the floral pattern, initials, and dating of the needlework convey.

The resonances between this form of needlework plotting and narrative plotting emerge especially in Richardson's novel when Pamela stays longer than she needs to on Mr. B's estate in order to finish "flowering" a waistcoat for him (44, 47–49). Though a skeptical reader might view this as an excuse induced by Pamela's unconscious attraction to and desire for Mr. B, despite her protestations that his sexual advances have made employment by him unbearable, her finishing the embroidery design is what advances Mr. B's plot and the narrative's own: by staying longer, she has made herself more vulnerable to his scheme to kidnap her on her way back to her parents' house and imprison her in his Lincolnshire home.

Costume collections cannot show what was carried inside eighteenth-century pockets, but Old Bailey proceedings reveal they frequently car-

FIGURE 4.6 Woman's pocket (one of a pair) and embroidery detail, England (1753). Wool, cotton, silk, linen. 13¾ × 8¼ in. (34.9 × 21 cm). Mrs. Alice F. Schott Bequest (M.67.8.90a–b). Photograph: Los Angeles County Museum of Art.

ried, in addition to notebooks, letters, and money, household goods. In 1739 and 1740, the period in which *Pamela* was written and published, the contents of stolen detachable pockets included such everyday objects as a little brass lamp, a half-pint mug, a pair of steel scissors, and, in the case of "one strip'd Cotton Pocket," "a Pair of Spectacles, three Brass Thimbles, an Iron Key, and 11s in Money."[52]

As organic extensions of the self—and of the environment—

eighteenth-century women's pockets possessed value less as objects than as spaces. Their operative feature was their capaciousness, as indicated by the Old Bailey inventories. Their size turned them into storehouses or portable cabinets, like Locke's figure for the perceiving mind. Pamela, for instance, in addition to stocking her pockets with "one Shift" and "two Handkerchiefs, and two Caps" when she runs away (170), hides in them the writing instruments that her fellow servant Mr. Longman gives her: "above forty Sheets of Paper, and a dozen Pens, and a little Phial of Ink, which last I wrapped in Paper and put in my Pocket, and some Wax and Wafers" (100). Moreover, in hiding her writing supplies, she places her pockets into the earth, thus distributing the fabric of her selfhood across Mr. B's landed property and appropriating it as her own space, an outcome borne out later in the novel.

The equivalence between female clothing and architectural space is in fact a time-honored one. Certainly, the fact that "fabric" before 1753 referred to a building rather than a textile article suggests this. And as Reyner Banham points out, the prosaic act of "wearing a coat in the rain" is akin to "getting in a tent out of the sun" insofar as both provide "partial solutions" to problems of environmental control that only "massive and apparently permanent structures" appear able to redress.[53] Architectural design is, more or less, "the deployment of technical sources" to "control the immediate environment." As such, one seeks in it the ability to "produce dryness in rainstorms, heat in winter, chill in summer, to enjoy acoustic and visual privacy, to have convenient surfaces on which to arrange one's belongings and sociable activities."[54] Just as pockets provide protection to Pamela's letters, clothing and rooms provide covering to her body, and furniture drawers and the rooms containing them do the same for the pieces of clothing themselves. Clothing, buildings, furniture, and letters exist on the same plane in this narrative insofar as they comprise the architectural function of enclosing and sheltering the self and its expressions. They also work to conceal the self, as Mr. B's use of closets, women's dress, and forged letters to disguise or hide his presence as a predatory man allow him to witness scenes and create situations that would otherwise be closed to him.

As significant as proper domestic architectural spaces are throughout the novel, the most privileged space for offering shelter to the interior self is the letter. In this regard, another commonly worn or carried accessory is presented as an equivalent to the letter: the fabric sewing roll used for housing domestic tools and known as a "housewife" (or "huswif," hence "hussy"). Used by both women and men, it contained a thimble, pincushion, scissors and knife, and other needlework tools. During her captivity on Mr. B's Lincolnshire estate, Pamela deploys her housewife to distract the maid and gain privacy to hide a letter for Mr. Williams to retrieve:

> So I went towards the Pond, the Wench following me, and dropt purposely my Hussy: And when I came near the Tiles, I said, Mrs. *Ann*, I have dropt my Hussy; be so kind to look for it. I had it by the Pond-side. The Wench went to look, and I slipt the Note between the Tiles, and cover'd them as quick as I could with the light Mould, quite unperceiv'd; and the Maid finding the Hussy, I took it, and saunter'd in again, and met Mrs. *Jewkes* coming to seek after me. (123–24)

This moment is significant not only because Pamela uses the hussy as a practical accessory, if in a manner altogether different from its customary usage, but also because Richardson presents the hussy—a variant of the woman's pocket—as equivalent to the letter. Structurally the huswif is similar to a letter insofar as the maneuvers of folding and unfolding allow one to close and open it, as well as store and carry it. As a decoy for a letter, it is fitting, for unlike the personal letter, which indicates Pamela's mental autonomy and ties independent of her employer's, it is equated with female domestic industry. Often made up of disparate scraps of fabric, it reflects the improvised nature of its composition, much like a letter to which one adds passages on unrelated topics as time goes on (an example of which is examined later in this chapter).

For Barbauld, the innovation of Richardson's representational technique lies in his use of the familiar letter to construct his narrative, which "gives the feelings of the moment as the writers felt them *at* the moment" (xxvi). Furthermore, as we recall, Richardson's style of writing his fictional letters has the property of "setting before the reader . . . every circumstance of what he means to describe" (cxxxvii). The contents of the familiar letter were as everyday as the contents of a detachable pocket or huswif in the eighteenth century. They were materials that were as voluble as they were ephemeral, internal, intimate, and raw; they were collected onto a paper sheet that functioned like a camera obscura screen for the mind's projections.

Epistolary Containment: Folding, Enclosing, and Archiving the Self

From the letter format, Richardson was in fact borrowing additional forms of interiority. With the size and folding of paper, the spaces between lines of writing, and the multidirectional flow of mind in the context of daily life, epistolary culture offered qualities of interiority that novels like *Pamela* attempt to capture. In passages such as the following, the letter writing medium and its materiality fuse with the active mind that discharges the writing:

> Tho' I dread to see him, yet do I wonder I have not. To be sure something is resolving against me, and he stays to hear all her Stories. I can hardly write; yet, as I can do nothing else, I know not how to forbear!—Yet I cannot hold my Pen!—How crooked and trembling the lines!—I must leave off, till I can get quieter Fingers!—Why should the Guiltless tremble so, when the Guilty can possess their Minds in Peace? (182)

The "crooked and trembling" lines—agitated handwriting the reader of the typeset novel is called on to imagine—express materially Pamela's interior state, even as she intends them to stay hidden from prying eyes within the letter's folds.

Watt sees Richardson's imitation of real epistolary practice in Pamela's "very garrulity," which is what in fact brings us intimately close to "Pamela's inner consciousness." For Watt, the "lack of selectiveness" in portraying her interior experiences encourages us to become more actively involved in what is described, on both internal and external levels. In doing so, as noted earlier in this chapter, "we have to pick significant items of character and behaviour out of a wealth of circumambient detail, much as in real life we attempt to gather meaning from the casual flux of circumstance."[55] Epistolary format, in other words, draws the reader into an interactive relationship with what appears to be a direct view to events in real life—or, I might add, the view a camera obscura would bring. Though he never refers to the device, Watt's subsequent elaborations on how epistolary fiction operates as a vehicle of mimesis offer further clues as to how we might connect it with the camera obscura's mimetic technology. Epistolary narrative's principle of heterogeneity and inclusiveness not only "induces" in readers a "kind of participation" but makes them feel they are "in contact not with literature but with the raw materials of life itself as they are momentarily reflected in the minds of the protagonists."[56] Importantly, however, the reader's contact with these fleeting thoughts is in fact mediated, by the physical book in the reader's possession and by the letters it fictionally contains.

Even as it points to the common ground between epistolary narrative and the camera obscura, insofar as both deal with and offer reflections on "the raw materials of life," Watt's observation allows us to make a key distinction: in themselves, epistolary fiction and the camera obscura are mirror reflections of each other. Whereas epistolary narratives make fiction appear to be "the raw materials of life," the camera obscura makes the raw materials of life appear to be fiction.

Actual epistolary correspondence is more akin to the camera obscura in offering the "raw materials of life" within the context of reality itself, though the veneer of fiction that accompanies the camera obscura's images is attenuated. A comparison of actual correspondence with epistolary fiction offers a chance to assess what forms of interiority Richardson was borrowing from the letter medium of his period. Furthermore, letters written following the publication of Richardson's novels suggest what letter writers might have been borrowing from the epistolary forms displayed in his novels.[57] In a real-world corollary of the long-ranging correspondences recreated in epistolary fiction, the actress-singer Mary Linley Tickell wrote to her sister Elizabeth Ann Linley Sheridan (also a singer, and playwright Robert Brinsley Sheridan's wife) nearly every day over the course of two years, from 1785 until 1787, the year Tickell died. One letter, in its irregularity of format (fig. 4.7), transmits visually the multidirectional flow of mind in the context of daily life that novels such as *Pamela* attempt to capture: Here, unlike other letters where she observes epistolary conventions, Tickell seems to begin and end quickly three distinct notes, perhaps deciding that she will say only one small thing, then deciding to add another on the same sheet—suggesting intrusions and breaks in her act of writing. In the center portion, which seems to be the original main part of the letter, she writes, "I send you the Ticket of admission to the little Theatre . . ." Beneath it, in a horizontal scrawl spanning the whole width of the page: "You are an ungrateful woman about the papers for I have never missed them one night—and whenever I have sent old ones it has been for you to read the Debates which kept them so long before they came out." On the vertical axis of the page, she writes yet another line: "again to the pantomime last night—it has been play'd twelve nights and to never less than 200£." Many directions of the mind— outward, inward, then outward again—are displayed in this letter, and signaled graphically by the directions of the very lines of writing themselves. At the same time, the impulse to continue using the same sheet of paper until its space becomes filled with writing suggests the relative high cost of paper at the time. It also evokes the Lockean notion of the white sheet of paper as a storehouse or camera obscura screen that registers the impressions of daily life as they enter the mind.

The practice of letter writing itself demonstrates both the mobility of interiority, in conveying the subjective experiences of the letter writer to another in a distant location, and the self-possession fostered by this form

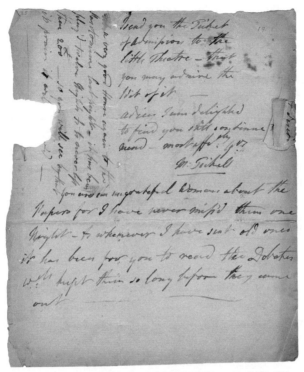

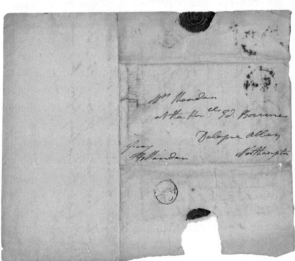

FIGURE 4.7 Letter, front and back, showing enclosure folds. Letters from Mary [Linley] Tickell to Elizabeth Ann Sheridan (ca.1785–1787), folder 2, number 19 (undated) (Y.d.35). Photograph used by permission of the Folger Shakespeare Library.

of literacy. The very act of presenting one's account of daily life sets boundaries of enclosure around the self and its world, as all of the happenings,
circumstances, and qualities presented pertain to the writer's subjective experience alone. At the moment such lines of enclosure are drawn
around the world as an aspect of the self's perceptions and experiences,
the individual is created. Within those lines lies the space of interiority.

Interiority lies as well within the lines created by the letter's folds.
These folds, taken for granted by scholars as features of the letter in its
mode as a flat sheet of paper, were in fact created in the early modern period to turn the sheet of paper on which the letter was written into its own
enclosure.[58] The folds of the letter, in other words, are what allow paper to
turn into a form of housing for the letter's written contents as it is transported to a different location. As MIT conservator Jana Dambrogio puts
it, the folds of early modern letters are what enable a two-dimensional
object to function as a three-dimensional one.[59] This capacity models
Locke's conception of a sheet of paper that, once the characters of writing
cover its surface, turns into a three-dimensional storehouse. The letter's
overlooked three-dimensionality is critical in establishing how it functions not so much as an object, but as a *space* that captures the passing
events of thoughts in everyday life.

Eighteenth-century letter writers themselves persistently made claims
for the apparently raw and unpremeditated quality of epistolary correspondence, as if the spaces of their letters were paper bedchambers. For
instance, in a November 1712 letter to John Caryll, Alexander Pope declared, "My style, like my soul, appears in its natural undress before my
friend."[60] A month later, he elaborated on this metaphor, describing his
letters to Caryll as filled with "thoughts just warm from the brain without any polishing or dress, the very déshabille of the understanding."[61]
Thomas Keymer, however, views metaphors equating the style of letter
writing with a state of undress as a ruse, for letter writing is "a rhetorical
act": "Far from being *undressed* . . . the letter is likely in the first place to
be *dressed* or adorned in conformity with the writer's chosen image of
himself, and moreover to be *addressed* to a reader on whom it will pursue
specific designs."[62]

In *Pamela*, we see an example of this rhetorical maneuver cast literally
as a sartorial one when the heroine locks herself up in her "little Room"
to "trick herself up," not in her dead mistress's handed-down finery but in
her own humble-seeming new garb:

And so, when I had dined, up Stairs I went, and locked myself into my
little Room. There I tricked myself up as well as I could in my new Garb,

and put on my round-eared ordinary Cap, but with a green Knot, however, and my homespun Gown and Petticoat, and plain-leather Shoes; but yet they are what they call Spanish Leather. A plain Muslin Tucker I put on, and my black Silk Necklace, instead of the *French* Necklace my Lady gave me; and put the Ear-rings out of my ear, and when I was quite 'quip'd, I took my Straw Hat in my Hand, with its two blue Strings, and look'd about me in the Glass, as proud as any thing.—To say Truth, I never lik'd myself so well in my life. (55)

This moment in the novel is remarkable for dramatizing Pamela's enterprise of fashioning herself as if she were her own doll—like a living Lady Clapham.[63] More interesting still is how the passage demonstrates the way in which epistolary narrative functions as a series of containers—or pockets—for the disparate objects of daily life. It exemplifies the fundamental qualities of prose as a remarkably elastic and capacious form of writing that, by virtue of its lack of metrical structure, readily incorporates thoughts and things as they occur. Though the passage conceivably narrates an important moment in the heroine's daily life, the moment is made up not so much by a set of remarkable actions but by the singular act of creating a collection of objects she deems her own. Complicating Watt's assertion that the epistolary medium lacks selectiveness, the recurring act of selection and enclosure in this passage at once makes those objects mobile, marshals them, and turns them into narrative itself, not just the subject matter of narrative. Here, we see a conception of containment that is dynamic and transforming. The spatial entities of things, in other words, are threaded together to stand in for the temporal dimension of actions.

Alongside Richardson's rhetorical strategy of presenting homely material objects as temporal entities that constitute the pockets of time in everyday life, pockets themselves mediate narrative drama insofar as they contain the written form of containers: Pamela's personal letters. At the beginning of volume II, and nearing the end of Pamela's imprisonment at Brandon Hall, Mr. B demands to know where she has hidden her "Written-papers," her "sawcy Journal" (233). While he guesses they may be "ty'd about your Knees with your Garters," and reveals he has "searched every Place above, and in your Closet" (235), he is emphatic in his apparent belief that they may be in her pockets:

We were standing most of this Time, but he then sat down, and took both my hands, and said, Well said, my pretty *Pamela, if you can help it!* But I will not let you help it. Tell me, are they in your Pocket?' 'No, sir,' said I,

my Heart up at my Mouth. Said he, 'I know you won't tell a downright
Fib for the world. . . . Answer me then, are they in *neither* of your Pockets? (233–34)

Indeed, Pamela is not fibbing; the papers are not in her pockets but,
rather, are sewn to her underclothes, which she reveals when writing earlier in her captivity, "But I begin to be afraid my Writings may be discover'd; for they grow large! I stitch them hitherto in my Under-coat, next
my Linen" (131).

While such a tactic secures her writings from being stolen without her
knowledge, it makes it impossible for Pamela to relinquish them without being stripped by Mr. B or undressing herself in front of him. Both
scenarios are intolerable to her. "I went to my Closet, and there I sat me
down, and could not bear the Thoughts of giving up my Papers. Besides,
I must all undress me in a manner to untack them," she writes (235). Yet,
undressing herself in private to untack the papers and hand them to Mr.
B without removing her clothes is preferable to being undressed by him
or undressing herself in front of him. The affordances of her detachable
pockets, which are still close to her body but can be removed from it, and
which is where she places her letters next, are what allow this.

The narration of Pamela's next movement curiously enacts for the
reader what might otherwise have been enacted by Mr. B: "so I took off
my Under-coat, and with great Trouble of Mind, unsew'd them from it"
(236). She proceeds then to renarrate the events we have already experienced with her in the earlier portion of the novel. Undressing herself
and "unsewing" the letters from her undercoat to transport them to her
pocket equates with providing access to her past inner experiences and,
indeed, to her whole being, as it is made up of stitched-together material
and revealed as a repository, an archive, for those very experiences.[64] She
has turned herself into a book.

If Pamela has turned herself and her experiences into a book by doing what a bookmaker might—sewing disparate sheets of paper together
to form a whole entity—she reverts to the original conception of her experiences as detachable epistles by gathering her papers into two parcels
and using her detachable pocket as their temporary container and binder
when delivering the papers to Mr. B In this way the distinction between
sewn-in letters and letters placed in pockets speaks to the differing forms
of containment, mediation, and remediation the novel sets in motion.
As a master printer, someone actively involved not just in the making of
books but in the making of his own books, Richardson would have been
aware of this. Whether the pockets were attached or tied on, factors dis-

cussed earlier, would bespeak differing levels of security in ensuring one's interiority and the ability to exert autonomy. Expecting her to bring him her papers in the garden after her negotiation with him, Mr. B says to Pamela when she arrives:

> But where are the Papers?—I dare say, you had them about you yesterday, for you say in those I have, that you will bury your Writings in the Garden, for fear you should be *search'd*, if you do not escape. This, added he, gave me a glorious Pretence to search you; and I have been vexing myself all Night, that I did not strip you, Garment by Garment, till I had found them. . . . I hope you have not now the Papers to give me; for I had rather find them myself, I'll assure you. (238)

In the face of Mr. B's clear statement that should she not hand over her letters, he will locate them on her body himself, Pamela eventually hands them over. In doing so, she distracts Mr. B from breaking the seal of her body by drawing his attention to the seal on the parcel:

> So I took out my Papers; and said, Here, Sir, they are. But, if you please to return them, without breaking the Seal, it will be very generous: And I will take it for a great Favour, and a good Omen.
>
> He broke the Seal instantly, and open'd them. So much for your Omen, said he. (239)

Although the text in the first edition does not make explicit that the first parcel of letters has come from her pocket, it is clear that the second does: "And so I gave him out of my Pocket the second Parcel" (314).[65] Despite his impertinence in breaking the seal of her letters against her explicit wishes, Mr. B begins to show receptiveness to the idea of internalizing Pamela as an individual subject when he puts the parcel into his own pocket ("He put them into his Pocket") (314). From this moment on, he assumes the position not just of suitor but also of sympathetic reader. As such, he assumes a position that readers of the novel are meant to have occupied all along, the "powerful vicarious identification of readers with the feelings of fictional characters."[66]

Beginning to read Pamela's writing in front of her in the garden, Mr. B retraces the steps she describes, taking both Pamela and her writing with his body, by walking to the side of the pond where she threw in her clothes, and with his heart. He reveals the latter not only by saying, "O my dear girl! you have touch'd me sensibly with your mournful Relation, and your sweet Reflections upon it," but also, by putting the papers in his pocket again when reading her reflections (241). The sense that he is put-ting Pamela herself into his pocket is reinforced when his embrace of her is identified as an act of "folding," as of a letter itself: "Then he most kindly folded me in his Arms" (241).

With these gestures, which merge the body and identity of a heroine with her material representatives, Mr. B's conversion from rake to future husband begins, and the contours of the domestic novel become legible as the marriage plot. If the original meaning of "plot" was a comprehen-sive description of a country house manor, then a plot turn also takes place in the way Mr. B can now regard the different parts of his estate only from the perspective of Pamela's past experiences. Her letters have effec-tively replotted his estate through her interior perspective and thereby made it hers. This conversion of both of Mr. B's plots is triggered by the activity of reading Pamela's letters, an activity mediated not only by pen and paper but by the very space that contains pen and paper and carries the letters to him—the mobile and expansive environment of Pamela's pockets. Thus, one of the novel's many metamorphoses takes place when a material object such as Pamela's pocket transforms into a space of pri-vacy, of intimacy, revelation, and movement. When it does so, it func-tions like a portable version of two sites of narrative action that are also among the most private spaces of country houses and, as such, sites for the workings of the camera obscura. The chain of connections between pockets, letters, rooms, and book exemplifies in its most expansive form the notion of the architextural, whereby environments of text, texture ("a woven fabric"), and architecture overlap.

Dark Rooms of Domestic Life

As pockets provide the setting for one's most private and practical be-longings, putting them into place for ready retrieval, rooms and clos-ets provide settings for people's actions as well as their possessions. To enter a room in order to spy on someone else's intimate activities and thoughts is akin to rifling through their pockets and letters. Like pockets, the rooms in *Pamela* have properties of both enclosure and movement. And like camera obscuras, they are spaces for processing outside experi-ences transported in, as well as for acquiring previously hidden or other-wise inaccessible information. In mediating projections and reflections of the real world, rooms in *Pamela* are not only like camera obscuras; they *are* camera obscuras.

Explaining to senior servant Mr. Longman why he must dismiss Pamela from the Lincolnshire estate, Mr. B voices his greatest anxiety regarding Pamela's writing: "I can't let her stay, I'll assure you; not only for her own Freedom of Speech; but her Letter-writing of all the Secrets of my Family" (72). Though the rooms themselves are not mentioned in this remark, in previous pages such rooms as the summer house and her lady's dressing room have been made so interchangeable with improper acts of his that must be kept secret, that to allow the secrets to move through social channels would be to give neighbors unlicensed views into the most private spaces of the estate.

It is not difficult to see why Pamela's writing might cause the landowning employer such anxiety: once she represents events in her own words, they become her story, her property, the work of her authorship. His character is in her hands to shape, whether in speech, with Mrs. Jervis, or in writing, to her parents. That he has no control over this confounds him: "And so I am to be exposed, am I, said he, *in* my House, and *out* of my House, to the whole World, by such a Sawcebox as you?" (31). Richardson's stressing of the prepositions "in" and "out" reveals Mr. B's unease over the mobility of Pamela's thoughts and language. Her thoughts have wings—within the great house through her speech, and outside of it through her letters, when they leave the space of her pockets. The letters themselves carry the rooms of the house he owns out into the world with them. And the stories about what happens inside those rooms reveal the ways in which the boundaries that make up domestic and social order are constantly tested, transgressed, or dissolved.

Because they are written from her perspective, the letters also serve as an aperture to the depths of Pamela's mind, revealing the elements of the outside world that have collected inside it, constituting the interiorized version of the world as her own. The effect is similar to the dreamscape of domestic interior life depicted in Emanuel de Witte's *Interior with a Woman Playing the Virginal*. From the Dutch Golden Age, like the Vermeer painting discussed in chapter 2, De Witte's painting produces its illusion of depth by creating a fictitious enfilade; it also creates a sense that the world outside has been incorporated fully into its space, the interior space of the house.

Most conducive to this impression is the light that streams through side windows, creating squares on the floor that merge with the black and white tiling, leaving open to question which elements of the resulting composite pattern are real and which a momentary illusion created by projections of light.[67] The painting depicts a moment of illumination. It is also a moment when an outsider may peer into the private space and see what it contains at that time. The white jug resting on the table, the gilt mirror, red curtains, canopied bed, and patterned carpet transmit the in-

FIGURE 4.8 Emanuel de Witte, *Interior with a Woman Playing the Virginal*
(ca. 1665–1670). Oil on canvas. 30½ × 41⅛ in. (77.5 × 104.5 cm).
Museum Boijmans Van Beuningen, Rotterdam. Wikimedia Commons.

teriority of the home's inhabitants insofar as they comprise the objects of
their perceptual awareness. That the occupants of the space are unaware
of the viewer's gaze heightens the scene's sense of interiority. They are
lost in their thoughts.

While one can see straight through—as in the "continued tube" of perspective views in Pope's garden—from the front room to a middle room,
and on to the back room, the window in this back room offers the eye a
release from the scene's sense of interior confinement by serving as the
painting's vanishing point. The dark recess of the bed's canopy reveals
very little of the man sleeping inside of it. The furnishings are aspects of
the inhabitants' interior setting, one of hidden and visible depths that is
as intimate as the realm of emotions and thoughts that incorporate them
into their space. The resemblance between the corridors of perspective
views in Pope's landscape garden and in De Witte's painting reminds us
that the forming of space, whether in reality or representation, allows us
greater access to the depths of our inner lives.[68]

The scene's simultaneous elements—the play of light, a maid sweeping the floor in the back room as her mistress plays the keyboard instrument in the front—relay an interior rhythm that is transient as well as specific to the inwardness of domestic activity. The space is populated by three solitary figures, withdrawn into separate activities—the man sleeps or rests alone, the women are bent to their tasks: one plays music, the other sweeps the floor. Not just lost in thought, each is in the dark closet of her or his own mind, with the soldier hidden inside the bed, reclining, dreaming, or dozing during the day, like the Duke of Lauderdale inside the curtained chair of his closet at Ham House. In addition to depicting humans completing "tasks" that make up "the constitutive acts of dwelling," as explored in chapter 2 with Cavendish, the painting demonstrates a scene that is but one of many "informal, fugitive moments" that make up the settings of domestic life.[69] Such moments, as Barbauld, Jeffrey, and others have claimed, form the very basis of Richardson's narrative in *Pamela*.

About Dutch painting interiors Svetlana Alpers observes, "It is here in the comfortable, enclosed, private setting of one's own home that experience is received and literally taken in." Evoking Cavendish's and Locke's figures for the mind as an architectural space to which sense impressions bring knowledge, which in turn evoke the function of the camera obscura, Alpers's observation helps formulate the observer's role as one who peers into or stands inside the space of the camera obscura when gazing at such an image as De Witte's *Interior with a Woman Playing the Virginal*.[70] The image, placing at its center the light effects created by sunlight pouring into a domestic interior, is one of projection and transience as it depicts a moment of illumination in one part of the home. We are outsiders— much like Marvell, Pamela, Parnell, or Elizabeth Bennet in approaching the estates they encounter as visitors—when gazing at such interior settings and their occupants.

Ultimately the De Witte painting, with its illusionistic positioning of light and space—in creating an enfilade that would not be found in actual houses of the period—thematizes the experience of reading novels such as *Pamela*. A virtual space has been created, on which, as Jeffrey observes, we drop in to watch and listen to the occupants as they go about their daily activities. Just as the painting, like the camera obscura, serves as a virtual space of interiority that, through its perspectival technique, effects apparent transformations between two- and three-dimensional space, the letter as a formal unit in epistolary narrative transforms the two-dimensional space of paper into private rooms. In this aspect, the letter accomplishes with language what it does, as a material form, with its folds, and what the pocket does with its fabric enclosure.

Likewise, the letters comprising an epistolary narrative bring the novel reader into the spaces and rooms in which events take place. In effect they function as projection devices, revealing to characters the thoughts of other characters at the same time that they reveal to readers Pamela's thoughts and experiences as they happen. Here and throughout Richardson's novel, Pamela's view of the external world—her view of "such things, as pass every day before our eyes," to quote Clara Reeve's description of the novel genre—is translated into an internal one, a function that is the camera obscura's own.[71]

Seeing with Dark Rooms

Since ancient times, the camera obscura has revealed what was previously unavailable to vision. Inside a camera obscura, celestial movements such as solar eclipses could be observed without damaging the eyes.[72] In the 1620s, Johannes Kepler made the portable camera obscura described by Henry Wotton, which allowed him to watch the sun from any location he pleased. Robert Boyle, referring to a "portable darkened room" in 1669, marveled at the way that "upon every turning of the instrument this way or that way, whether it be in the town or open fields, one may discover new objects and sometimes new landscapes upon the paper."[73] Abbé Nollet, in *Leçons de physique experimentale* (1764), describes how using a room-size camera obscura amplifies the effects of such scientific demonstrations as diffracting a ray of light through a sphere of water to produce a rainbow.[74] Similarly, *Pamela* demonstrates how the architectural design of the country house might implicitly turn into camera obscuras, or rooms where external information can be brought to view, namely, the information of someone else's inner feelings and thoughts. In this case, the small room turns not just into a hiding place for a character but into the very space of the mind described by Locke, in which ideas and sense are "acquired" and "enter."

Throughout, characters sit inside closets and other hidden rooms, eavesdropping on the conversations of others and spying on their activities. Pamela herself does this when she overhears the "fine ladies" of the neighborhood who come to visit Mr. B's home talking about her and her celebrated beauty. Wishing to evade their notice, she "did step into the Closet" when they came to Mrs. Jervis's office to visit her (52). In being so close to the subjects of interest without being detected by them, she can perceive their personalities in a way that direct contact would not bring. The space of the closet in this sense works as a perspective device as she occupies the role of a narrator, reporting to her parents the ladies' behavior and recording the conversation and behavior of others.

The most dramatic moments of closet hiding occur when the dweller of the closet is Mr. B. In one of the two harrowing bedroom scenes, he uses the closet to spy on Pamela as she undresses to get ready for bed with Mrs. Jervis, her bedmate. The conversation she has with Mrs. Jervis is about Mr. B and her frustration with his repeated attempts to "subdue" her virtue (62). During the course of the conversation, Pamela hears a rustling in the closet. Dismissing the notion after the noises stop, she removes her clothing, "all to an Under-petticoat," at which point she hears the rustling again (63). Announcing her plan to inspect the closet, she is met with a shocking sight: "O dreadful! out rushed my Master, in a rich silk and silver Morning Gown" (63).

The emphasis on the clothing worn in the scene and the physical positioning of the bodies wearing the clothes works to reconstruct the moment for those who could not be there. Yet even if Mr. B is in the room with Pamela when the events take place, he cannot be in the one room to which he does not have access but we as readers of her letters do, which is the room of her mind that perceives and reflects on those events. On one hand, the scene reconfigures the space of a country house into a camera obscura, in that it presents a viewer occupying a dark room a means to see something that is impossible to look at directly. On the other, it brings the reader into the position of being in the moment, seeing an internal space—Pamela's mind—taken over by incoming impressions of phenomena in the world around it as they are being experienced. It is mediated narration.

As happens frequently in the Gothic narratives that *Pamela* precedes, the aperture to the heroine's mind closes when she loses consciousness. Presumably this happens because the mind is so flooded with impressions disturbing to her conscious awareness that it ceases its operations: "I found his Hand in my Bosom, and when my Fright let me know it, I was ready to die; and I sighed, and scream'd, and fainted away" (63). Conscious awareness remains unsustainable during the ordeal of Mr. B's intrusion, and she faints several more times—"for I knew nothing more of the Matter, one Fit following another" (63). In the absence of her own conscious awareness during these moments, Mrs. Jervis is the one to report the scene to her.

That the account of the episode is as close as possible to Pamela's first-hand experience of it is indicated by her ending the letter, "I must leave off a little, for my Eyes and my Head are greatly disordered" (64). As with the moments of fainting, which shut down conscious awareness of external circumstances, the letter shuts down as her mind becomes just as disordered from recollecting and processing the scene. Throughout both cases, her mind is the space that mediates the viewing of the scene. There is a mind within a mind here—the mind that writes down the letter as it describes the mind that experiences what is being described. The epistolary format is the device for this effect.

In the green-room episode, wherein Mr. B hides in a "Closet, with a Sash-door, and a Curtain before it," readers are informed that he has joined them in "slip[ping] invisible" into the room to watch the interactions between Pamela and Mrs. Jervis (78). Much as the closet in Mrs. Jervis's bedroom is described, so too is the closet here: "for there [Mrs. Jervis] puts her Sweet-meats and such Things" (78). Adjacent to these household items is the human figure who, in keeping with the novel's "keyhole view of life," wishes to hear Pamela's thoughts, candidly expressed, and observe her unguarded behavior. This positioning of Mr. B, hiding next to the pantry items of his great house, physicalizes Watt's equation between "the delineation of the domestic life and the private experience of the characters who belong to it."[75]

Hiding in the space where the most mundane items of quotidian life are stored, Mr. B has found a direct route to the inner domain of Pamela's mind. Paradoxically, this domain is designated not by her feelings and thoughts alone as she shares them with Mrs. Jervis, but also by her archival process of describing and arranging items of clothing in her possession into numbered bundles that signify different parts of her life. Organizing her clothing into parcels allows her to claim the identity she wishes while setting apart the one she wishes to reject, such as the "second wicked Bundle" of clothing belonging to her lady that Mr. B had given her (79). Throughout this exchange, too, Mr. B is often the subject of conversation. Pamela's belief that she is speaking to Mrs. Jervis in private allows her to say, while hugging her "dear third Bundle" (containing the most humble and practical clothing) to her bosom, "And I beg you'll say nothing of all this till I am gone, that my Master mayn't be so angry, but that I may go in Peace, for my Heart" (81). The link between emotional life and domestic details is ever indissoluble in this novel.

The architectural setting of the closet in all three episodes described evokes Locke's "dark room," the would-be camera obscura of the understanding, where images of the outside world are carried into the room and projected onto its own wall. Mr. B and Pamela alike resemble the figure in Athanasius Kircher's illustration of a walk-in camera obscura insofar as in this model, the viewer needs to enter the box itself, which is the size of a small closet, in order to experience its effects. Slipping into various closets of the Bedfordshire house to experience reality in a mediated, socially detached, and private format, Mr. B and Pamela recreate domestic reality for themselves as they observe but do not participate in it, as the viewer might in regarding the dream-world version of domestic reality that De Witte's painting depicts. By hiding in closets to remain undetected while discovering the intentions of others, Mr. B and Pamela experience their domestic world as an incalculable sequence of sounds and moving images. Such sounds and images recall the qualities of camera obscuras discerned by such natural philosophers and polymaths of a much earlier age as Giambattista Della Porta.

Della Porta, in his evocative description in *Magia Naturalis* (1558) of the camera obscura's operation, calls attention to the narrative quality of its moving images and the possibility of staging fanciful scenes to appear on its "white sheet":

> Let there be over against that Chamber, where you desire to represent these things, some spacious Plain, where the Sun can freely shine; Upon that you shall set Trees in Order, also Woods, Mountains, Rivers, and Animals, that are really so, or made by Art, of Wood, or some other matter. You must frame little children in them, as we bring them in when Comedies are Acted: and you must counterfeit Stages, Bores, Rhinocerets, Elephants, Lions, and what other creatures you please: Then by degrees they must appear, as coming out of their dens, upon the Plain: The Hunter he must come with his hunting Pole, Nets, Arrows, as other necessaries, that may represent hunting.[76]

Prevalent here are the desire, agency, and "spectatorial pleasures" characteristic of the camera obscura.[77] There are elements of narrative pleasure too, with the establishment of a setting, the insertion of human figures and animals, and the promise of a story, set in motion by the counterfeit animals and the Hunter appearing only "by degrees."[78] For the same reason that the camera obscura in Della Porta's description resembles the dreamlike metamorphoses of early modern masques, replete with special machinery, preconceived roles, and background scenery, it also aligns with cinematic experience, as film theorists have pointed out. For Giuliana Bruno, for instance, the camera obscura's kinship with the cinema has less to do with its relation to the technology of the movie camera itself than to the space in which the images recorded by the camera are viewed, "a movie house," as it is known.[79]

That the space of the camera obscura is an architectural one—as the meaning of *camera* in Latin indicates—is critical. So much so that the legacy of the device—its "very semiotic imprint"—is inherited by cinema and other forms of spectatorial experience as a virtual architecture.[80] The idea of the movie, television, or computer screen—to use Anne Friedberg's taxonomy of contemporary screen types—as having architectural properties goes against expectation, considering the screen's very quality of flatness.[81] A far cry from eighteenth-century England's silently but freely roaming Mr. Spectator, today's spectator sits or stands immobilized before images moving on a screen hanging from the ceiling, propped on a tripod or desk, or held in the hand. Architecture, on the other hand, affords an experience of bodily movement through space: "using, visiting, inhabiting a building involves movement in, through, up, down, out."[82] And yet the movie screen, with immaterial images of physical experiences and built environments projected onto it, imports the camera obscura's architectural aspect, subsisting as an "architectonic element" that invites viewers to dwell in its virtual spaces and assume its points of view and identities. Such an insight allows us to understand just how novels, which in early printings frequently appeared with frontispiece illustrations showing domestic interior views, might be likened to virtual architectures and spaces too.

The critical distinction between camera obscuras as they are customarily used and Della Porta's conception of them as a moving sequence of artificially constructed tableaus is that in their traditional usage, the images are based on figures and features "that are really so." But what makes the camera obscura's remediation so beguiling is that it makes those elements, though from the viewer's own reality, appear as if they have emerged from a dream. A similar effect takes place when characters hide themselves in closets to eavesdrop and spy on other characters. When Mr. B and Pamela do so, one appears to be pursuing the thrills of voyeurism, the other indulging her bashful curiosity. Yet they also evince desire for the camera obscura view of life, a view that presents "the delights and pleasures of watching images of events as they unfold."[83] How do others, and how do I, appear in that beguiling sequence of images projected into the space of a small room?

Richardson's novel demonstrates how keen the desire to know the answer to this question is, and uses the spaces of privacy in the country house to create the conditions for answering it. It is fair to say that in the closet scenes, Mr. B is a character who appears as interested—if not more so—in what Pamela has to say about him, whether in speech or writing, as in her body. Even as he bemoans "the Liberty she has taken with [his] Character, out of the House and in the House" (58), and scolds her repeatedly for it, he remains fascinated by the images of himself projected by her words. Evidence of this fascination lies in the numerous instances in which Pamela's letters disappear because he has stolen them from her. As Pamela herself admits, "There is a secret Pleasure one has to hear one's self prais'd" (15).

Richardson's friend Arthur Young reveals in a letter of 1767 that Pamela and Mr. B were far from alone as fictional characters who transformed the everyday spaces around them into dark rooms for perceiving their reality. He suggests that he too wished to experience life through the perspective of the camera obscura and therefore found the means to create it out of landscape structures: "'The next opening in the hedge (I should tell you, by the by, that these breaks and openings are all natural, none stifly artificial) gives you at one small view, all the picturesque beauties of a natural camera obscura.'"[84]

The model of the camera obscura, in which life is experienced indirectly through its mediation, works in concert with the self-consciously novelistic view of her or his life that each character seeks to create and consume. Initially they do so on their own terms; more than once Mr. B makes this claim. Take, for instance, the scene just before his conversion: "Besides, said he, there is such a pretty Air of Romance, as you relate them, in your Plots, and my Plots, that I shall be better directed in what manner to wind up the Catastrophe of the pretty novel" (232). Pamela also registers the potential of her life to be mediated as a novel when she proclaims to her parents, "My Story surely would furnish out a surprizing kind of Novel, if it was to be well told" (246).

If, in offering a mediated view of reality, the arrangement of words on a page that form Richardson's novel corresponds with the camera obscura's play of light in its dark room, their mutual reliance on the existence of a bounded space, a room, demands consideration. So much of the narrative in *Pamela* is organized not just by the temporal-spatial units of letters but also by those of rooms. Throughout, pivotal moments take place and then become encoded in conversation as the rooms or spaces of the manor houses themselves, especially ones in which Mr. B has made his sexual advances on Pamela. After Mr. B's private presentation to her of his mother's intimate garments, Pamela refers to the closet in which the transaction took place as "my good Lady's Dressing-room, a Room I once lov'd, but then as much hated" (33). In addition, when Mrs. Jervis informs Pamela that her employer resents her for talking about his misbehavior to others, she refers to his actions by the names of the rooms themselves accordingly: "consider it was the Truth; if he does not love to hear of the Summer-house and the Dressing room, why should he not be asham'd to continue in the same Mind" (62). "Why," says she, "he was very angry at your hints of the summer-house, and dressing-room" (94).[85] Much later in the novel, long after Pamela is released as Mr. B's sexual prey and has been instated in her role as his wife as well as mistress of his property, she continues to perceive each room as a figure for the events that took place in it. As architectural units, the rooms are condensed narratives of the past: "We went up; and in every Room, the Chamber I took Refuge in, when my master pursu'd me, my Lady's Chamber, her Dressing-room, Mrs *Jervis's* Room, (not forgetting her Closet, my own little Bed-chamber, the Green-room, and in each of the others, I kneeled down severally, and blessed God for my past Escapes, and present Happiness" (459). Itemizing the rooms of her home in this way entails describing her own internal thought process, insofar as each room is shown to correspond with the memory of a past event, like the rooms of a Renaissance memory palace.[86] In this way, the rooms and landscape spaces on the estate are vital as settings for states of mind.

For Robin Evans, rooms provide "an edge to perception."[87] The camera obscura supports this notion not just by modeling the process by which perceptions take place, but also by supplying the spatial context in which its effects can be perceived at all. Without an enclosed structure, the device would neither work nor exist. By the same token, without the designated spaces in which the events of the narrative take place, from the dressing room, green-room, and library to the pasture, pond, and garden, there would be no context for the action and interactions that drive the activities of the heroine's mind, the predominating enclosed space that provides readers with an edge to their perceptions. In the 1801 edition, the attempt to create a camera obscura–like sense of simultaneity between Pamela's experiences as they take place and her reflections of them on the page is keenly registered when she writes, "I write the very words I said."[88] (111). Enclosed by the boundaries of the character's consciousness and the rooms and landscape spaces she occupies, readers find themselves immersed in the images on the wall of a dark room. As Soame Jenyns's 1752 poem about the camera obscura indicates, the surfaces of the mind and the camera obscura, including its sheet of paper for receiving projections, were viewed as one:

> Like the fair empty sheet he hangs to view,
> Void, and unfurnish'd, 'till inspir'd by you:
> O let one beam, one kind inlight'ning ray
> At once upon his mind, and paper play![89]

When "slip[ping] invisible, into the domestic privacy of his characters," to revisit Jeffrey's description of Richardson that began this chapter, we have not so much picked up a book as walked into a camera obscura's play of projection and reality.

Yet the virtue of the camera obscura and of the book is their ability to be fashioned into and used as portable possessions. If the duodecimo format afforded the novel movability, Kepler's little black tent, Hooke's "picture box," and Boyle's "portable darkened room" did the same for the camera obscura.[90] James Mann's pocket microscope camera obscura, publicized in 1755, was claimed to be "easy for Carriage," with all its parts "contained in a small Case, which may easily be carried in the Pocket."[91] Frances Terpak points out that the camera obscura, whether as a room or a handheld device, gave individuals a sense of owning "their own moving images, long before the modern film and video industry would make that a commonplace."[92] It should be added that unlike many of the products of the modern movie industry, the moving images created by the camera obscura came from the individual's immediate world, not from a world created by a scriptwriter and producer. This attribute of the camera obscura primed viewers to see reality in an unreal guise, and so to be receptive to the novel's streaming of its virtual world, a real-seeming unreality. Another important aspect of the camera obscura's cultural influence, Terpak points out, is that it "encouraged individuals to look at physical phenomena through an aperture."[93] Such an expectation found its literary counterpart in the technique of point of view, wherein the conception of a fictional world made to seem real is rendered through the singular perspective of an individual subject.

The transfer of a domestic setting from its "real-world" origins to a wall, page, or canvas, whether through a camera obscura, novel, or painting, entails translating a three-dimensional referent into two dimensions. One might observe that this process reverses the maneuver of letters, which render two-dimensional sheets of paper into three-dimensional containers, like pockets, for thoughts and feelings, whether through folds or the act of writing itself. The hand-press printing process of Richardson's time entailed the use of folds to turn two dimensions into three insofar as individual sheets of paper were folded to create the multiple leaves that comprise the text block of a book. In the case of the camera obscura, as Friedberg puts it, the translation is one that moves from "three-dimensional materiality to two-dimensional virtuality." Moreover, the virtual images "carried" by the light penetrating through the camera obscura's pinhole are in motion.[94] Concurrently, the transference—or projection—of words on a page leads to a mode in itself of filling up white space with a stream of ideas. Writing, after all, is a method of transporting words "from the world of sounds" to "visual surfaces," and print "locks words into position" in the space of those surfaces, as Walter Ong puts it.[95] The act of writing a novel is a means of verbally processing the stream of perceptions a camera obscura mediates visually, but the act of printing the novel is a method for preserving the stream in a way the camera obscura cannot. The result is a portable private world that one might enter in the same way the novel in turn enters the pocket that carries it.

Richardson's novel's movements—situating spaces of interiority from rooms to things and, in doing so, turning things into rooms of their own—contribute to its critical role in the conjoined histories of subjectivity, material culture, and the history of the novel genre. *Pamela* led a pattern of movement in the novel-reading experience in which the novel as a readable object transforms into an internal space of everyday life. This movement colludes with the social and political developments in the status of property in eighteenth-century England and with the proliferation of portable camera obscuras in the marketplace. Literary criticism might, in this light, reenvision the meaning of such categorical terms as "domestic fiction." In capturing the spatial dimensions and temporal rhythms of the everyday, domestic fiction allows a new form of homemaking to take place whereby the internal world that the novel creates introjects the reader so deeply into its space that it becomes another home in itself. It does so, above all, as a portable space of interiority.

My analysis of Richardson's novel in effect redefines C. B. Macpherson's *possessive individualism* in terms of gender, materiality, and interiority.[96] A concept originating in seventeenth-century political discourse, possessive individualism views the individual as "the proprietor of his own person or capacities" or, more simply, "an owner of himself."[97] If "the human essence is freedom from the dependence on the wills of others and freedom is a function of possession," then Richardson's Pamela richly demonstrates the notion of freedom that underpins liberal democracy's possessive individualism when she describes herself as declaring to her "master," Mr. B, after he pretends to confuse her with someone else: "O Sir, said I, I am *Pamela*, indeed I am: Indeed I am *Pamela, her own self!*" (56)

I have demonstrated that, ultimately, Pamela lays claim to her selfhood not through such words alone but also by effecting a dynamic wherein her movable possessions—her pockets and letters, in particular—become spatial regions of the self that challenge the authority of land ownership conferred to her social superiors. She effects, in other words, a shift in social relations as defined by property and marriage. She does so by turning the interiority found in the everyday possessions and the spaces around her into an estate of the self, or, as she puts it, *"her own self!"*

The following chapter explores further the fabric of fiction as an architectural structure, but one that is meant to be beheld by many viewers in an exterior, landscape setting. Despite the external setting of follies, or artificial ruins used as landscape garden ornamentation, they were meant to stimulate internal contemplation and fantasies about a far removed past. The mobility of interior spaces is redistributed so that although the space remains stationary, the body of the subject is in motion, and the devices for perceiving and recording the space are ever more portable.

Folly

FICTIONS OF GOTHIC SPACE
IN LANDSCAPE AND TEXT

One of the most psychologically suggestive forms of historical fiction resides not in a textual product but in the small buildings in the Gothic style known as follies. These structures, looking like medieval fortresses, castles, or ruins but designed and created in the eighteenth century, began catching the eye and ornamenting the landscapes of private estates late in the second decade of that century. Overlooking the Claremont estate in Surrey, England, is the castellated Belvedere Tower, which appears to be from the Middle Ages but was built in about 1717 by John Vanbrugh. On the approach to Castle Howard in York, also designed by Vanbrugh, an imposing series of fortified towers built in 1719 lures those who enter the grounds into thinking they are visiting a medieval castle, not the Baroque masterwork that serves as the actual house. And deep in the woods of Cirencester Park, Gloucestershire, a walk of two and a half hours from the main house, sits Alfred Hall, now in poorer condition than originally intended. Designed in 1721 by Lord Bathurst with the help of Alexander Pope, it was the first full-scale sham-ruined castle. Seeming to have chronological origins and purposes different from their apparent ones, follies are temporal as well as spatial fictions. As they produce an air of mystery and hauntedness, they transform the interiority of those who gaze at, enter, or walk around their profoundly fictive spaces.

Despite the existence of these and other faux Gothic structures built several decades before its publication, Horace Walpole's 1764 novel *The Castle of Otranto* is commonly viewed as the first Gothic fiction and the paradigm of the Gothic genre. Elements of the genre include the narrative ruse of medieval origins and the textual manufacturing of an "atmosphere" ostensibly derived from a "dark," unenlightened, anticlassical culture.[1] To what extent was it necessary to the conception of the Gothic novel that the architectural forms of Gothic fiction had already been formed, perceived, and experienced?

FIGURE 5.1 After Thomas Robins, King Alfred's Hall [Gloucestershire] (ca. 1763). Engraving (RCIN 701438). Photograph: Royal Collection Trust, © Her Majesty Queen Elizabeth II 2021.

The best-known example of an architectural Gothic fiction is Walpole's own house, Strawberry Hill, which he began remodeling in 1749 and called his "little Gothic castle." Yet, as landscape and domestic architecture designs by Vanbrugh, Bathurst, Sanderson Miller, and others indicate, he was not the first or only man of property to use architecture as the medium for enacting fantasies of the Middle Ages. Architectural fictions of the Gothic had appeared in the landscapes of private estates decades before Walpole's ventures in Gothic domestic design and literature, and well before the 1790s mania for Gothic fiction that allowed Jane Austen to conceive a character like Catherine Morland, the avid Gothic-reading heroine of *Northanger Abbey* (1817), who confuses fiction and its structures for reality and is shamed for doing so.

The provenance of Gothic fiction in the form of architectural follies demonstrates that the desire to recreate the distant Middle Ages had become environmentally pervasive in early eighteenth-century culture. Without such models in actual space, textual articulations of the same desire would not exist: the use of landscape space, building materials, and idioms of architectural style as the media for fictions of Gothic spatial form provided the model for novelistic excursions into spatial formalism—that is, experiments with spatial environments in and as text. Experimentation in fictional spatial constructs was, indeed, an intermedial endeavor shared by literature *and* landscape architecture, even if novelists such as Walpole trailed builders like Vanbrugh by some fifty years.

Gothic fiction, beginning with architectural follies and realized later in textual narratives, treats and presents space as the medium through which stories emerge and take place. While this was also a feature of the spaces explored in prior chapters, follies are distinctive in being self-consciously temporal as well as material deceptions. Simply put, they emulate something they are not: edifices built in the medieval period. Eighteenth-century follies thereby illuminate how space is used as a medium for the extratextual dimensions of fiction as a mode of embodied and materially responsive interiority. By making manifest in everyday spaces fantasies of a past that never happened, "of ruins where there was never a house," follies shed new light on how fiction creates environments for the inner lives of human subjects.[2]

The camera obscura is a critical artifact for understanding the ways follies work as Gothic fiction and, in turn, how Gothic fiction works as follies. Jayne Lewis's examination of atmosphere as a "key gothic signature" helps elucidate this point.[3] Lewis's own concept of atmosphere, which includes the Gothic's "architectural forms and models of inwardness," is developed as a "dimension of literary experience for which we now possess no stable vocabulary," unlike "character, plot, or even style."[4] Finding in scientific discourses on air a rich source for contextualizing and understanding literature's developing technique of atmosphere, she examines how air "mediates between material and immaterial, literal and figurative, registers of reality."[5] Striking in Lewis's insightful and original conceptualizations of the most ineffable yet haunting aspects of literary settings and environments is their assonance with the qualities of experience associated with the camera obscura. These include their projection of images that mediate between reality and imagination, clarity and blurriness, and proximity and distance, making indistinguishable the internal perception of something and its dreamy rendering as an external, real-seeming image. If atmosphere, like air itself, is difficult to capture in concrete and material terms, so is the impression of spatial reality produced by the camera obscura. The camera obscura transforms real spaces into atmosphere, and, as this chapter will reveal, its technology of atmospheric transformation was directly and indirectly complicit with the creation and experience of Gothic follies, not only of Gothic fictional narratives.

Pope makes an early foray into equating literary with architectural Gothic style when, in "Preface to Shakespeare," he likens Shakespeare's drama and its "irregularity" to "an ancient majestick piece of *Gothick* Architecture."[6] Compared with the "elegant and glaring" features of a "neat Modern building," Pope observes, the "strong and solemn" ones of a Gothic building display "greater variety" and "much the nobler apartments," though "dark, odd, and uncouth passages" frequently serve as their conductors.[7] By extending these terms to Shakespeare's drama, Pope lays hold of its aesthetic qualities but, further, presents a literary work as a building with habitable rooms. Robert Harbison articulates what impulse might impel one to create such an equation in the case of fiction, if not drama as well: "A strong concern with architecture signifies in fiction as it does outside a concern with protection, a desire for established existence and a home for consciousness."[8]

Gothic narrative form is usually understood in terms of a formula first evident in Walpole's *Castle of Otranto* and continued in the works of Sophia Lee, Ann Radcliffe, William Beckford, and Matthew Lewis. Although there are variations, Gothic fiction is usually identified by its contents, or what it "has": supernatural phenomena and occurrences, uncanny doublings and repetitions, patriarchal oppression, lost mothers, abused sons and daughters, sublime moments of horror and terror, social or sexual transgression, intricate architectural structures that figure almost like characters themselves, and human characters, usually female, imprisoned or hiding within them. But Gothic fiction in its original eighteenth-century setting was also an everyday fiction of domestic design and interiority that preceded and extended beyond Walpole's admittedly great, but by no means singular, influence on the Gothic Revival in architecture and design.

When literary critics acknowledge the relevance of architecture to Gothic fiction, they have tended to focus on how Gothic architecture emerges as a represented construct in the setting, plot, and symbolism of Gothic narrative.[9] Early on, however, Gothic architecture and Gothic fiction served as mutual constructs for the play of fiction and, at the same time, environments for the play of the mind—a shared project of counterfeiting the status of both *as* Gothic. Play, in Johan Huizinga's telling, is an act of "stepping out of 'real' life into a temporary sphere of activity with a disposition all of its own."[10] The Gothic folly is an especially suggestive architectural form for exploring the interrelation of buildings and books as media for the plays of fiction and mind. The sham Gothic building or ruin, whether as narrative or as architecture, lives out the extratextual definition of "fiction" put forth by Rousseau in *Reveries of the Solitary*

Walker: "To lie without benefit or harm to oneself or to others is not to lie: it is not a lie, but a fiction."[11]

Architectural design books functioned as visual sources for the fiction of Gothic housing. One of the eight chimneypiece designs in landscape designer and architectural writer Batty Langley's *Ancient Architecture, Restored, and Improved* (1742; republished in 1747 as *Gothic Architecture*), is especially representative of this chapter's vision of the Gothic. For Langley, who insisted the tribe known as "the Goths" would more accurately be called "the Saxons," the impetus to create this first book of Gothic Revival design and architecture came from a desire to "restore and illustrate the beauties of the Saxon Architecture, for the good of posterity."[12] His effort was successful insofar as his example led such writers as William Halfpenny, Thomas Overton, Paul Decker, and William Wrighte to write their own books on Gothic design.[13] Moreover, his published designs made their ways into lived reality. Architectural historian Eileen Harris finds evidence of this in "doorways at Great Fulford, Devon, and the Ludlow police station; fireplaces at Shobdon church, Herefordshire and Tissington Hall, Derbyshire; the Gothic temple at Bramham Park, Yorkshire; and the 'show' front of the gate at Castletown, co. Kildare."[14]

On the Palladian foundation of one of Langley's chimneypiece designs, Gothic trefoil and quatrefoil motifs and rosette roundels are combined with the flourishing acanthus-leaf swags associated with the contemporary Rococo style (fig. 5.2). By integrating an arcane visual mode with modern and classical ones, the chimneypiece transposes elements from religious architecture to the secular space of the domestic interior. These intermixtures of time and space prefigure, through material means, Walpole's "attempt to blend the two kinds of romance, the ancient and the modern," when writing *The Castle of Otranto*, two decades later. Visual idioms and architectural functions are mixed in other ways as well in Langley's chimneypiece. For instance, the trefoil arch one might see as the tracery design for a church window is used as the frame for a singularly eighteenth-century image that is both Gothic and picturesque: a landscape scene of a ruined ancient building. The ruin's appearance of age and dilapidation is reinforced by the vegetal growth seeming to spring from its form. Whether the ruin depicted is real or a simulacrum of a ruin is immaterial. Its appearance within a frame self-consciously stylized as Gothic endows it with the spirit of the folly. In any case, the design makes the temporally distant space of the Gothic coextensive with a contemporary domestic one. It suggests that the activity of looking at a folly, despite its external situation, can be translated as an act of looking inward, within the space of a notional or real home, through a frame of Gothic design.

FIGURE 5.2 Batty Langley, Chimney Piece, Plate XLVII, *Gothic Architecture* (1747). Photograph: Getty Research Institute, Los Angeles.

In this way the chimneypiece design, camera obscura–like, brings inside, and thus internalizes, architectural features that one usually sees when outside or looking outward.

This view of the Gothic and its representative eighteenth-century architectural structure, the folly, within an idealized domestic setting reveals the limitations in standard literary accounts of formal or domestic realism as the master genre for novelistic interiority. Accounts that privilege the novel's representations of domestic or private life as central aspects of the new literary genre, including most prominently the works of Watt and Armstrong, leave out the Gothic entirely. In doing so, they contribute to criticism's tendency to sideline the Gothic novel as a subgenre that stands more as a Romantic or proto-nineteenth-century construct than as an eighteenth-century one. The Gothic novel, with its incorporation of supernatural and implausible occurrences, is seen as running counter to the "Age of Reason," a cultural-intellectual moment considered the natural progenitor of realist narrative technique. Against this notion, Lewis has argued that the atmospheric mist of the Gothic that "creeps into the poetry and literary romance of the 1790s" develops *out of* rather than in defiance of "Enlightenment assumptions that the world is immediately available to the senses."[15]

The Gothic novel, then, warrants a place in the lineage of novelistic forms conducive to the psychological interiority that is viewed as paradigmatic of modern subjectivity and fiction. If realism is designated by its fidelity to the spatiality and temporality of everyday life—as readers experience it themselves—then Gothic fiction warrants consideration as a form of realism in its own right, which spatial formalism makes detectable. As the instances of built ruins and Gothic Revivalism in contemporary architectural design demonstrate, Gothic forms and fictions were features of everyday life in eighteenth-century England, well before the age of Romanticism. Gothic form in landscape experience demonstrates that the interactive nature of spatial environments, as products of creative design and agents of imaginative experience in material culture, serves as the very grounds on which Gothic fiction could be textually imagined and developed by Walpole and the novelists who followed him.[16]

Insofar as, throughout this book, spatial formalism reconfigures Watt's "formal realism" to register the psychic affordances of form that dwell in spatial elements of the material world—in texts, landscape, or architecture—the Gothic readily serves its objectives. By conceiving or representing spatial details and features precisely to enable a viewer, reader, or dweller to engage psychologically with a given structure, creators of Gothic fictions in both architectural and narrative art provide ideal examples for the examination of spatial formalism. Gothic fiction, whether in buildings or in texts, in other words, exemplifies Ingold's notion of the architextural, whereby the textural aspects of "verbal composition," and not just the textual, achieve significance. Considerations of the "textural"—the "tissue of lines" that appears in the patterns of words on a page, as well as the pattern of movements into, out of, and around buildings and texts themselves—render the textual and architectural into the architextural. Entanglements between built structures and the subjects who enact movements toward, through, and within them take place. Such entanglements have been found in all of the spaces explored in earlier chapters, from the writing closets of seventeenth-century subjects, providing enclosure and freedom within which the mind could create new worlds out of text, to the detachable pockets of eighteenth-century women, rendering privacy portable through their capacity to carry letters and other personal items. Nowhere, though, were these architextural entanglements and slippages from space to text more deliberately mediated and pursued than in the creation of eighteenth-century Gothic follies.

Follies and Associationism

Fundamentally, a folly is an ornamental building whose main purpose is to provide a visual point of interest within the greater composition of a private landscape garden. Many also served practical functions, as, for example, a hunting lodge, a teahouse or summer house for entertainment, a library, a dovecote, a small castle for dogs, or a barn. Overall, it is the element of irony, of appearing to be one sort of building and functioning as another, that distinguishes the folly and its experience not just as fiction but as Gothic fiction. Such a mixture of apparent frivolity and day-to-day function is precisely what motivates the writing of the *Castle of Otranto*. Remarking that he intended to "blend" the ancient and modern "kinds of romance," Walpole explains that fancy and the supernatural characterizes the ancient mode of narrative, while the natural and common life characterizes the modern.

Though follies began appearing in late sixteenth- and early seventeenth-century landscape gardens of private English estates, the form is very much associated with the eighteenth century, and most were built in the eighteenth and early nineteenth centuries.[17] It was then, in the age of Enlightenment, that the folly became a requisite element in the most fashionable landscape gardens and parks of country manor estates. If one were to stretch the definition of follies, they might include as well other subgenres of garden buildings: grottoes, hermitages, pyramids, obelisks, Turkish tents and Chinese pagodas, bridges. By and large, however, faux medieval structures were most prevalent, and that attribute remains part of the canonical definition.

Several scholars have explored and accounted for the political and nationalistic motivations underlying the emergence of follies from the 1710s to the 1760s. The taste for the "new" Gothic signified a turn away from classical influences to embrace an aesthetic tradition derived from the "true" forebears of Britain, the Goths. Hence, Gothic style came to be associated mainly with Whig values of national pride, freedom from absolutism, and constitutional government. By the last quarter of the century, worries about a Jacobite resurgence had subsided to the extent that the building of mock ruins was no longer driven by political motivations. Instead, they were created to fulfill a desire for picturesque landscape objects.[18] The forties were an especially active period of folly design and building: James Gibbs's Gothic Temple (also known as the Temple of Liberty) was built at Stowe House in 1741, Daniel Garrett's Culloden Tower at York House in 1746, and Sanderson Miller's influential Radway Tower and its accompanying suite of ruins in 1746–1747 on his estate. All of these structures, as well as earlier landscape buildings of the 1710s and 1720s, can be said to lay claim to the Gothic past for ideological purposes, accomplishing acts of nation-building through the very process of incorporating British history into the lived environment.[19] According to this line of scholarship, garden buildings made to resemble medieval towers, castles, and ruins held primary importance as signifiers of British national identity and vehicles for asserting political alliances and values.[20]

Even in their role as instruments of political ideology, follies served and generated more subjective ends and experiences, including the longing to "perpetuate self-seclusion" and experience changes in the mind's spaces.[21] The choice of Gothic style timelessly coheres with, as Harbison puts it, "the gloom and darkness of a self which wants to convert its feeling of being embattled to literal fortifications."[22] The very principle of associationism underlying the use of a faux ruin even as a vehicle for political or nationalistic expression bespeaks its quality of stimulating experiences of the mind. For instance, the ability to recognize the historical and political significance of the location of Radway Tower on Edge Hill, where the first battle of the English Civil War took place, might invite an inward meditation on "the drama of the making and unmaking of kings and constitution, played out within the terms of gothic and feudal principles."[23] The ability of Radway Tower (1745) to evoke a past made romantic and mysterious by its distance and difference from the current period is intensified by the set of ruined buildings that surround the octagonal, castellated tower. These include a thatched cottage built two years earlier, with a ruined stone facade, Gothic windows, and round bastions, and a "ruinous wall," with doors and medieval-style windows.

Miller's antiquarianism indicates the folly's function as a prompt for historical associations, as does a remark by William Shenstone: "Surely I approve his design. He will, by this means, turn every bank and hillock of his estate there, if not into *classical*, at least into historical ground."[24] By virtue of taking place in contiguity and enacting a train of ideas, the historical associations of such follies as Radway Tower enlist the imagination and its pleasures. As Joshua Reynolds puts it, because "we have naturally a veneration for antiquity, whatever buildings bring to our remembrances ancient customs and manners . . . such as the Castles of the Barons of ancient chivalry, is sure to give delight." At the same time, these delightful remembrances are entirely subjective—different for each subject—which is the very nature of associationism; for Locke, "this strong Combination of *Ideas*, not ally'd by nature, the Mind makes in it self either voluntarily, or by chance, and hence it comes in different Men to be very different, according to their different Inclinations, Educations, Interest, *etc.*"[25]

At bottom, whether conceived to generate associations of a political, historical, or purely imaginative nature, the association of ideas is as much a fiction-making process as a subjective one, occasioned by engaging with the sensorial features of one's environment that enlist as well as stimulate the imagination. Addison, applying Locke's empiricist psychology to aesthetic experience in his "Pleasures of the Imagination" essays, identifies this engagement in the sequences of ideas that ensue when one perceives the elements of an evocative object, such as "the veins of marble" that might reveal "accidental Landskips of Trees, Clouds and Cities."[26] In general, broad expanses of landscape are the settings that prompt the imagination's associationist tendencies: "The Beauties of the most stately Garden or Palace lie in a narrow Compass, the Imagination immediately runs them over, and requires something else to gratifie her; but, in the wide Fields of Nature, the Sight wanders up and down without Confinement, and is fed with an infinite variety of images." Among the most propitious landscape "images" to feed the imagination through the channel of sight were those of ruins, whether real or fabricated.

Addison addresses this notion in *Spectator* 110, when walking alone at dusk in a setting where abbey ruins are "scattered up and down on every Side, and half covered with Ivy and Eldar-Bushes." Here, one might observe a grazing cow and construe it to be "a black Horse without an Head."[27] With this example of a rich set of conditions in which an association of ideas might take place, Addison, as Mr. Spectator, relates the Gothic setting of ruins to the subject matter most commonly aligned with Gothic fiction, its "Spectres and Apparitions" and "supernumerary Horrours." In doing so, he places what would later be formulated as the narrative experience of Gothic fiction within the context of quotidian life. "I was taking a Walk in this Place last Night between the Hours of Nine and Ten, and could not but fancy it one of the most proper Scenes in the World for a Ghost to appear in." Here, as in the description of Pamela's first encounter with Mr. B's Lincolnshire home, the specified details of time and place situate Mr. Spectator's Gothic encounter in a prosaic setting, but one where realism intersects with Gothic fantasy. Both examples, predating Walpole's *Castle of Otranto*, reinforce the notion that the Gothic is a fictional mode central to the development of domestic realism, if not a form of domestic realism in itself. Whereas Pamela herself prefigures the young abducted females who feature as Gothic heroines, similar to Isabel Thwaites in *Upon Appleton House*, her apprehensive description of Mr. B's Lincolnshire home as a Gothic edifice involves a supernatural element: an "old, and lonely Mansion, that looks made for Solitude and Mischief . . . with all its brown nodding Horrors of lofty Elms and Pines about it." Yet the absence of a Gothic architectural edifice in passages such as Addison's indicates the way that Gothic fiction subsists as a quality of atmosphere that alters familiar contexts, similar to the way the camera obscura serves as a tool for viewing what is actually there, but modifies it so it appears unreal. Each, the Gothic (whether as narrative or as architecture) and the camera obscura, works as a medium for making reality appear as if it were imagined.

In an early essay into his influential enunciation of the picturesque aesthetic, William Gilpin expresses through a dialogue between Callophilus and Polython the impression that the sight of built ruins in a landscape, the Hermitage and Octagon Lake Cascade at Stowe (1728–1729), makes on the imagination:

"Has not that ruin," says he, "a good effect? How romantick is yon Hermitage? Those pines which hang nodding over those broken Arches, that murmuring cascade, and those Fauns and Satyrs dancing to its sound, I assure you begin to raise very wild ideas in my head. Whence is it, my friend that the imagination, even of a god-natured man, is more enraptured with these rude appearances of Nature, these prospects of the ruinous kind, than with the most smiling views of plenty and prosperity?"[28]

The passage demonstrates the direct connection of the visual and aural elements of the ruin with the experience of the mind, identifying the ruin's overall appearance of roughness as the factor that makes it conducive to activating the imagination. The "very wild ideas" that are raised comprise the mental fictions that emerge in associative response to the ruin. Though fictive, and failing to correspond with what is physically present, these ideas are shaped and prompted by the materiality of what is.

Other elements of follies also contribute to their fictionality, including both their very status as imposters of something else and the embodied process of this discovery. One of the most remarked-upon aspects of experiencing follies is the inevitable discovery or detection that their assertion of ancient origins is a fraud. The arc of this realization comprises an experience of fiction. Todorov's conception of fiction as fundamentally a form of grammar that moves from disequilibrium to equilibrium applies here.[29] Joseph Heely, whose visit to Hagley is documented in *A Description of Hagley Park* (1775), recounts his cognitive and emotional experience of encountering a folly, and of recognizing that it is one.[30] The folly in question is an artificial ruined castle, designed in 1747 by Sanderson Miller for Sir George Lyttelton. After passing through a "gay, irregular, and sylvan area" that was Pope's favorite spot and where an urn dedicated to him stands, one begin the approach to the "castle":

> While with cheerful step you climb the side-mantled hill, a seat within a knot of old and crooked alders will invite you to it, where your eye will ... delighted, repose ... on the remains of an old dusky building, solemn and venerable, rearing its gothic turret among the bushy trees, called
>
> THE RUIN

> Upon the first glimpse of this becoming object, which adds so much dignity to the scene, one cannot resist an involuntary pause—struck with its character, the mind naturally falls into reflections, while curiosity is on the wing, to be acquainted with its history; and I make no doubt that an antiquarian ... would sigh to know in what era it was founded, and by whom:—what sieges it had sustained—what blood had been spilt upon its walls:—and would lament that hostile discord, or the iron hand of all-mouldering time, should so rapaciously destroy it.

Throughout his account of visiting Hagley, Heely provides a first-person narrative of the forms of physical and mental movement the landscape garden affords. When he encounters "the ruin," the account becomes particularly rich in its flow of psychological responses and modes, from curious and delighted, to impressed and reflective. Temporality becomes complex as well. The "involuntary pause" that accompanies the "first glimpse" of the ruin disrupts the present moment as he reflects on its supposed history, speculating on events of the distant past, only to come into the awareness that the imagined time never existed:

> Believe me, the appearance of this antique pile has the power of stamping these impressions on the mind, so masterly is it executed to deceive; for in reality it is nothing but a deception, designed and raised here by the

late noble possessor . . . it is a modern structure, intended not merely as an object only, to give a livelier consequence to the landscape, but for use; being a lodge for the keeper of the park . . . the large and massy stones, which have seemingly tumbled from the tottering and ruinous walls, are suffered to lie about the different parts of the building, in the utmost confusion. This greatly preserves its intention as a ruin, and the climbing ivy which already begins to embrace the walls with its gloomy arms will soon throw a deeper solemnity over the whole, and make it carry the strongest face of antiquity.

The folly's status as an element that gives the landscape "a livelier consequence" hinges on this ability to create a fiction of temporality, which spurs the mind into a state first of curiosity, then of reflection, and finally of comprehension—a recognition of the reality of the ruin. Heely's reverie then turns to detachment as he observes the material aspects that compose the false "face of antiquity." Initially, fiction is generated through associative response, as the visitor wonders about the history of the ruin and "what blood had been spilt upon its walls." Subsequently, fiction subsists in its "deception," its masquerade of age and decrepitude. This fiction enfolds a material deception into a temporal one insofar as the temporal fiction is effected by the very materials that make up the ruin. In the case of the ruin at Hagley, Heely writes, its "massy stones" and the ivy that covers them conspire to affirm its "intention as a ruin."

In contrast, Gilpin, who considered ruins, whether real or fake, to be essential components of picturesque landscapes, would not regard ivy or massy stones as sufficient to make a built ruin appear authentic:

There is great art, and difficulty also in *executing* a building of this kind. It is not every man, who can build a house, that can execute a ruin. To give the stone it's [*sic*] mouldering appearance—to make the widening chink run naturally through all the joins—to mutilate the ornaments—to peel the facing from the internal structure—to shew how correspondent parts have once united; tho now the chasm run wide between them—and to scatter heaps of ruin around with negligence and ease; are great efforts of art; much too delicate for the hand of a common workman; and what we very rarely see performed.[31]

Gilpin here draws attention to follies as products of artifice. In stressing artifice over design, he illuminates the paradox of materiality that lies at the heart of follies: to "execute" a ruin, one uses human hands to "make up" materials to resemble those in the process of being "unmade" by nature and time. Rather than a product of natural decay and arbitrary force and violence, the folly's apparent authenticity depends on artisanal skill and technique. The sense of authenticity also requires an awareness of how materials scatter, erode, and settle over time, and of how to compose stones so that they appear to be in a state of decomposition. Follies are fictions of time at the level of their material qualities and spatial dispositions.

The technique used in Gothic novels, corollary to that of making materials in a construction appear older than they are, is the found-text or manuscript convention, whereby the narrative is presented as coming from an authentic medieval document. Writers of Gothic novels convey this faux-archival identity by referring to superficial quirks that reveal their texts' "ancient" status. Walpole, for instance, in his preface to the first edition of *The Castle of Otranto*, refers to the "black letter" (or Gothic) typeface in which the text originally appeared, and infamously pretends to the world that his novel had been "found in the library of an ancient Catholic family."

Likewise, Radcliffe's *A Sicilian Romance*, published in 1790, presents itself as a "solemn history . . . contained in a manuscript" housed in the library of an old Italian castle. Most dramatically, Sophia Lee's *The Recess*, published in 1783, offers the notion that stories of the past are subject to the same erosions of time as architecture, which can render them ruins too. The advertisement that opens *The Recess* claims the narrative came from "extracts" of a manuscript. Between these, "the depredations of time have left chasms in the story." As in architectural ruins, such chasms increase the interior richness of experiencing the artifact, for, as the advertisement states, they "only heighten the pathos."

Insofar as the found-manuscript tradition of Gothic narrative shares with mock Gothic ruins a stress on the material elements of production, whether figural or real, the fictionality they mutually generate is one of fabrication. The French word for the landscape folly, *fabrique,* makes this association explicit. Throughout Radcliffe's novels, especially *A Sicilian Romance*, the word used to refer to buildings is "fabric" (indeed, "an edifice, a building" is the *OED*'s first definition for the word). For example: "After much wandering and difficulty they arrived, overcome with weariness, at the gates of a large and gloomy fabric."[32] As in *Pamela*, the term operates in the Gothic novel in a multivalent fashion, commensurate with the imbrication of different structural entities, from textual, textural, and architectural bodies to narrative itself. All these architextural entities conform to the basic definition of fabric as "a product of skilled workmanship."

Other definitions for the term *fabric* also apply to the variants of the Gothic examined in this chapter. These include its guise as "a manufactured material" (the ruinated stones of follies) and a "body formed by the conjunction of dissimilar parts" (the "ancient and the modern" forms of romance "blended" to create the narrative genre conceived by Walpole).[33] To consider the Gothic in all its permutations as a "fabric" is to open it further to the analysis of fiction's materiality. This is especially evident in the frame narrative that opens *A Sicilian Romance*, which reproduces a description of encountering ruins such as might be found in a guidebook like Heely's. The novel's first paragraph begins with a third-person narrative perspective on the remains of the Mazzini castle as it then stands in the middle of a small bay on Sicily's northern shore. Having established the castle's general location, the passage shifts into the first person, like Heely's guidebook passage, to assess the ruins:

> As I walked over the loose fragments of stone, which lay scattered through the immense area of the fabric, and surveyed the sublimity and grandeur of the ruins, I recurred, by a natural association of ideas, to the times when these walls stood proudly in their original splendor, when the halls were the scenes of hospitality and festive magnificence, and when they resounded with the voices of those whom death had long since swept from the earth. "Thus," said I, "shall the present generation—he who now sinks in misery—and he who now swims in pleasure, alike pass away and be forgotten." My heart swelled with the reflection.[34]

This description of a fictional encounter with a "real" ruin, like Heely's real encounter with a faux ruin, depicts the "natural association of ideas" that leads to speculation on past events that took place inside the once-intact building, as well as to a general state of contemplation. Here, too, the ruin is personified and configured as a witness and auditor. The novel's epigraph, from *Hamlet*, "I could a tale unfold," spoken by the ghost of Hamlet's father, reinforces the anthropomorphized status of the ruined castle as a ghostly entity. Not only can it see and hear things; recalling the nunnery ruins at Nun Appleton, it has the ability to speak, to craft a story of all that has passed within its walls.

The fabric of the building coincides architexturally with the fabric of the narrative the castle "unfolds." The "loose fragments of stone" that make up the ruins of the castle are commensurate in function and value with the pieces of the castle's history taken as "abstracts" from the purported manuscript, as well as "conversation with the abate" who brought it to the narrator.[35] The "following pages," having been "arranged" by the narrator—who functions in effect as an archivist—compose the central narrative known as *A Sicilian Romance*. They also constitute the work undertaken to imagine the ruined structure as whole again. Such is the framework of the folly built by Radcliffe.

Space and Psyche

Landscape follies, as mentioned earlier, though ornamental, frequently fulfill basic roles of buildings in general, providing shelter, for example, or storage, or a setting in which to carry out a specific activity. The faux ruin at Hagley, for instance, served as a lodge for the park's keeper, and so has "a neatly fitted-up room in the tower, which intentionally is left in a perfect state."[36] At times follies not only function as fictions but serve as fictions of function. Sir George Lyttelton, owner of Hagley, indicates this in a letter directing Miller, his architect, as to how he might design a folly for Lyttelton's friend, Lord Chancellor Hardwicke, on his Wimpole Hall estate. Lyttelton would prefer, he writes, that Miller not copy his folly at Hagley, and he explains that Hardwicke himself has a unique idea: "he wants no house nor even room in it, but merely the walls and semblance of an old castle to make an object from his house."[37]

So fixated is Hardwicke on the idea that his folly at Wimpole Hall should have minimal practical function that Lyttelton reiterates those wishes in another letter to Miller, elaborating on the extent to which the building will *prohibit* habitation:

> The view of Wimpole which you have seen will give you a pretty just idea. . . . It is a hill about half a mile from the house to which the ground rises gently all the way. My Ld. agrees with your notion of having some firrs before part of the walls. As the back view will be immediately closed by the wood there is no regard to be had to it, nor to the left side, but only to the front and right side as you look from the house. As my Lord designs it merely as an object, he would have no staircase nor leads in any of the towers, but merely the walls so built as to have the appearance of a ruined castle.[38]

Nothing in the folly's external appearance prevents one from imagining the possibility of ascent once inside the structure. But Hardwicke's desire to construct a building that eliminates basic internal features of a building, to allow it to function solely as an attractive "object [to be regarded] from his house," reveals the extent to which the built ruin's status is ficti-

FIGURE 5.3 Sanderson Miller, Castle in Hagley Park (ca. 1747),
Hagley, Worcestershire. Photograph by Philip Halling,
Wikimedia Commons (CC BY-SA 2.0).

tious. Referring to the owner of Shugborough Hall and the "pile of artificial ruins" that the windows of his house "look towards," Gilpin in fact
uses the word *fictitious*: "But Mr. Anson has been less happy in fabricating
fictitious ruins; than in restoring such as are real."

Gilpin details the complexities involved in planning a folly. The designer of a ruin meant to be seen from "some distant, inaccessible place,"
he points out, may proceed with only "one or two points of view" in mind.
A folly "presented *on the spot*," however, as is Shugborough Hall's, becomes
"a matter of great difficulty," for "the spectator may walk round it, and survey it on every side—perhaps enter it."[39] Yet, despite this distinction, the
folly built "merely as an object" still yields the attributes of a space. It does
so precisely because its owner has envisioned its purpose as only "to have
the appearance of a ruined castle"; serving as a distant and unfinished
fiction, it invites the mind to imagine the space that might have been.[40]

Gilpin helps explain how the spatial evocativeness of the Wimpole
Hall folly lies in its status as an incomplete built ruin whose interior stays
resolutely uninhabitable. Discerning the capacity for incomplete buildings and "rough plans" of houses to stimulate the imagination, he writes:

Again, on the same supposition, one would imagine, that the rude beginning, or rough plan of a house, would please us more than the compleat pile; for the *imagination is entertained with the promise of something more* ... we see why the *sketch* may please beyond the *picture;* tho the *unfinished fabric* disappoints. An elegant house is a *compleat object.* The imagination can rise no higher. It receives full satisfaction.[41]

The notion that a folly's value as a building lies mainly in its ability to *appear* as one in actual space resonates with Harbison's observation that Gothic style expresses the projections of an "embattled" self longing for "literal fortifications." The folly, in other words, embodies the psyche's need to encounter the manifestation of a wished-for dwelling that would never be practical to inhabit or otherwise realize. The emotional projections that Gothic-style buildings draw out are also evident in Gilpin's delineation of the two types that appear frequently in picturesque landscapes: "Castles, and abbeys have different situations, agreeable to their respective uses. The castle, meant for defence, stands boldly on the hill: the abbey, intended for meditation, is hid in the sequestered vale."[42] With this personifying description of defensive castles and meditative abbeys, an equation is made between the spaces of buildings and the spaces of psyches.

Thus, as a prompt for psychological desires rather than an actual edifice for practical dwelling, the folly reinforces the spatial dimensions of the mind, filling it with attractive notions by means of association. Thomas Gray's 1758 letter to William Palgrave asking him to describe the picturesque landscape scenes he comes across during his travels in Scotland demonstrates that such scenes were in fact viewed as filling up and furnishing the space of the mind as a "Gothic apartment":[43]

In the meantime I congratulate you on your new acquaintance with the *savage,* the *rude,* and the tremendous. Pray, tell me, is it anything like what you had read in your book, or seen in two-shilling prints? Do not you think a man may be the wiser (I had almost said the better) for going a hundred or two of miles; and that the mind has more room in it than most people seem to think, if you will but furnish the apartments? I almost envy your last month, being in a very insipid situation myself, and desire you would not fail to send me some furniture for my Gothic apartment, which is very cold at present.[44]

A landscape scene perceived by someone else and conveyed through their report, Gray's letter suggests, nevertheless stimulates ideas and fantasies about scenes as spaces, furnishing and enlivening the "Gothic apartment" that is the receiver's mind.

Spaces as Objects

As suggested by Lord Hardwicke's desire to use a built ruin to "make an object from his house," the folly functioned as much as an architectural object as an architectural space by providing a visual point of interest within the fabric of the landscape garden. Landscape-design guides throughout the century referred to garden buildings precisely as "objects" to engage the eye *as well as* the imagination. Echoing Joseph Addison's principles of the pleasures of the imagination, expressed in *The Spectator*, Batty Langley, in his 1728 book on garden design, *New Principles of Gardening*, writes, "The End and Design of a good Garden, is to be both profitable and delightful; wherein should be observed, that its Parts should be always presenting new Objects, which is a continued Entertainment to the Eye, and raise a Pleasure of Imagination."[45]

This "continued Entertainment," the sequence of effects determined by relationships among the garden's parts, depends for its perception on the positions, experiences, and movements of the observer's body: "Now as the Beauty of Gardens in general depends upon an elegant Disposition of all their Parts, which cannot be determined without a perfect Knowledge of its several Ascendings, Descendings, Views, &c. How is it possible any Person can make a good Design for any Garden, whose Situation they never saw?"[46] One must experience the parts of a landscape firsthand, Langley insists, to apprehend subjectively the progressively revealed features and qualities of its "disposition" as a composed entity. Radcliffe's narrator, as mentioned earlier, presents a similar notion in *A Sicilian Romance* when explaining that the ensuing narrative had not arrived in one piece, readymade, but rather was "arranged" out of "abstracts" of a found "history." In contrast to textual narrative, landscape narrative hinges on the subjective experiences of one's body as it moves through space, and of one's mind as it perceives the internal responses to the resulting "Ascendings, Descendings, Views, &c." Landscape objects work to mediate this embodied narrative of spatial experience and discovery.

Thomas Whately, in *Observations on Modern Gardening* (1770), places an even greater emphasis on the role of small buildings as objects in garden design, but he also recognizes their value as physical spaces.[47] By this time, follies had become common landscape features, built more for "lavish display" than for utility. Reflecting on their origin as spaces offering "shelter against the wind" or a "sudden shower" to walkers in distant parts of the landscape, he advocates that follies be "considered both as beautiful objects, and as agreeable retreats." In expressing this view, Whately reveals an awareness both of the qualities that render the folly an object and of the qualities that render it a space. On one hand, "it is by their exterior that they become *objects*." On the other, it is through attentiveness to the "interior of buildings" that they function as spaces. And yet, because his main concern is landscape design and the relationships of the parts that make up the whole, Whately is most concerned with the function of garden buildings as objects—and consequently as the elements of a spatial rhetoric.[48] "As objects," he writes, they "are designed either to *distinguish*, or to *break*, or to *adorn*, the scenes to which they are applied."[49] Far from frivolous, garden buildings such as follies are essential to landscape design, functioning as a sort of punctuation:

> The difference between one wood, one lawn, one piece of water, and another; are not always very apparent; the several parts of a garden would, therefore, often seem similar, if they were not distinguished by buildings; but these are so observable, so obvious at a glance, so easily retained in the memory, they mark the spots where they are placed with so much strength, they attract the relation of all around with so much power; that parts thus distinguished can never be confounded together.[50]

By viewing garden buildings as formative elements in a grammatical as well as a visual composition, akin to the marks that distinguish phrases and make writing more intelligible, Whately opens the possibility of understanding landscape experience as a textual experience. The landscape is occupied and viewed as a series of interconnected sentences and phrases. He also opens a view to landscape's textural qualities, showing how it is composed of disparate material elements to form a visual pattern.

The textual and textural aspects of follies account for why they have spatial and narrative resonances, even when they are conceived and regarded as objects. In their function as visually engaging landscape objects, they stimulate the mind and turn it into a vivid and active domain. Whately suggests this too when describing our response to seeing a decaying building:

> We naturally contrast its present to its former state, and delight to ruminate on the comparison. It is true that such effects properly belong to real ruins; but they are produced in a certain degree by those which are fictitious, the impressions are not strong, but they are exactly similar; and the

representations, though it does not present facts to the memory, yet suggests subjects to the imagination.[51]

Here, Whately, like Heely, indicates the associationist logic by which a folly as a ruined building might enter and engage the psyche while inviting it to enter its own space in turn. Such entrance is made through the implied activity of the imagination as it wonders what happened to, and inside, the building, ineluctably creating a story in doing so. For Whately, the status of the ruin as "fictitious" or authentic makes little difference, as each type issues the same effect. Taking a slightly different tack, I am suggesting that even if the building is a true ruin, it bears the properties of a folly insofar as it too stimulates and affords the mode of fiction by suggesting so much to the imagination. It too works to turn the mind into the space of a Gothic romance. Within philosophical and aesthetic systems of the eighteenth century, fiction is a permutation of the everyday acts of thinking that take place continually when living and being in material environments. The fiction-generating interactions between Gothic edifices and individual minds are only marked enactments of this notion.

Empiricist Experience as Gothic Fiction

In *Spectator* 413, one of Addison's 1712 essays on the pleasures of the imagination, the Gothic is already being presented to popular culture as a paradigm and means for questioning the different ways in which the mind is understood as perceiving its physical world. In a reflection on Locke's notion that material reality and the different qualities of light and colors one perceives in it are dissociated from each other—"those Ideas which are different from any thing that exists in the Objects themselves"—Addison uses stock elements of the Gothic romance to underscore the reluctance with which he accepts this concept.[52] The experience of perception in itself provides pleasures that are spectacular: "We are every where entertained with pleasing Shows and Apparitions, we discover imaginary Glories in the Heavens, and in the Earth, and see some of this Visionary Beauty poured out upon the whole Creation." In this world, life is nothing short of a Gothic narrative: "our Souls are at present delightfully lost and bewildered in a pleasing Delusion, and we walk about like the Enchanted Hero of a Romance, who sees beautiful Castles, Woods and Meadows; and at the same time hears the warbling of Birds, and the purling of Streams." Yet allowing "that great Modern Discovery," Locke's idea that secondary qualities, "as apprehended by the Imagination, are only

Ideas in the Mind, and not Qualities that have any Existence in Matter," one will find nature's "Colouring disappear, and the several Distinctions of Light and Shade vanish." The outcome is a melancholy one, a vision of ruin after the breaking of an enchantment: "but upon the finishing of some secret Spell, the fantastic Scene breaks up, and the disconsolate Knight finds himself on a barren Heath, or in a solitary Desart."[53]

Locke himself uses the language of "phantasm" when referring to ideas, implicating them with fiction as well as with what would emerge as Gothic narrative and its own ghosts in the following century. At the beginning of *An Essay Concerning Human Understanding*, he informs the reader that the word *Idea* will frequently appear in his "following Treatise," for the term "serves best to stand for whatsoever is the Object of the Understanding when a Man thinks." He has "used it to express whatever is meant by *Phantasm, Notion, Species*, or whatever it is, which the Mind can be employ'd about in thinking."[54] That the experience of phantasms is a regular part of the mental experience of daily life is underscored in Locke's theory of primary and secondary qualities and the distinction between them.

As Addison indicates in *Spectator* 413, light and color are of the class Locke identifies as "secondary qualities," those "powers" that cause the mind to perceive an object. Other secondary qualities include sounds, smells, tastes, and heat and cold. Unlike the ideas of "primary qualities"— bulk, figure, texture, and motion—which "really do exist in the Bodies themselves," those of secondary qualities "have no resemblance of them at all."[55] Thus, for Locke, the color and coldness of a snowball, the smell and color of a violet, and the heat of fire are but fictions. He writes, "What I have said concerning *Colours* and *Smells*, may be understood also of *Tastes* and *Sounds* . . . which, whatever reality we, by mistake, attribute to them, are in truth nothing in the Objects themselves, but Powers to produce various Sensations in us."[56] In the moment of accepting this, we are all "disconsolate Knight[s]" alone in a desolate landscape.

Yet not just the different qualities of things in the world but the manner in which they traverse, through "*Sensation*" and "*Reflection*," the mind register as ideas. Succession, for instance, is an "idea" that is "offered us, by what passes in our Minds." We can identify it if "we look immediately into our selves, and reflect on what is observable there." Therein, "our Ideas [are] always, whilst we are awake, or have any thought, passing in train, one going, and another coming, without intermission."[57] The successive nature of thinking is a quality that narrative, in distinction from other literary modes yet in concert with the camera obscura's projections, possesses as well. Whereas thinking entails the "passing" of ideas in our minds, narrative entails a passing of events. Thus, just as the experience of thinking might resemble narrative, the experience of narrative, in its successive structure, resembles thinking itself. The perception of material reality, then, and its secondary qualities especially, can be a deeply fictive experience.

Camera Obscura and Claude Glass: Picturesque Space, Surface, and Scene

Even more indicative of the successive and narrative nature of the mind's activities in its perceptions of secondary qualities is the camera obscura. For Locke, Hume, and Cavendish, the dark space of the camera obscura is the space of the mind. Dark space can also be understood as the space of Gothic experience. For instance, William Thomas, author of *Original Designs in Architecture* (1783), refers to "the Night of Gothic Ignorance" as a stage in architectural history.[58] Others, such as Alexander Pope, viewed the darkness of Gothic settings, and of the camera obscura, as generative of visions of the imagination, as is apparent in Pope's grotto as well as *Eloisa to Abelard*.[59] For period commentators on architecture, design, and landscape, the elements of darkness, Gothic design, and, directly or indirectly, the camera obscura were mutually implicated as generators of psychological activity.

Langley, in *New Principles of Gardening* (1728), conceived of proto-picturesque garden design by insisting on the creation of dark spaces, as well as irregular lines. Not until 1742, however, in his *Ancient Architecture, Restored, and Improved*, would he directly address Gothic style and provide the means by which buyers of his book could incorporate it into their house designs. Although Langley emphasizes Gothic architectural designs in *Ancient Architecture*, providing many illustrated plates, his textual commentary is minimal, limited mainly to a chronological summary of major buildings erected during the reigns of medieval-era kings. It is the earlier treatise, *New Principles of Gardening*, with its emphasis on shade, irregularity, and ruins as elements of attractive garden design, that serves as an indirect exposition of Gothic form.

For Langley, "there is nothing more agreeable in a Garden than good *Shade*, and without it *a Garden is nothing*."[60] Not only does shade provide gardens with beauty; it serves, as well, as a covering for the land itself: "*Without a Shade no Beauty Gardens know; / And all the Country's but a naked Show*."[61] And yet most critical to landscape design is how it facilitates movement between different parts of the garden, allowing visitors to "pass and repass" through "proportionable Avenues" from the house to the groves and wildernesses. Originally the only shaded parts of the garden, and traditionally on its outskirts—as we know from Marvell's *Upon Appleton House*—wildernesses and groves demanded that visitors "pass thro' the *scorching Heat of the Sun*" to reach them.[62] While fulfilling the practical function of giving visitors a more physically comfortable means of reaching such regions, the incorporation of shade throughout landscape gardens makes them more conducive to contemplative states of being, allowing minds to settle into the body's rhythm of walking: "Indeed, 'tis oftentimes necessary to place *Groves* and open *Wildernesses* in such remote Parts of Gardens, from when *pleasant Prospects are taken*; but then we should always take care to plant *proportionable Avenues* leading them from the House to them, under whose *Shade* we might with Pleasure pass and repass at any time of the day."[63]

At the same time that the body "might with Pleasure pass and repass" under the shade of avenues, so too, and in unison with the body's movement, might ideas of the mind in the successive activity of thinking. The body in the dark avenues and wildernesses of the landscape garden is in league with the motions of ideas in the dark space of the mind. By creating shade for protection from sun and heat, the space of the landscape garden becomes like a camera obscura, mediating the body and mind in conjoined passings and repassings.

While Langley never states that dark landscapes could be designed to promote the conditions and experience of the camera obscura, William Gilpin makes direct claims that the process of observing and recording scenes of picturesque landscape leads toward turning the mind into a camera obscura. Gilpin, following Locke, explains that through the experience of repeatedly encountering these scenes and the natural objects therein, such as different oak trees, we acquire "correct knowledge of objects," whereby "we get [the natural object] more by heart" and may represent "by a few strokes in a sketch, those ideas, which have made the most impression upon us." Building one's inner "fund" of natural objects, adding them to our "collection" and getting them "by heart," leads to the ability to do something altogether different—to create and represent "*scenes of fancy*" that are "more a work of creation, than copying from nature." It is with this power that the

imagination becomes a camera obscura, only with this difference, that the camera represents objects as they really are while the imagination, impressed with the most beautiful scenes, and chastened by rules of art, forms it's [*sic*] pictures, not only from the most admirable parts of nature; but in the best taste.[64]

By depicting the camera obscura as a medium for idealized objects as opposed to real ones, Gilpin indicates a shift in attitudes toward the device. The mind is no longer merely similar to a camera obscura but has become one.[65] At the same time, the projections that filter into the device no longer come directly from the outside world; rather, they are the products of the mind's development of the most tasteful and "admirable parts of nature." The process by which such development takes place turns the camera obscura of the imagination into a workroom of sorts. This workroom is created when the eye is "half-closed" and "shut[s]" out further external input so that the "imagination, active and alert, collects its scattered ideas, transposes, combines, and shifts them into a thousand forms, producing such exquisite scenes, such sublime arrangements, such glow, and harmony of colouring and brilliant lights, such depth, and clearness of shadow."[66] These self-generating scenes, surpassing any that might be found in real life, but indebted to it for their origins, echo Addison's claim that on account of the faculties of sight and the imagination, a man trapped in a dungeon is able to divert himself with landscapes more beautiful than what can be found in nature.[67]

Gilpin's conception of a camera obscura whose projections derive from images already stored within its space seems to contradict the very principle of the device, for its projected images can only derive from what exists in external reality. As Friedrich Kittler puts it, "The *camera obscura* only works in the real world." The fact that it evolved into the photographic camera, which "cannot record anything that does not exist," confirms this.[68] In this regard, Gilpin's camera obscura of the imagination might seem more to resemble a magic lantern, whose images are drawn beforehand. Yet the fact that the idealized images of his camera obscura could originate only from directly experienced picturesque travel and the repeated observation of natural scenes and objects sustains the principle of the traditional camera obscura. As he insists in an earlier work, picturesque observations can only be "taken warm from the scenes of nature, as they arise."[69] Gilpin's definition of picturesque observation in this context sheds light on his figuration of the imagination as a camera obscura that projects images meeting the highest aesthetic standards. For Gilpin, observing landscape according to "the rules of picturesque beauty" is an act of "adapting the description of natural scenery to the principles of artificial landscape."[70] The dark space of the imagination as a camera obscura in this case serves as the medium for picturesque observation itself, as it too "adapts" images originating from reality to meet aesthetic criteria.

Gilpin's notion of the picturesque imagination functioning as a camera obscura comes, no doubt, from picturesque tourists' practice of using portable camera obscuras to record the sights they encountered on their travels. Yet the Claude glass, a pocket-size convex mirror with a black tain that transformed the landscape into a luminous, ideal scene when one looked into it, was the more portable, and more widely used, viewing device on picturesque tours. Gilpin himself used Claude glasses, and the horizontally oriented oval shape of the picturesque views in his books derives from a common shape for Claude glass frames. The box-size camera obscura was also used by picturesque tourists and artists to record the scenes at which they gazed. If the Claude glass transformed landscape scenes with a golden tint and mellowed hues, the camera obscura gave them a "great breadth of light" and a "minute finish," to use the terminology of Joshua Reynolds.[71] Just as the user of a Claude glass turns away from the scene in order to see its reflection on the mirror's surface, so too does the portable camera obscura user avert her eyes from the scene itself in order to see its projection inside a detached enclosed space.

With both devices, Kittler explains, the optical transmission of information is "automatic," but they also enable its storage by way of a "manual" process.[72] It is the manual process of drawing the images reflected or projected by the Claude glass and camera obscura that turns them into storage devices. Locke comments on the evanescence of unrecorded projections and reflections, deeming them as meaningless as thoughts that are forgotten. A looking glass, he writes, "constantly receives variety of Images, or *Ideas*, but retains none; they disappear and vanish, and there remain no footsteps of them; the Looking-glass is never the better for such *Ideas*, nor the Soul for such Thoughts."[73]

Though the objectives and uses of the two instruments for picturesque tourism were quite similar, some basic factors distinguish them. Whereas the Claude glass focuses on and frames an element of the landscape, the camera obscura projects its more immersive image within the enclosure of a dark, three-dimensional space. The experience of the camera obscura in the outdoor space of a landscape is, in this sense, a uniquely interiorizing one. Whether the viewer stands outside the box and looks in or stands inside the box, the experience is one of absorption by the image, which replicates the world "as it is" while revealing new aspects of it.

Although scholars have repeatedly characterized the camera obscura as cutting the viewer off from the world, the examples of the picturesque and other scenes throughout this book demonstrate the device's creative aspect, which affords viewers access to their own inner worlds, bringing them more deeply inside the self, and thereby bringing them as well to a new way of engaging with the external world. Gilpin registers this aspect of picturesque experience when he remarks that there is "more plea-

FIGURE 5.4 Claude Lorrain mirror (Wellcome transfer no. B1640), oval, in red
leather–covered case (ca. 1737–1767). Copper (alloy), glass, leather, padding,
textile, wood. Open case, ⅝ × 5¾ × 9 in. (1.5 × 14.5 × 23 cm). 1980-1746/2.
Photograph: Science Museum Group, © The Board of Trustees
of the Science Museum (CC Attrib. 4.0).

sure in recollecting, and recording, from a few transient lines, the scenes
we have admired, than in the present enjoyment of them."[74] The state of
presence entailed in using the camera obscura works similarly, effecting
a removal of presence from a directly perceived time or space in order to
open oneself up to an interior, mental representation of time and space.
In circumscribing an interior world visible only to oneself at the time the
images are created, and rendering the external world in all its movements
and colors, but on a reduced scale, the camera obscura, according to Gilpin, does not so much promote the activity of the imagination as exist as
the imagination itself.

The picturesque emphasis on the use of optical devices, not just as
aids for drawing but also for capturing and intensifying fleeting moments,
demonstrates their specific use as a journal of sorts. As one might use a
pocket-size notebook to record one's impressions, as John Parnell, John

Byng, and other great house tourists did, or a smartphone, as one would today, one might also use a camera obscura or Claude glass. This practice renders the camera obscura and mirror not just as metaphors for the mind but also—if one makes the extra effort of tracing and copying by hand their momentary images—as practical aids to enhance one of the mind's essential faculties: memory.

That an extra, manual step is necessary to preserve the transitory records created by the camera obscura and Claude glass indicates that, even as the picturesque offers moments of pleasure, it also entails the loss of those moments. Picturesque travel, as an essentially mobile experience undertaken on foot or by horse or carriage, is a fundamentally transient experience. Accordingly, the scenes, as viewed through Claude glasses from within a moving vehicle, "are like the visions of the imagination; or the passing landscapes of a dream. Forms, and colours, in brightest array, fleet before us."[75] Gilpin's description of fleeting landscape views on picturesque tours resembles Addison's depiction of the false reality one perceives—as an "Enchanted Hero of a Romance, who sees beautiful Castles, Woods and Meadows"—before submitting to the Lockean notion that enchanting secondary qualities of shade and color are divorced from reality. The states of "false consciousness" in Locke's system of empirical reality and Gilpin's picturesque reality, in their transience, intersect above all at the point of their identifications as fiction.

Throughout his writings on the picturesque, Gilpin expresses admiration for Gothic architecture and ruins as the most sought-after and rewarding objects of "the picturesque eye": "But among all the objects of art, the picturesque eye is perhaps most inquisitive after the elegant relics of ancient architecture; the ruined tower, the Gothic arch, the remains of castles and abbeys. These are the richest legacies of art."[76] These too are the sources for the ideal Gothic buildings and ruins that are re-formed and reappear in the camera obscura of the imagination as conceived by Gilpin. As ideas that enter the mind without leaving a trace, the scenes of Gothic architecture and ruins undergo the same fate as the buildings themselves—they are objects of ruin and decay, or of memory itself, as revealed in Locke's depiction:

> The Memory in some Men, 'tis true, is very tenacious, even to a Miracle: But yet there seems to be a constant decay of all our *Ideas*, even of those which are struck deepest, and in Minds the most retentive; so that if they be not sometimes renewed by repeated Exercise of the Senses, or Reflection on those kind of Objects, which at first occasioned them, the Print wears out, and at last there remains nothing to be seen. Thus the *Ideas*, as

well as Children, of our Youth, often die before us: And our minds repre-
sent to us those Tombs, to which we are approaching; where though the
Brass and Marble remain, yet the Inscriptions are effaced by time; and the
Imagery moulders away. *The Pictures drawn in our Minds, are laid in fading
Colours*; and if not sometimes refreshed, vanish and disappear.[77]

Here, memory is intensely material, rendered as print, inscriptions in
brass and marble, moldering images, and fading paint. If a number of follies in the first half of the eighteenth century were built to commemo-
rate military victories and assert political and national identity, they also
spoke to a dominant concept of memory that saw in both real and fake
ruins the very model of what happens to ideas as memories. The folly was
not only a prompt for associative ideas but a striking embodiment of their
eventual fate in and as memories. In outdoor spaces, structures like ruins
and built ruins allowed new spaces of fiction and interiority to be created
in the fissures and fragments of once whole and complete forms.

Lady Scott's Landscape in a Box

A 1780 painting in gouache of Roslin Castle by topographical artist Paul
Sandby shows the camera obscura in use as a medium and recorder of picturesque scenes, replete with a ruin (fig. 5.5). Here, against the backdrop
of the castle's ruins, eight miles south of Edinburgh, surrounded by estate workers, we see two women in riding habits together on the bank of
the River North Esk. Lady Frances Scott, an amateur artist, stands above
a camera obscura, holding in her right hand what looks to be a drawing
implement and drawing the image that appears on the top of the machine.
Lady Elliott sits on the bank, wearing a feathered hat, and stares steadily
at the artist painting her and her companion. An earlier watercolor and
graphite study of the two figures enlarges their expressions and activities
in the midst of the scenery (plate 7); a few details differ, including the
white sheet of paper Lady Scott holds in the earlier work, and the bolder
expression on Lady Elliott's face.[78]
    Lady Scott's serious, introspective, downward gaze and Lady Elliott's
frank stare both demonstrate the contrast between the inward concentration and absorption induced by the camera obscura and the free-ranging,
intersubjective engagement that viewing the world with one's own eyes
affords. Where Lady Elliott is free to interact with Sandby, Lady Scott is
lost in intersubjective engagement with the camera obscura and its inner
world. It is also the world of her creativity, which will give her something
to show for that moment of mediated viewing—a rendering of the scene

FIGURE 5.5 Paul Sandby, *Roslin Castle, Midlothian* (ca. 1780). Gouache on medium laid paper, mounted on board. Sheet: 18⅛ × 25⅛ in. (46 × 63.8 cm). Photograph: Yale Center for British Art, Paul Mellon Collection (B1975.4.1877).

in the form of her own tracing and drawing, a visual creation that coincides with another, in which she appears as a subject, Sandby's painting.

As an act that furthers the relationship with the camera obscura, the picture Lady Scott is involved not so much in making as in *making out*, enables her mind to become a camera obscura, seeing the scene through its vision and recharacterizing the world with a new scale, finish, and light.[79] Sandby could very well have been using a camera obscura himself to execute his drawing of Lady Scott using a camera obscura in front of Roslin Castle. The mastery of perspective and scale in *Roslin Castle, Midlothian* suggests that the use of a technological aid is not out of the question. Paul Sandby's older brother, Thomas, was known for his accomplished use of the camera obscura in his work, and the clean and precise perspectival layout of his drawings and paintings reflect this. Paul was also known to use the camera obscura—if less regularly—and most definitely used one for the panoramic extended views he drew, such as *Ben Lomond, View near Dumbarton* (ca. 1747).

If an actual camera obscura cannot be proven to have been in use when Paul drew *Roslin Castle*, one might say that a camera obscura of the imagination was, in that the artist executed the drawing with an eye well acquainted with, if not trained by, the device. Accordingly, another form of depth of vision, that of mise en abîme, is thus enacted in the way Sandby sketches and paints the "lady artist" at work, using her camera obscura to depict a landscape scene, as an element of his own topographical scene, whose main subject is, in fact, a ruined castle. In this and other drawings of ruined castles, the authenticity of the castle as a ruin is immaterial as long as the effect produced is consistent with the ideals of what a ruined castle should do in a picturesque landscape. Because Roslin Castle is a represented castle in Sandby's drawing, an object of illusion and not the castle itself, its status will always be akin to that of a folly.

In Sandby's drawing, Lady Scott's body and gaze are turned away from the castle to focus on another scene. Yet the castle—outside the frame of the drawing she undertakes in Sandby's drawing, though represented in his drawing of her doing so—is still implicated in the field of vision of Lady Scott's camera obscura as a possible object of focus for another day.

Less straightforward than a mirror reflection, whose lateral reversal is the main symptom of its status as representation, the camera obscura's image, without correcting devices, is not only vertically and horizontally reversed, but also projected onto a surface that is radically displaced from the site of the original subject. I experienced this when using an early nineteenth-century pocket-size wooden camera obscura from Erkki Huhtamo's collection of optical devices. The vase of flowers sitting on the tabletop I'd been looking at a few seconds earlier, for instance, materialized unexpectedly in my hands as I looked down at the viewfinder on top of the device. With every slight movement inside the room, another aspect of the domestic setting in which I held the camera obscura manifested uncannily in my hands. Recognizing that the image of a small white sphere one is holding in one's hand—bobbing up in a space that had been dark and gray—is of the crinkled paper globe, used as a lampshade and hanging overhead, sparks a moment of alarm and eventually wonder. In this way, the camera obscura turns everyday reality into the stuff of Gothic fiction, in which prosaic entities are uncannily doubled, disappearing and rematerializing in places where you least expect to encounter them. The device reorders, resizes, and ultimately rewrites the elements of one's immediate environment, performing through the optical medium what the Gothic novel does with a textual creation that eventually exists as a print object.

As Pope's camera obscura grotto demonstrates, translating the Thames and its boats into a domestic interior, the encounter with the camera obscura's representation of reality is as apparitional as the ghost of Abelard that Eloisa believes for a moment is real and embraces. In the case of the portable camera obscura, such spectral transpositions are transportable and invite a sense of appropriating the world. If worlds can be kept and carried inside women's detachable pockets and the letters they carry, the medium for conjuring them as visual scenes can be carried in boxes and witnessed, if not stored, inside them. Both detachable pockets and portable camera obscuras reflect a time in which the portability of interiority through the innovation of material designs meant the ability to house, carry, or stimulate interior experiences was on the rise. The interior world offered by the portable camera obscura was as miniaturized and illusionistic as the medieval worlds simulated by mock ruins.

Walpole's Accurate Delineator

Fittingly, it is Horace Walpole who provides a vivid example of the camera obscura's miniaturization of Gothic environments. In a letter to the Honorable H. S. Conway, he expresses his delight and wonder over a new camera obscura he has acquired called the Accurate Delineator, invented by William Storer:

> I have got a delightful plaything, if I had time for play. It is a new sort of camera-obscura for drawing the portraits of persons, or insides of rooms, and does not depend on the sun or anything.... To be sure, the painted windows and the prospects, and the Gothic chimneys, &c. &c., were the delights of one's eyes, when no bigger than a silver penny.[80]

On a technical level, Storer's design is remarkable; it needs neither sun in the daytime nor candlelight at night to function as a camera obscura. Yet the true source of Walpole's delight is the machine's ability to convey to the eyes interior and exterior views of his home in miniature. While Strawberry Hill, in its status as a mock Gothic structure, is already a reduced version of a Gothic castle, and faux ruins in general are even more reduced renditions of Gothic buildings in states of decay, Storer's Accurate Delineator reduces Walpole's Gothic buildings and environments to an ultimate state of miniaturization: the appearance of being no bigger than the size of a silver penny.

In a letter to William Mason, written a few days later, Walpole elaborates on the visual effects and practical features of his new camera obscura:

It will be the delight of your solitude. . . . Sir Joshua Reynolds and West are gone mad with it, and it will be their own faults if they do not excel Rubens in light and shade, and all the Flemish masters in truth. It improves the beauty of trees,—I don't know what it does not do—everything for me, for I can have every inside of every room here drawn minutely in the size of this page. Mr. Storer fell as much in love with Strawberry Hill as I did with his instrument. The perspectives of the house, which I studied so much, are miraculous in this camera. The Gallery, Cabinet, Round Drawing Room, and Great Bed Chamber, make such pictures as you never saw. The painted glass and trees that shade it are Arabian tales . . . and with it you may take a vase or the pattern of a china jar in a moment; architecture and trees are its greatest beauty; but I think it will perform more wonders than electricity, and yet it is so simple as to be contained in a trunk, that you may carry in your lap in your chaise, for there is such contrivance in that trunk that the filbert in the fairy tales which held such treasures was a fool to it.[81]

In noting that the Accurate Delineator transforms his stained glass and the trees surrounding it into "Arabian tales," Walpole concurs with the notion that the camera obscura makes fictions out of everyday space. His space was itself conceived as a fiction, as a "'little Gothic castle," "built to please my own taste, and in some degree to realize my own vision."[82] The idea that the camera obscura offered a means by which Walpole was able to scale the dimensions of his Gothic rooms to fit a sheet of writing paper demonstrates an essential technique of his Gothic fiction enterprise. This was to correlate and integrate the architectural Gothic with the textual to produce an "architextural" fabric—that is, a fiction whose conception and internal experience are derived from self-conscious acts of fabrication, construction, and material formation with the media of both physical materials and words. The subject's engagement with the fiction and the fiction itself are engendered by the motion through space—going *into* and *out of* different domains—that both physical and textual spaces entail. Hume describes the associative passage of thoughts activated with such motions:

> But notwithstanding the empire of the imagination, there is a secret tie or union among particular ideas, which causes the mind to conjoin them more frequently together, and makes the one, upon its appearance, introduce the other . . . hence the connection of writing; and hence that thread, or chain of thought, which a man naturally supports even in the loosest *reverie*.[83]

When entering and engaging with Gothic architextural fabrics, the "thread[s], or chain[s] of thought," create a weave. The rooms offered by pages, physical rooms, buildings, landscapes, and minds interpenetrate within Gothic frameworks to create a dense fabric of fiction.

Sir Walter Scott, in his introduction to the 1811 edition of *The Castle of Otranto*, cites the architectural design and decoration of Gothic spaces as conducive to a mindset susceptible to supernatural sounds and stories:

> He who, in early youth, has happened to pass a solitary night in one of the few ancient mansions which the fashion of more modern times has left undespoiled of their original furniture, has probably experienced, that the gigantic and preposterous figures dimly visible in the defaced tapestry, the remote clang of the distant doors which divide him from living society, the deep darkness which involves the high and fretted roof of the apartment, the dimly-seen pictures of ancient knights . . . the varied and indistinct sounds which disturb the silent desolation of a half-deserted mansion; and, to crown all, the feeling that carries us back to ages of feudal power and papal superstition, join together to excite a corresponding sensation of supernatural awe, if not terror.[84]

Such dark and evocatively furnished settings countervail the "garish light of sun-shine" and the general "dissipating sights and sounds of everyday life" that discourage people from taking supernatural stories seriously. They produce instead a susceptibility to the "contagion" of superstition and a willingness to "listen with respect, and even with dread" to legends that might otherwise be dismissed as "sport." In his description of the paradigmatic Gothic domestic space, Scott is nearly as meticulous as Walpole was in setting the scene for both his own Gothic castle and his paper and leather-bound one. Yet, rather than the stone of true Gothic buildings, Walpole's home was made more of paper than one would expect, for it included papier-mâché fan-vault ceilings and painted wallpaper. This shared medium of paper works further to co-identify Gothic romance and Gothic home as mutual fictions. Scott himself is alert to the correspondences between the formal features of the new genre of literature Walpole invented and the design of his famed home. Both "intermix" elements of the ancient and the modern, the fantastic and the real:

> His mind being thus stored with information, accumulated by researches into the antiquities of the middle ages, and inspired, as he himself informs us, by the romantic cast of his own habitation, Mr. Walpole resolved to

give the public a specimen of the Gothic style adapted to modern literature, as he had already exhibited its application to modern architecture.

As, in his model of a Gothic modern mansion, our author had studi-
ously endeavoured to fit to the purpose of modern convenience, or luxury, the rich, varied, and complicated tracery and carving of the ancient
cathedral, so, in *The Castle of Otranto*, it was his object to unite the marvelous turn of incident and imposing tone of chivalry, exhibited in the
ancient romance, with that accurate exhibition of human character, and
contrast of feelings and passions, which is, or ought to be, delineated in
the modern novel.[85]

The mixture of the material and the mental in Walpole's living environment, its Gothic designs and features resulting from his applying as a spatial formalist the information and images stored in his head, recalls the
example of Pope, also a resident of Twickenham. Walpole's spatial formalism entailed as well the application of ancient-style elements to a modern space, but through that exercise, his home became a fertile source and
model for the fictional design of his novel.[86]

Yet more can be said about what particular relationships the buildings,
as architectural entities in lived reality, have to the fictional narratives that
represent them and are generated by them. The idea that a building is interchangeable with fiction, and a narrative entirely dependent on a building, is confirmed by Gothic novels themselves. In *The Castle of Otranto*,
for instance, the first mention of the castle is in relation to spatial affordances that allow characters to move from one part of the story to another, just as the spaces themselves allow characters to move from one
part of the castle to another. Viewed through the eyes of Isabella, the castle reveals itself in terms of its capacity for providing escape routes and
hiding spaces:

> That lady, whose resolution had given way to terror the moment she had
> quitted Manfred, continued her flight to the bottom of the principal stair-
> case. There she stopped, not knowing whither to direct her steps, nor how
> to escape from the impetuosity of the prince. The gates of the castle she
> knew were locked, and guards placed in the court. . . . Yet where con-
> ceal herself? How avoid the pursuit he would infallibly make throughout
> the castle? As these thoughts passed rapidly through her mind, she recol-
> lected a subterraneous passage which led from the vaults of the castle to
> the church of St. Nicholas. Could she reach the altar before she was over-
> taken, she knew even Manfred's violence would not dare to profane the
> sacredness of the place, and she determined, if no other means of deliv-

erance offered, to shut herself up for ever among the holy virgins, whose convent was contiguous to the cathedral. In this resolution, she seized a lamp that burned at the foot of the staircase, and hurried towards the secret passage.[87]

The design of the castle reveals itself through Isabella's apprehension or fear; in this way, the castle is as much a product of her interiority as a structure of objective reality and a medium for action within the narrative. Furthermore, the "atmosphere" is produced not so much by the castle's features alone—the staircase, locked gates, subterraneous passages, and vaults—as by her perceptions of them. This is to say that the novel functions as a camera obscura for her experience of Gothic space; it mediates her experience of the castle for the reader to experience in turn. Coleridge's well-known estimation of the novel genre, mentioned earlier, applies. Accordingly, the novel functions precisely as "a sort of mental *camera obscura* manufactured at the printing office, which, *pro tempore* fixes, reflects, and transmits the moving phantasms of one man's delirium, so as to people the barrenness of a hundred other brains."

Yet, lacking in Coleridge's assessment of the novel as a camera obscura that "transmits the moving phantasms of one man's delirium" is the awareness that such phantasms are a function not merely of daydreaming but of perceiving space in day-to-day life, whether rendered or conceived as Gothic or not. The fact that men of property created buildings on their estates to shape such spatial perceptions as Gothic demonstrates this notion. The Gothic was foremost a *spatial* medium and not just a textual genre for thinking that shows what the mind does in material environments. As such, it operates as both a dark mirror and room for these experiences. The landscape folly constituted an effort to recreate this space for the mind that predated the emergence of the Gothic in the narrative medium.

This chapter has shown inherent sympathy to the project of Catherine Morland, the heroine of Jane Austen's *Northanger Abbey*, by exploring how the Gothic was incorporated into eighteenth-century landscapes of the everyday. In the novel's pivotal scene, Henry reads Catherine's mind, understanding its passages in the way Walpole's Matilda and other Gothic heroines and heroes come to understand those of the castles in which they live. He reprimands her for imagining that his father has imprisoned his wife, Henry's mother, and kept her in an unused part of his home, telling everyone she has died. Reinforcing the sense that her mistake is a failure of mental reasoning, the word used repeatedly to refer to Catherine's misreading is "folly," which Johnson's 1756 *Dictionary of the English Language* defines as "want of understanding; weakness of intellect."[88]

Whereas Catherine is made to experience private shame for her folly of perceiving prosaic reality in terms of Gothic narrative conventions, replete with villainous patriarch, imprisoned wife, and the haunted wing of a vast and old house, this chapter provides her with company. Included are the eighteenth-century landowning men who embraced and promoted folly in their own lives by creating architectural spaces and ruins that proposed a fictitious Gothic reality, and the visitors who gazed at and lingered around them in wonder while reflecting on their fabrications. While the power, wealth, and land ownership that allowed such men to build follies in the first place differentiate them from the likes of Catherine Morland, their impulse to create and live with follies evinces a susceptibility to the Gothic imaginary, as well as heightened sensitivity to its physical dispositions and forms. In this, such men share this female character's will to manipulate the forms of current realities to recreate the Gothic's shadowy yet materially and emotionally vivid environments—its "dark, odd, and uncouth passages"—for the mind, the body, and the buildings designed for their habitation and exploration. They are spatial formalists too.

The folly, like the other structure of landscape architecture considered in this book, the grotto, exemplifies what landscape designer and historian Diane Balmori calls "intermediate structures." Essentially a "designed piece" placed in the landscape, the intermediate structure was "quasi-architectural" and "quasi-landscape" in its nature.[89] As an intermediate structure, the eighteenth-century folly mediated between the aesthetic realms identified by Balmori, as well as the imagination and reality, the solid and the atmospheric, and the past and the present. The folly was foremost a medium in its intermediating quality. This is to say, it channeled the abstract contents of inner life into the realm of the concrete, making the made-up and the ephemeral real for as long as it was able to stand, appearing to be a stone fiction of an ancient ruin and the interior fantasies it stimulates.

Epilogue

In *Spectator* 414 (1712), Joseph Addison upholds the camera obscura as a fitting example of the pleasures of the imagination. For him, just as nature obtains more value for resembling art, so too does art for resembling nature. Thus, the "prettiest Landskip" he has ever seen is one found, not in nature itself, but in a camera obscura, "drawn on the Walls of a dark Room." In this room, the world outside is magically brought inside and projected in miniature, in motion, and in color: "there appeared the Green Shadows of Trees, waving to and fro with the Wind, and Herds of Deer among them in Miniature, leaping about upon the Wall."[1] Citing the landscape "drawn" with the camera obscura as an "experiment" that is "very common in Opticks," he confesses that although he enjoys its "novelty," it is above all its improvement on "other pictures," in giving "the Motion of the Things it represents" and not just "the Colour and Figure," that brings pleasure to the imagination. Addison not only underscores the camera obscura's faculty of reproducing the world in its endless state of movement; he values it for doing so. Movement, after all, is a fundamental aspect of thinking and experience—thoughts move, just as bodies do in the very condition of being alive. If the camera obscura models the operation of the mind and its interior workings, it does so in its state of aliveness to the activities and features of the living world as it moves.

To distinguish the camera obscura as a prominent model for the experience of interiority in eighteenth-century England, as this book has done, confirms the status of the everyday as the very source of wonder for eighteenth-century subjects.[2] The eighteenth century was a time when the idea that the everyday and its details could be represented at all was radically new. Encounters with the mimetically precise renderings of everyday life in narrative fiction gave readers the new and fascinating experience of familiarity and difference felt simultaneously. Representations and projections of everyday life, whether in camera obscuras, novels, or the empiricist mind, furnished novel spaces and experiences of interiority while giving eighteenth-century subjects a sense of "home" in unexpected places.

Today, a prevailing narrative about the camera obscura is that it exists mainly as a precursor to the more advanced media technologies of photography and cinema. Yet, the fact that many late twentieth- and early twenty-first-century artists and photographers, including Zoe Leonard, Leslie Hewitt, Abelardo Morell, Olafur Eliasson, and Vera Lutter, have embraced it in their work suggests that what it offers exceeds its status as merely a technological precedent. In itself, the camera obscura work of Leonard is remarkable for its ambition and its ability to engage and intrigue twenty-first-century audiences; the room-size camera obscura she installed at the 2014 Whitney Biennial won the Whitney Museum's Bucksbaum Award. More remarkable for this book is Leonard's commitment to experimenting with the camera obscura as an imaginative medium of possessive interiority that reframes and reorganizes space and time, recalling the very qualities that captivated seventeenth- and eighteenth-century English subjects.

In a recent interview with art critic Elisabeth Lebovici, Leonard explains that the creation of her camera obscuras derived from her desire as a contemporary photographer to ask, in the context of "an incredibly image-saturated culture," questions "about how we see, how we look, and what we take for granted about sight." The fact that the camera obscura "offers us a way of seeing that does *not* have to result in a fixed image— such as a photograph or a film"—presents an opportunity to explore such questions.[3] Although Leonard's standpoint as a woman creating art during the first quarter of the twenty-first century gives her the perspective of one accustomed to using the photographic medium as an image-making device, it is her understanding of what makes the camera obscura unique that resonates with what its eighteenth-century viewers and visitors found so fascinating. The camera obscura, she points out, as a medium for "photographic seeing," is above all a "spatial, temporal experience, a space that can be entered and inhabited."[4]

From 2011 to 2014 Leonard made six installations of room-size camera obscuras across Western Europe and the United States. The locations of these installations were, in chronological order, Cologne, London, Venice, the Chelsea neighborhood in New York City, Marfa, Texas, and again in New York, on the Upper East Side. Indicating how inextricable the location of the camera obscura was from its experience, the title for each installation is the address of the gallery or museum space that housed it.

And aligning with the ephemeral nature of the camera obscura as a performative medium, the installations themselves have disappeared. The fact that some of the spaces have ceased to exist at all—including the Whitney's former dwelling at 945 Madison Avenue and the now-closed Chelsea gallery Murray Guy—intensifies further the ephemerality of the work's existence as both experience and space.

Leonard's camera obscuras momentarily captured the qualities of the spaces in which they were installed, pulling in and projecting exterior views onto the interior space and mixing their features, much like the landscape views brought into Pope's grotto camera obscura. In *Campo San Samuele*, Leonard's installation in Venice's Pallazo Grassi, the boats moving through the polluted but mythic Grand Canal outside became part of the sumptuous interior of the palace installation space. The camera obscura thus rendered everyday reality—the commercial, contemporary world of the boat traffic outside—indistinguishable from the fantasy space of the luxurious historical palace.[5] Just as the drama and play of the imagination was a significant feature of Leonard's camera obscuras, so was space a critical component of setting that play into motion. At the same time, Leonard's attitude toward these installations implicitly refutes Jonathan Crary's claims that the camera obscura presents an "orderly projection of the world" that cuts the viewer off from the world around her.[6] In an interview she states, "The camera [obscura] reflects what's happening outside, so it asks us to engage with the world."[7]

As with Pope and Addison, or any of the other figures in this study, the experience of the camera obscura as a medium for a sensorially and emotionally intensified experience of reality is critical to Leonard's project. Unlike artists who, for centuries before her, used the device, and its provision of ready-made perspective lines, to produce greater reality effects in paintings, Leonard deploys it as a projector not just of images but of mystified sensory information that induces wonder and underscores its property of mediating reality itself as a possible fiction. In another interview at the time of the Venice installation, she explains that while images are projected from the outside, so too is sound, the experience of which becomes intensified in the dark: "the longer you stay in the space, the more you become conscious of the sound: the sounds of a small city in Cologne, the sound of a busy high street in London. . . . There is a slow and quiet feeling in the camera that allows your listening and looking to be fully engaged. You know what you're looking at, but at the same time things feel a bit unfamiliar."[8]

Distinguishing Leonard's camera obscuras from those described in eighteenth-century accounts is the fact that hers are avowedly public spaces, installed in the public settings of galleries and museums where strangers congregate, not in private homes. They are meant to be "occupied ... with other people," so that the "experience of looking and understanding is shared." In those spaces, she observes, "you watch each other." Furthermore, "as the image moves and changes, it becomes a temporal experience." Within the camera obscura, that is, you watch each other watching the image created by the device that encloses you, so the temporal experience is a narrative one: observing the changes one undergoes internally in perceiving the image as it materializes on the wall, and observing the reactions of others in their own process of perceiving and wondering. The projective experience of the camera obscura is thus distributed as well as deepened in Leonard's installations.

And yet the fact that the camera obscura is a space for observing subjectivity is what holds Leonard's attention the most. Ending her interview with Lebovici, she brings up the novels of Virginia Woolf, finding in them a remarkable feature of their characters' interiority: "She fully describes the interior of a character's mind—what they are thinking, feeling, their internal dialogue, the reality of their consciousness—and at the same time, her characters move through the world; they interact. She doesn't give up the exterior world, the narrative, the social situation that's outside. She keeps us present in that moment of interaction—where your whole subjective interior meets and interacts with the outside world." Having described, unwittingly, free indirect discourse, the very innovation of narrative technique for which eighteenth-century novelists are held responsible, Leonard states, "This is what I'm interested in, the way we live in an interior and an exterior life, simultaneously and continuously."[9]

From camera obscuras of the eighteenth century to those created and experienced in Leonard's and our time, the representational mechanism is the same, but the contexts of viewing are vastly different. Technological innovations, changes in architectural style, and shifts in social norms yield different experiences of space as well as different relationships to sound, light, and time. New methods for projecting and focusing light, and changing characteristics of manufactured glass and mirrors, lead to different qualities of projections. Leonard, as her early modern predecessors might have, had lenses custom-made to fit into the windows of each of her sites. Today's fascination with the camera obscura's ability to transform everyday spaces into dreamscapes that recreate reality entangles eighteenth-century perspectives with twenty-first-century ones. Furthermore, Leonard's citation of Woolf's narrative technique reminds us that although the camera obscura largely fell out of favor in the intervening centuries and was replaced by other visual technology and media, the eighteenth-century legacy of mediating interiority in enclosed spaces remains apparent in our continued appreciation and consumption of an ever-portable yet capacious home for the imagination: the novel.

This book has shown that the eighteenth century was an age in which material designs and media for cultivating interior life proliferated diversely in domestic architecture and landscape, dress, letter writing culture, and imaginative writing. It was also the age of the camera obscura. Though the camera obscura is essentially an ancient natural phenomenon, as Leonard has pointed out, cultural fascination with the medium rose unmistakably during the eighteenth century.[10] Throughout this era the device had a role in multiple areas of life having to do with experiences of pleasure and curiosity that hinged on seeing the everyday world anew from within enclosures. These ranged from popular entertainment venues and touristic travels to domestic diversions. The fact that the camera obscura was both a long-standing device for creating realistic visual images and an eighteenth-century medium for generating surprise and astonishment suggests there was something inherently wondrous about the aesthetic effects of realism during the period that witnessed "the rise of the novel." As explored in chapter 4, these include not just the novel's properties of making fiction seem like everyday life, but also the camera obscura's capacity to make everyday life seem like a fiction.

From the mid- to late seventeenth century and throughout the eighteenth, the camera obscura as a source of entertainment and knowledge was an inescapable material and conceptual paradigm for designing and inhabiting diverse spaces of imaginative experience. These experiences were located in physical contexts, implied and suggested on one hand, directly embodied and represented on the other, in architectural, artefactual, literary, and pictorial spaces. On a fundamental level, the camera obscura's model of making interior and exterior realms, as well as the real and the represented, continuous with each other influenced the way people viewed the world and understood their relationships to what they saw as objects of perception, as well as of projection.

Most important to this study, both of the camera obscura's manifestations during the period—as an architectural chamber to enter and inhabit, and a device to carry—produced an understanding that space can function as a medium of psychological projection and therefore of fiction that goes beyond textual models. The *OED*'s definition of "medium" as a "pervading or enveloping substance or 'element' in which an organism lives; hence . . . one's environment, conditions of life," suggests the mediating role of spaces that this book has examined.[11] Yet more evocative is Giuliana Bruno's notion of medium, which leans on its etymological background as a "condition of 'betweenness' and a quality of 'becoming' as a connective, pervasive, or enveloping substance. As an intertwining matter through which impressions are conveyed to the senses, a medium is a living environment of expression, transmission, and storage."[12]

As media in their own right, the spaces in my book serve as living environments for relationships of interactive copresence between space and self in diverse settings of private life, from women's detachable pockets to follies and cottages on country house estates. Beginning with Marvell's country house poem *Upon Appleton House* and Cavendish's domestic verse, letters, and narratives, once literature became aware of itself as a projective space and medium for real living environments, interiority rooted in everyday environments began to develop as an aesthetic framework. I have referred to this as "possessive interiority," wherein inner life emerges and self-possession ensues when subjects are placed in interactive relationship with the formal dimensions of particular spaces. I have maintained that this interiority can be made legible in literary works only by taking the critical approach of spatial formalism. Its underlying premise is that interiority is relational and works interdependently with the spatial forms and settings of a historically defined material world. Rather than static, as it tends to be characterized, spatial "setting" is, in my book, generative and interactive, functioning as an agent of form and feeling, and not just a fixed backdrop for narrative or dramatic action.

By demonstrating the interrelations between spaces (diversely conceived) of lived reality and literary texts as mediating channels for inner life throughout the eighteenth century, I reframe the novel's historical significance as a genre of interiority and as a site of domestic fiction. Its interiority derives not so much from details of spatial description as from the ways in which it registered the interiorizing relationships with domestic space that eighteenth-century subjects experienced as a consequence of changes in built environments and in material and visual culture. Experiencing domestic life as a virtual experience through such structures as follies and writing closets that take their inhabitants to new internal worlds is a form of eighteenth-century "domestic fiction" that had yet to be examined.

The great novelty of eighteenth-century literature lies not so much in the depiction of domestic interiors in novels alone as in their acts of generating the fictive and imaginal properties of these spaces in the very act of including them in diverse textual genres and fabrics. These properties include their architextural roles as conductors and associates of internal experiences, in both literary representation and lived reality. Here such roles are exemplified in the spaces of Pope's grotto, the detachable pockets that carry records of private experience in Richardson's *Pamela*, and the artificial ruins whose presence stimulates reveries about the past.

Returning to where this book began, the Santa Monica Camera Obscura, I would like to consider a claim made in the information sheet for visitors: "When you enter the Camera Obscura you are in effect inside the body of a camera."[13] Such an arresting notion evokes what Walter Benjamin helps us remember in regard to the photographic camera: it sees life's most minute motions, its split-second gestures and moments, which, without its mediation, would be all but lost to us.[14] Stretching and compressing time and space, the camera "introduces us to unconscious optics," the domain of dreams.[15] The photographic camera, in other words, like the camera obscura, operates as a tool for seeing things in the world that one would not otherwise discern. But it is the camera obscura that allows one to notice the ways in which one perceives the everyday happenings of the world as a direct consequence of dwelling inside or peering into its dark chamber in the very course of their unfolding. Contemporary practices of living in mediated and virtual realities are deeply indebted to the seventeenth- and eighteenth-century developments of new spatial forms for wandering and being alone with one's thoughts while seeing the world become stranger, richer, and more vivid to one's own eyes.

Acknowledgments

This book has been with me for several years and has gone through deep transformations. The sustenance of family, friends, and colleagues helped ensure it got written. My first and last sustainers are my parents, especially my father, to whom this book is dedicated. He passed away a year before I delivered my manuscript to the Press to begin the production process. This book, and knowing just in time that it would be published, meant everything to him. His model of goodness, courage, inner vision, and grit will always be mine to emulate. I owe him for much more than that, including his never faltering love and support, especially of my books and other dreams.

At the University of Chicago Press, I am thankful to Alan Thomas and Randolph Petilos for being responsive and wise editors, and for their dedication to publishing this book. I am especially grateful to Alan for supporting this book early on and for understanding its spirit and contributions. Joel Score, senior manuscript editor at the Press, was meticulous and gracious, and made the text stronger and sharper than it would otherwise have been. Meredith Nini, promotion manager, has brought clarity and enthusiasm to the marketing process. My external readers gave me the opportunity to improve my argument with their illuminating reports and the encouragement they offered.

Important friends to this project and me include George Boulukos, Robin Schuldenfrei, Alexander Edmonds, Aaron Kunin, Robert Mack, and Ellen Wayland Smith. A special acknowledgement goes to George Boulukos for his keen and insightful readings of multiple drafts and for understanding exactly what I was trying to say from beginning to end of this book's journey. A special note of gratitude also goes to Robin Schuldenfrei for being my transatlantic writing companion, and for her unfailing readiness to help me keep going. Ruth Mack, Jason Pearl, Suzanne Pucci, Diana Solomon, and Courtney Weiss Smith offered helpful comments on drafts as fellow eighteenth-century scholars. Generative and serendipitous conversations with Rebecca Bullard, Naomi Milthorpe, and Elizabeth Eger brought valuable elements to the book at different stages. I owe thanks to Liza Blake, Joanie Eppinga, James Fitzmaurice, Karen Harvey, Moira Killoran, Jonathan Lamb, Ed Park, Jacqueline Reid-Walsh, Peter Schmader, Crosby Stevens, David Taylor, and Lindsay Waters for the help and good will they provided this project along the way. Martin White, who has indexed all of my books including this one, deserves special thanks for creating another index that captures and understands more corners, details, and contours of my argument than I could ever imagine possible. For giving me this book's title, I must thank legendary editor William Germano. He is a friend who can tell me when he does not like something—such as the former title—and nimbly make it better.

True to its argument, the story behind this book is as filled with significant spaces and places as it is with people. Several fellowships allowed me to research and write the book in culturally rich locations with equally rich research repositories, surrounded by remarkable scholars. One of my biggest debts goes to the Folger Shakespeare Library, where I spent a year as a long-term fellow and wrote my seventeenth-century chapters. Meeting Michael Witmore, the director of the Folger, and Pamela Long, an eminent historian in my long-term fellows cohort, changed my life. Mike and Pam realize things that no one thinks of as possibilities, and showed me how it is done. The firmness of Mike's support has been a precious resource to me. Carol Brobeck, Raz Chen-Morris, Miriam Jacobson, Christopher Johnson, Louise Noble, Diane Purkiss, and Lyn Tribble also offered friendship and care that touched me when it mattered the most.

A long-term fellowship in the Materialities, Texts and Images program at the Huntington Library and Caltech brought me a year to focus on the conceptual aspects of my book in a vibrant location for eighteenth-century studies, Los Angeles. I am indebted to the directors of the MTI Program, John Brewer and Steve Hindle, for giving me an opportunity to develop *My Dark Room* in ways that would have been impossible elsewhere. John read several chapters and would-be chapters and offered his counsel and encouragement freely. He is without peer in many ways, not least in his loyalty as a friend and sagacity as a mentor. As director of research at the Huntington, Steve created an environment of open warmth and high intellectual energy and generously supported my endeavors as a scholar. My fellow MTI fellow, Susan Barbour, brightened my year even further with her ideas, insights, and talent in many things, including positive thinking.

A Social Sciences and Humanities Research Council Standard Research Grant and a Howard Foundation fellowship allowed me to develop an early version of this book, which led to short-term research library fellowships at the Folger and the Huntington that preceded the long-term ones, as well as at the Getty Research Institute and Dumbarton Oaks Library and Archives. I am grateful to John Beardsley, director of research at Dumbarton Oaks, for supporting my project and creating a warm environment where connections of many kinds could be made among and between scholars of landscape design history. The closest I have been to paradise was at Dumbarton Oaks, where fellows have private access to Beatrix Farrand's garden in the mornings. Farrand's masterpiece garden design, which gives one the sense of wandering through a fascinating and beautiful brain, made it impossible for me not to recognize that the ties between mind, soul, space, and body could be made exquisitely intimate.

Early on, a scholarship from the American Friends of the Attingham Trust to attend the Attingham Summer School for the Study of Historic Country Houses in the United Kingdom was crucial to heightening my awareness of the phenomenology of historical interiors. I owe much to the Trust for awarding a place to me, a literature scholar, in a program geared toward museum curators, architects, architectural historians, historic house specialists, and conservators.

No less transformative in bringing me directly to the material dimensions of interiority was Erkki Huhtamo, media archaeologist and owner of an important collection of eighteenth- and nineteenth-century optical devices. I am grateful to Peter Lunenfeld and to Shawn Vancour for introducing us. Without spending time with Erkki's collection, his cabinet of wonders, in Los Angeles, my understanding of how camera obscuras work would be missing critical dimensions, not least, their qualities as an embodied experience. And without my time in Los Angeles, with its extraordinary light, I would not have developed the appreciation for life as an experience that can appear more imagined than real, one of this book's central notions. Also in Los Angeles, I had inspiring conversations with Jonathan Furner and Anne Gilliland about the camera obscura; I thank them for giving me more insights into its properties as a device for the imagination.

Sharing my work at different institutions with multidisciplinary audiences has been an important part of its development. Ewa Lajer-Burcharth and Beate Söntgen invited me to present an early version of chapter 2 for their Interiors and Interiority workshop at the Radcliffe Institute of Advanced Study in 2011. I thank Ewa and Beate for inviting me to take part as a literature scholar in a heady international gathering made up largely of art historians. For their feedback and attention, I am grateful also to audiences at the University of Sydney; University of Buffalo; Early Modern Center at the University of California, Santa Barbara; Southern California Eighteenth-Century Group; Group for the Study of Early Cultures at the University of California, Irvine; Center for 17th- and 18th-Century Studies and Clark Library; and Open Digital Seminar in Eighteenth-Century Studies at the University of Reading. I thank Vanessa Smith, Ruth Mack, Rachael King, Felicity Nussbaum, Lyle Massey, Sarah Kareem and Davide Panagia, and Rebecca Bullard for their respective invitations and their hospitality.

Cathy Jurca, executive officer for the humanities at Caltech during my time at the Huntington and Caltech, ensured I had support. I thank her for her conscientiousness as a senior administrator, for her general good will, and for helpful feedback on an early version of chapter 4. A group of talented scholars were my intellectual companions and moral supporters at the Huntington, including Dympna Callaghan, Adria Imada, Susan Juster, Matthew Kadane, and Kevin Lambert, as well as Melissa Bailes, Alice Fahs, Dena Goodman, and Tawny Paul. Dena took the time to read my introduction carefully and shared her incisive and extensive comments with me. Matt also helped me clarify my argument by asking me important questions about my analytical framework. The interdisciplinary input of these two historians was invaluable to the growth of my project. I am grateful to Roy Ritchie for supporting an early version of my project while he was still director of research at the Huntington. Staff members Christopher Adde, Juan Gomez, Leslie Jobsky, Carolyn Powell, and Samuel Wylie helped make the Huntington feel like a second home.

I brought this project with me to New York in late 2019, where I worked as a rare books curator in the Special Collections Center of New York University's Elmer Holmes Bobst Library. At NYU, the support of Lisa Gitelman, Charlton McIlwain, Farooq Niazi, and Charlotte Priddle helped me bring the project to an important stage of its development. I am also indebted to Mobina Hashmi, Meredith Martin, Shannon O'Neill, Bob Seidel, Carolina Velez-Grau, and Yanyi for the pleasures of their camaraderie during an unforgettable time.

Many curators and librarians—clavigers for prized materials of cultural heritage—directed their knowledge, expertise, and generosity toward helping me develop my project. These include Georgianna Ziegler of the Folger Shakespeare Library, Isotta Poggi of the Getty Research Institute, Melinda McCurdy, Mary Robertson, Alan Jutzi, and Gayle Richardson of the Huntington Library, Leigh Wishner of the Los Angeles County Museum of Art, and Linda Eaton and Rosemary Krill of Winterthur Museum, Garden and Library. I am grateful to them for sharing their extensive knowledge of their repository holdings with me. Robert Youngs, treasurer of the Pope's Grotto Trust, made a long-standing dream come true by giving me a private tour of Pope's grotto. The landscape workers of Goldney Hall at the University of Bristol made a dream I did not even know I had come to life by showing me the secret marvels of Thomas Goldney's grotto.

I am fortunate to have met Julia Lupton and Alexander Nemerov during my time in California. They both inspire me with their individualism, poetic and creative approach to scholarship, and dedication to thinking big for the humanities. I thank Julia for her steadfast backing as well as for exemplifying what it means to pursue eudaimonia and virtue in scholarly life. To Alex I owe special thanks for urging me to embrace states of wonder and conviction as a mode of scholarly being. Another fortunate aspect of living in Los Angeles was being close to Jayne Lewis, an equally important source of influence and encouragement, and a trusted friend with a staggering mind and heart. Long-standing Southern California colleagues in eighteenth-century studies Robert Folkenflik and Maximillian Novak, who to me represent the warmth and generosity of both the region and the field, encouraged and supported me too, for which I am grateful.

My gratitude extends to many more friends who showed up in significant ways during the event-filled years it took for me to write this book. Vanessa Smith and Guy Davidson are a whole world away in Australia, but the easy understanding, loyalty, and lightness of being their friendship brings nevertheless has made a difference. Joanna Picciotto read one of the earliest versions of the book prospectus and helped the project gather momentum with her sparks of brilliance and enthusiasm. My oldest friends in England, Elizabeth and Andrew Ross, readily gave me a place to stay in London during my visits, lots of moral support, and a sense that my work mattered. Brendan Moore was gracious, attentive, and generous with his resources whenever I came to visit his country in search of paper ephemera at the British Museum, where he was a curator. The numerous stray cats I adopted, from Whiskey and Fanny, to Fibo, Fabritius, and Mavis, deserve acknowledgement for ensuring the spaces at home in which I wrote *My Dark Room* were filled with play, warmth, and love.

Many student assistants at both McMaster University and Vassar College helped me research this book. I am grateful for their help: Alicia Kerfoot, Pouria Tabrizi, Tara McGrath, Gina Morrow, Marissa Schwartz, Elena Hersey, and Hayden Dinges. The members of my Vassar Senior Seminar, Interior Worlds of Eighteenth-Century England—Jon Fuller, Alicia Hyman, Mercedes Elkoff, Kathleen Dwyer, and Danielle Unger—

were thoughtful and spirited interlocutors who helped me see the project's different dimensions at its earliest stage. I am also grateful to my colleagues at Vassar College for their support: Beth Darlington, Yvonne Elet, Wendy Graham, David Kennett, Lisa Paravasini, and above all Tyrone Simpson. Yvonne gave me comments on the earliest drafts of this book, and the pleasures of being a kindred spirit in landscape design studies and cat rescue. I thank the History of Science Museum, National Trust, Orleans House Gallery, Royal Collection Trust, and Winterthur Museum, Garden and Library for waiving reproduction fees for this book as a scholarly publication.

I would never have predicted how long, transformative, and meandering the path from beginning to end of this book would be. But anything more direct would have made it less rich, and bereft of the insights and wonders I encountered in the many spaces and communities that gave the book its form and purpose. The most cherished gift the years of working on this book has brought me is the opportunity to learn how to create and inhabit my own dark rooms in the spaces around me. It is my hope that the book makes the intellectual journey of understanding what that meant in seventeenth- and eighteenth-century England also a wonder-filled one for its readers.

Notes

Introduction

1. More specifically, light enters through an aperture on the side of the turret, strikes a mirror angled at forty-five degrees, and passes through a convex lens that focuses an image of the outside world on the surface of the table.

2. The translation appears in the visitor's account of visiting the grotto after Pope's death, published in the January 1748 issue of *The Newcastle General Magazine, or Monthly Intelligencer*, 1:25–28; reprinted in Maynard Mack, *The Garden and the City* (Toronto: University of Toronto Press, 1969), 237–43; 240.

3. Alexander Pope to Edward Blount, June 2, 1725, in *The Correspondence of Alexander Pope*, ed. George Sherburn (Oxford: Clarendon Press, 1956), 2:256–57.

4. Robert Dodsley, *Verses on the Grotto at Twickenham* (London: R. Dodsley, 1743), 16.

5. For an illustration of how this phenomenon was created and conceived in the eighteenth century, see Benjamin Martin, *Philosophia Britannica; or, A New and Comprehensive System of the Newtonian Philosophy* ... (London: W. Strathan, J & F Rivington, et al., 1771), 3:83, plate 49. The camera obscura's feature of visual subversion has invited later critics, from Karl Marx to Sarah Kofman and Jill Casid, to insist on its aptness as a figure for the workings of ideology.

6. On the history of the relationship between interiority and notions of property, see Nancy Armstrong and Leonard Tennenhouse, "The Interior Difference: A Brief Genealogy of Dreams, 1650–1717," in "The Politics of Difference," ed. Felicity Nussbaum, special issue of *Eighteenth-Century Studies* 23, no. 4 (Summer 1990): 458–78. On individual subjectivity and property, see also Alan Macfarlane, *The Origins of English Individualism* (New York: Cambridge University Press, 1978), and C. B. Macpherson, *The Political Theory of Possessive Individualism* (Oxford: Oxford University Press, 1962).

7. I developed this term as a reformulation of Macpherson's "possessive individualism."

8. Henry Mackenzie, *Mirror* 61, December 7, 1779 (Edinburgh: William Creech; W. Strahan and T. Cadell, 1779), 224–29; 228, 229.

9. Mackenzie, *Mirror* 61, 224, 225, 227.

10. Mackenzie, *Mirror* 61, 228, 224.

11. Mackenzie, *Mirror* 61, 227.

12. Thomas Hobbes, *Leviathan*, ed. Richard Tuck (Cambridge: Cambridge University Press, 1991), 16.

13. Danielle Bobker similarly takes a material culture approach to a historical spatial construct, the closet, by tracing the way it shaped eighteenth-century life. Whereas Bob-

ker's study emphasizes social life, my study stresses internal life, as well as the *mutually constitutive* relationship between space and self. See Bobker, *The Closet* (Princeton, NJ: Princeton University Press, 2020).

14. Other works that followed Watt in studying the interrelationships between domestic space and the development of the novel include Nancy Armstrong, *Desire and Domestic Fiction* (Oxford: Oxford University Press, 1987); Christina Marsden Gillis, *The Paradox of Privacy: Epistolary Form in* Clarissa (Gainesville: University Presses of Florida, 1984); Charlotte Grant, "Reading the House of Fiction: From Object to Interior," *Home Cultures* 2, no. 3 (2005): 233–50; Karen Lipsedge, *Domestic Space in Eighteenth-Century British Novels* (Houndmills, Basingstoke, Hampshire: Palgrave Macmillan, 2012); Michael McKeon, *The Secret History of Domesticity* (Baltimore: Johns Hopkins University Press, 2005); Philippa Tristram, *Living Spaces in Fact and Fiction* (London: Routledge, 1989); and Simon Varey, *Space and the Eighteenth-Century English Novel* (Cambridge: Cambridge University Press, 1990). Cynthia Wall has examined the question of when domestic interiors began to emerge as objects of narrative description in the late eighteenth and early nineteenth centuries, and is unique in focusing more on the rhetorical history of description than on interiors and the novel genre in themselves. See Wall, *The Prose of Things* (Chicago: University of Chicago Press, 2006). Mimi Yiu makes the case that architectural changes in the Renaissance, including the inception of architecture as a field, intersected with drama to produce early modern interiority in her luminous *Architectural Involutions* (Evanston, IL: Northwestern University Press, 2015).

15. Sarah Fielding and Jane Collier, *The Cry*, 2 vols. (Dublin: Printed for George Faulkner, 1754), 1:9,7.

16. See Ian Watt, *The Rise of the Novel* (Berkeley: University of California Press, 1957); Wall, *Prose of Things* and "Details of Space: Narrative Description in Early Eighteenth-Century Novels," *Eighteenth-Century Fiction* 10, no. 4 (July 1998): 387–405; and D. S. Bland, "Endangering the Reader's Neck: Background Description in the Novel," *Criticism* 3, no. 2 (Spring 1961): 121–39.

17. On the increasing orientation of domestic space and life around privacy in the eighteenth century, see Amanda Vickery, "Thresholds and Boundaries at Home," in *Behind Closed Doors* (New Haven, CT: Yale University Press, 2009), 25–48, and Lawrence Stone, *The Family, Sex and Marriage in England 1500–1800* (New York: Harper & Row, 1977).

18. Meredith Martin, "The Ascendancy of the Interior in Eighteenth-Century French Architectural Theory," in *Architectural Space in Eighteenth-Century Europe: Constructing Identities and Interiors*, ed. Meredith Martin and Denise Baxter (Farnham, Surrey: Ashgate, 2010), 15–34.

19. This interior self is aligned with the notion of a modern self. See Charles Taylor, *Sources of the Self* (Cambridge, MA: Harvard University Press, 1989), and Dror Wahrman, *The Making of the Modern Self* (New Haven, CT: Yale University Press, 2004). For Taylor, "by the turn of the eighteenth century, something recognizably like the modern self is in process of constitution" (185).

20. John Locke, *An Essay Concerning Human Understanding*, ed. Peter H. Nidditch (Oxford: Clarendon Press, 1975), book 2, chap. 11, §17, 162–63.

21. See more recent works such as Brad Pasanek, *Metaphors of Mind* (Baltimore: Johns Hopkins University Press, 2015), and Sean Silver, *The Mind Is a Collection* (Philadelphia: University of Pennsylvania Press, 2015).

22. This conception of life is indebted to Ingold, for whom life resides in "the move-

ment of becoming—the growth of the organism, the unfolding of the melody, the motion of the brush and its trace . . ." Life is above all "open-ended: its impulse is not to reach a terminus but to keep on going." See Tim Ingold, *Being Alive* (London: Routledge, 2011), 83.

23. Silver's persistent description of the camera obscura as a "gadget" is rather misleading. The term diminishes the device and erases its architectural and spatial dimensions. See Anne Friedberg, *The Virtual Window* (Cambridge, MA: MIT Press, 2006), 71.

24. John Hammond, *The Camera Obscura* (Bristol: Adam Hilger, 1981), 17.

25. Hammond, *Camera Obscura*, 16.

26. Elizabeth Graeme Ferguson's account of her 1764 visit to Goldney Hall in Milcah Martha Moore's commonplace book. See Moore, *Milcah Martha Moore's Book*, ed. Catherine La Courreye Blecki and Karin A. Wulf (University Park, PA: Pennsylvania State University Press, 1997), 209. I thank Stephen Hague for informing me about this source.

27. Thomas Goldney III, Copy Inventory of furniture and effects at Goldney House, 1768, University of Bristol Inventory of 1768. I am grateful to Stephen Hague for this reference as well. For a discussion of this camera obscura, see Hague, *The Gentleman's House in the British Atlantic World, 1680–1780* (Basingstoke: Palgrave Macmillan, 2015), 15.

28. John Harris, *Lexicon Technicum: or, An Universal English Dictionary of Arts and Sciences*, 2nd ed., vol. 1 (London: Printed for Dan. Brown et al., 1708), "OBL" page.

29. Harris, *Lexicon Technicum*, "OBS" page.

30. Abraham Rees, *Cyclopædia: or, An Universal Dictionary of Arts and Sciences*, vol. 4, Plates (London: Longman, Hurst, Rees, Orme and Brown, 1786), under "OPTICS Camera Obscura," plate 3.

31. These boxes were meant to be attached to the side of the roof and manipulated by a wooden pyramidal trunk, if one lacked a dome-shaped one.

32. "Camera Obscura," in *The Beauties of Poetry Display'd* (London: J. Hinton, 1757), 1:206; John Cuff, "Verses, Occasion'd by the Sight of a Chamera Obscura" (1747), a poem found in a British Museum ms., quoted in Marjorie Nicolson and G. S. Rousseau, *"This Long Disease, My Life": Alexander Pope and the Sciences* (Princeton, NJ: Princeton University Press, 1968), 284–85n88.

33. Friedberg's analysis in *The Virtual Window* (70–71) is an exception in emphasizing the quality of movement as well as color in camera obscura images. These accounts serve as evidence of the camera obscura's role as a "viewing machine" that stimulates the imagination, not just a "perspective machine" that aids attempts at Crary's notion.

34. Ephraim Chambers, *Cyclopædia: or, An Universal Dictionary of Arts and Sciences* (London, 1728) 2: 143. I will discuss Addison's *Spectator* 414 comments on the camera obscura in chapter 3.

35. Robert Boyle, "Of the Systematical and Cosmical Qualities of Things," in *The Works of the Honourable Robert Boyle*, ed. Richard Boulton (London: J. Phillips and J. Taylor, 1699), 239–49; 245.

36. Edmund Stone, *A New Mathematical Dictionary* (London: J. Senex et al., 1726), under "CA." As will be discussed in chapter 3, Joshua Reynolds would later decry the camera obscura as a source for inferior art. See Reynolds, Discourse XII, in *Discourses on Art*, ed. Robert R. Wark (New Haven, CT: Yale University Press, 1959), 237.

37. Other words used to describe the camera obscura's actions in eighteenth-century poetry about the device include "carrying," "radiating," "painting," "exhibiting," and "staining."

38. For a discussion of the lineage of this view, see Friedberg, *Virtual Window*, 70.

39. See *OED*, s.v. "project, *v.*," def. 9b.

40. See *OED*, s.v. "project, *v.*," def. 9c (emphasis in original).

41. See *OED*, s.v. "project, *v.*," def. 9d.

42. The *OED* cites eighteenth-century usages (1704 and 1745) of the verb "project" to mean "to throw, cast, or shoot forwards or onwards" in works of technical and experimental philosophy that refer to "the curve of a parabola," for instance, or the projection of a ball in a certain direction. See "project, *v.*," def. 6a.

43. Max Novak, "Introduction," in *The Age of Projects*, ed. Max Novak (Toronto: University of Toronto Press, 2008), 3–25; 3.

44. Novak, *Age of Projects*, 7. For a more recent study of seventeenth- and eighteenth-century projects as "visionary schemes," see David Alff, *The Wreckage of Intentions: Projects in British Culture, 1660–1730* (Philadelphia: University of Pennsylvania Press, 2017).

45. "Camera Obscura," in *Beauties of Poetry Display'd*, 1:206.

46. *The Conjuror's Repository* (London: J. D. Dewick, 1795), 29.

47. Robin Evans, *The Projective Cast: Architecture and Its Three Geometries* (Cambridge, MA: MIT Press, 1995), 368 (emphasis mine).

48. Evans, *Projective Cast*, 368.

49. Locke, *Essay*, book 2, chap. 1, §2, 104

50. Locke, *Essay*, book 2, chap. 11, §17, 162–63 (emphasis mine).

51. "Sketches No. 1: To the Editor of the European Magazine," *European Magazine* 74 (1782): 21.

52. *The Museum*, vol. 13 (London: R. Dodsley, 1746–1747), 339.

53. Henry Temple Croker et al., *The Complete Dictionary of Arts and Sciences*, 3 vols. (Dublin: Printed for the authors, and sold by J. Wilson & J. Fell et al., 1764), 1:40v.

54. Hobbes, *Leviathan*, 14–15. According to Hobbes, what "the Latines call Imagination" is what "the Greeks call . . . Fancy" (15).

55. Hobbes, *Leviathan*, 14.

56. For his description of a portable camera obscura and how it functions, see Boyle, "Of the Systematical and Cosmical Qualities," 245.

57. Johann Zahn, *Oculus Artificialis Telediotricus sive Telescopium*, 3 vols. (Herbipoli [Würzburg, Germany]: Sumptibus Quirini Heyl, 1685–1686), I:181.

58. Watt, *Rise of the Novel*, 196.

59. Samuel Taylor Coleridge, *Biographia Literaria*, pt. 1, vol. 7 of *The Collected Works of Samuel Taylor Coleridge*, ed. James Engell and W. Jackson Bate (Princeton, NJ: Princeton University Press, 1983), 48.

60. Alexandra Neel interprets this passage as an instance where Coleridge positions the camera obscura as a figure for passive creative agency; see Neel, "'A *Something-Nothing* Out of Its Very Contrary': The Photography of Coleridge," *Victorian Studies* 49, no. 2 (2007): 208–17.

61. This reading goes against the grain of M. H. Abrams's famous interpretation of Locke's camera obscura as upholding a passive approach to perception, as reflection, rather than the romantics' approach to subjective perception as projection, a "more creative" faculty. Abrams's assessment may stem from a misunderstanding of how the camera obscura works; as my study shows, both its operation and its effect of perceptual illusion are strongly based on projection. See Abrams, *The Mirror and the Lamp* (New York: Oxford University Press, 1953).

62. Hester Thrale, May 19, 1782, *Thraliana*, vol. 1, 1776–1784, ed. Katharine C. Balderston (Oxford: Clarendon Press/Huntington Library, 1942), 536.

63. See Bernard Aikema and Boudewijn Bakker, *Painters of Venice: The Story of the Venetian "Veduta"* (Amsterdam: Rijksmuseum, 1990), and Casper J. Erkelens, "Perspective on Canaletto's Paintings of Piazza San Marco in Venice," *Art and Perception* 8, no. 1 (2020): 49–67.

64. Jonathan Crary, *Techniques of the Observer* (Boston: MIT Press, 1990), 41.

65. Crary, *Techniques*, 41.

66. Crary, *Techniques*, 42–43.

67. Crary, *Techniques*, 42, 46.

68. Friedberg is careful to trace the "dual" history of the camera obscura, both as a "scientific instrument and as a device for illusion"; *Virtual Window*, 61.

69. In the last twenty or so years, scholarship in the humanities and social sciences has been preoccupied with examining the relationship between humans and the material world through the study of objects and "things." My own previous book studied objects as vital media, in collaboration with the novel, for fashioning the eighteenth-century self. See Julie Park, *The Self and It* (Stanford, CA: Stanford University Press, 2010).

70. Sociologist Erving Goffman offers a corresponding term for "setting" with his frame theory, which sees social situations as theatrical. Subjects behave as "actors" within the "frames" that shape "the organization of experience." See Goffman, *Frame Analysis* (New York: Harper & Row, 1975), 10–11.

71. Robin Evans, "Figures, Doors and Passages," in *Translations from Drawing to Building and Other Essays* (London: Janet Evans and Architectural Association Publications, 1997), 56–91; 88.

72. Tim Ingold, *The Perception of the Environment* (London: Routledge, 2000), 200.

73. Ingold, *Perception of the Environment*, 171.

74. See *OED*, s.v. "text."

75. Ingold, *Being Alive*, 84. Ingold in turn cites Henri Lefebvre's *The Production of Space*, trans. D. Nicholson-Smith (Oxford: Blackwell, 1991), 117–18. My emphasis is on Ingold's conception, not Lefebvre's.

76. *OED*, s.v. "space, $n.^1$," def. 11e.

77. Julia Lupton's work offers a conceptual model of embodied space, by way of considering early modern drama through the theory of affordances, as a field of rich phenomenological interactivity and affiliations. See Lupton, *Shakespeare Dwelling: Designs for the Theater of Life* (Chicago: University of Chicago Press, 2018).

78. David Kurnick, *Empty Houses: Theatrical Failure and the Novel* (Princeton, NJ: Princeton University Press, 2011), 1. For a comprehensive and authoritative account of the eighteenth-century rise of design and the domestic interior, see Charles Saumarez Smith, *Eighteenth-Century Decoration* (New York: Harry N. Abrams, 1993).

79. See *OED*, s.v. "medium," defs. 4a, 5b.

80. *OED*, s.v. "interiority." See Lover of Truth, *Truth and Error Contrasted* (London: Printed by and for James Phillips, 1776), and John Norris, *An Essay Towards the Theory of the Ideal or Intelligible World*, part II (London: Printed for Edmund Parker, 1704).

81. Carole Straw, *Gregory the Great: Perfection in Imperfection* (Berkeley: University of California Press, 1988), 129. I am grateful to Benjamin Saltzman for this reference.

82. Katharine Eisaman Maus articulates this point throughout her introduction to *Inwardness and Theater in the English Renaissance* (Chicago: University of Chicago Press, 1995), 1–34; 3–4, 11–14.

83. See Michael C. Schoenfeldt, *Bodies and Selves in Early Modern England* (Cambridge: Cambridge University Press, 1999).

84. For an elaboration on this tension, see Patricia Dailey, *Promised Bodies: Time, Language, and Corporeality in Medieval Women's Mystical Texts* (New York: Columbia University Press, 2013), 11. I am indebted to Benjamin Saltzman for this citation as well.

85. Both Burton and Bacon are cited in Schoenfeldt, *Bodies and Selves*, 25. Robert Burton, *Anatomy of Melancholy*, ed. Thomas C. Faulkner, Nicholas Kiessling, and Rhonda Blair, 2 vols. (London: Printed for Henry Cripps, 1632; Oxford: Clarendon Press, 1989), 1:144–46 (citations refer to the Oxford edition); Francis Bacon, *Historia Vitae et Mortis*, vol. 5 of *Works*, ed. James Spedding et al. (Cambridge, MA: Hurd and Houghton, 1869), 5:294.

86. Edward Wettenhall, *Enter into Thy Closet*, 5th rev. ed. (London: R. Bentley, 1684), 69, 76. For a recent literary-cultural history of the closet as an increasingly pervasive site of politicized intimacy that shaped social relations throughout seventeenth- and eighteenth-century England, see Bobker, *Closet*.

87. Wettenhall, *Enter into Thy Closet*, 8.

88. Wettenhall, *Enter into Thy Closet*, 3, 69; Richard Rambuss, *Closet Devotions* (Durham, NC: Duke University Press, 1998), 105. See also, e.g., Oliver Heywood, *Closet-Prayer a Christian Duty* (London: A. M. for Tho. Parkhurst, 1671), and Samuel Slater, *A Discourse of Closet (or Secret) Prayer* (London: Jonathan Robinson, 1691).

89. See Lena Cowen Orlin, *Locating Privacy in Tudor England* (Oxford: Oxford University Press), 3, 309–25.

90. Roger North, *Of Building: Roger North's Writings on Architecture*, ed. Howard Colvin and John Newman (Oxford: Oxford University Press, 1981). Among the manuscripts by North in this collection are "Architecture" (ca. 1690) and "Of Building" (ca. 1695–1696).

91. John Fowler and John Cornforth, *Eighteenth-Century Decoration* (Princeton, NJ: Pyne Press, 1974), 27.

92. These include Jones's designs for chimneypieces in the Queen's House at Greenwich (ca. 1637) and Webb's designs for the King's Bedchamber (1667) for the rebuilding of Greenwich Palace. See Saumarez Smith, *Eighteenth-Century Decoration*, 12, 14–15 (plate 2), 16–17 (plate 4).

93. Saumarez Smith, *Eighteenth-Century Decoration*, 63. A notable instance of the cutaway section emerged in Colen Campbell's *Vitruvius Britannicus: or, The British Architect* (1715–1725).

94. Martin, "Ascendancy," 22.

95. Evans, *Projective Cast*, 203.

96. Evans, *Projective Cast*, 203.

97. For analyses of Shakespearean stage sets and scenography as sites of interactive engagement and interpretation, see Lyn Tribble, *Cognition in the Globe: Attention and Memory in Shakespeare's Theatre* (New York: Palgrave Macmillan, 2011), and Lupton, "Reading Dramaturgy in *Romeo and Juliet*," in *Shakespeare Dwelling*, 46–84.

98. In examining the interpenetrating developments of atmosphere as an object of knowledge in natural philosophy and as a feature of imaginative writing during the long eighteenth century, Jayne Lewis defines atmosphere as "the making apparent, if not strictly visible, of an otherwise invisible medium." See Lewis, *Air's Appearance* (Chicago: University of Chicago Press, 2012), 5.

99. Maurice Merleau-Ponty, *The Phenomenology of Perception*, trans. Colin Smith (London: Routledge & Kegan Paul, 1982), 243.

100. In broadening the category of space to incorporate experiential spaces as well as

textual ones, my project is sympathetic to Caroline Levine's project of expanding literary considerations of form to relate to nonliterary ones. See Levine, *Forms* (Princeton, NJ: Princeton University Press, 2015).

101. Mieke Bal, *Narratology: Introduction to Theory of Narrative*, 3rd ed. (1985; Toronto: University of Toronto Press, 2009), 139.

102. Bal, *Narratology*, 138.

103. Bland, "Endangering," 124.

104. This aspect of spatial formalism, relating spatial environments in lived reality to those represented in word and image, coheres with Henri Lefebvre's view that representational space and lived spaces are, along with representations of space (or conceptualized space), "interconnected." See Lefebvre, *Production of Space*, 40.

105. Watt's terms for interiority include "private experience," "train of thought," and "inner consciousness."

106. Watt, *Rise of the Novel*, 26.

107. Georg Lukács, *Theory of the Novel*, trans. Anna Bostock (Cambridge, MA: MIT Press, 1971).

108. Watt, *Rise of the Novel*, 175.

109. Wall, "Details of Space," 394.

110. Wall, *Prose of Things*, 123. In making this argument, Wall counters Rachel Trickett's observation that eighteenth-century narrative, unlike poetry, lacked a visual idiom not just for spatial description but also for the act of "relating the poet's discourse to his environment." For Wall, eighteenth-century prose was rich with an idiom of spatial description, to which contemporary readers were cognitively attuned but post-nineteenth-century readers are not. See Trickett, "'Curious Eye': Some Aspects of Visual Description in Eighteenth-Century Literature," in *Augustan Studies: Essays in Honor of Irwin Ehrenpreis*, ed. Douglas Lane Patey and Timothy Keegan (Newark: University of Delaware Press, 1985): 239–52; 245.

111. Wall, "Details of Space, 394.

112. This is a notion suggested by her playful, Fieldingesque reference to description as "the foundling" in her chapter headings and framing of her study. See Wall, *Prose of Things*, chap. 1, "A History of Description, a Foundling," and chap. 8, "The Foundling as Heir."

113. M. H. Abrams, *A Glossary of Literary Terms* (Fort Worth, TX: Harcourt Brace Jovanovich College, 1993).

114. John Bender's argument about the influence of fiction on the management of prisoners through prison architecture design certainly resonates with spatial formalism. But Bender's study lacks the prevailing concern with the phenomenology of embodied interactions with architectural forms of space that defines spatial formalism. Rather, his emphasis lies in tracing ideological nuances in prison reform discourse, with space as a formal and material construct remaining a side issue. See Bender, *Imagining the Penitentiary: Fiction and the Architecture of Mind in Eighteenth-Century England* (Chicago: University of Chicago Press, 1987).

115. Armstrong, *Desire and Domestic Fiction*; McKeon, *Secret History of Domesticity*.

116. Bland, "Endangering," 135. For a contemporary account of a visit to Nun Appleton that makes comparisons between the extant landscape and places described in the poem, see J. Mark Heumann, "Andrew Marvell and the Experience of Nunappleton," *Andrew Marvell Society Newsletter* 3, no. 1 (Summer 2011), https://marvell.wp.st-andrews.ac.uk /newsletter/j-mark-heumann-andrew-marvell-and-the-experience-of-nunappleton/. See

also Jonathan Post, "'On each pleasant footstep stay': A Walk about 'Appleton House,'" *Ben Jonson Journal* 11, no. 1 (2004): 163–205.

117. The camera obscura is in the collection of Erkki Huhtamo.

118. Kaja Silverman points out that the flow of the camera obscura's images "existed only in the 'now' in which it appeared." Because "the viewer had to enter the camera obscura in order to see it, the two were spatially as well as temporally co-present." See Silverman, *The Miracle of Analogy; or, The History of Photography* (Stanford, CA: Stanford University Press, 2015).

Chapter One

1. The aforementioned estates from novels appear, respectively, in Henry Fielding's *Tom Jones*, Tobias Smollett's *Humphry Clinker*, Evelyn Waugh's *Brideshead Revisited*, and Ian McEwan's *Atonement*.

2. I echo the locution J. Paul Hunter uses for his book title: *Before Novels: The Cultural Contexts of Eighteenth-Century English Fiction* (New York: Norton, 1990). On the conservatism of country house poetry, see Isabel Rivers, *The Poetry of Conservatism, 1600–1745: A Study of Poets and Public Affairs from Jonson to Pope* (Cambridge: Rivers Press, 1973).

3. G. R. Hibbard, "The Country House Poem of the Seventeenth Century," *Journal of the Warburg and the Courtauld Institutes* 19, nos. 1–2 (1956): 159–74. Although Aemilia Lanyer's "The Description of Cookham" (1610) is now regarded as the first country house poem, Ben Jonson's "To Penshurst" (1616) was the most influential, generating similar poems by his followers.

4. Kari Boyd McBride, *Country House Discourse in Early Modern England: A Cultural Study in Landscape and Legitimacy* (Burlington, VT: Ashgate, 2001), 11.

5. Hibbard, "Country House Poem," 159.

6. Hibbard, "Country House Poem," 159.

7. Hibbard, "Country House Poem," 171.

8. See Hibbard's discussion of *Epistle to Burlington* in "Country House Poem," 172–74.

9. For a collection of these late seventeenth-century and eighteenth-century estate poems, see Alastair Fowler, ed., *The Country House Poem* (Edinburgh: Edinburgh University Press, 1994). For a study of eighteenth-century estate poetry as a subgenre of topographical poetry, see Robert Arnold Aubin, *Topographical Poetry in XVIII-Century Poetry* (New York: Modern Language Association of America, 1966).

10. If the scholars are correct who believe that Marvell lived in the new house or at least was present while work on it was beginning, then he would have encountered an architectural space that incorporated principles of the double pile design, or the plans for such a space. It may have been too early for him to perfect the double pile plan by the time he worked on Nun Appleton House, but Webb was already designing with a view toward creating more freedom of movement and circulation, as his plan for the house he worked on just before, Maiden Bradley (1646–1640), demonstrates.

11. Rosalie Colie describes Marvell's poem, with its rich generic mixture, or *genera mixta*, as a "generic anthology." Its range of incorporated genres includes locodescriptive poem, masque, treatise, historical narrative, allegory, homily, and emblem book. See Colie, *The Resources of Kind: Genre-Theory in the Renaissance* (Berkeley: University of California Press, 1973), 38.

12. Hibbard, "Country House Poem," 164.

13. Hibbard, "Country House Poem," 164.

14. I borrow the phrase "life of the community" from Hibbard, "Country House Poem," 169.

15. Gervase Jackson-Stops, *The English Country House: A Grand Tour* (Boston: Little, Brown, 1985), 46.

16. For histories of private life and privacy in early modern Europe, see Roger Chartier, *Passions of the Renaissance*, vol. 3 of *A History of Private Life*, trans. Arthur Goldhammer, series ed. Philippe Ariès and Georges Duby (Cambridge, MA: Belknap Press, 1989), and Orlin, *Locating Privacy*.

17. Jackson-Stops, *English Country House*, 44, 46.

18. Andor Gomme and Alison Maguire, *Design and Plan in the Country House from Castle Donjons to Palladian Boxes* (New Haven, CT: Yale University Press, 2008), 82.

19. Initially, in the sixteenth century, staircases were built as a functional construct to allow family members to pass from the great hall to the solar or great chamber, where they could dine separately from the community. As the family continued to distance itself from the communal experience of the great hall, and the great chamber grew in significance, the staircase leading to it became bigger and more impressive in design. See Jackson-Stops, *English Country House*, 64.

20. Macfarlane, *Origins of English Individualism*, 40.

21. Caroline van Eck, "Artisan Mannerism: Seventeenth-Century Rhetorical Alternatives to Sir John Summerson's Formalist Approach," in *Summerson and Hitchcock: Centenary Essays on Architectural Historiography*, ed. Frank Salmon (New Haven, CT: Yale University Press, 2006), 85–104; 90.

22. Henry Wotton, *The Elements of Architecture* (Charlottesville: University of Virginia Press/Folger Shakespeare Library, 1968), 4.

23. Vincenzo Scamozzi, *L'idea della architettura universal* (Venice: n.p., 1615), 138; Kimberley Skelton, *The Paradox of Body, Building and Motion in Seventeenth-Century England* (Manchester: Manchester University Press, 2015), 4–5. For an extended consideration of the idea expressed in *L'idea*, see Scamozzi, *Discorsi sopra l'antichità di Roma* (Venice: Appresso Francesco Ziletti, 1582).

24. See Skelton, *Paradox of Body*, 4–5.

25. John Bold, "Privacy and the Plan," in *English Architecture Public and Private: Essays for Kerry Downes*, ed. John Bold and Edward Chaney (London: Hambledon, 1993), 107–19, 118.

26. Evans, "Figures, Doors and Passages," in *Translations from Drawing to Building*, 79.

27. For an in-depth examination of this debate, see Jane Partner, "'The Swelling Hall': Andrew Marvell and the Politics of Architecture at Nun Appleton House," *Seventeenth Century* 23, no. 2 (October 2008): 225–43.

28. The last two lines referred to in "To Penshurst" are as follows: "Those proud, ambitious heaps, and nothing else, / May say, their lords have built, but thy lord dwells." The critical contrast between "building" and "dwelling" is also enlarged on, though not in relation to Jonson's poem, by Martin Heidegger and then by Tim Ingold. See Heidegger, *Poetry, Language, Thought*, trans. Albert Hofstadter (New York: Harper Colophon, 1971), and Ingold, *Perception of the Environment*, 185–87.

29. For a discussion of this time in Marvell's life, see Nigel Smith, *Andrew Marvell: The Chameleon* (New Haven, CT: Yale University Press, 2010): 88–101.

30. Such polarities include those between "build" and "dwell," "touchstone" and "country stone," "volunteer" and "trapped," "give" and "take," and "admire" and "envy."

31. Andrew Marvell, *Upon Appleton House*, in *The Poems of Andrew Marvell*, ed. Nigel

Smith (London: Longman 2003), 210–41. All references to *Upon Appleton House* are to this edition.

32. See Marvell, *Upon Appleton House*, 216 (note to lines 6–8).

33. See Erwin Panofsky, "The History of the Theory of Human Proportions as a Reflection of the History of Styles," in *Meaning in the Visual Arts* (Garden City, NY: Anchor Books, 1955), 55–107, and George Dodds and Robert Tavernor, eds., *Body and Building: Essays on the Changing Relationship of Body and Architecture* (Cambridge, MA: MIT Press, 2003). In *De re aedificatoria* (1443–1452), Leon Battista Alberti views buildings as analogues of human bodies. See Alberti, *On the Art of Building in Ten Books*, trans. Joseph Rykwert, Neil Leach, and Robert Tavernor (Cambridge, MA: MIT Press, 1988).

34. Anne Cotterill, "Marvell's Watery Maze: Digression and Discovery at Nun Appleton," *ELH* 69, no. 1 (Spring 2002): 103–32.

35. Morris Croll, "The Baroque Style in Prose," in *Style, Rhetoric, and Rhythm: Essays by Morris W. Croll*, ed. J. Max Patrick et al. (Princeton, NJ: Princeton University Press, 1966), 207–33. I am grateful to Christopher Johnson for informing me of Croll's work.

36. Croll, "Baroque Style," 213, 216.

37. Croll, "Baroque Style," 209.

38. Croll, "Baroque Style," 221.

39. Colie, *Resources of Kind*, 182. For more on the contradiction between the poem's formal neatness and its internal irregularity, see Post, "On each pleasant footstep stay," 169, and Cotterill, "Marvell's Watery Maze," 103.

40. With "period," Croll uses the term in rhetoric for a "grammatically complete sentence" (*Oxford English Dictionary*).

41. Colie comments on the "arcimboldesque" qualities in the magic lantern effects of the meadow scene. See Colie, *Resources of Kind*, 212.

42. Douglas Chambers has commented on the slippage between bibliographical and architectural terminology in Marvell's "frontispiece of poor." See "'To the Abyss': Gothic as a Metaphor for the Argument about Art and Nature in 'Upon Appleton House,'" in *On the Celebrated and Neglected Poems of Andrew Marvell*, ed. Claude J. Summers and Ted-Larry Pebworth (Columbia: University of Missouri Press, 1992), 139–53.

43. See Smith, *Marvell: The Chameleon*.

44. See Cotteril, "Marvell's Watery Maze," on deviance as a wider-ranging theme in Marvell's poem.

45. Michel Conan, "Landscape Metaphors and Metamorphosis of Time," in *Landscape Design and the Experience of Motion*, ed. Michel Conan (Washington, DC: Dumbarton Oaks Research Library and Collection, 2003), 287–317; 302.

46. For the history of the Fairfax family's possession of Nun Appleton, see James Holstun, "'Will you rent our ancient love asunder?' Lesbian Elegy in Donne, Marvell, and Milton," *ELH* 54, no. 4 (1987): 835–67; 847. On the Acts of Dissolution and their effects on the architecture of sixteenth-century England, see Maurice Howard, *The Building of Elizabethan and Jacobean England* (New Haven, CT: Yale University Press/Paul Mellon Centre for Studies in British Art, 2007).

47. The phrase and notion derive from Michael McKeon's *The Secret History of Domesticity*.

48. Howard, *Building*, 13.

49. Howard, *Building*, 15.

50. See Sarah Monette, "Speaking and Silent Women in *Upon Appleton House*," *SEL* 42, no. 1 (2002): 155–71; 9.

51. T. Katharine Sheldahl Thomason, "Marvell, His Bee-Like Cell: The Pastoral Hexagon of *Upon Appleton House*," *GENRE* 16, no. 1 (Spring 1983): 39–56; 47.

52. Lord Fairfax's nineteenth-century biographer affirms Marvell's plot when describing Nun Appleton's topography: "on the south side were the ruins of the old nunnery, the flower garden, and the low meadows called *ings*, extending to the banks of the Wharfe." See Clements R. Markham, *Life of the Great Lord Fairfax* (London: Macmillan, 1870), 366.

53. Timothy Raylor, "'Paradice's Only Map': A Plan of Nun Appleton," *Notes and Queries* 44, no. 2 (1997): 186–87. The map Raylor found was made about fifty years earlier, in 1596, as part of a survey of Bolton Percy, a Yorkshire parish, and is held in the Borthwick Institute for Archives, University of York. Raylor writes, "It is clear from the Bolton Percy map that Marvell's poem is, among other things, an entirely plausible account of a sinuous yet circular walk through the Fairfax estate at Nun Appleton" (187).

54. See Heumann, "Marvell and the Experience of Nunappleton." Heumann makes comparisons between the extant landscape and places described in the poem.

55. See Heumann, "Marvell and the Experience of Nunappleton."

56. For a recent interpretation of the garden section of the poem as Marvell's form of engaging with contemporary military technology and theory, especially with regard to siegecraft and fortifications, see Julianne Werlin, "Marvell and the Strategic Imagination: Fortification in *Upon Appleton House*," *Review of English Studies* 63, no. 260 (2012): 370–87.

57. Cawood Castle itself had a dramatic Civil War history. A Royalist garrison, it was captured three times and used by Lord Fairfax as a prisoner of war camp.

58. Wotton, *Elements*, 109–10.

59. Colie uses the term "scalar shift" throughout her analysis of *Upon Appleton House* in *My Echoing Song*.

60. Alastair Fowler, *Renaissance Realism* (Oxford: Oxford University Press, 2003), 14.

61. Frances Yates, *The Art of Memory* (Chicago: University of Chicago Press, 1966), 132.

62. Military elements such as fortifications and battlements were common in garden designs of the period. See Fowler, *Country House Poem*, 6. For more on the integration of military design in Nun Appleton's garden and its correspondences with protocols of diagramming, see Katherine O. Acheson, "Military Illustration, Garden Design, and Marvell's *Upon Appleton House*," *English Literary Renaissance* 45, no. 1 (January 2011): 146–88. For an analysis of battleground imagery in the garden section of *Upon Appleton House* and proleptic evocation of Laurence Sterne's *Tristram Shandy*, see Tom Keymer, "Horticulture Wars: *Tristram Shandy* and *Upon Appleton House*," *Shandean* 11 (1999–2000): 38–46.

63. See Ann Berthoff, *The Resolved Soul* (Princeton, NJ: Princeton University Press, 1970), and Muriel Bradbrook, "Marvell and the Masque," in *Tercentenary Essays in Honor of Andrew Marvell*, ed. Kenneth Friedenreich, 204–23 (Hamden, CT: Archon, 1977).

64. See Curtis Whitaker, "Fairfax, Marvell, and the Mowers of Nun Appleton," *Ben Jonson Journal* 20, no. 1 (2013): 72–94.

65. Bradbrook acknowledges that an advantage in Marvell's choice of using poetry to examine the political and moral gesture of retreat and reframe it as "measured advance, dominance, triumph," is that he avoids "the social ritual of the old masque," which was "too often an instrument for self-delusion." "Marvell and the Masque," 221.

66. See Smith, *Poems of Andrew Marvell*, note 446.

67. A. W. Johnson, *Ben Jonson: Poetry and Architecture* (Oxford: Clarendon Press, 1994), 53.

68. Hobbes, *Leviathan*, 17.

69. Hobbes, *Leviathan*, 20.

70. *Leviathan* was published in 1651, a year that overlapped with Marvell's time at Nun Appleton.

71. Hobbes, *Leviathan*, 20.

72. David Hume, *A Treatise of Human Nature*, ed. Peter H. Nidditch (Oxford: Clarendon Press, 1978), book 1, pt. 4, §6, 253.

73. Henry Wotton, *The Life and Letters of Sir Henry Wotton*, ed. Logan Pearsall Smith, 2 vols. (Oxford: Clarendon Press, 1907), 2:205.

74. Wotton, *Life*, 2:206.

75. Wotton, *Life*, 2:206.

76. Svetlana Alpers discusses the distinction between drawings using the camera obscura and geometrical perspective. See Alpers, *The Art of Describing* (Chicago: University of Chicago Press, 1983), 31–32. For a historical study of geometrical perspective, beginning with Brunelleschi, see Martin Kemp, *The Science of Art* (New Haven, CT: Yale University Press, 1990).

77. See Alpers, *Art of Describing*.

78. Denis Diderot and Jean le Ronde D'Alembert, *Encyclopédie ou dictionnaire des sciences, des arts et des métiers*, vol. 3 (Paris: Briasson, 1753).

79. Quoted in Kemp, *Science of Art*, 192.

80. Colie, *Resources of Kind*, 211–17.

81. Joanna Picciotto points out that such serial mediations underscore how, for Marvell, the way things look are not so much givens as creations of "particular perceptual conditions" that "themselves become the object of scrutiny." See Picciotto, *Labors of Innocence* (Cambridge, MA: Harvard University Press, 2010), 358.

82. Claudio Guillén, "On the Concept and Metaphor of Perspective," in *Comparatists at Work: Studies in Comparative Literature*, ed. Stephen G. Nichols Jr. and Richard B. Vowles (Waltham, MA: Blaisdell, 1968), 28–90; 29.

83. Friedberg, *Virtual Window*, 48. In *De Pictura* (1435), Alberti likened the visual composition of a painting to what is viewed within a picture frame. See Leon Battista Alberti, *On Painting*, trans. Cecil Grayson (London: Penguin, 1972).

84. Joseph Moxon, *Practical Perspective; or, Perspective Made Easie* (London: Joseph Moxon, 1670), B.

85. Moxon, *Practical Perspective*, B.

86. Jean Dubreuil, *Perspective Practical; or, A Plain and Easie Method of True and Lively Representing all Things to the Eye at a distance, by the Exact Rules of Art* (London: Robert Pricke, 1698), 6.

87. I borrow the notion of the wood as a camera obscura from James Turner, *The Politics of Landscape* (Cambridge, MA: Harvard University Press, 1979). Turner writes, "The wood is like a camera obscura, where daylight is barred so tightly that 'light Mosaicks' of the outside world are projected" (78).

88. For a discussion of air's significance as a medium for movement, see Tim Ingold, "Footprints through the Weather-World: Walking, Breathing, Knowing," *Journal of the Royal Anthropological Institute*, n.s., 16 (2010): S121–S139.

89. See Guita Lamsechi, "Freiberg's Tulip Pulpit: Hybrid Nature and Civic Politics," in *The Book of Nature and Humanity in the Middle Ages and the Renaissance*, ed. David Hawkes et al. (Turnhout, Belgium: Brepols, 2013), 157–79.

90. For exemplary acts of animating affordance and design theory within the context of literary criticism, see Lupton, *Shakespeare Dwelling*, and Caroline Levine, *Forms*.

91. The quoted lines are, respectively, from stanza 67, l. 530; stanza 72, l. 575; stanza 65, l. 513–14; and stanza 66, l. 523.

92. In finding a place to settle his mind, he is more able to lay claim consciously to his thoughts as his own through inserting the word *methinks*. Not only does the poet actively possess his thoughts with this word; with this indirect narration of mental activity, he also prefigures narrative discourse. Such a rhetorical maneuver would grow in cultural importance as the concept and practice of private property became fully dominant in the eighteenth century, with the peasant class—the object of Marvell's gaze in the meadow—dying out by the first half of the century. See Macfarlane, *Origins of English Individualism*, 43.

93. Locke, *Essay*, book 2, chap. 2, §2, lines 3–5.

94. Locke, *Two Treatises of Government* and *A Letter Concerning Toleration*, ed. Ian Shapiro (1689; New Haven, CT: Yale University Press, 2003), 111.

95. Michel de Certeau, *The Practice of Everyday Life*, trans. Steven Rendall (Berkeley: University of California Press, 1984), 174.

96. Certeau, *Practice*, xxi.

97. Certeau, *Practice*, 115.

98. Ingold, "Footprints," S129.

99. Ingold, "Footprints," S122.

100. Ingold, "Footprints," S122.

101. Wotton, *Elements*, 4.

102. Guillén, "Concept and Metaphor," 28–90; 71.

103. Guillén, "Concept and Metaphor," 64.

104. See Rayna Kalas, *Frame, Glass, Verse* (Ithaca, NY: Cornell University Press, 2007). See also Debora Shuger, "The 'I' of the Beholder: Renaissance Mirrors and the Reflexive Mind," in *Renaissance Culture and the Everyday*, ed. Patricia Fumerton and Simon Hunt (Philadelphia: University of Pennsylvania Press, 1999), 21–41. Shuger argues that the new level of clarity in reflection brought by the technological innovation of crystal, clear glass mirrors in the sixteenth century engendered a self-reflexiveness that was relational, not direct. In the Renaissance, she writes, "one encounters one's own likeness only in the mirror of the other" (37).

105. See Kalas, *Frame, Glass, Verse*, 110–11.

106. Turner, *Politics of Landscape*, 80.

107. On the cultural history of the dressing room, see Tita Chico, *Designing Women: The Dressing Room in Eighteenth-Century English Literature and Culture* (Lewisburg, PA: Bucknell University Press, 2005).

108. Isabel Thwaites, for instance, was saved by William Fairfax only after she had already succumbed to the nuns' enticements, converting in doing so from Protestantism to Catholicism.

109. Jane Austen, *Pride and Prejudice* (Oxford: Oxford University Press, 1970), 185. See Cynthia Wall's reading of this scene in *Grammars of Approach* (Chicago: University of Chicago Press, 2018).

110. See Ann Banfield, *Unspeakable Sentences: Narration and Representation in the Language of Fiction* (Boston: Routledge & Kegan Paul, 1982), on represented speech and thought in fiction. I borrow the phrase "the mental and the material" from Ingold, "Footprints," S129.

111. Certeau, *Practice*, 170, 174, xxi.

112. Austen, *Pride and Prejudice*, 216.

113. Colie, *Resources of Kind*, 182–83.

114. It is scholars such as Colie and Kitty Scoular who reveal to us that Marvell's images throughout *Upon Appleton House* reference verbally the visual art of emblems created earlier in the century. His image of fishers who, carrying canoes on their backs, resemble tortoises recalls Zacharias Heyns's emblem showing a human figure using a gigantic tortoise shell to create a shelter for himself on a beach, while another rows a boat in the water. See Colie, *Resources of Kind*, 196–98, 201; Scoular, *Natural Magic* (Oxford: Clarendon Press, 1965); and Zacharias Heyns, *Emblemata* (Rotterdam: P. van Waesberghe, 1625), 7.

Chapter Two

1. The copy of the frontispiece in question appears in the Huntington Library copy of Margaret Cavendish, *Philosophical and Physical Opinions* (London: J. Martin and J. Allestrye, 1655). Page citations will be from original editions, except for *The Blazing World* (1666), *A True Relation of My Birth, Breeding, and Life* (1656), and *CCXI Sociable Letters* (1664), which I cite frequently, and which are widely available in modern editions in paper. Text of original editions is available on the open web through the Early English Books Online–Text Creation Partnership, as are digital editions for select other titles.

2. These are some of the artists analyzed by Svetlana Alpers in "Looking at Words: The Representation of Texts in Dutch Art," chap. 5 in *Art of Describing*, 169–221.

3. Known books include *Philosophical and Physical Opinions* and *Worlds Olio*. Two other images depicting Cavendish were commonly used as frontispieces for her body of work. According to James Fitzmaurice, "There is, interestingly, little pattern to the way in which frontispieces appear in her books: that is, virtually any book may be found with any of the three frontispieces or with none at all. Nevertheless, the frontispieces are commonly if not uniformly present in the books." See Fitzmaurice, "Fancy and the Family: Self-Characterizations of Margaret Cavendish," *Huntington Library Quarterly* 53, no. 3 (Summer 1990): 198–209; 202.

4. On the putti as embodied thoughts, see Lucy Worsley, *Cavalier* (London: Faber and Faber, 2007), 218.

5. Margaret Cavendish, *Sociable Letters*, ed. James Fitzmaurice (Peterborough, ON: Broadview, 2004), Letters #192, 258; #195, 262; #74, 128. Subsequent citations of this source appear in the body of the text.

6. Anna Battigelli, *Margaret Cavendish and the Exiles of the Mind* (Lexington: University of Kentucky Press, 1998), 85.

7. Margaret Cavendish, *Observations upon Experimental Philosophy. To Which Is Added, The Description of a New Blazing World* (London: A. Maxwell, 1666).

8. For book-length works on Cavendish, see Lisa Sarasohn, *The Natural Philosophy of Margaret Cavendish* (Baltimore: Johns Hopkins University Press, 2010), and Battigelli, *Cavendish and the Exiles*.

9. Cavendish, *The Life of the Thrice Noble, High and Puissant Prince William Cavendishe* (London: A. Maxwell, 1667), 76.

10. The image of a putto or putti bringing a laurel wreath to rest on a human figure's head was a conventional means of marking an elevated person or allegorical being throughout the seventeenth century.

11. Margaret Mulvihill, in her keynote lecture for the 2013 Cavendish Society Conference at Sundance, Utah, observed that Cavendish's contrapposto pose in the frontispiece contributed to her classical self-fashioning. Katie Whitaker remarks that Cavendish's plain dress in the writing closet image evokes the "simple black commonly worn by scholars and clergymen." See Whitaker, *Mad Madge* (New York: Basic Books, 2002), 174.

12. In this way, Cavendish's frontispiece operates like the *voorhuis*, the front house section of Netherlandish homes that served as a zone of mediation between exterior and interior spaces. See Mariët Westermann's discussion of the *voorhuis* in "'Costly and Curious, Full off pleasure and home contentment': Making Home in the Dutch Republic," in *Art and Home: Dutch Interiors in the Age of Rembrandt*, ed. Mariët Westermann (Zwolle, Netherlands: Waanders/Denver Art Museum and Newark Museum, 2001), 15–81; 27–31. I am indebted to Guita Lamsechi for sharing this source with me.

13. Mary Baine Campbell, *Wonder and Science* (Ithaca, NY: Cornell University Press, 1999), 206.

14. Ingold, *Being Alive*, 10.

15. Heidegger, *Poetry, Language, Thought*, 158–59.

16. Heidegger, *Poetry, Language, Thought*, 160–61.

17. Cavendish, *The Blazing World and Other Writings*, ed. Kate Lilley (London: Penguin, 1992), 185.

18. Cavendish, "To the Grace the Duke of Newcastle," in *Life of the Thrice Noble*, (b)1r–v.

19. See Carolyn Steedman's discussion of Vermeer's *Lady Writing a Letter, with Her Maid* and its relationship with epistolary narrative in "A Woman Writing a Letter," in *Epistolary Selves*, ed. Rebecca Earle (Aldershot, UK: Ashgate, 1999), 111–33.

20. Richard Flecknoe, "On the Duchess of Newcastle's Closet," in Fowler, *Country House Poem*, 179–80.

21. Alastair Fowler makes this hypothesis. See *Country House Poem*, 180.

22. Flecknoe, "On the Duchess of Newcastle's Closet," 179.

23. Cavendish, *A True Relation of My Birth, Breeding, and Life* (1656), in *Paper Bodies: A Margaret Cavendish Reader*, ed. Sylvia Bowerbank and Sara Mendelson (Peterborough, ON: Broadview, 2000), 57.

24. Cavendish, "Similizing Thoughts," in *Poems, and Fancies, written by the Right Honourable, the Lady Margaret Newcastle* (London: J. Martin and J. Allestrye, 1653), 145.

25. Cavendish, *True Relation*, 57.

26. Cavendish, *True Relation*, 57.

27. Cavendish, *True Relation*, 57.

28. Cavendish, *True Relation*, 59.

29. Cavendish, *Poems, and Fancies*, 213.

30. In addition, there are no floor plans from the seventeenth century. I am indebted to Gareth Hughes, Collections Manager, Portland Collection of the Welbeck Estates Company Limited, for providing me with this information.

31. Thornton refers to Fiennes's account of seeing the Burghley House curiosity cabinet in her 1702 travel memoir. See *The Illustrated Journeys of Celia Fiennes, c. 1682–1712*, ed. Christopher Morris (Exeter: Webb and Bower, 1982).

32. Peter Thornton, *Seventeenth-Century Interior Decoration in England, France and Holland* (New Haven, CT: Yale University Press, 1978), 301.

33. North, *Of Building*, 73.

34. North, *Of Building*, 70.

35. North, *Of Building*, 84.

36. North, *Of Building*, 86.

37. North, *Of Building*, 134.

38. North, *Of Building*, 134.

39. Peter Thornton and Maurice Tomlin, *The Furnishing and Decoration of Ham House* (London: Furniture History Society, 1980), 62.

40. Thornton and Tomlin write, "These curtains must have served to exclude the light and increase the comfort of the Duke when reposing on the couch"; *Furnishing and Decoration*, 62.

41. Cavendish, "The Body, Time, and Minde, disputed for Preheminency," in *Natures Pictures Drawn by Fancies Pencil to the Life* (London: J. Martin and J. Allestrye, 1656), 153–55; 154.

42. As Thornton put it, "Their outrageous conformation is presumably the result of an imaginative attempt to produce chairs in an Oriental style. No known Oriental chairs look like these and they must be the fruit of a rich Carolean fantasy"; *Seventeenth-Century Interior Decoration*, 84.

43. See Whitaker, *Mad Madge*, 169–71.

44. Cavendish, *Philosophical and Physical Opinions*, 80.

45. For a discussion of the Renaissance notion of "images in the air" as it applies to Johannes Kepler's system of distinction between the two forms of image, *picture* and *imago*, see Sven Dupré, "Inside the *Camera Obscura*: Kepler's Experiment and Theory of Optical Imagery," *Early Science and Medicine* 13 (2008): 219–44.

46. Giambattista Della Porta, *Natural Magic* (London: Printed for Thomas Young, and Samuel Speed, 1658). I borrow Leni Katherine Robinson's notion that "the camera obscura evokes the marvel of the . . . technicolor brilliance of Cavendish's exotic and paradisal Blazing World." See "A Figurative Matter: Continuities between Margaret Cavendish's Theory of Discourse and Her Natural Philosophy," unpublished dissertation, University of British Columbia, 2009, 250n851.

47. Francesco Algarotti, *An Essay on Painting* (London: L. David and C. Reymer, 1764), 62.

48. Cavendish, *Blazing World*, 132.

49. Cavendish, *Blazing World*, 110.

50. Catherine Gallagher, "The Rise of Fictionality," in *The Novel*, ed. Franco Moretti (Princeton, NJ: Princeton University Press, 2006), 1:336–63.

51. Della Porta, *Natural Magic*, 364.

52. Cavendish, *Blazing World*, 193–94, 222.

53. Cavendish, *Blazing World*, 132.

54. Saumarez Smith, *Eighteenth-Century Decoration*, 12, 27.

55. Timothy Raylor, "'Pleasure Reconciled to Virtue': William Cavendish, Ben Jonson, and the Decorative Scheme of Bolsover Castle," *Renaissance Quarterly* 52 (1999): 402–39; 423.

56. Margaret Cavendish, *Worlds Olio* (London: J. Martin and J. Allestrye, 1655), 3.

57. Cavendish, "Thought Similized," in *Poems and Phancies* (London: William Wilson, 1664), 178.

58. Marvell, *Upon Appleton House*, stanza 76, line 602.

59. Cavendish, *True Relation*, 59.

60. Cavendish, "Body, Time, and Minde," in *Natures Pictures*, 153.

61. Cavendish, *Poems, and Fancies*, 45.

62. Quoted in Norma Wenczel, "The Optical Camera Obscura II: Images and Texts," in *Inside the Camera Obscura*, ed. Wolfgang Lefèvre (preprint 333, Max-Planck-Institut für Wissenschaftsgeschichte, 2007), 19, https://www.mpiwg-berlin.mpg.de/Preprints /P333.PDF.

63. Della Porta, *Natural Magic*, 364.

64. Cavendish, "A Dialogue betwixt a Contemplatory Lady and a Poet," in *Natures Pictures*, 175–77; 176.

65. The term "interior parts" is used throughout to describe nearly every natural object examined in Cavendish, *Observations*. See, for example, 12, 20, 42, 43, 57, 121.

66. This is a critical point in Cavendish's argument against the Royal Society's program of experimental science and its veneration of such scientific instruments as the microscope. I discuss at greater length her contention with the Royal Society's celebration of microscopes in Julie Park, "Marching Thoughts on White Paper: Margaret Cavendish's Tools of Inwardness," in *Interiors and Interiority*, ed. Ewa Lajer-Burcharth and Beate Söntgen (Berlin: De Gruyter, 2015), 119–38.

67. Cavendish, *Observations*, 12.

68. In *The Blazing World*, for instance, the Duchess is described as making worlds based on different philosophic systems that have a direct material effect on her mind. Hobbes's "opinion" on her mind makes "all the parts of this imaginary world c[o]me to press and drive each other." They seem "like a company of wolves that worry sheep, or like so many dogs that hunt after hares" (188).

69. On the background of Dutch Golden Age painting in nineteenth-century realist novels, see Ruth Bernard Yeazell, *Art of the Everyday: Dutch Painting and the Realist Novel* (Princeton, NJ: Princeton University Press, 2008).

70. Anna Laetitia Barbauld, *The Correspondence of Samuel Richardson . . . To Which Are Prefixed, A Biographical Account of That Author, and Observations on His Writings* (London: Richard Phillips, 1804), 1:cxxxvii.

71. See Catherine Gallagher and Lubomir Doležel, "Mimesis and Possible Worlds," in "Aspects of Literary Theory," special issue of *Poetics Today* 9, no. 3 (1988): 475–96.

72. Cavendish, *Sociable Letters*, 42. Subsequent citations will appear in the body of the text.

73. Lara Dodds, *The Literary Invention of Margaret Cavendish* (Pittsburgh: Duquesne University Press, 2013), 30, 27.

74. Dodds, *Literary Invention*, 28.

75. See B. G. MacCarthy, *Women Writers: Their Contribution to the English Novel 1621–1744* (Cork: Cork University Press, 1944), 137. I am grateful to James Fitzmaurice for informing me of this source.

76. Quoted in MacCarthy, *Women Writers*, 137. See J. J. Jusserand, *The English Novel in the Time of Shakespeare*, trans. Elizabeth Lee (London: Unwin, 1890).

77. Alpers, *Art of Describing*, 192.

78. Watt, *Rise of the Novel*, 192.

79. Alpers, *Art of Describing*, 192. For a book chapter that takes as its subject the actual epistolary correspondence of a real person, William Cowper, and compares the descriptions of his daily life with seventeenth-century Dutch paintings of domestic interiors, see Bruce Redford, "William Cowper: Invitations to the Microcosm," in *The Converse of the Pen* (Chicago: University of Chicago Press, 1986), 49–92. For Redford, Cowper's use of

"painterly descriptions" in his textual language served as a strategy for opening his private life to his intimates (52).

80. Alpers, *Art of Describing*, 192.

81. Alpers, *Art of Describing*, 200.

82. Quoted in Alpers, *Art of Describing*, 200.

83. Ingold, *Perception of the Environment*, 195.

84. Ingold, *Perception of the Environment*, 197.

85. Susanne Langer, *Feeling and Form: A Theory of Art* (New York: Scribner's 1953), 80.

86. Westermann, "Costly and Curious," 72.

87. Westermann, "Costly and Curious," 74.

88. Ingold, *Perception of the Environment*, 195.

89. Andrew Douglas and A.-Chr. Engels-Schwarzpaul point this out in the introduction to their special issue, "Unstable Containers: Aspects of Interiority," for *Interstices* 12 (2011), http://interstices.ac.nz/wp-content/uploads/2011/11/INT12_intro.pdf.

90. René Descartes, *The Philosophical Writings of Descartes*, trans. J. Cottingham et al. (Cambridge: Cambridge University Press, 2007), 1:116.

91. Descartes, *Philosophical Writings*, 2:12.

92. Cavendish, "An Epiloge to My Philosophical Opinions," in *Philosophical and Physical Opinions*, B3v.

93. Cavendish, *Grounds of Natural Philosophy* (London: A. Maxwell, 1668), A2v, and "To the Reader," in *Poems, and Fancies*, A7v.

94. For a discussion of Cavendish's work within the history of the book, see Randall Ingram, "First Words and Second Thoughts: Margaret Cavendish, Humphrey Moseley, and 'the Book,'" *Journal of Medieval and Early Modern Studies* 30, no. 1 (Winter 2000): 101–24. For Ingram, "Rather than point readers toward a self-contained, self-containing monument, Cavendish's prefatory material embeds the printed object within a specific subjectivity" (111).

95. Cavendish, *Natures Pictures*, A1r

96. Cavendish, *Natures Pictures*, A1r.

97. Cavendish, *Natures Pictures*, A2r, lines 1–8.

98. Cavendish, *Natures Pictures*, A2r.

99. Cavendish, *Natures Pictures*, A2v, A2r.

100. Cavendish, *Natures Pictures*, A3v.

101. Cavendish, "Epistle to the Reader," in *Philosophical and Physical Opinions*, 2nd ed. (London: William Wilson, 1663), b3v.

102. Cavendish, "Epistle to the Reader," b1r, b3v, b1v.

103. Cavendish, *Observations*, c2r.

104. Cavendish describes this episode in *A True Relation*, 51.

105. Cavendish, "To the Reader," in *Poems, and Fancies*, A7r.

106. Battigelli, *Cavendish and the Exiles*, 7.

107. Battigelli, *Cavendish and the Exiles*, 9.

108. Cavendish, *Life of the Thrice Noble*, a1v (emphasis mine).

109. Cavendish, "The Preface," in *Sociable Letters*, 43. All preceding quotations in the paragraph are from the preface.

110. Heidegger, *Poetry, Language, Thought*, 156.

111. Sarasohn, *Natural Philosophy*, 11, 55.

112. Cavendish, *True Relation*, 55, 59

113. See Peter Beals, *In Praise of Scribes* (Oxford: Clarendon Press, 1998).

Chapter Three

1. *Select Fables of Esop and Other Fabulists* (London: R. and J. Dodsley, 1761).

2. Pope to William Borlase, March 9, 1740, in Pope, *Correspondence*, 4:228.

3. Owen Ruffhead, *The Life of Alexander Pope, Esq.* (London: C. Bathurst et al., 1769), 152.

4. The grotto survives in its dilapidated condition and can be seen during Twickenham's Festival Week in the second week of June each year, during Open House London in September, and by appointment during the few months of the year when the girls' school now on the grounds is out of session. A major restoration has been undertaken by the Pope's Grotto Preservation Trust.

5. Stephanie Ross, *What Gardens Mean* (Chicago: University of Chicago Press, 2001), 173.

6. J. Dixon Hunt, *The Figure in the Landscape* (Baltimore: Johns Hopkins University Press, 1976), 80. For a study of the implications of the ha-ha as a shaper of psychological perspective in narrative form, see Julie Park, "What the Eye Cannot See: Watching Interior Landscapes in *Mansfield Park*," *Eighteenth Century: Theory and Interpretation* 54, no. 2 (Summer 2013): 169–81.

7. Mack, *Garden and the City*, 8.

8. Hunt, *Figure in the Landscape*, 77.

9. I am referring, respectively, to Mark A. Cheetham and Elizabeth D. Harvey, "Obscure Imaginings: Visual Culture and the Anatomy of Caves," *Journal of Visual Culture* 1, no. 1 (April 2002): 105–26; Karen Lang, "The Body in the Garden," in *Landscapes of Memory and Experience*, ed. Jan Birksted (London: Spon Press, 2000), 107–27; and Helen Deutsch, "Twickenham and the Landscape of True Character," in *Resemblance and Disgrace* (Cambridge, MA: Harvard University Press, 1996), 83–135. See also Anthony Beckles Willson, "Alexander Pope's Grotto in Twickenham," *Garden History* 26, no. 1 (Summer 1998): 31–59.

10. Mack, *Garden and the City*, 82.

11. In contrast, for Silver, the camera obscura provides Pope with "a conceptual metaphor" for the mind. See Silver, *Mind Is a Collection*, 86.

12. Silver, *Mind Is a Collection*, 98.

13. Silver, *Mind Is a Collection*, 88.

14. Pope to John Caryll Jr., December 5, 1712, in Pope, *Correspondence*, 1:163.

15. Pope, *An Essay on Man in Four Epistles*, in *Alexander Pope*, ed. Pat Rogers (Oxford: Oxford University Press, 1995), 270–309; 270. All poems by Pope cited in the chapter are from this collection; lines will be cited in the body of the text.

16. Pope, *Essay on Man*, 270.

17. Pope, *Essay on Man*, 271.

18. See *OED*, s.v. "design, *n.*," def. 7a.

19. In the history of design, William Morris is best known as a source for earlier manifestoes on uniting beauty with function. See for example Morris, *Art and Its Producers, and The Arts and Crafts of To-day: Two Addresses Delivered before the National Association for the Advancement of Art* (London: Longmans & Co., 1901).

20. Bruno Munari, *Design as Art*, trans. Patrick Creagh (1972; London: Penguin, 2008), 25–26.

21. Ambrose Heal, *London Tradesmen's Cards of the XVIII Century* (London: Batsford, 1925) and *The London Furniture Makers, from the Restoration to the Victorian Era* (Lon-

don: Batsford, 1953). See also Akiko Shimbo, *Furniture-Makers and Consumers in England, 1754–1851: Design as Interaction* (London: Routledge, 2015).

22. Samuel Johnson, *A Dictionary of the English Language*, 2 vols. (London: Printed by W. Strahan, 1755–1756); emphasis mine.

23. Munari, *Design as Art*, 30.

24. Munari, *Design as Art*, 35.

25. Samuel Johnson, "The Life of Pope," in *The Life of the Most Eminent English Poets*, vol. 4, ed. Roger Lonsdale (Oxford: Oxford University Press, 2006).

26. See Robert Boyle, *Tracts Written by the Honourable Robert Boyle* (Oxford: Printed by W. H. for Ric. Davis, 1671).

27. Hunt, *Figure in the Landscape*, 67; Walpole to Horace Mann, June 20, 1760, in *The Letters of Horace Walpole, Fourth Earl of Orford*, ed. Paget Jackson Toynbee and Helen Wrigley Toynbee (Oxford: Clarendon Press, 1901–1905), 4:397.

28. Horace Walpole, *A History of the Modern Taste in Gardening*, ed. I. W. U. Chase (Princeton, NJ: Princeton University Press, 1943), 28–29.

29. Mack, *Garden and the City*, 26.

30. Northrop Frye, *The Anatomy of Criticism* (Princeton, NJ: Princeton University Press, 1957), 263.

31. Locke, *Essay*, book 2, chap. 10, §9, 154.

32. See Ingold, "Footprints." See also Peter de Bolla, "The Leasowes and Hagley Park," in *The Education of the Eye* (Stanford, CA: Stanford University Press, 2003), 104–50. De Bolla sees in Horace Walpole's *History of the Modern Taste in Gardening* a history for experiencing the English landscape garden as a "narrative of looking" as well an "education of the eye" (110, 111). Other sources on the phenomenological experience of the English landscape garden's circuit walk include Wall, *Grammars of Approach*, esp. chaps. 1 and 5, and Stephen Daniels, *Humphry Repton* (New Haven, CT: Yale University Press, 1999), 47.

33. Robert Pogue Harrison, *Gardens: An Essay on the Human Condition* (Chicago: University of Chicago Press, 2008), 95.

34. *The Newcastle General Magazine, or Monthly Intelligencer*, January 1748, 1:25–28; reprinted in Mack, *Garden and the City*, 237–43.

35. *Newcastle General Magazine*, in Mack, 237, 239.

36. *Newcastle General Magazine*, in Mack, 239.

37. *Newcastle General Magazine*, in Mack, 239.

38. *Newcastle General Magazine*, in Mack, 239.

39. For a comprehensive examination of the grotto and landscape architecture drawings extra-illustrating the Huntington Library's copy (RB 106623) of John Serle, *A Plan of Mr. Pope's Garden* (London: R. Dodsley, 1745), see Vanessa Lyon, "'A Relic from the Cave of Pope': Drawings of the Grotto in an Extra-Illustrated *Plan of Mr. Pope's Garden* in the Huntington Library," *Huntington Library Quarterly* 78, no. 3 (Autumn 2015): 441–77.

40. Naomi Miller, *Heavenly Caves* (New York: George Braziller, 1982), 17.

41. Miller, *Heavenly Caves*, 27, 20.

42. See Miller, *Heavenly Caves*, 37, and Claudia Lazzaro, *The Italian Renaissance Garden* (New Haven, CT: Yale University Press, 1990).

43. See Luke Morgan, "Landscape Design in England Circa 1610: The Contribution of Salomon de Caus," *Studies in the History of Gardens & Designed Landscapes* 23, no. 1 (2003): 1–21; *Nature as Model: Salomon de Caus and Early Seventeenth-Century Design* (Philadelphia: University of Pennsylvania Press, 2007); and "Isaac de Caus Invenit," *Stud-*

ies in the History of Gardens & Designed Landscapes 29, no. 3 (2009): 141–51. See also Paige Johnson, "Producing Pleasantness: The Waterworks of Isaac de Caus, Outlandish Engineer," *Studies in the History of Gardens & Designed Landscapes* 29, no. 3 (June 2009): 169–91.

44. J. Dixon Hunt, *Garden and Grove* (Philadelphia: University of Pennsylvania Press, 1996), 133.

45. Fiennes, *Illustrated Journeys*, 38–39.

46. Hunt, *Garden and Grove*, 138.

47. Quoted in Hunt, *Garden and Grove*, 138.

48. Hunt, *Garden and Grove*, 138.

49. Quoted in Barbara Jones, *Follies and Grottoes*, 2nd ed. (London: Constable, 1974), 15.

50. Jones, *Follies and Grottoes*, 15.

51. Hunt, *Garden and Grove*, 114.

52. John Worlidge, *Systema Horti-Culturae; or, The Art of Gardening in Three Books*, 4th ed. (London: Printed for W. Freeman, 1700), 52.

53. Worlidge, *Systema Horti-Culturae*, 53.

54. Jones, *Follies and Grottoes*, 149.

55. Thomas Oswald, "Goldney Hall, Clifton—II," *Country Life* 104 (August 13, 1948), 328–31; 328.

56. Jones, *Follies and Grottoes*, 149.

57. J. Dixon Hunt, "Emblem and Expressionism in the Eighteenth-Century Landscape Garden," *Eighteenth-Century Studies* 4, no. 3 (Spring 1971): 294–317.

58. Stephen Switzer, *Ichnographia Rustica: or, The Nobleman, Gentleman, and Gardener's Recreation*, 3 vols. (London: D. Browne, 1718), II: 197.

59. Pope to Edward Blount, June 2, 1725, in Pope, *Correspondence*, 2:297.

60. Chapter 5 will examine the picturesque at greater length.

61. Switzer, *Ichnographia Rustica*, 1:xxi.

62. Miller, *Heavenly Caves*, 78.

63. Miller, *Heavenly Caves*, 78.

64. Switzer, *Ichnographia Rustica*, 1:xxxvi.

65. Miller, *Heavenly Caves*, 78.

66. Frances Hutcheson, *An Inquiry into the Original of Our Ideas of Beauty and Virtue; in Two Treatises* (London: J. Darby et al., 1726), 59.

67. Hutcheson, *Inquiry*, 50.

68. Pope, *Essay on Criticism*, in *Alexander Pope* (ed. Rogers), 17–39, line 52.

69. William Borlase, *The Natural History of Cornwall* (Oxford: W. Jackson, 1757), iv.

70. Borlase, *Natural History*, iii.

71. Borlase, *Natural History*, iv.

72. Borlase, *Natural History*, iv.

73. Pope to Jervas, December 12, 1718, in Pope, *Correspondence*, 2:24.

74. Munari, *Design as Art*, 30.

75. See Benjamin Boyce, "Mr. Pope, in Bath, Improves the Design of His Grotto," in *Restoration and Eighteenth-Century Literature*, ed. Camden Carroll, 143–53 (Chicago: University of Chicago Press/William Marsh Rice University, 1963), and Morris Brownell, *Alexander Pope and the Arts of Georgian England* (Oxford: Clarendon Press, 1978). Both focus on this element of Pope's grotto improvement. While I agree that Pope's renovation of his mind focused on displaying geological splendors as well as emulating nature, I find that his equal emphasis on beauty, "glitter," and "dazzle"—words used in his letters for the

effects he desired—preclude the idea that his intention was wholly to refashion the grotto into a mine or quarry. See Pope to William Borlase, March 9, [1739/40]: "I would be glad to make the Place . . . dazzle a Gazing, Spectator" (Pope, *Correspondence*, 4:228); Pope to Dr. Oliver, May 27, [1740]: "I would ask him for some of the metallic kind that are most common. So they do but *shine* and *glitter*" (4:244); Pope to William Borlase, June 8, 1740: "I wish it were glittering tho' not curious" (4:246).

76. See Evans, *Projective Cast*.

77. Jeremy Voorhees, "The Projective Credibility of Fictions: Robin Evans' Methodological Excursions," in ARCC 2013, *The Visibility of Research*, 180–87; 180. http://www.arcc-journal.org/index.php/repository/article/view/142/110.

78. Mohsen Mostafavi, "Paradoxes of the Ordinary," in Evans, *Translations from Drawing to Building*, 9.

79. Pope to Jervas, December 12, 1718, in Pope, *Correspondence*, 2:24.

80. Pope to Jervas, December 12, 1718, in Pope, *Correspondence*, 2:23.

81. Jones, *Follies and Grottoes*, 36.

82. Quoted in Robert J. G. Savage, *Natural History of the Goldney Garden Grotto Clifton, Bristol*, reprinted from *Garden History* 17, no. 1 (Spring 1989): 1–40; 34.

83. Addison, *Spectator* 414, Wednesday, June 25, 1712, in *The Spectator*, ed. Donald F. Bond, 5 vols. (Oxford: Clarendon Press, 1965), 3:550.

84. Pope to Allen, June 17, 1740, in Pope, *Correspondence*, 4:247.

85. Pope to William Borlase, March 9, [1739/40], in Pope, *Correspondence*, 4:228–29.

86. Borlase, *Natural History*, iii.

87. Robert A. Aubin, "Grottoes, Geology and the Gothic Revival," *Studies in Philology* 31, no. 3 (July 1934): 408–16.

88. Hannah Robertson, *The Young Ladies School of Arts*, 2nd ed. (Edinburgh, 1767?).

89. Mary Delany, *The Autobiography and Correspondence of Mary Granville, Mrs. Delany*, ed. Lady Llanover, 3 vols. (London: Bentley, 1861), 1:570.

90. See Beth Fowkes Tobin, *The Duchess's Shells: Natural History Collecting in the Age of Cook's Voyages* (New Haven, CT: Yale University Press, 2014). At least four other grottoes are attributed to Delany.

91. See Boyce, "Mr. Pope, in Bath," and Brownell, *Pope and the Arts*.

92. Pope to Edward Blount, June 2, 1725, in Pope, *Correspondence*, 2:297.

93. Quoted in Helen Sard Hughes, "Mr. Pope on His Grotto," *Modern Philology* 28, no. 1 (August 1930): 100–104; 103. The letter is in the Wellesley College library.

94. Quoted in Richard D. Altick, "Mr. Pope Expands His Grotto," *Philological Quarterly* 21, no. 4 (October 1942): 427–30; 430.

95. Savage, *Natural History*, 27.

96. Savage, *Natural History*, 26.

97. See Savage, *Natural History*, for detailed inventories and tables of the natural objects in Goldney's grotto.

98. See Lang, "Body in the Garden."

99. Gaston Bachelard, *The Poetics of Space*, trans. Maria Joas (Boston: Beacon Press, 1958), 123.

100. Bachelard, *Poetics of Space*, 124.

101. Pope to Blount, June 2, 1725, in Pope, *Correspondence*, 2:297.

102. Pope, *The Rape of the Lock*, canto 1, in *Alexander Pope* (ed. Rogers), 77–100; 80.

103. Pope to Blount, June 2, 1725, in Pope, *Correspondence*, 2:296.

104. *Newcastle General Magazine*, in Mack, 240.

105. Pope to Bolingbroke, September 3, 1740, in Pope, *Correspondence*, 4:262.

106. Translated in the *Newcastle General Magazine*, January 1748, account of visiting the grotto. In Mack, *Garden and the City*, 240.

107. Pope to Borlase, June 8, 1740, in Pope, *Correspondence*, 4:245.

108. Pope to Caryll, February 1712/13?, in Pope, *Correspondence*, 1:174.

109. Pope to Lady Mary Wortley Montague, 1718, in Pope, *Correspondence*, 1:507.

110. Pope to Blount, June 2, 1725, in Pope, *Correspondence*, 2:296–97.

111. Hunt, "Emblem and Expressionism," 310.

112. Reynolds, Discourse XII, in *Discourses on Art*, 237.

113. Reynolds, Discourse XII, 237.

114. Willson, "Alexander Pope's Grotto," 33.

115. Quoted in Willson, "Alexander Pope's Grotto," 33.

116. Pope to Caryll, December 5, 1712, in Pope, *Correspondence*, 1:163.

117. Pope, *Correspondence*, 1:163.

118. Soame Jenyns, "A Translation of Some Latin Verses on the Camera Obscura," in *Poems. By ****** (London: R. Dodsley, 1752), 179.

119. Pope to Lady Mary Wortley Montague, June 1717, in Pope, *Correspondence*, 1:405.

120. Pope to Lady Mary Wortley Montague, June 1717, in Pope, *Correspondence*, 1:406.

121. Pope to Caryll, November 19, 1712, in Pope, *Correspondence*, 1:156.

122. Murray Krieger, "'Eloisa to Abelard': The Escape from Body or the Embrace of Body," in "The Eighteenth-Century Imagination," ed. Ronald Paulson, special issue of *Eighteenth-Century Studies* 3, no. 1 (Autumn 1969): 28–47; 34.

123. Krieger, "Eloisa to Abelard," 34.

124. J. Paul Hunter, "Couplets," in *Oxford Handbook of British Poetry*, ed. Jack Lynch (Oxford: Oxford University Press, 2016), 374–85; 377, 379.

125. Steven Connor, *Dumbstruck* (Oxford: Oxford University Press, 2000), 5.

126. Robert Havell, *The Natuorama; or, Nature's Endless Transposition of Views on the Thames* (London: Havell, 1820), 20.

127. See Pierpont Morgan Library 4239, extra-illustrated copy of Alexander Pope, *The Poetical Works*, 3 vols. in 5 (Andrew Foulis: Glasgow, 1785), 4:79. As with the *Newcastle General Magazine* account of visiting Pope's grotto, Maynard Mack is responsible for discovering this sketch, which he believes was made ca. 1760–1770 based on the depiction of the willow tree, which stopped appearing in illustrations of Pope's home after 1782. The Morgan Library, however, dates the sketch to ca. 1800–1810, perhaps on the basis of a conservation assessment.

Chapter Four

1. For a cultural analysis of the novel as a pivotal genre of the everyday in its status as a new medium for popular entertainment in eighteenth-century England, see William Warner, *Licensing Entertainment* (Berkeley: University of California Press, 1998).

2. This stands in contrast with Nancy Armstrong, Vineta Colby, and Helen Thompson, who use the label "domestic fiction" in their studies of novels focusing on women and their roles in the home. For Colby and Armstrong, Richardson's *Pamela* lays the groundwork for Victorian literature. See Armstrong, *Desire and Domestic Fiction*; Colby, *Yesterday's Woman* (Princeton, NJ: Princeton University Press, 1974); and Thompson, *Ingenuous Subjection* (Philadelphia: University of Pennsylvania Press, 2005).

3. Watt, *Rise of the Novel*, 204, 200.

4. Watt, *Rise of the Novel*, 174. Watt's eloquent formulation invites a more extended examination of just how the detailed delineation of domestic space in fiction leads to a greater sense of what it is like to inhabit a character's consciousness, yielding new insights altogether.

5. Barbauld, *Correspondence of Samuel Richardson*, 1:xx.

6. Barbauld, *Correspondence of Samuel Richardson*, 1:cxxxvii.

7. Samuel Richardson, *Pamela: or, Virtue Rewarded*, ed. Thomas Keymer (Oxford: Oxford University Press, 2008), 60, 63. This edition, based on the original 1740 edition, is used in this study unless explicitly noted, and hereafter cited parenthetically in the body of the chapter.

8. *OED*, s.v. "setting, $n.^1$," definition 6b.

9. Watt, *Rise of the Novel*, 193.

10. Francis Jeffrey, review of *The Correspondence of Samuel Richardson*, ed. Anna Laetitia Barbauld, *Edinburgh Review*, October 1804, in *Contributions to the Edinburgh Review* (London: Longman, Brown, Green, and Longmans, 1844), 1:302–23.

11. Jeffrey, review, 321.

12. Aaron Betsky, *Building Sex* (New York: William Morrow, 1995), 78.

13. See Hammond, *Camera Obscura*, for a record of portable camera obscuras—unprecedented in previous centuries—mentioned and appearing in the aforementioned sources.

14. "John Cuff, Optician, Spectacle, and Microscope Maker, at the Sign of the RE-FLECTING MICROSCOPE and SPECTACLES, against *Serjean's-Inn* Gate in *Fleet-street*," London, 1745? in Bodleian Library, and Cuff, "Verses, Occasion'd by the Sight of a Chamera Obscura."

15. Cuff, *Verses Occasion'd*, 6.

16. See Warner, *Licensing Entertainment*, on the novel's small format as an essential feature of its predominance as a popular genre.

17. See, for instance, Amaranth Borsuk's definition of the book as "a portable data storage and distribution method." She also quotes definitions from Frederick Kilgour ("a storehouse of human knowledge intended for dissemination in the form of an artifact that is portable") and Thomas Vogler ("records in portable form"). Borsuk, *The Book* (Cambridge, MA: MIT Press, 2018), 1, 2, 8; Kilgour, *The Evolution of the Book* (Cary: Oxford University Press, 1998); Vogler, "When a Book Is Not a Book," in *A Book of the Book: Some Works and Projections about the Book and Writing*, ed. Jerome Rothenberg and Steven Clay, 448–66 (New York: Granary Books, 2000).

18. German nineteenth-century architect Gottfried Semper decried the coextensive relationship between ancient dress and architecture, exemplified in Egyptian capitals imitating female hair in their ornament details. Semper, *The Four Elements of Architecture and Other Writings*, trans. Henry Francis Mallgrave and Wolfgang Herrmann (Cambridge: Cambridge University Press, 1989), 241.

19. Evans, *Translations from Drawing to Building*, 89.

20. Ingold, *Being Alive*, 12.

21. Armstrong writes, "It is also reasonable to claim that the modern individual was first and foremost a female"; *Desire and Domestic Fiction*, 66.

22. Wolfram Schmidgen, *Eighteenth-Century Fiction and the Law of Property* (Cambridge: Cambridge University Press, 2002), 7.

23. Schmidgen, *Eighteenth-Century Fiction*, 9–10.

24. J. G. A. Pocock, *Virtue, Commerce, and History* (Cambridge: Cambridge University Press, 1985), 103.

25. Pocock, *Virtue, Commerce, and History*, 54.

26. Armstrong and Tennenhouse, "Interior Difference," 460.

27. Armstrong and Tennenhouse, "Interior Difference," 458, 463, 458.

28. For a history of the transformation of "virtue" into a gendered property, see, in addition to Watt, April Alliston, "Female Quixotism and the Novel: Character and Plausibility, Honesty and Fidelity," in "The Drift of Fiction," ed. Julie Park, special issue of *Eighteenth Century: Theory and Interpretation* 52, nos. 3–4 (2011): 249–69.

29. On the marriage market as a critical element in the eighteenth-century landowning system, see G. E. Mingay, *English Landed Society in the Eighteenth Century* (London: Routledge & Kegan Paul, 1963).

30. For Pocock, the relation between immovable and movable property was more "dialectical" than the "unidirectional transformation of thought" that Macpherson, in *The Political Theory of Possessive Individualism*, describes as causing "market assumptions" to condition ideas and attitudes in seventeenth-century political discourse and "economic man" to prevail (59, 70). At the same time, Pocock's claim, in *Virtue, Commerce, and History*, about the "confrontation" between "real and mobile property" is more nuanced; rather than being based on the "marketable" quality of mobile property, the conflict had to do with the fact that mobile property entailed dependence on government support, meaning it threatened the "independence and virtue" that landed property had originally conferred (68).

31. Schmidgen, *Eighteenth-Century Fiction*, 11.

32. See John Plotz, *Portable Property* (Princeton, NJ: Princeton University Press, 2005), for a literary-historical study of movable property in Victorian Britain.

33. Vickery, "Thresholds and Boundaries," 46.

34. Deidre Shauna Lynch, "The Novel: Novels in the World of Moving Goods," in *A Concise Companion to the Restoration and Eighteenth Century*, ed. Cynthia Wall, (Malden, MA: Blackwell, 2008), 121–43; 126. Warner, *Licensing Entertainment*, also analyses the small dimensions of novels as key features of their popularity in eighteenth-century England.

35. Lynch, "Novel," 123.

36. Lynch, "Novel," 125.

37. For an account of the mobility of reading practices in eighteenth-century England, see John Brewer, "John Marsh's History of My Private Life, 1752–1828," *History and Biography: Essays in Honour of Derek Beales*, ed. Tim Blanning and David Cannadine (Cambridge: Cambridge University Press, 1996), 72–87.

38. Barbauld, *Correspondence of Samuel Richardson*, 1:lviii.

39. Tobias Smollett, preface to *The Adventures of Roderick Random*, in *Novel Definitions*, ed. Cheryl L. Nixon (Peterborough, ON: Broadview, 2009). Smollett was not the originator of this turn of phrase. At least two other works used the locution before Smollett published *The Adventures of Roderick Random*. They include a dictionary of moral precepts, *The Universal Monitor* (London: J. Hartley, 1702), and a conduct book, *The Ladies Library, written by a Lady* (London: J. Tonson, 1714).

40. Thomas Thoughtless [pseud.], advertisement to *The Fugitive of Folly*, in Nixon, *Novel Definitions*, 75–76; 76.

41. Certainly the capturing of homely details is a feature of travel narratives and diaries

of the period, including those mentioned in this study, from Celia Fiennes and John Byng to Mary Delany, as well as Daniel Defoe's *Tour through the Whole Island of Great Britain* (1724–1727). See Carole Fabricant, "The Literature of Domestic Tourism and the Public Consumption of Private Property," in *The New Eighteenth Century*, ed. Felicity Nussbaum and Laura Brown (New York: Methuen, 1987), 254–75, and Adrian Tinniswood, *The Polite Tourist: Four Centuries of Country House Visiting* (London: National Trust, 1998).

42. John Parnell, "An account of the many fine seats of noblemen etc. I have seen with other observations made during my residence in [southern] England, 1763 December 23," M.a.11, Folger Shakespeare Library, Washington, DC.

43. Locke, *Essay*, 104. Hereafter, page numbers in *Essay* are cited parenthetically in the body of the chapter.

44. For a history of description, especially as it pertains to spaces, in eighteenth-century literature and culture, see Wall, *Prose of Things*.

45. Armstrong writes that the novel's rise as a "respectable" genre, beginning with Richardson's *Pamela*, entailed the creation of "a cultural fantasy" concerning "a private domain of culture that was independent of the political world and overseen by a woman; *Desire and Domestic Fiction*, 98.

46. For a study of the significance of dress in *Pamela*, see Chloe Wigston Smith, *Women, Work and Clothes in the Eighteenth-Century Novel* (Cambridge: Cambridge University Press, 2013).

47. I am grateful to Aaron Kunin for reminding me of this first pocket.

48. Yolanda Van de Krol, "'Ty'ed about my middle, next to my smock': The Cultural Context of Women's Pockets," MA diss., University of Delaware, 1994, 13.

49. Ariane Fennetaux, "Women's Pockets and the Construction of Privacy in the Eighteenth Century," in "Interiors," ed. Julie Park, special issue of *Eighteenth-Century Fiction*, 20, no. 3 (Spring 2008): 307–34; 329. See also Barbara Burman and Ariane Fennetaux, *The Pocket: A Hidden History of Women's Lives* (New Haven, CT: Yale University Press, 2019).

50. I am indebted to Leigh Wishner of the Los Angeles County Museum of Art and Linda Eaton of Winterthur for answering my questions about this issue.

51. Ephraim Chambers, *Cyclopædia*, 3rd ed., vol. 2 (Dublin: Richard Gunne et al., 1740).

52. Old Bailey Online, *The Proceedings of the Old Bailey, 1674–1913*, University of Sheffield Humanities Research Institute, http://www.oldbaileyonline.org/: Johanna Baker, Theft, July 9, 1740, ref. no. t174000709-41; Elizabeth Davis, Theft, July 9, 1740, ref. no. 17400709; Elizabeth Green, Theft, September 3, 1740, ref. no. t17400903-10; [no name], Theft, December 5, 1739, ref. no. t17391205-37.

53. Reyner Banham, *The Architecture of the Well-Tempered Environment* (1969; Chicago: University of Chicago Press, 1984), 18.

54. Banham, *Architecture*, 18.

55. Watt, *Rise of the Novel*, 193.

56. Watt, *Rise of the Novel*, 193.

57. For the case study of Jane Johnson (1706–1759), an upper-middling-class provincial woman whose correspondence reveals an interactive relationship with Richardson's novels, see Susan Whyman, *The Pen and the People: English Letter Writers, 1660–1800* (Oxford: Oxford University Press, 2009).

58. According to John Donne scholar Daniel Starza Smith, "open and flat, for being written and read are how we think of the letter." Smith presented this view in his lecture at the Workshop on Early Modern Letterlocking. Jana Dambrogio and Daniel Starza Smith,

coordinators, sponsored by the Materialities, Texts and Images Program of Caltech and the Huntington Library on October 8, 2014, in the Preservation and Conservation Department of the Huntington Library.

59. Dambrogio, *Letterlocking Workshop*.

60. Pope, *Correspondence*, 1:155.

61. Pope, *Correspondence*, 1:160.

62. Thomas Keymer, *Richardson's* Clarissa *and the Eighteenth-Century Reader* (Cambridge: Cambridge University Press, 1992), 12.

63. In my previous book I explored this aspect of the passage in more detail as an example of reverse anthropomorphism; Pamela turns herself into an object, her own doll, to generative effect. See Park, *Self and It*.

64. Although the scene of Pamela placing her letters into her pocket after unsewing them from her undercoat is not explicitly narrated, it is implied that is what she does, for when the packet of letters reappears, it emerges from her pocket.

65. The version of the scene in the Penguin edition, which is based on the 1801 edition of the novel, with incorporated corrections made in 1810, much more sharply renders this scene as one that issues from Pamela's using her pocket in a strategic manner. It is immediately mentioned and presented as a mechanism for guarding Pamela against Mr. B's encroachment on her body: "I did not like this way of talk; and thinking it best, to cut it short, pulling the first parcel out of my pocket, 'Here, sir,' said I, 'since I cannot be excused, is the parcel, that goes on with my fruitless attempt to escape . . .'" See Samuel Richardson, *Pamela: or, Virtue Rewarded*, ed. Peter Sabor (London: Penguin, 1985), 274.

66. Watt, *Rise of the Novel*, 206.

67. I am indebted to Aaron Betsky's reading of this painting. See *Building Sex*, 108–10.

68. According to Didier Maleuvre, "depth of space is depth of soul." See Maleuvre, *The Horizon: A History of Our Infinite Longing* (Berkeley: University of California Press, 2011), 147.

69. Ingold, "The Temporality of the Landscape," in *Perception of the Environment*, 195; Bold, "Privacy and the Plan," 118.

70. This comparison makes sense in light of De Witte's membership in the Delft school, which was known for its use of the camera obscura. See Jane Turner, ed., *From Renaissance to Impressionism: Styles and Movements in Western Art, 1400–1900*, Grove Dictionary of Art (Oxford: Oxford University Press, 2000), 73.

71. Clara Reeve, *The Progress of Romance*, 2 vols. (London: Printed for the author, by W. Keymer, 1785), 1:111.

72. Alpers, *Art of Describing*, 33.

73. Robert Boyle, "Of the Systematical and Cosmical Qualities of Things," in *The Works of the Honourable Robert Boyle* (London, 1772), 3:312.

74. Barbara Stafford and Frances Terpak, *Devices of Wonder* (Los Angeles: Getty Research Institute, 2001), 309.

75. Watt, *Rise of the Novel*, 175.

76. Quoted in Friedberg, *Virtual Window*, 87.

77. I borrow "spectatorial pleasures" from Giuliana Bruno, *Atlas of Emotion* (New York: Verso, 2002), 139.

78. Bruno, *Atlas of Emotion*, points out that Della Porta's rendering of the camera obscura "prefigured narrative space," for he viewed it as being made up of "moving scenes that unfold to tell a story sequentially."

79. Bruno, *Atlas of Emotion*, 140. See also Friedberg, *Virtual Window*.

80. Bruno, *Atlas of Emotion*, 140.

81. Friedberg, *Virtual Window*, 150.

82. Friedberg, *Virtual Window*, 150.

83. Stafford and Terpak, *Devices of Wonder*, 313.

84. Letter dated July 13, 1767. Quoted in Stafford and Terpak, *Devices of Wonder*, 313.

85. Robert Folkenflik points out that such substitutions of rooms for actions are not only euphemistic, for the rooms themselves are described with feeling, and the sexual attacks impassively. See Folkenflik, "A Room of Pamela's Own," *ELH* 39 (1972): 582–96; 587.

86. See Yates, *Art of Memory*.

87. Evans, *Translations from Drawing to Building*, 69.

88. Richardson, *Pamela* (ed. Sabor), 111.

89. Jenyns, "Translation of some Latin Verses," 176.

90. On Hooke's "picture-box" see Wolfgang Lefèvre, "The Optical Camera Obscura I: A Short Exposition," in Lefèvre, *Inside the Camera Obscura*, 15.

91. James Mann and James Ayscough, *The Description of a Pocket Microscope . . .* (London: n.p., 1750?), n.p.

92. Frances Terpak, "Objects and Contexts," in Stafford and Terpak, *Devices of Wonder*, 143–364; 313.

93. Terpak, "Objects and Contexts," 313.

94. Friedberg, *Virtual Window*, 151.

95. Walter Ong, *Orality and Literacy* (London: Routledge, 1982), 129, 119.

96. Macpherson, *Political Theory of Possessive Individualism*.

97. Macpherson, *Political Theory of Possessive Individualism*, 3.

Chapter Five

1. Lewis, *Air's Appearance*.

2. Tom Stoppard, *Arcadia* (London: Faber and Faber, 1993), 12.

3. Lewis, *Air's Appearance*, 7.

4. Lewis, *Air's Appearance*, 7.

5. Lewis, *Air's Appearance*, 8.

6. Alexander Pope, "Preface to the Works of Shakespeare," in *The Works of Alexander Pope*, 10 vols. (Berlin: Printed for Fredrik Nicolai Bookseller, [1762]–1764), 6:356.

7. Pope, "Preface to the Works of Shakespeare," 6:356–57.

8. Robert Harbison, *Eccentric Spaces* (Cambridge, MA: MIT Press, 2000), 73.

9. See, for instance, Warren Hunting Smith, *Architecture in English Fiction* (New Haven, CT: Yale University Press, 1934). For a feminist psychoanalytic approach to the symbolism of the castle in Gothic fiction, see also Claire Kahane, "Gothic Mirrors and Feminine Identity," *Centennial Review* 24, no. 1 (Winter 1980): 43–64.

10. Johan Huizinga, *Homo Ludens* (Boston: Beacon Press, 1950), 8.

11. Jean-Jacques Rousseau, *Reveries of the Solitary Walker*, trans. Russell Goulbourne (Oxford: Oxford University Press, 2011), 38.

12. Batty Langley, *Gothic Architecture* (London: John Millan, 1747).

13. For Langley's Gothic influence on other architectural writers, see Eileen Harris, "Langley, Batty," in *Oxford Dictionary of National Biography*, https://www.oxforddnb .com, and Hanno-Walter Kruft, *History of Architectural Theory* (New York: Princeton Architectural Press, 1994), 249.

14. Harris, "Langley, Batty."

15. Lewis, *Air's Appearance*, 4.

16. Here, as elsewhere, I am indebted to Julia Lupton's work in using the terms of design theory to interpret literary form and representation.

17. See Jones, *Follies and Grottoes*, 5.

18. See Lauren Kaplan, "Exotic Follies: Sanderson Miller's Mock Ruins," *Frame: A Journal of Visual and Material Culture*, no. 1 (Spring 2011), 54–68; 67.

19. See Chris Brooks, *Gothic Revival* (London: Phaidon, 1999). He writes, "Garden gothic rose by the power of historical association—national, patriotic and increasingly naturalized" (69).

20. See Kaplan, "Exotic Follies"; Brooks, *Gothic Revival*; Margot Finn, "The Homes of England," in *The Cambridge History of English Romantic Literature*, ed. James Chandler (Cambridge: Cambridge University Press, 2009); and Michael McCarthy, *The Origins of the Gothic Revival* (New Haven, CT: Yale University Press, 1987).

21. Harbison, *Eccentric Spaces*, 23.

22. Harbison, *Eccentric Spaces*, 23.

23. See Brooks, *Gothic Revival*, 19.

24. Duncan Mallam, ed., *Letters of William Shenstone* (London: Oxford University Press, 1939), 400. Quoted in McCarthy, *Origins of the Gothic Revival*, 118.

25. Locke, *Essay*, book 2, chap. 33, "Of the Association of Ideas," 396.

26. Addison, *Spectator* 414, June 25, 1712, 3:550.

27. Addison, *Spectator* 110, July 6, 1711, 1:454.

28. [William Gilpin], *Stow: The Gardens of the Right Honourable the Lord Viscount Cobham* (London: Printed for B. Seeley, Buckingham . . . , 1751), 29.

29. Tzvetan Todorov, *The Poetics of Prose* (Ithaca, NY: Cornell University Press, 1977).

30. Joseph Heely, *A Description of Hagley, Envil and the Leasowes* (Birmingham: M. Swinney, 1775). For an extensive analysis of the gardens and garden literature of the period as instances of a wider project of "public visual culture," including Heely's *Letters on the Beauties of Hagley, Envil, and the Leasowes*, see de Bolla, "Leasowes and Hagley Park."

31. William Gilpin, *Observations, Relative Chiefly to Picturesque Beauty, Made in the Year 1772*, 2nd ed., 2 vols. (London: R. Blamire, 1788), 1:73.

32. Ann Radcliffe, *A Sicilian Romance* (Oxford: Oxford University Press, 1993), 89.

33. See *OED*, s.v. "fabric."

34. Radcliffe, *Sicilian Romance*, 1

35. Radcliffe, *Sicilian Romance*, 2.

36. Heely, *Description of Hagley*, 79, 78.

37. Letter from Sir George Lyttelton to Sanderson Miller regarding Lord Chancellor Hardwicke's plans for a folly at Wimpole, in Jones, *Follies and Grottoes*, 75.

38. Lyttelton letter, in Jones, *Follies and Grottoes*, 75.

39. Gilpin, *Observations, Relative Chiefly to Picturesque Beauty*, 1:72.

40. For a study of the late eighteenth-century fragmentary form, see Elizabeth Wanning Harries, *The Unfinished Manner* (Charlottesville: University of Virginia Press, 1994).

41. Gilpin, *Observations, Relative Chiefly to Picturesque Beauty*, 1:16–17.

42. William Gilpin, *Observations on the River Wye, and Several Parts of South Wales, etc. Relative to Picturesque Beauty, Made in the Summer of the Year 1770* (London: R. Blamire, 1782).

43. For a full-length study of spatial metaphors of the mind in the eighteenth century, see Silver, *Mind Is a Collection*.

44. Quoted in Hunt, *Figure in the Landscape*, 150–51.

45. Langley, *New Principles of Gardening* (London: A. Bettesworth and J. Batley et al., 1728), 193.

46. Langley, *New Principles*, 194.

47. Thomas Whately, *Observations on Modern Gardening* (Dublin: John Exshaw, 1770).

48. Cynthia Wall takes up Whately's spatial rhetoric in her recent study, seeing in his own sentences a grammatical channel for the spatial experience of the landscape designs they describe. See *Grammars of Approach*, 31–32.

49. Whately, *Observations on Modern Gardening*, 124.

50. Whately, *Observations on Modern Gardening*, 124.

51. Whately, *Observations on Modern Gardening*, 138–39.

52. Addison, *Spectator* 413, 3:546.

53. Addison, *Spectator* 413, 3:546–47.

54. Locke, *Essay*, 47.

55. Locke, *Essay*, 137.

56. Locke, *Essay*, 137. Locke repeats the second half of the sentence with a slight variation on page 135: "Such *Qualities*, which in truth are nothing in the Objects themselves, but Powers to produce various Sensations in us."

57. Locke, *Essay*, 131.

58. William Thomas, *Original Designs in Architecture* (London: Printed for the Author, No. 5, Portland Road, 1783).

59. Pope also wrote about Gothic architecture in "Temple of Fame" (see lines 119–36).

60. Langley, *New Principles*, x.

61. Langley, *New Principles*, x.

62. Langley, *New Principles*, xi.

63. Langley, *New Principles*, xi.

64. William Gilpin, *Three Essays: On Picturesque Beauty; On Picturesque Travels; and On Sketching Landscape* (London: R. Blamire, 1792), 52.

65. See Pasanek, *Metaphors of Mind*, and Silver, *Mind Is a Collection*, for reflections on the correspondences made between "the mind" and camera obscura in cultural discourse of the period.

66. Gilpin, *Three Essays*, 54.

67. Addison, *Spectator* 411, 3:537.

68. Friedrich Kittler, *Optical Media: Berlin Lectures 1999*, trans. Anthony Enns (Cambridge: Polity, 2002), 61.

69. Gilpin, *Observations on the River Wye*, 1.

70. Gilpin, *Observations on the River Wye*, 1.

71. Joshua Reynolds, *The Works of Sir Joshua Reynolds: Containing His Discourses, Idlers, A Journey to Flanders and Holland* . . . (Edinburgh: William Forrester, 1867), 200–201.

72. Kittler, *Optical Media*, 63.

73. Locke, *Essay*, 112.

74. Gilpin, *Three Essays*, 51.

75. William Gilpin, *Remarks on Forest Scenery and Other Woodland Views (Relative to Picturesque Beauty)* (London: R. Blamire, 1794).

76. Gilpin, *Three Essays*, 46.

77. Locke, *Essay*, 151–52.

78. Paul Sandby RA, *Lady Frances Scott and Lady Elliott*, ca. 1770, Yale Center for British Art, Paul Mellon Collection, 5 × 5⅛ inches, accession number B1977.14.4410.

79. As an amateur artist, Lady Scott (1750–1817) drew picturesque views of castles and ruins situated atop dramatically high Scottish promontories. Upon her marriage to Archibald James Edward Douglas, first Baron Douglas of Douglas, in 1783, she lived at Bothwell Castle, next to one of the most striking ruined medieval castles in Scotland. Paul Sandby used Bothwell Castle as the subject of a topographical view at least twice, and Scott herself seems to have executed a stylized rendition of it after Robert Adam's pen-and-ink depiction in 1782. The reduced scale of the immense expanse of building and landscape would be difficult to achieve freehand; that and the depth of perspective suggest that this work, too, was conceived and carried out with a camera obscura.

80. Walpole to the Hon. H. S. Conway, Tuesday evening, September 16, 1777, in *Letters*, 10:107–8.

81. Walpole to the Rev. William Mason, Strawberry Hill, September 21, 1777, *Letters*, 10:115–16.

82. Walpole, "A Description of Strawberry-Hill," in *The Works of Horatio Walpole, Earl of Orford* (London: G. G. and J. Robinson, and J. Edwards, 1798), 2:398.

83. From *Abstract of "A Treatise of Human Nature,"* quoted in Sarah Winter, *The Pleasures of Memory: Learning to Read with Charles Dickens* (New York: Fordham University Press, 2011), 47.

84. Walter Scott, introduction to *The Castle of Otranto* (Edinburgh: James Ballantyne, 1811), iii–xxxvi; reprinted in Horace Walpole, *The Castle of Otranto*, ed. Michael Gamer (London: Penguin, 2001), 132–41; 136.

85. Scott, introduction, 134.

86. See Horace Walpole, *Description of the Villa at Strawberry Hill* (Twickenham, London, England, 1774), and Michael Snodin, ed., *Horace Walpole's Strawberry Hill* (New Haven, CT: Yale University Press, 2009).

87. Walpole, *Castle of Otranto*, 25.

88. Samuel Johnson, *Dictionary of the English Language*, vol. 1 (London: J. Knapton et al., 1756), 3C2.

89. Diana Balmori, "Architecture, Landscape, and the Intermediate Structure: Eighteenth-Century Experiments in Mediation," *Journal of the Society of Architectural Historians* 50, no. 1 (March 1991): 38–56; 39.

Epilogue

1. Addison, *Spectator* 414, 3:530–31.

2. See Sarah Kareem, *Eighteenth-Century Fiction and the Reinvention of Wonder* (Oxford: Oxford University Press, 2014).

3. Zoe Leonard, "The Politics of Contemplation," interview by Elisabeth Lebovici, in *Photography and the Optical Unconscious*, ed. Shawn Michelle Smith and Sharon Sliwinski (Durham, NC: Duke University Press, 2017), 93–103; 94.

4. Leonard, "Politics of Contemplation," 94.

5. Leonard, "Politics of Contemplation," 100.

6. Crary, *Techniques*, 46.

7. Zoe Leonard, interview by Shannon Ebner, *BOMB*, no. 127 (April 2014), https://bombmagazine.org/articles/shannon-ebner-and-zoe-leonard/.

8. Leonard, "Politics of Contemplation," 107.

9. Leonard, "Politics of Contemplation," 103.

10. Leonard, "Politics of Contemplation," 99.

11. *OED*, s.v. "medium," def. 5b.

12. Giuliana Bruno, *Surface* (Chicago: University of Chicago Press, 2014), 5.

13. "Welcome to Santa Monica's Historic Camera Obscura!" unpublished information sheet, Camera Obscura Art Lab.

14. Walter Benjamin, "The Work of Art in the Age of Mechanical Reproduction," in *Illuminations*, ed. Hannah Arendt, trans. Harry Zohn (New York: Schocken, 1969), 1–26.

15. Benjamin, "Work of Art," 16. See Sigmund Freud, *The Interpretation of Dreams*, trans. James Strachey (New York: Basic Books, 2010).

Bibliography

Primary Sources

Addison, Joseph. *The Spectator*. Edited by Donald F. Bond. 5 vols. Oxford: Clarendon Press, 1965.

Alberti, Leon Battista. *On the Art of Building in Ten Books*. Translated by Joseph Rykwert, Neil Leach, and Robert Tavernor. Cambridge, MA: MIT Press, 1988.

———. *On Painting*. Translated by Cecil Grayson. London: Penguin, 1972.

Algarotti, Francesco. *An Essay on Painting*. London: L. David and C. Reymer, 1764.

Austen, Jane. *Pride and Prejudice*. Oxford: Oxford University Press, 1970.

Bacon, Francis. *Historia Vitae et Mortis*. Vol. 5 of *Works*. Edited by James Spedding et al. Cambridge, MA: Hurd and Houghton, 1869.

Barbauld, Anna Laetitia. *The Correspondence of Samuel Richardson . . . To Which Are Prefixed, A Biographical Account of That Author, and Observations on His Writings*. 6 vols. London: Richard Phillips, 1804.

Borlase, William. *The Natural History of Cornwall*. Oxford: W. Jackson, 1757.

Boyle, Robert. "Of the Systematical and Cosmical Qualities of Things." In *The Works of the Honourable Robert Boyle*. 6 vols. London: Printed for J. and F. Rivington et al., 1772.

———. *Tracts Written by the Honourable Robert Boyle*. Oxford: Printed by W. H. for Ric. Davis, 1671.

———. *The Works of the Honourable Robert Boyle*. Edited by Richard Boulton. London: J. Phillips and J. Taylor, 1699.

Burton, Robert. *Anatomy of Melancholy*. Vol. 1. Edited by Thomas C. Faulkner, Nicholas Kiessling, and Rhonda Blair. London: Printed for Henry Cripps, 1632; Oxford: Clarendon Press, 1989.

"Camera Obscura." In *The Beauties of Poetry Display'd*, vol. 2. London: J. Hinton, 1757.

Cavendish, Margaret. *The Blazing World and Other Writings*. Edited by Kate Lilley. London: Penguin, 1992.

———. *Grounds of Natural Philosophy*. London: A. Maxwell, 1668.

———. *The Life of the Thrice Noble, High and Puissant Prince William Cavendishe*. London: A. Maxwell, 1667.

———. *Natures Pictures Drawn by Fancies Pencil to the Life*. London: J. Martin and J. Allestrye, 1656.

———. *Observations upon Experimental Philosophy. To Which Is Added, The Description of a New Blazing World*. London: A. Maxwell, 1666.

————. *Philosophical and Physical Opinions*. London: J. Martin and J. Allestrye, 1655. 2nd ed., London: William Wilson, 1663.

————. *Poems, and Fancies, written by the Right Honourable, the Lady Margaret Newcastle*. London: J. Martin and J. Allestrye, 1653.

————. *Poems, and Phancies*. London: William Wilson, 1664.

————. *Sociable Letters*. Edited by James Fitzmaurice. Peterborough, ON: Broadview, 2004.

————. *A True Relation of My Birth, Breeding, and Life* (1656). In *Paper Bodies: A Margaret Cavendish Reader*, edited by Sylvia Bowerbank and Sara Mendelson. Peterborough, ON: Broadview, 2000.

————. *The Worlds Olio*. London: J. Martin and J. Allestrye, 1655.

Chambers, Ephraim. *Cyclopædia: or, An Universal Dictionary of Arts and Sciences*. London: Printed for James and John Knapton et al., 1728.

————. *Cyclopædia*. 3rd edition. Vol. 2. Dublin: Richard Gunne et al., 1740.

Coleridge, Samuel Taylor. *Biographia Literaria*. Part 1, vol. 7, of *The Collected Works of Samuel Taylor Coleridge*, edited by James Engell and W. Jackson Bate. Princeton, NJ: Princeton University Press, 1983.

Conjuror's Repository, The. London: J. D. Dewick, 1795.

Cuff, John. "John Cuff, Optician, Spectacle, and Microscope Maker, at the Sign of the REFLECTING MICROSCOPE and SPECTACLES, against *Serjean's-Inn* Gate in *Fleet-street*." Trade card. London: n.p., 1745?

————. "Verses, Occasion'd by the Sight of a Chamera Oscura" (1747). In Marjorie Nicolson and G. S. Rousseau, *"This Long Disease, My Life": Alexander Pope and the Sciences*. Princeton, NJ: Princeton University Press, 1968.

Descartes, René. *The Philosophical Writings of Descartes*. 2 vols. Translated by J. Cottingham et al. Cambridge: Cambridge University Press, 2007.

Delany, Mary. *The Autobiography and Correspondence of Mary Granville, Mrs. Delany*. Edited by Lady Llanover. 3 vols. London: Bentley, 1861.

Della Porta, Giambattista. *Natural Magic*. London: Printed for Thomas Young, and Samuel Speed, 1658.

Diderot, Denis, and Jean le Ronde D'Alembert. *Encyclopédie ou dictionnaire des sciences, des arts et des métiers*. Vol. 3. Paris: Briasson, 1753.

Dodsley, Robert. *Verses on the Grotto at Twickenham*. London: R. Dodsley, 1743.

Dubreuil, Jean. *Perspective Practical; or, A Plain and Easie Method of True and Lively Representing all Things to the Eye at a distance, by the Exact Rules of Art*. London: Robert Pricke, 1698.

Fielding, Sarah, and Jane Collier. *The Cry*. 2 vols. Dublin: Printed for George Faulkner, 1754.

Fiennes, Celia. *The Illustrated Journeys of Celia Fiennes, c. 1682–1712*. Edited by Christopher Morris. Exeter: Webb and Bower, 1982.

Flecknoe, Richard. "On the Duchess of Newcastle's Closet." In *The Country House Poem*, edited by Alastair Fowler, 179–80. Edinburgh: Edinburgh University Press, 1994.

Gilpin, William. *Observations on the River Wye, and Several Parts of South Wales, etc. Relative to Picturesque Beauty, Made in the Summer of the Year 1770*. London: R. Blamire, 1782.

————. *Observations, Relative Chiefly to Picturesque Beauty, Made in the Year 1772*. 2nd edition. 2 vols. London: R. Blamire, 1788.

———. *Remarks on Forest Scenery and Other Woodland Views (Relative to Picturesque Beauty)*. London: R. Blamire, 1794.

———. *Stow: The Gardens of the Right Honourable the Lord Viscount Cobham*. London: Printed for B. Seeley, Buckingham; and sold by John and James Rivington; and Robert Sayer, 1751.

———. *Three Essays: On Picturesque Beauty; On Picturesque Travels; and On Sketching Landscape*. London: R. Blamire, 1792.

Goldney, Thomas, III. Copy Inventory of furniture and effects at Goldney House, 1768. University of Bristol Inventory of 1768.

Harris, John. *Lexicon Technicum, or An Universal English Dictionary of Arts and Sciences*. 2nd edition. Vol. 1. London: Printed for Dan. Brown et al., 1708.

Havell, Robert. *The Natuorama; or, Nature's Endless Transposition of Views on the Thames*. London: Havell, 1820.

Heely, Joseph. *A Description of Hagley, Envil and the Leasowes*. Birmingham: M. Swinney, 1775.

Heyns, Zacharias. *Emblemata*. Rotterdam: P. van Waesberghe, 1625.

Heywood, Oliver. *Closet-Prayer a Christian Duty*. London: A. M. for Tho. Parkhurst, 1671.

Hume, David. *A Treatise of Human Nature*. Edited by Peter H. Nidditch. Oxford: Clarendon Press, 1978.

Hutcheson, Frances. *An Inquiry into the Original of Our Ideas of Beauty and Virtue; in Two Treatises*. London: J. Darby et al., 1726.

Jeffrey, Francis. Review of *The Correspondence of Samuel Richardson*, edited by Anna Laetitia Barbauld. *Edinburgh Review*, October 1804. In *Contributions to the Edinburgh Review*, 4 vols., 1:302–23. London: Longman, Brown, Green, and Longmans, 1844.

Jenyns, Soame. "A Translation of Some Latin Verses on the Camera Obscura." In *Poems. By *****. London: R. Dodsley, 1752.

Johnson, Samuel. *A Dictionary of the English Language*. 2 vols. London: Printed by W. Strahan, 1755–1756.

———. *A Dictionary of the English Language*. 2 vols. London: J. Knapton et al., 1756.

———. *The Lives of the Most Eminent English Poets*. 4 vols. Edited by Roger Lonsdale. Oxford: Oxford University Press, 2006.

Kircher, Athanasius. *Physiologia Kircheriana Experimentalis*. Amstelodami: Ex officinâ Janssonio-Waesbergiana, 1680.

Ladies Library, written by a Lady, The. London: J. Tonson, 1714.

Langley, Batty. *Ancient Architecture, Restored, and Improved*. 1741–1742. Republished as *Gothic Architecture*. London: John Millan, 1747.

———. *New Principles of Gardening*. London: A. Bettesworth and J. Batley et al., 1728.

Lover of Truth. *Truth and Error Contrasted*. London: Printed by and for James Phillips, 1776.

Mackenzie, George. *Mirror* 61, December 7, 1779, 224–29. Edinburgh: William Creech; W. Strahan and T. Cadell, 1779.

Mallam, Duncan, ed. *The Letters of William Shenstone*. London: Oxford University Press, 1939.

Mann, James, and James Ayscough. *The Description of a Pocket Microscope*. London: n.p., 1750?

Martin, Benjamin. *Philosophia Britannica: or, A New and Comprehensive System of the Newtonian Philosophy . . .* 3 vols. London: W. Strathan, J. & F. Rivington, et al., 1771.

Marvell, Andrew. *The Poems of Andrew Marvell.* Edited by Nigel Smith. London: Longman, 2003.

Moore, Milcah Martha. *Milcah Martha Moore's Book.* Edited by Catherine La Courreye Blecki and Karin A. Wulf. University Park, PA: Pennsylvania State University Press, 1997.

Morris, William. *Art and Its Producers, and The Arts and Crafts of To-day: Two Addresses Delivered before the National Association for the Advancement of Art.* London: Longmans & Co., 1901.

Moxon, Joseph. *Practical Perspective; or, Perspective Made Easie.* London: Joseph Moxon, 1670.

Museum, The. Vol. 13. London: R. Dodsley, 1746–1747.

Newcastle General Magazine, or Monthly Intelligencer, The, January 1748, 1:25–28. Reprinted in Maynard Mack, *The Garden and the City,* 237–43. Toronto: University of Toronto Press, 1969.

Norris, John. *An Essay Towards the Theory of the Ideal or Intelligible World.* Part II. London: Printed for Edmund Parker, 1704.

North, Roger. *Of Building: Roger North's Writings on Architecture.* Edited by Howard Colvin and John Newman. Oxford: Oxford University Press, 1981.

Old Bailey Online. *The Proceedings of the Old Bailey, 1674–1913.* University of Sheffield Humanities Research Institute. https://www.oldbaileyonline.org/

Parnell, John. "An account of the many fine seats of noblemen etc. I have seen with other observations made during my residence in [southern] England." December 23, 1763. M.a.11, Folger Shakespeare Library, Washington, DC.

Pope, Alexander. *Alexander Pope.* Edited by Pat Rogers. Oxford Authors. Oxford: Oxford University Press, 1995.

———. *The Correspondence of Alexander Pope.* Edited by George Sherburn. Oxford: Clarendon Press, 1956.

———. *The Poetical Works of Alexander Pope.* Andrew Foulis: Glasgow, 1785. Extra-illustrated copy, vol. 4 of 5. Pierpont Morgan Library 4239.

———. *The Works of Alexander Pope.* 10 vols. Berlin: Printed for Fredrik Nicolai Bookseller, [1762]–1764.

Radcliffe, Ann. *A Sicilian Romance.* 1790. Oxford: Oxford University Press, 1993.

Rees, Abraham. *Cyclopædia: or, An Universal Dictionary of Arts and Sciences.* Vol. 4, Plates. London: Longman, Hurst, Rees, Orme and Brown, 1786.

Reeve, Clara. *The Progress of Romance.* 2 vols. London: Printed for the author, by W. Keymer, 1785.

Reynolds, Joshua. *Discourses on Art.* Edited by Robert R. Wark. New Haven, CT: Yale University Press, 1959.

Richardson, Samuel. *Pamela: or, Virtue Rewarded.* 1740. Edited by Thomas Keymer. Oxford: Oxford University Press, 2008.

———. *Pamela: or, Virtue Rewarded.* 14th edition, "based on the 1801 text and incorporating corrections made in 1810." Edited by Peter Sabor. London: Penguin, 1985.

Rousseau, Jean-Jacques. *Reveries of the Solitary Walker.* Translated by Russell Goulbourne. Oxford: Oxford University Press, 2011.

Robertson, Hannah. *The Young Ladies School of Arts.* 2nd edition. Edinburgh, 1767?
Ruffhead, Owen. *The Life of Alexander Pope, Esq.* London: C. Bathurst et al., 1769.
Scamozzi, Vincenzo. *Discorsi sopra l'antichità di Roma.* Venice: Appresso Francesco Ziletti, 1582.
———. *L'idea della architettura universal.* Venice: n.p., 1615.
Scott, Walter. Introduction to *The Castle of Otranto,* iii–xxxvi. Edinburgh: James Ballantyne, 1811. Reprinted in Horace Walpole, *The Castle of Otranto,* edited by Michael Gamer, 132–41. London: Penguin, 2001.
Select Fables of Esop and Other Fabulists. London: R. and J. Dodsley, 1761.
Serle, John. *A Plan of Mr. Pope's Garden.* London: R. Dodsley, 1745. Extra-illustrated copy, Huntington Library 106623.
"Sketches No. 1: To the Editor of the European Magazine." *European Magazine* 74 (1782): 21.
Slater, Samuel. *A Discourse of Closet (or Secret) Prayer.* London: Jonathan Robinson, 1691.
Stone, Edmund. *A New Mathematical Dictionary.* London: J. Senex et al., 1726.
Stoppard, Tom. *Arcadia.* London: Faber and Faber, 1993.
Switzer, Stephen. *Ichnographia Rustica: or, The Nobleman, Gentleman, and Gardener's Recreation.* 3 vols. London: D. Browne, 1718.
Thomas, William. *Original Designs in Architecture.* London: Printed for the Author, No. 5, Portland Road, 1783.
Thoughtless, Thomas [pseud.]. Advertisement to *The Fugitive of Folly,* 1793. In *Novel Definitions,* edited by Cheryl L. Nixon, 75–76. Peterborough, ON: Broadview, 2009.
Thrale, Hester. *Thraliana.* Vol. 1, 1776–1784. Edited by Katharine C. Balderston. Oxford: Clarendon Press/Huntington Library, 1942.
Universal Monitor, The. London: J. Hartley, 1702.
Walpole, Horace. *The Castle of Otranto.* Edited by Michael Gamer. London: Penguin, 2001.
———. *Description of the Villa at Strawberry Hill.* Twickenham, London, 1774.
———. *Descriptions of Strawberry Hill.* In *The Works of Horatio Walpole, Earl of Orford.* London: G. G. and J. Robinson, and J. Edwards, 1798.
———. *A History of the Modern Taste in Gardening.* Edited by I. W. U. Chase. Princeton, NJ: Princeton University Press, 1943.
———. *The Letters of Horace Walpole, Fourth Earl of Orford.* Edited by Paget Jackson Toynbee and Helen Wrigley Toynbee. 16 vols. Oxford: Clarendon Press, 1901–1905.
Wettenhall, Edward. *Enter into Thy Closet.* 5th edition, revised. London: R. Bentley, 1684.
Woolridge, John. *Systema Horti-Culturae; or, The Art of Gardening, in Three Books.* 4th edition. London: Printed for W. Freeman, 1700.
Wotton, Henry. *The Elements of Architecture.* Charlottesville: University of Virginia Press/Folger Shakespeare Library, 1968.
———. *The Life and Letters of Sir Henry Wotton.* Edited by Logan Pearsall Smith. 2 vols. Oxford: Clarendon Press, 1907.
Zahn, Johann. *Oculus Artificialis Telediotricus sive Telescopium.* Vol. 1. Herbipoli [Würzburg, Germany]: Sumptibus Quirini Heyl, 1685–1686.

Secondary Sources

Abrams, M. H. *A Glossary of Literary Terms*. 6th edition. 1957; Fort Worth, TX: Harcourt Brace Jovanovich College, 1993.

———. *The Mirror and the Lamp*. New York: Oxford University Press, 1953.

Acheson, Katherine O. "Military Illustration, Garden Design, and Marvell's *Upon Appleton House*." *English Literary Renaissance* 45, no. 1 (January 2011): 146–88.

Aikema, Bernard, and Boudewijn Bakker. *Painters of Venice: The Story of the Venetian "Veduta."* Amsterdam: Rijksmuseum, 1990.

Alff, David. *The Wreckage of Intentions: Projects in British Culture, 1660–1730*. Philadelphia: University of Pennsylvania Press, 2017.

Alliston, April. "Female Quixotism and the Novel: Character and Plausibility, Honesty and Fidelity." In "The Drift of Fiction," special issue edited by Julie Park. *Eighteenth Century: Theory and Interpretation* 52, nos. 3–4 (2011): 249–69.

Alpers, Svetlana. *The Art of Describing*. Chicago: University of Chicago Press, 1983.

Altick, Richard D. "Mr. Pope Expands His Grotto." *Philological Quarterly* 21, no. 4 (October 1942): 427–30.

Armstrong, Nancy. *Desire and Domestic Fiction*. Oxford: Oxford University Press, 1987.

Armstrong, Nancy, and Leonard Tennenhouse. "The Interior Difference: A Brief Genealogy of Dreams, 1650–1717." In "The Politics of Difference," special issue edited by Felicity Nussbaum. *Eighteenth-Century Studies* 23, no. 4 (Summer 1990): 458–78.

Aubin, Robert Arnold. "Grottoes, Geology and the Gothic Revival," *Studies in Philology* 31, no. 3 (July 1934): 408–16.

———. *Topographical Poetry in XVIII-Century England*. New York: Modern Language Association of America, 1966.

Bachelard, Gaston. *The Poetics of Space*. Translated by Maria Joas. Boston: Beacon Press, 1958.

Bal, Mieke. *Narratology: Introduction to Theory of Narrative*. 3rd edition. 1985; Toronto: University of Toronto Press, 2009.

Balmori, Diana. "Architecture, Landscape, and the Intermediate Structure: Eighteenth-Century Experiments in Mediation." *Journal of the Society of Architectural Historians* 50, no. 1 (March 1991): 38–56.

Banfield, Ann. *Unspeakable Sentences: Narration and Representation in the Language of Fiction*. Boston: Routledge & Kegan Paul, 1982.

Banham, Reyner. *The Architecture of the Well-Tempered Environment*. 2nd ed. 1969; Chicago: University of Chicago Press, 1984.

Battigelli, Anna. *Margaret Cavendish and the Exiles of the Mind*. Lexington: University of Kentucky Press, 1998.

Beals, Peter. *In Praise of Scribes*. Oxford: Clarendon Press, 1998.

Bender, John. *Imagining the Penitentiary: Fiction and the Architecture of Mind in Eighteenth-Century England*. Chicago: University of Chicago Press, 1987.

Benjamin, Walter. "The Work of Art in the Age of Mechanical Reproduction." In *Illuminations*, edited by Hannah Arendt and translated by Harry Zohn, 1–26. New York: Schocken, 1969.

Berthoff, Ann. *The Resolved Soul*. Princeton, NJ: Princeton University Press, 1970.

Betsky, Aaron. *Building Sex*. New York: William Morrow, 1995.

Bland, D. S. "Endangering the Reader's Neck: Background Description in the Novel." *Criticism* 3, no. 2 (Spring 1961): 121–39.

Bobker, Danielle. *The Closet: The Eighteenth-Century Architecture of Intimacy*. Princeton, NJ: Princeton University Press, 2020.

Bold, John. "Privacy and the Plan." In *English Architecture Public and Private: Essays for Kerry Downes*, edited by John Bold and Edward Chaney, 107–19. London: Hambledon, 1993.

Borsuk, Amaranth. *The Book*. Cambridge, MA: MIT Press, 2018.

Boyce, Benjamin. "Mr. Pope, in Bath, Improves the Design of His Grotto." In *Restoration and Eighteenth-Century Literature*, edited by Camden Carroll, 143–53. Chicago: University of Chicago Press/William Marsh Rice University, 1963.

Bradbrook, Muriel. "Marvell and the Masque." In *Tercentenary Essays in Honor of Andrew Marvell*, edited by Kenneth Friedenreich, 204–23. Hamden, CT: Archon, 1977.

Brewer, John. "John Marsh's History of My Private Life, 1752–1828." In *History and Biography: Essays in Honour of Derek Beales*, edited by Tim Blanning and David Cannadine, 72–87. Cambridge: Cambridge University Press, 1996.

Brodey, Inger Sigrun. *Ruined by Design: Shaping Novels and Gardens in the Culture of Sensibility*. New York: Routledge, 2008.

Brooks, Chris. *Gothic Revival*. London: Phaidon, 1999.

Brownell, Morris. *Alexander Pope and the Arts of Georgian England*. Oxford: Clarendon Press, 1978.

Bullard, Rebecca. "Gatherings in Exile: Interpreting the Bibliographical Structure of *Natures Pictures Drawn by Fancies Pencil to the Life* (1656)," *English Studies: A Journal of English Language and Literature* 92, no. 7 (November 2011): 786–805.

Bruno, Giuliana. *Atlas of Emotion*. New York: Verso, 2002.

———. *Surface*. Chicago: University of Chicago Press, 2014.

Burman, Barbara, and Ariane Fennetaux. *The Pocket: A Hidden History of Women's Lives*. New Haven, CT: Yale University Press, 2019.

Camera Obscura Art Lab. "Welcome to Santa Monica's Historic Camera Obscura!" Unpublished, undated information sheet. Obtained June 24, 2018.

Campbell, Mary Baine. *Wonder and Science*. Ithaca, NY: Cornell University Press, 1999.

Casid, Jill. *Scenes of Projection: Recasting the Enlightenment Subject*. Minneapolis: University of Minnesota Press, 2015.

Certeau, Michel de. *The Practice of Everyday Life*. Translated by Steven Rendall. Berkeley: University of California Press, 1984.

Chambers, Douglas. "'To the Abyss': Gothic as a Metaphor for the Argument about Art and Nature in 'Upon Appleton House.'" In *On the Celebrated and Neglected Poems of Andrew Marvell*, edited by Claude J. Summers and Ted-Larry Pebworth, 139–53. Columbia: University of Missouri Press, 1992.

Chartier, Roger, ed. *Passions of the Renaissance*. Vol. 3 of *A History of Private Life*. Translated by Arthur Goldhammer, series edited by Philippe Ariès and Georges Duby. Cambridge, MA: Belknap Press, 1989.

Cheetham, Mark A., and Elizabeth D. Harvey. "Obscure Imaginings: Visual Culture and the Anatomy of Caves." *Journal of Visual Culture* 1, no. 1 (2002): 105–26.

Chico, Tita. *Designing Women: The Dressing Room in Eighteenth-Century English Literature and Culture*. Lewisburg, PA: Bucknell University Press, 2005.

Colby, Vineta. *Yesterday's Woman*. Princeton, NJ: Princeton University Press, 1974.

Colie, Rosalie. *My Echoing Song: Andrew Marvell's Poetry of Criticism*. Princeton, NJ: Princeton University Press, 1970.

————. *The Resources of Kind: Genre-Theory in the Renaissance.* Berkeley: University of California Press, 1973.

Conan, Michel. "Landscape Metaphors and Metamorphosis of Time." In *Landscape Design and the Experience of Motion,* edited by Michel Conan, 287–317. Washington, DC: Dumbarton Oaks Research Library and Collection, 2003.

Connor, Steven. *Dumbstruck.* Oxford: Oxford University Press, 2000.

Cotterill, Anne. "Marvell's Watery Maze: Digression and Discovery at Nun Appleton." *ELH* 69, no. 1 (Spring 2002): 103–32.

Crary, Jonathan. *Techniques of the Observer.* Boston: MIT Press, 1990

Croll, Morris. "The Baroque Style in Prose." In *Style, Rhetoric, and Rhythm: Essays by Morris W. Croll,* edited by J. Max Patrick and Robert O. Evans, with John M. Wallace and R. J. Schoeck, 207–33. Princeton, NJ: Princeton University Press, 1966.

Dailey, Patricia. *Promised Bodies: Time, Language, and Corporeality in Medieval Women's Mystical Texts.* New York: Columbia University Press, 2013.

Daniels, Stephen. *Humphry Repton.* New Haven, CT: Yale University Press, 1999.

de Bolla, Peter. "The Leasowes and Hagley Park." In *The Education of the Eye,* 104–50. Stanford, CA: Stanford University Press, 2003.

Dodds, George, and Robert Tavernor, eds. *Body and Building: Essays on the Changing Relationship of Body and Architecture.* Cambridge, MA: MIT Press, 2003.

Dodds, Lara. *The Literary Invention of Margaret Cavendish.* Pittsburgh: Duquesne University Press, 2013.

Deutsch, Helen. *Resemblance and Disgrace.* Cambridge, MA: Harvard University Press, 1996.

Douglas, Andrew, and A.-Chr. Engels-Schwarzpaul, eds. "Unstable Containers: Aspects of Interiority." Special issue, *Interstices* 12 (2011).

Dupré, Sven. "Inside the *Camera Obscura*: Kepler's Experiment and Theory of Optical Imagery." *Early Science and Medicine* 13 (2008): 219–44.

Eck, Caroline van. "Artisan Mannerism: Seventeenth-Century Rhetorical Alternatives to Sir John Summerson's Formalist Approach." In *Summerson and Hitchcock: Centenary Essays on Architectural Historiography,* edited by Frank Salmon, 85–104. New Haven, CT: Yale University Press, 2006.

Erkelens, Casper J. "Perspective on Canaletto's Paintings of Piazza San Marco in Venice." *Art and Perception* 8, no. 1 (2020): 49–67.

Evans, Robin. *Translations from Drawing to Building and Other Essays.* London: Janet Evans and Architectural Association Publications, 1997.

————. *The Projective Cast: Architecture and Its Three Geometries.* Cambridge, MA: MIT Press, 1995.

Fabricant, Carole. "The Literature of Domestic Tourism and the Public Consumption of Private Property." In *The New Eighteenth Century,* edited by Felicity Nussbaum and Laura Brown, 254–75. New York: Methuen, 1987.

Fennetaux, Ariane. "Women's Pockets and the Construction of Privacy in the Eighteenth Century." In "Interiors," special issue edited by Julie Park. *Eighteenth-Century Fiction* 20, no. 3 (Spring 2008): 307–34.

Finn, Margot. "The Homes of England." In *The Cambridge History of English Romantic Literature,* edited by James Chandler. Cambridge: Cambridge University Press, 2009.

Fitzmaurice, James. "Fancy and the Family: Self-Characterizations of Margaret Cavendish." *Huntington Library Quarterly* 53, no. 3 (Summer 1990): 198–209.

Folkenflik, Robert. "A Room of Pamela's Own." *ELH* 39 (1972): 582–96.

Fowler, Alastair, ed. *The Country House Poem*. Edinburgh: Edinburgh University Press, 1994.

———. *Renaissance Realism*. Oxford: Oxford University Press, 2003.

Fowler, John, and John Cornforth. *Eighteenth-Century Decoration*. Princeton, NJ: Pyne Press, 1974.

Friedberg, Anne. *The Virtual Window*. Cambridge, MA: MIT Press, 2006.

Freud, Sigmund. *The Interpretation of Dreams*. Translated by James Strachey. New York: Basic Books, 2010.

Frye, Northrop. *The Anatomy of Criticism*. Princeton, NJ: Princeton University Press, 1957.

Gallagher, Catherine. "Embracing the Absolute: Margaret Cavendish and the Politics of the Female Subject in Seventeenth-Century England." *Genders* 1 (March 1988): 24–29.

———. "The Rise of Fictionality." In *The Novel*, edited by Franco Moretti, 1:336–63. Princeton, NJ: Princeton University Press, 2006.

Gallagher, Catherine, and Lubomir Doležel. "Mimesis and Possible Worlds." In "Aspects of Literary Theory," special issue. *Poetics Today* 9, no. 3 (1988): 475–96.

Gillis, Christina Marsden. *The Paradox of Privacy: Epistolary Form in* Clarissa. Gainesville: University Presses of Florida, 1984.

Goffman, Erving. *Frame Analysis*. New York: Harper & Row, 1975.

Gomme, Andor, and Alison Maguire. *Design and Plan in the Country House from Castle Donjons to Palladian Boxes*. New Haven, CT: Yale University Press, 2008.

Grant, Charlotte. "Reading the House of Fiction: From Object to Interior." *Home Cultures* 2, no. 3 (2005): 233–50.

Guillén, Claudio. "On the Concept and Metaphor of Perspective." In *Comparatists at Work: Studies in Comparative Literature*, edited by Stephen G. Nichols Jr. and Richard B. Vowles, 28–90. Waltham, MA: Blaisdell, 1968.

Hague, Stephen. *The Gentleman's House in the British Atlantic World, 1680–1780*. Basingstoke: Palgrave Macmillan, 2015.

Hammond, John. *The Camera Obscura*. Bristol: Adam Hilger, 1981.

Harbison, Robert. *Eccentric Spaces*. Cambridge, MA: MIT Press, 2000.

Harries, Elizabeth Wanning. *The Unfinished Manner*. Charlottesville: University of Virginia Press, 1994.

Harris, Eileen. "Langley, Batty." In *Oxford Dictionary of National Biography*. https://www.oxforddnb.com

Harrison, Robert Pogue. *Gardens: An Essay on the Human Condition*. Chicago: University of Chicago Press, 2008.

Heal, Ambrose. *The London Furniture Makers, from the Restoration to the Victorian Era*. London: Batsford, 1953.

———. *London Tradesmen's Cards of the XVIII Century*. London: Batsford, 1925.

Heidegger, Martin. *Poetry, Language, Thought*. Translated by Albert Hofstadter. New York: Harper Colophon, 1971.

Heumann, J. Mark. "Andrew Marvell and the Experience of Nunappleton." *Andrew Marvell Society Newsletter* 3, no. 1 (Summer 2011). https://marvell.wp.st-andrews.ac.uk/newsletter/j-mark-heumann-andrew-marvell-and-the-experience-of-nunappleton/

Hibbard, G. R. "The Country House Poem of the Seventeenth Century." *Journal of the Warburg and the Courtauld Institutes* 19, nos. 1–2 (January–June 1956): 159–74.

Hobbes, Thomas. *Leviathan*. Edited by Richard Tuck. Cambridge: Cambridge University Press, 1991.

Holstun, James. "'Will you rent our ancient love asunder?' Lesbian Elegy in Donne, Marvell, and Milton." *ELH* 54, no. 4 (1987): 835–67; 847.

Howard, Maurice. *The Building of Elizabethan and Jacobean England*. New Haven, CT: Yale University Press/Paul Mellon Centre for Studies in British Art, 2007.

Hughes, Helen Sard. "Mr. Pope on His Grotto." *Modern Philology* 28, no. 1 (August 1930): 100–104; 103.

Huizinga, Johan. *Homo Ludens*. Boston: Beacon Press, 1950.

Hunt, J. Dixon. "Emblem and Expressionism in the Eighteenth-Century Landscape Garden." *Eighteenth-Century Studies* 4, no. 3 (Spring 1971): 294–317.

———. *The Figure in the Landscape*. Baltimore: Johns Hopkins University Press, 1976.

———. *Garden and Grove*. Philadelphia: University of Pennsylvania Press, 1996.

Hunter, J. Paul. *Before Novels: The Cultural Contexts of Eighteenth-Century English Fiction*. New York: Norton, 1990.

———. "Couplets." In *Oxford Handbook of British Poetry*, edited by Jack Lynch, 374–85. Oxford: Oxford University Press, 2016.

Ingold, Tim. *Being Alive*. London: Routledge, 2011.

———. "Footprints through the Weather-World: Walking, Breathing, Knowing." *Journal of the Royal Anthropological Institute*, n.s., 16 (2010): S121–S139.

———. *The Perception of the Environment*. London: Routledge, 2000.

Ingram, Randall. "First Words and Second Thoughts: Margaret Cavendish, Humphrey Moseley, and 'the Book.'" *Journal of Medieval and Early Modern Studies* 30, no. 1 (Winter 2000): 101–24.

Jackson-Stops, Gervase. *The English Country House: A Grand Tour*. Boston: Little, Brown, 1985.

Johnson, A. W. *Ben Jonson: Poetry and Architecture*. Oxford: Clarendon Press, 1994.

Johnson, Paige. "Producing Pleasantness: The Waterworks of Isaac de Caus, Outlandish Engineer." *Studies in the History of Gardens & Designed Landscapes* 29, no. 3 (June 2009): 169–91.

Jones, Barbara. *Follies and Grottoes*. London: Constable, 1974.

Jusserand, J. J. *The English Novel in the Time of Shakespeare*. Translated by Elizabeth Lee. London: Unwin, 1890.

Kahane, Claire. "Gothic Mirrors and Feminine Identity," *Centennial Review* 24, no. 1 (Winter 1980): 43–64.

Kalas, Rayna. *Frame, Glass, Verse*. Ithaca, NY: Cornell University Press, 2007.

Kaplan, Lauren. "Exotic Follies: Sanderson Miller's Mock Ruins." *Frame: A Journal of Visual and Material Culture*, no. 1 (Spring 2011), 54–68; 67.

Kareem, Sarah. *Eighteenth-Century Fiction and the Reinvention of Wonder*. Oxford: Oxford University Press, 2014.

Kemp, Martin. *The Science of Art*. New Haven, CT: Yale University Press, 1990.

Keymer, Tom. "Horticulture Wars: *Tristram Shandy* and *Upon Appleton House*." *Shandean* 11 (1999–2000): 38–46.

———. *Richardson's* Clarissa *and the Eighteenth-Century Reader*. Cambridge: Cambridge University Press, 1992.

Kilgour, Frederick. *The Evolution of the Book*. New York: Oxford University Press, 1998.

Kittler, Friedrich *Optical Media: Berlin Lectures 1999*. Translated by Anthony Enns. Cambridge: Polity, 2002.

Kofman, Sarah. *Camera Obscura: Of Ideology*. Translated by Will Straw. Ithaca, NY: Cornell University Press, 1999.

Krieger, Murray. "'Eloisa to Abelard': The Escape from Body or the Embrace of Body." In "The Eighteenth-Century Imagination," special issue edited by Ronald Paulson. *Eighteenth-Century Studies* 3, no. 1 (Autumn 1969): 28–47.

Kruft, Hanno-Walter. *History of Architectural Theory*. Translated by Ronald Taylor, Elsie Callander, and Antony Wood. New York: Princeton Architectural Press, 1994.

Kurnick, David. *Empty Houses: Theatrical Failure and the Novel*. Princeton, NJ: Princeton University Press, 2011.

Lamsechi, Guita. "Freiberg's Tulip Pulpit: Hybrid Nature and Civic Politics." In *The Book of Nature and Humanity in the Middle Ages and the Renaissance*, edited by David Hawkes and Richard G. Newhauser, with Nathaniel Bump, 157–79. Turnhout, Belgium: Brepols, 2013.

Lang, Karen. "The Body in the Garden." In *Landscapes of Memory and Experience*, edited by Jan Birksted, 107–27. London: Spon Press, 2000.

Langer, Susanne. *Feeling and Form: A Theory of Art*. New York: Scribner, 1953.

Lazzaro, Claudia. *The Italian Renaissance Garden*. New Haven, CT: Yale University Press, 1990.

Lefebvre, Henri. *The Production of Space*. Translated by D. Nicholson-Smith. Oxford: Blackwell, 1991.

Lefèvre, Wolfgang. "The Optical Camera Obscura I: A Short Exposition." In *Inside the Camera Obscura: Optics and Art under the Spell of the Projected Image*, edited by Wolfgang Lefèvre. Berlin: Max Planck Institute for the History of Science, 2007. https://www.mpiwg-berlin.mpg.de/Preprints/P333.PDF

Leonard, Zoe. Interview with Shannon Ebner. *BOMB*, no. 127 (April 2014). https://bombmagazine.org/articles/shannon-ebner-and-zoe-leonard/

———. "The Politics of Contemplation." Interview by Elisabeth Lebovici. In *Photography and the Optical Unconscious*, edited by Shawn Michelle Smith and Sharon Sliwinski, 93–103. Durham, NC: Duke University Press, 2017.

Levine, Caroline. *Forms*. Princeton, NJ: Princeton University Press, 2015.

Lewis, Jayne. *Air's Appearance*. Chicago: University of Chicago Press, 2012.

Lipsedge, Karen. *Domestic Space in Eighteenth-Century British Novels*. Houndmills, Basingstoke, Hampshire: Palgrave Macmillan, 2012.

Locke, John. *An Essay Concerning Human Understanding*. Edited by Peter H. Nidditch. Oxford: Clarendon Press, 1975.

———. *Two Treatises of Government* and *A Letter Concerning Toleration*. Edited by Ian Shapiro. 1689; New Haven, CT: Yale University Press, 2003.

Lukács, Georg. *Theory of the Novel*. Translated by Anna Bostock. Cambridge, MA: MIT Press, 1971.

Lupton, Julia. *Shakespeare Dwelling: Designs for the Theater of Life*. Chicago: University of Chicago Press, 2018.

Lynch, Deidre Shauna. "The Novel: Novels in the World of Moving Goods." In *A Concise Companion to the Restoration and Eighteenth Century*, edited by Cynthia Wall, 121–143. Malden, MA: Blackwell, 2008.

Lyon, Vanessa. "'A Relic from the Cave of Pope': Drawings of the Grotto in an Extra-Illustrated *Plan of Mr. Pope's Garden* in the Huntington Library." *Huntington Library Quarterly* 78, no. 3 (Autumn 2015): 441–77.

MacCarthy, B. G. *Women Writers: Their Contribution to the English Novel 1621–1744.* Cork: Cork University Press, 1944.

Macfarlane, Alan. *The Origins of English Individualism.* New York: Cambridge University Press, 1978.

Mack, Maynard. *The Garden and the City.* Toronto: University of Toronto Press, 1969.

Macpherson, C. B. *The Political Theory of Possessive Individualism.* Oxford: Oxford University Press, 1962.

Maleuvre, Didier. *The Horizon: A History of Our Infinite Longing.* Berkeley: University of California Press, 2011.

Markham, Clements R. *Life of the Great Lord Fairfax.* London: Macmillan, 1870.

Martin, Meredith. "The Ascendancy of the Interior in Eighteenth-Century French Architectural Theory." In *Architectural Space in Eighteenth-Century Europe: Constructing Identities and Interiors,* edited by Meredith Martin and Denise Baxter, 15–34. Farnham, England: Ashgate, 2010.

Maus, Katharine Eisaman. *Inwardness and Theater in the English Renaissance.* Chicago: University of Chicago Press, 1995.

McBride, Kari Boyd. *Country House Discourse in Early Modern England: A Cultural Study in Landscape and Legitimacy.* Burlington, VT: Ashgate, 2001.

McCarthy, Michael. *The Origins of the Gothic Revival.* New Haven, CT: Yale University Press, 1987.

McKeon, Michael. *The Secret History of Domesticity.* Baltimore: Johns Hopkins University Press, 2005.

Merleau-Ponty, Maurice. *The Phenomenology of Perception.* Translated by Colin Smith. London: Routledge & Kegan Paul, 1982.

Miller, Naomi. *Heavenly Caves.* New York: George Braziller, 1982.

Mingay, G. E. *English Landed Society in the Eighteenth Century.* London: Routledge & Kegan Paul, 1963.

Monette, Sarah. "Speaking and Silent Women in *Upon Appleton House.*" *SEL* 42, no. 1 (2002): 155–71.

Moore, Shawn, and Jacob Tootalian, directors. *Digital Cavendish.* digitalcavendish.org

Morgan, Luke. "Isaac de Caus Invenit." *Studies in the History of Gardens & Designed Landscapes* 29, no. 3 (2009): 141–51.

———. "Landscape Design in England Circa 1610: The Contribution of Salomon de Caus." *Studies in the History of Gardens & Designed Landscapes* 23, no. 1 (2003): 1–21

———. *Nature as Model: Salomon de Caus and Early Seventeenth-Century Design.* Philadelphia: University of Pennsylvania Press, 2007.

Munari, Bruno. *Design as Art.* Translated by Patrick Creagh. 1972; London: Penguin, 2008.

Neel, Alexandra. "'A *Something-Nothing* Out of Its Very Contrary': The Photography of Coleridge." *Victorian Studies* 49, no. 2 (2007): 208–17.

Nixon, Cheryl L., ed. *Novel Definitions: An Anthology of Commentary on the Novel, 1688–1815.* Peterborough, ON: Broadview, 2009.

Novak, Maximillian. "Introduction." In *The Age of Projects,* edited by Maximillian Novak, 3–25. Toronto: University of Toronto Press, 2008.

Ong, Walter. *Orality and Literacy.* London: Routledge, 1982.

Orlin, Lena Cowen. *Locating Privacy in Tudor England.* Oxford: Oxford University Press, 2008.

Oswald, Thomas. "Goldney Hall, Clifton—II." *Country Life* 104 (August 13, 1948): 328–31.

Panofsky, Erwin. "The History of the Theory of Human Proportions as a Reflection of the History of Styles." In *Meaning in the Visual Arts*, 55–107. Garden City, NY: Anchor Books, 1955.

Park, Julie. "Marching Thoughts on White Paper: Margaret Cavendish's Tools of Inwardness." In *Interiors and Interiority*, edited by Ewa Lajer-Burcharth and Beate Söntgen, 119–38. Berlin: De Gruyter, 2015.

———. *The Self and It*. Stanford, CA: Stanford University Press, 2010.

———. "What the Eye Cannot See: Watching Interior Landscapes in *Mansfield Park*." *Eighteenth Century: Theory and Interpretation* 54, no. 2 (Summer 2013): 169–81.

Partner, Jane. "'The Swelling Hall': Andrew Marvell and the Politics of Architecture at Nun Appleton House." *Seventeenth Century* 23, no. 2 (October 2008): 225–43.

Pasanek, Brad. *Metaphors of Mind*. Baltimore: Johns Hopkins University Press, 2015.

Picciotto, Joanna. *Labors of Innocence*. Cambridge, MA: Harvard University Press, 2010.

Plotz, John. *Portable Property*. Princeton, NJ: Princeton University Press, 2005.

Pocock, J. G. A. *Virtue, Commerce, and History*. Cambridge: Cambridge University Press, 1985.

Post, Jonathan. "'On each pleasant footstep stay': A Walk about 'Appleton House.'" *Ben Jonson Journal* 11, no. 1 (2004): 163–205.

Rambuss, Richard. *Closet Devotions*. Durham, NC: Duke University Press, 1998.

Raylor, Timothy. "'Paradice's Only Map': A Plan of Nun Appleton." *Notes and Queries* 44, no. 2 (1997): 186–87.

———. "'Pleasure Reconciled to Virtue': William Cavendish, Ben Jonson, and the Decorative Scheme of Bolsover Castle." *Renaissance Quarterly* 52 (1999): 402–39.

Redford, Bruce. *The Converse of the Pen*. Chicago: University of Chicago Press, 1986.

Rivers, Isabel. *The Poetry of Conservatism, 1600–1745: A Study of Poets and Public Affairs from Jonson to Pope*. Cambridge: Rivers Press, 1973.

Ross, Stephanie. *What Gardens Mean*. Chicago: University of Chicago Press, 2001.

Sanders, Julie. "'The Closet Opened': A Reconstruction of 'Private' Space in the Writings of Margaret Cavendish." In *A Princely Brave Woman*, edited by Stephen Clucas, 127–40. Aldershot, UK: Ashgate, 2003.

Sarasohn, Lisa. *The Natural Philosophy of Margaret Cavendish*. Baltimore: Johns Hopkins University Press, 2010.

Saumarez Smith, Charles. *Eighteenth-Century Decoration*. New York: Harry N. Abrams, 1993.

Savage, Robert J. G. *Natural History of the Goldney Garden Grotto Clifton, Bristol*. Reprinted from *Garden History* 17, no. 1 (Spring 1989): 1–40.

Schmidgen, Wolfram. *Eighteenth-Century Fiction and the Law of Property*. Cambridge: Cambridge University Press, 2002.

Schoenfeldt, Michael C. *Bodies and Selves in Early Modern England*. Cambridge: Cambridge University Press, 1999.

Scoular, Kitty W. *Natural Magic*. Oxford: Clarendon Press, 1965.

Semper, Gottfried. *The Four Elements of Architecture and Other Writings*. Translated by Henry Francis Mallgrave and Wolfgang Herrmann. Cambridge: Cambridge University Press, 1989.

Shanahan, John. "The Indecorous Virtuoso: Margaret Cavendish's Experimental Spaces." *Genre* 35 (Summer 2002): 221–52.

Shimbo, Akiko. *Furniture-Makers and Consumers in England, 1754–1851: Design as Interaction.* London: Routledge, 2015.

Shuger, Debora. "The 'I' of the Beholder: Renaissance Mirrors and the Reflexive Mind." In *Renaissance Culture and the Everyday,* edited by Patricia Fumerton and Simon Hunt, 21–41. Philadelphia: University of Pennsylvania Press, 1999.

Silver, Sean. *The Mind Is a Collection.* Philadelphia: University of Pennsylvania Press, 2015.

Silverman, Kaja. *The Miracle of Analogy; or, The History of Photography, Part I.* Stanford, CA: Stanford University Press, 2015.

Skelton, Kimberley. *The Paradox of Body, Building and Motion in Seventeenth-Century England.* Manchester: Manchester University Press, 2015.

Slater, Samuel. *A Discourse of Closet (or Secret) Prayer.* London: Printed for Jonathan Robinson and Tho. Cockerill, 1691.

Smith, Nigel. *Andrew Marvell: The Chameleon.* New Haven, CT: Yale University Press, 2010.

Smith, Warren Hunting. *Architecture in English Fiction.* New Haven, CT: Yale University Press, 1934.

Snodin, Michael, ed. *Horace Walpole's Strawberry Hill.* New Haven, CT: Yale University Press, 2009.

Stafford, Barbara, and Frances Terpak. *Devices of Wonder.* Los Angeles: Getty Research Institute, 2001.

Steedman, Carolyn. "A Woman Writing a Letter." In *Epistolary Selves,* edited by Rebecca Earle, 111–33. Aldershot, UK: Ashgate, 1999.

Stone, Lawrence. *The Family, Sex and Marriage in England 1500–1800.* New York: Harper & Row, 1977.

Straw, Carole. *Gregory the Great: Perfection in Imperfection.* Berkeley: University of California Press, 1988.

Taylor, Charles. *Sources of the Self.* Cambridge, MA: Harvard University Press, 1989.

Thomason, T. Katharine Sheldahl. "Marvell, His Bee-Like Cell: The Pastoral Hexagon of *Upon Appleton House.*" *GENRE* 16, no. 1 (Spring 1983): 39–56.

Thompson, Helen. *Ingenuous Subjection.* Philadelphia: University of Pennsylvania Press, 2005.

Thornton, Peter. *Seventeenth-Century Interior Decoration in England, France and Holland.* New Haven, CT: Yale University Press, 1978.

Thornton, Peter, and Maurice Tomlin, *The Furnishing and Decoration of Ham House.* London: Furniture History Society, 1980.

Tinniswood, Adrian. *The Polite Tourist: Four Centuries of Country House Visiting.* London: National Trust, 1998.

Tobin, Beth Fowkes. *The Duchess's Shells: Natural History Collecting in the Age of Cook's Voyages.* New Haven, CT: Yale University Press, 2014.

Todorov, Tzvetan. *The Poetics of Prose.* Ithaca, NY: Cornell University Press, 1977.

Tribble, Lyn. *Cognition in the Globe: Attention and Memory in Shakespeare's Theatre.* New York: Palgrave Macmillan, 2011.

Trickett, Rachel. "'Curious Eye': Some Aspects of Visual Description in Eighteenth-Century Literature." In *Augustan Studies: Essays in Honor of Irwin Ehrenpreis,* edited by Douglas Lane Patey and Timothy Keegan. Newark: University of Delaware Press, 1985.

Tristram, Philippa. *Living Spaces in Fact and Fiction*. London: Routledge, 1989.

Turner, James. *The Politics of Landscape*. Cambridge, MA: Harvard University Press, 1979.

Turner, Jane, ed. *From Renaissance to Impressionism: Styles and Movements in Western Art, 1400–1900*. Grove Dictionary of Art. Oxford: Oxford University Press, 2000.

Van de Krol, Yolanda. "'Ty'ed about my middle, next to my smock': The Cultural Context of Women's Pockets." MA dissertation, University of Delaware, 1994.

Varey, Simon. *Space and the Eighteenth-Century English Novel*. Cambridge: Cambridge University Press, 1990.

Vickery, Amanda. "Thresholds and Boundaries at Home," 25–48. In *Behind Closed Doors*. New Haven, CT: Yale University Press, 2009.

Vogler, Thomas. "When a Book Is Not a Book." In *A Book of the Book: Some Works and Projections about the Book and Writing*, edited by Jerome Rothenberg and Steven Clay, 448–66. New York: Granary Books, 2000.

Voorhees, Jeremy. "The Projective Credibility of Fictions: Robin Evans' Methodological Excursions." ARCC 2013, *The Visibility of Research*, 180–87. http://www.arcc -journal.org/index.php/repository/article/view/142/110

Wahrman, Dror. *The Making of the Modern Self*. New Haven, CT: Yale University Press, 2004.

Wall, Cynthia. "Details of Space: Narrative Description in Early Eighteenth-Century Novels." *Eighteenth-Century Fiction* 10, no. 4 (July 1998): 387–405.

———. *Grammars of Approach: Landscape, Narrative, and the Linguistic Picturesque*. Chicago: University of Chicago Press, 2018.

———. *The Prose of Things*. Chicago: University of Chicago Press, 2006.

Warner, William. *Licensing Entertainment*. Berkeley: University of California Press, 1998.

Watt, Ian. *The Rise of the Novel*. Berkeley: University of California Press, 1957.

Wenczel, Norma. "The Optical Camera Obscura II: Images and Texts." In *Inside the Camera Obscura*, edited by Wolfgang Lefèvre. Berlin: Max-Planck-Institut für Wissenschaftsgeschichte, 2007. https://www.mpiwg-berlin.mpg.de/Preprints/P333.PDF

Werlin, Julianne. "Marvell and the Strategic Imagination: Fortification in *Upon Appleton House*." *Review of English Studies* 63, no. 260 (2012): 370–87.

Westermann, Mariët. "'Costly and Curious, Full off pleasure and home contentment': Making Home in the Dutch Republic." In *Art and Home: Dutch Interiors in the Age of Rembrandt*, edited by Mariët Westermann, 15–81. Zwolle, Netherlands: Waanders/ Denver Art Museum and Newark Museum, 2001.

Whately, Thomas. *Observations on Modern Gardening*. Dublin: John Exshaw, 1770.

Whitaker, Curtis. "Fairfax, Marvell, and the Mowers of Nun Appleton." *Ben Jonson Journal* 20, no. 1 (2013): 72–94.

Whitaker, Katie. *Mad Madge*. New York: Basic Books, 2002.

Whyman, Susan. *The Pen and the People: English Letter Writers, 1660–1800*. Oxford: Oxford University Press, 2009.

Wigston Smith, Chloe. *Women, Work and Clothes in the Eighteenth-Century Novel*. Cambridge: Cambridge University Press, 2013.

Willson, Anthony Beckles. "Alexander Pope's Grotto in Twickenham." *Garden History* 26, no. 1 (Summer 1998): 31–59.

Winter, Sarah. *The Pleasures of Memory: Learning to Read with Charles Dickens*. New York: Fordham University Press, 2011.

Worsley, Lucy. *Cavalier*. London: Faber and Faber, 2007.

Yates, Frances. *The Art of Memory*. Chicago: University of Chicago Press, 1966.

Yeazell, Ruth Bernard. *Art of the Everyday: Dutch Painting and the Realist Novel*. Princeton, NJ: Princeton University Press, 2008.

Yiu, Mimi. *Architectural Involutions*. Evanston, IL: Northwestern University Press, 2015.

Index

Page numbers in italics refer to illustrations.